Barclay Head

Catalogue of the Greek coins of Caria, Cos, Rhodes & c.

With one map and forthy five autopype plates.

Barclay Head

Catalogue of the Greek coins of Caria, Cos, Rhodes & c.
With one map and forthy five autopype plates.

ISBN/EAN: 9783741176913

Manufactured in Europe, USA, Canada, Australia, Japa

Cover: Foto ©Andreas Hilbeck / pixelio.de

Manufactured and distributed by brebook publishing software (www.brebook.com)

Barclay Head

Catalogue of the Greek coins of Caria, Cos, Rhodes & c.

A CATALOGUE

OF

THE GREEK COINS

IN

THE BRITISH MUSEUM.

CATALOGUE

OF THE

GREEK COINS OF CARIA, COS, RHODES, &c.

BY

BARCLAY V. HEAD, D.C.L., Ph.D.,
KEEPER OF THE DEPARTMENT OF COINS AND MEDALS.

WITH ONE MAP AND FORTY FIVE AUTOTYPE PLATES.

LONDON:
PRINTED BY ORDER OF THE TRUSTEES OF THE BRITISH MUSEUM.
B. QUARITCH, 15, Piccadilly, W.;
HENRY FROWDE, Oxford University Press Warehouse, Amen Corner, E.C.
C. ROLLIN & FEUARDENT, 6, Bloomsbury St., W.C., and
4, Rue de Louvois, Paris; A. ASHER & CO.;
KEGAN PAUL, TRENCH, TRÜBNER & CO.; LONGMANS, GREEN & CO.

1897.

[*All rights reserved.*]

LONDON:
PRINTED BY GILBERT AND RIVINGTON, LD.,
ST. JOHN'S HOUSE, CLERKENWELL ROAD, E.C.

PREFACE.

This volume of the Catalogue of the Greek Coins in the British Museum comprises the money of the South-Western regions of Asia Minor, anciently known as Caria, and of the adjacent islands, Astypalaea, Calymna, Carpathos, Cos, Megiste, Nisyros, Rhodes, &c.

The Map which accompanies the work is by Mr. B. V. Darbishire. In its physical features it is mainly based on Kiepert's *Formae Orbis antiqui*, 1894 (Map ix.); but, owing to the kindness of Mr. J. L. Myres, the results of his recent explorations in the country to the north of the Ceramic gulf have been placed at the disposal of Mr. Darbishire, and have enabled him to make some important modifications in these regions, and to mark correctly the sites of the towns of Caryanda, Telmessus, and Chalcetor. The sites, as indicated on the map, of Bargasa, Euippe, Hyllarima, and Astyra (κατὰ 'Ρόδον), are more or less conjectural. I have not ventured to place on the map the positions of Euralium, Callipolis, and Pyrnus, of which places there are no coins in the British Museum.

A few of the more remarkable and interesting coins not in the British Museum are figured on Pl. xlv., among which, however, the tetradrachm of Cnidus (Fig. 7) has been added to the Collection since the Plate was printed.

The size of the coins is given in inches and tenths, and the weight of all gold and silver coins in Eng. Troy grs. Tables for converting grains into grammes, as well as into the measures of Mionnet's scale, are placed at the end of the volume.

In the revision of the work, I have received material assistance from Mr. Warwick Wroth and Mr. G. F. Hill, Assistants in the Department of Coins and Medals.

BARCLAY V. HEAD.

BRITISH MUSEUM.
July, 1896.

CONTENTS.

	PAGE
PREFACE .	v
INTRODUCTION .	xxv

§ I. GEOGRAPHICAL LIMITS OF CARIA . . . xxv.
§ II. NUMISMATIC HISTORY OF THE GREEK AND CARIAN TOWNS OF SOUTH-WESTERN ASIA MINOR . . xxvi

Alabanda	xxvi
No coinage before B.C. 197	xxvii
Name changed to Antiochia	xxvii
Resumption of its original name, *circ.* B.C. 189 . .	xxviii
Alexandrine tetradrachms struck at Alabanda . .	xxviii
Cultus of 'Roma' and games in her honour from B.C. 170	xxix
Probable cessation of coinage between B.C. 133 and Imperial times . . . . . . ,	xxix
Imperial coinage, Augustus—Philip and Otacilia . .	xxix
Alinda	xxx
Strong fortress in the district called Hidrias . . .	xxx
Ceded by Ada to Alexander	xxx
Coinage of the 2nd cent. B.C.	xxx
Imperial coinage, Augustus to Caracalla and Plautilla .	xxx
Amyzon	xxxi
Site, N.W. of Alinda	xxxi
Coinage probably belongs to the Imperial period . .	xxxi
Antiochia ad Maeandrum	xxxi
Probably founded by Antiochus Soter . . .	xxxi
Alexandrine tetradrachms &c., before B.C. 168 .	xxxi
Autonomous coinage after B.C. 168 . . .	xxxi
Early Imperial coins struck in the name of the Συναρχία	xxxii

CONTENTS.

	PAGE
Aphrodisias and Plarasa	xxxiii
Rights of ἐλευθερία and ἀτέλεια conferred upon it B.C. 39—35	xxxiii
Silver drachms of the time of Augustus tariffed as equivalent to Roman denarii	xxxiv
Bronze coins, Augustus to Gallienus . . .	xxxiv
Titles of magistrates. Dedicatory issues. Agonistic festivals, &c.	xxxv
Famous temple of Aphrodite	xxxvi
Apollonia Salbace	xxxvi
Doubtful attribution of coins with Maeander symbol	xxxvi
Reverse type, Sabazios or Amazon ?	xxxvii
List of strategi of Apollonia	xxxvii
Astyra	xxxviii
Probable site on the mainland opposite Rhodes .	xxxviii
Coinage before and after the foundation of Rhodus (B.C. 408) .	xxxix
Attuda	xxxix
Site and limits of its territory . . .	xxxix
Second or first century silver drachms	xl
Imperial coinage	xl
Cultus of Mên Karou at Attuda	xli
Use of διά in place of ἐπί before magistrates' names peculiar to a small group of towns in N.E. Caria.	xli
Titles of magistrates, Υἱὸς πόλεως, Ἱέρεια, Asiarch . .	xlii
Bargasa	xlii
Site still doubtful	xlii
Coins exclusively Imperial .	xlii
Bargylia	xlii
Ruins on the southern shore of the gulf of Bargylia	xlii
No inscribed coins known earlier than the 1st cent. B.C. .	xliii
Temple of Artemis Kindyas . .	xliii
Callipolis	xliii
Probably situate on the S. coast	xliii
Bronze coins of the 2nd or 1st century B.C. .	xliii

CONTENTS. ix

	PAGE
Caryanda	xliii
Discovery of site near Telmessus	xliii
Small bronze coins of the 4th cent. B.C.	xliii
Caunus	xliii
Important-naval station	xliv
Archaic staters probably struck at Caunus	xliv
A possession of the Ptolemies from B.C. 309	xliv
Purchased by the Rhodians, *circ.* B.C. 189	xliv
Revolts from Rhodes, B.C. 167	xliv
Coinage	xliv
Ceramus	xlv
Situation	xlv
An important member of the Chrysaorean Confederacy	xlv
Old road from Ceramus to Stratonicea through Panamara	xlv
Silver and bronze 2nd or 1st century coins, similar to those of Stratonicea	xlv
Types on Imperial coins of Zeus Chrysaoreus and of Zeus Stratios or Labraundos	xlv
Chalcetor(?)	xlv
Site fixed at *Kara-koyoun*	xlv
Small bronze coins, either of Chalcetor or of the island of Chalce	xlv
Chersonesus	xlvi
The Κοινὸν Χερσονασίων as distinct from Cnidus, separately assessed in Athenian Tribute Lists	xlvi
Coins anterior to B.C. 500, of the Aeginetic Standard	xlvi
Cidramus	xlvi
Probably situate near the Lydian and Phrygian frontiers S. of the Maeander	xlvi
Cultus of Zeus Lydios	xlvi
Imperial coinage, Augustus to Julia Maesa, Magistrates' names preceded by διά	xlvii
Family of Seleucus, Polemo, Pamphilus, &c.	xlvii

CONTENTS.

	PAGE
Cnidus	xlvii
Member of the Dorian Hexapolis	xlvii
B.C. 700-650. Stater with very archaic head of Aphrodite (Pl. xiii. 7)	xlvii
B.C. 650-480. Series of drachms and smaller divisions of Aeginetic weight. *Obv.*, Forepart of Lion, symbol of the Triopian Apollo. *Rev.*, Archaic head of Aphrodite in incuse square (Pl. xiii. 8-13, Pl. xiv. 1-4)	xlviii
B.C. 480-412. Cessation of coinage during the Athenian hegemony	xlix
B.C. 412-400. Revolt from Athens	xlix
Cnidus again strikes drachms (Pl. xiv. 5) . .	xlix
B.C. 400-390. Adoption of the Rhodian Standard, 4 Dr., 2 Dr., 1 Dr. (Pl. xiv. 6-8), and Federal 3 Dr., inscribed ΣΥΝ, in alliance with Ephesus, Iasus, Samos and Rhodes (Pl. xiv. 9), with head of Aphrodite Εὐπλοία	xlix
B.C. 390-300. Renewed activity of the Cnidian mint, 4 Drs., Drs., &c. (Pl. xv. 1-8, and Montagu Sale Cat. Pl. viii. 599)	xlix
Heads of Aphrodite, doubtful copies of that of the famous statue by Praxiteles	l
B.C. 300-190. Five beautiful 4 Drs. assigned to this period, of which two are figured Pl. xlv. 7, 8, and numerous Drachms, &c., Pl. xv. 9-13. First issue of Bronze coins, Pl. xv. 14-19. Active trade with Egypt	l
B.C. 190-167. Assimilation of the Cnidian coinage to that of Rhodes (Pl. xvi. 1)	li
Issue during this period of Alexandrine 4 Drs. (Müller, nos. 1151-2)	li
After B.C. 167. Cessation of silver coinage at Cnidus, and remarkable decrease during the 1st cent. B.C. of bronze issues	li
Extreme rarity of Imperial coinage	li

CONTENTS.

	PAGE
Cys. Site fixed at *Béli-Pouli*	lii
Small autonomous bronze coins of Roman times. Inscr. KY, KYI, KYITΩN and [K]YEITΩN. (*Hist. Num.*, p. 525)	lii
Euippe	lii
Site not ascertained, but probably near Alabanda . . Rare bronze coins of 2nd or 1st cent. B.C., and of Imperial times (Pl. xvii. 1, 2)	lii lii
Euralium. Identified by Borrell (*Num. Chron.*, ix. 151) with the Uranium of Pliny. Coin of Caracalla reading ΕΥΡΑΛΕΩΝ(?) of doubtful attribution . .	liii
Euromus	liii
Site fixed at *Ayakli*, near Mylasa	liii
Local cult of Zeus Euromeus	liii
Bronze coins from 2nd cent. B.C. to Imperial times .	liii
Gordiuteichos	liii
Site probably at *Karasu*, near Aphrodisias . . .	liii
Rare bronze coins of the 2nd cent. B.C. (Pl. xvii. 9) .	liii
Halicarnassus	liv
Scanty coinage before the time of Mausolus, B.C. 367 .	liv
Residence of the Satraps of Caria	liv
Destroyed by Alexander	lv
Rebuilt in the 3rd cent. B.C. while under Ptolemaic rule. (Bronze coins, Pl. xviii. 9-10)	lv
B.C. 188-166 and later. Drachms of the Rhodian type, &c. (Pl. xviii. 14-16)	lv
Imperial times. Halicarnassus almost deserted . .	lv
Harpasa	lvi
Coinage almost wholly of Imperial times . . .	lvi
The title Ἀρχίατρος	lvi
Heraclea Salbace	lvi
Site fixed at *Mahuf*, at the foot of Mt. Salbacus, and overlooking the plain of Tabae	lvi

CONTENTS.

	PAGE
Its territory bounded on the W. by the R. Timeles	lvi
Imperial coinage. Remarkable types	lvii
Hydisus	lviii
Correct form of name	lviii
Bronze coins of the 1st cent. B.C.	lviii
Hyllarima	lviii
Uncertainty as to site	lviii
Bronze of early Imperial times	lviii
Iasus	lix
Site opposite Bargylia, on the northern shore of the gulf	lix
Tetradrachm struck there by Tissaphernes (*Cat. Ionia*, Pl. xxxi. 6), probably in B.C. 395	lix
B.C. 394-390. Federal coinage in alliance with Ephesus, Samos, Cnidus, and Rhodus	lx
B.C. 390-250. No coinage in this period	lx
B.C. 250-190. Drachms (82 grs.). Origin of the type of Hermias and the Dolphin	lx
B.C. 190-168. Iasus under Rhodian dominion. Cessation of coinage till Imperial times	lxi
Principal coin types	lxi
Idyma	lxi
Site at the head of the Ceramic gulf	lxi
Archaic drachms of Aeginetic weight probably struck at Idyma	lxii
B.C. 437-400. Drachms of the Phœnician standard (Pl. xxi. 8-9)	lxii
After B.C. 400. Drachms of later style (Pl. xxi. 10)	lxii
Mylasa	lxii
Strabo's description of its site	lxii
Chief city of Caria under Hecatomnus	lxii
Temples of Zeus Osogoa (Ζηνοποσειδῶν), Zeus Stratios or Labraundos	lxiii
B.C. 314. Bronze, perhaps struck at Mylasa by Eupolemus, General of Cassander (Pl. xxxi. 11)	lxiii

CONTENTS. xiii

	PAGE
After B.C. 190. Alexandrine tetradrachms and gold Philippi, struck at Mylasa	lxiii
Imperial coinage	lxiv
Medallions of Asia	lxiv

Myndus lxiv
   Site identified by Leake at *Gumishli* lxiv
   Circ. B.C. 190. Unique tetradrachm in the Hague
   collection (Pl. xlv. 9) lxiv
   2nd and 1st cent. B.C. Series of drachms, &c., of Attic
   weight with numerous Magistrates' names in nominative case lxiv
   Imperial coins down to Sept. Severus . . . lxv

Neapolis Myndiorum(?) lxv
   Site uncertain, but near Myndus lxv
   Unique bronze coin of the 2nd or 1st cent. B.C. . . lxv

Neapolis ad Harpasum lxv
   Site fixed at *Ineboli*, in the lower valley of the Harpasus lxv
   Prevalent confusion between coins of this city and those
   of Neapolis Aurelia in Ionia lxv
   Imperial coinage, Gordian to Volusian . . . lxvi

Orthosia lxvii
   Site fixed at *Ortas* by Kubitschek and Reichel . . lxvii
   Bronze coins from the 3rd cent. B.C., with Magistrates'
   names, and Imperial without them . . . lxvii

Sebastopolis lxvii
   Site fixed at *Kizilje* lxvii
   Imperial coinage from time of Vespasian to that of Sept.
   Severus lxvii

Stratonicea lxviii
   A Macedonian settlement. Site fixed at *Eski-Hissar* . lxviii
   Temples in the Stratonicean territory, of Hekate at
   Lagina, of Zeus Chrysaoreus or Karios near the city,
   and of Zeus Panamaros at Panamara lxviii

CONTENTS.

	PAGE
B.C. 189-168. Coins of the Alexandrine type	lxix
After B.C. 168. Stratonicea a free city.	lxix
Autonomous hemidrachms, &c., of Rhodian weight	lxix
B.C. 88-84. Stratonicea faithful to Rome during the Mithradatic war	lxx
Freedom confirmed B.C. 81	lxx
After B.C. 81. Silver and bronze coins:—Stater or Tridrachm (166 grs.); Drachm 52·3 grs. (Pl. xxiii. 17), and bronze coins	lxx
Resists Labienus B.C. 40	lxxi
Ancient rights confirmed by Decrees of the Senate, B.C. 39 and A.D. 22	lxxi
Silver coins of Imperial times (Pl. xxiv. 1, 5)	lxxi
Prevalent types (Æ and Æ), Zeus Panamaros on horseback, and Hekate	lxxii
Coins reading INΔI, INΔЄI, &c., wrongly attributed to Stratonicea in Caria	lxxii
Countermark ΘЄΟΥ on large bronze coins	lxxiii

Syangela? lxxiv
Site near Halicarnassus lxxiv
Doubtful attribution of coins assigned to it . . . lxxiv

Tabae lxxiv
Site at the modern *Davas* lxxiv
Rewarded for fidelity to Rome during the Mithradatic war (*circ.* B.C. 82) lxxv
Silver drachm and bronze of this time lxxvi
Imperial times. Re-commencement of a silver coinage, which lasted probably from *circ.* B.C. 39 to Nero's time lxxvi
Magistrates lxxvii
Chief types lxxvii

Telmessus lxxvii
Site near Halicarnassus lxxvii
Coins sometimes assigned to it belong to Telmessus in Lycia lxxvii

	PAGE
Termera	lxxvii
Site west of Halicarnassus	lxxvii
Governed by Tymnes, *circ.* B.C. 500 .	lxxvii
,, Histiaeus, *circ.* B.C. 480 . .	lxxvii
,, Tymnes II. (?), before B.C. 450 . . .	lxxviii
Silver coin of Tymnes II., of Persic weight (Pl. xxvii. 2)	lxxviii
Cessation of coinage under Athenian dominion . .	lxxviii
B.C. 367. Absorption in Halicarnassus . .	lxxviii
Trapezopolis	lxxviii
Site on the northern slopes of Mt. Salbacus . .	lxxviii
Coinage wholly of Imperial times	lxxviii
Principal types	lxxix
Alliance with Attuda	lxxix
§ III. SATRAPS OF CARIA :—	
Hecatomnus, *circ.* B.C. 395-377	lxxxi
Mausolus, B.C. 377-353	lxxxi
B.C. 367 ? Synoikismos of Halicarnassus . .	lxxxi
Artemisia, B.C. 353-351	lxxxiii
Hidrieus, B.C. 351-344	lxxxiii
Ada, B.C. 344-340	lxxxiii
Pixodarus, B.C. 340-334	lxxxiii
Orontobates, B.C. 334-333	lxxxiv
§ IV. ISLANDS OF CARIA :—	
Astypalaea	lxxxv
Bronze coins from the 3rd cent. B.C. . . .	lxxxv
Alexandrine gold staters and tetradrachms struck at Astypalaea	lxxxvi
B.C. 105. Constituted a Civitas Fœderata . .	lxxxvi
Calymna	lxxxvi
B.C. 600-550. Archaic silver staters (Pl. xxix. 8) .	lxxxvi
Plentiful silver coinage in the 3rd cent. B.C .	lxxxvii
Carpathos	lxxxviii
Archaic coins of the city of Posidium	lxxxviii

CONTENTS.

	PAGE
Chalce or Chalcia	lxxxix
Small bronze coins usually assigned to this island described under Chalcetor (p. 79)	lxxxix
Cos	lxxxix
7th cent. B.C. Small electrum and silver coins (Stater and Diobol, Pl. xxx. 1, 2) of Aeginetic weight . .	lxxxix
The Crab as a symbol of Herakles	xc
5th cent. B.C. Tetradrachms of Attic weight. The Discobolus an agonistic type connected with the Triopian games (Pl. xxx. 3-5)	xci
B.C. 366. Foundation of the new city of Cos at the eastern end of the island	xci
Coinage after B.C. 366 on the Rhodian (reduced Attic) standard (Pl. xxx. 6-15), with names of the eponymous magistrates	xciii
B.C. 300-190. Coins characterized by the Lysippean style of the head of Herakles	xciv
B.C. 190-166. Tetradrachms of the Alexandrine type of Attic weight. Smaller denominations of the Rhodian standard (Pl. xxxi. 13-16)	xcv
Archaic form KΩION replaced by KΩIΩN . .	xcv
B.C. 166-88. Tetradrachm of Attic weight in the Hunter Collection (Pl. xlv. 6)	xcv
Introduction of Asklepian types	xcv
Restoration of the incuse square on the drachms, &c. (Pl. xxxii. 1-5)	xcvi
Magistrates' names perhaps those of the Προστάται .	xcvi
Initial letters of the officinae of the mint ? . . .	xcvi
B.C. 88-50. Silver coins without incuse square, and bronze (Pl. xxxii. 7-12)	xcvii
B.C. 50. Time of Augustus. Bronze coins bearing portrait of the tyrant Nikias (Pl. xxxii. 13)	xcvii
Imperial times. Bronze coins ranging from the time of Augustus to that of Philip. Remarkable types . .	xcviii

CONTENTS. xvii

	PAGE
Megiste	xcviii
Autonomous silver and bronze coins of Rhodian types (Pl. xxxiv. 1-3).	xcviii
The island probably attached to Lycia after B.C. 166	xcviii
Nisyros	xcviii
Autonomous silver and bronze of the latter half of the 4th cent. B.C.	xcix
Rhodes	c
Lindus, Ialysus, and Camirus	c
6th and 5th century coinages	c
B.C. 408. Foundation of Rhodus	cii
Coin-types	cii
B.C. 408-333. Coinage falls into three groups: (i.) Tetradrachms of light Attic wt., 260 grs. (Pl. xxxvi. 1 and xlv. 1); (ii.) Federal Tridrachms of Rhodian wt., in alliance with Ephesus, Samos, Iasus and Cnidus (Pl. xlv. 2); (iii.) Tetradrachms, &c., of the Rhodian standard (240 grs.) (Pl. xxxvi. 6, 7) .	ciii
Origin of the Rhodian standard	civ
Gold coinage of the 4th cent. B.C. . . .	civ
Classification of the various series of silver coins . .	cv
Re-introduction of the incuse square in the 2nd cent. B.C.	cvi
Later drachms, with head of Helios in profile . .	cvi
B.C. 189. Re-organization of Asia, and restoration of the Alexandrine tetradrachm	cvii
Re-issue of gold Philippi in the 2nd cent. B.C. .	cviii
Rhodes deprived of her possessions on the mainland	cix
Monetary reforms after B.C. 166	cix
The Drachm raised in weight	cx
B.C. 87-84. Rhodes faithful to Rome during the Mithradatic War.	cxi
Restoration of the Peraea to Rhodes	cxii
Latest Rhodian silver coins	cxii
Valuations of the Rhodian drachm in Roman money	cxii
Silver drachms superseded by large bronze coins	cxiii

xviii   CONTENTS.

	PAGE
Indefinite use of the term 'Drachm' . .	cxiv
Date of the introduction of heavy bronze money . .	cxv
Policy of Rhodes during the civil war between Pompey and Caesar . . .	cxv
Capture of the city by Cassius	cxvi
B.C. 43. His extortions . . .	cxvi
B.C. 42. Final ruin of Rhodian commerce	cxvi
Rhodian coinage under the Empire . .	cxvi
Magistrates in autonomous and Imperial times	cxvi
Adjunct symbols	cxvii
Final reduction of the Rhodian bronze coinage	cxvii
Syme. (See Syangela)	cxvii
Telos. Bronze coins of the 4th cent. B.C., published by Imhoof-Blumer	cxxiii

CATALOGUE OF COINS :—
   CARIA :

Alabanda	1
Alinda	10
Amyzon	13
Antiochia ad Maeandrum	14
Aphrodisias and Plarasa	25
Aphrodisias	28
Aphrodisias with Ephesus .	53
Aphrodisias with Antiochia	53
Apollonia Salbace	54
Astyra	59
Attuda	62
Bargasa	70
Bargylia	71
Caunus	74
Ceramus	77
Chalcetor (?)	79
Chersonesus Cnidia	80
Cidramus	81
Cnidus	84

	PAGE
Euippe	98
Euromus	99
Gordiuteichos	101
Halicarnassus	102
Halicarnassus with Samos	112
Halicarnassus with Cos	112
Harpasa	113
Heraclea Salbace	116
Hydisus	122
Hyllarima	123
Iasus	124
Idyma	127
Mylasa	128
Myndus	134
Neapolis Myndiorum (?)	140
Neapolis ad Harpasum	141
Orthosia	143
Plarasa (see Aphrodisias).	
Sebastopolis	146
Stratonicea	147
Tabae	160
Termera	176
Trapezopolis	177

SATRAPS OF CARIA:

Hecatomnus	180
Mausolus	181
Hidrieus	183
Pixodarus	184

ISLANDS OF CARIA:

Astypalaea	186
Calymna	188
Carpathos (Posidium)	192
Cos	193
Megiste	221
Nisyros	222

CONTENTS.

	PAGE
Rhodes:	
Camirus	223
Ialysus	226
Lindus	228
Rhodus	230
APPENDIX	271
Alabanda	271
Aphrodisias and Plarasa	271
Cnidus	272
Cos	272
Rhodus	272
INDEXES:—	
I. Geographical	275
II. Types	277
III. Symbols and Countermarks	293
IV. A. Kings and Rulers	297
B. Magistrates' Names on Autonomous Coins	298
C. Magistrates' Names on Imperial Coins	308
V. Roman Magistrates' Names	317
VI. Engravers' Names	317
VII. Remarkable Inscriptions	318
Table for converting English Inches into Millimètres and the Measures of Mionnet's Scale	323
Tables of the Relative Weights of English Grains and French Grammes	324

LIST OF PLATES.

I. Alabanda.
II. Alabanda, Alinda.
III. Amyzon, Antiochia ad Macandrum.
V. Antiochia ad Maeandrum.
V. Aphrodisias and Plarasa.
VI. Aphrodisias.
VII. Aphrodisias.
VIII. Aphrodisias.
IX. Apollonia-Salbace.
X. Astyra, Attuda.
XI. Attuda, Bargasa, Bargylia.
XII. Caunus, Ceramus.
XIII. Chersonesus, Cidramus, Cnidus.
XIV. Cnidus.
XV. Cnidus.
XVI. Cnidus.
XVII. Euippe, Euromus, Gordiuteichos.
XVIII. Halicarnassus.
XIX. Halicarnassus, Harpasa, Heraclea-Salbace.
XX. Heraclea Salbace, Hydisus, Hyllarima.
XXI. Iasus, Idyma, Mylasa.
XXII. Mylasa, Myndus.
XXIII. Neapolis Myndiorum (?), Neapolis ad Harpasum, Orthosia, Sebastopolis, Stratonicea.
XXIV. Stratonicea.
XXV. Tabae.
XXVI. Tabae.
XXVII. Termera, Trapezopolis.

XXVIII. Satraps of Caria.
XXIX. Astypalaea, Calymna, Carpathos.
XXX.—XXXIII. Cos.
XXXIV. Megiste, Nisyros, Camirus.
XXXV. Ialysus, Lindus.
XXXVI.—XLIII. Rhodus.
XLIV. Caria. Alliance Coins.
XLV. Coins not in the British Museum.

MAP OF CARIA, &c.

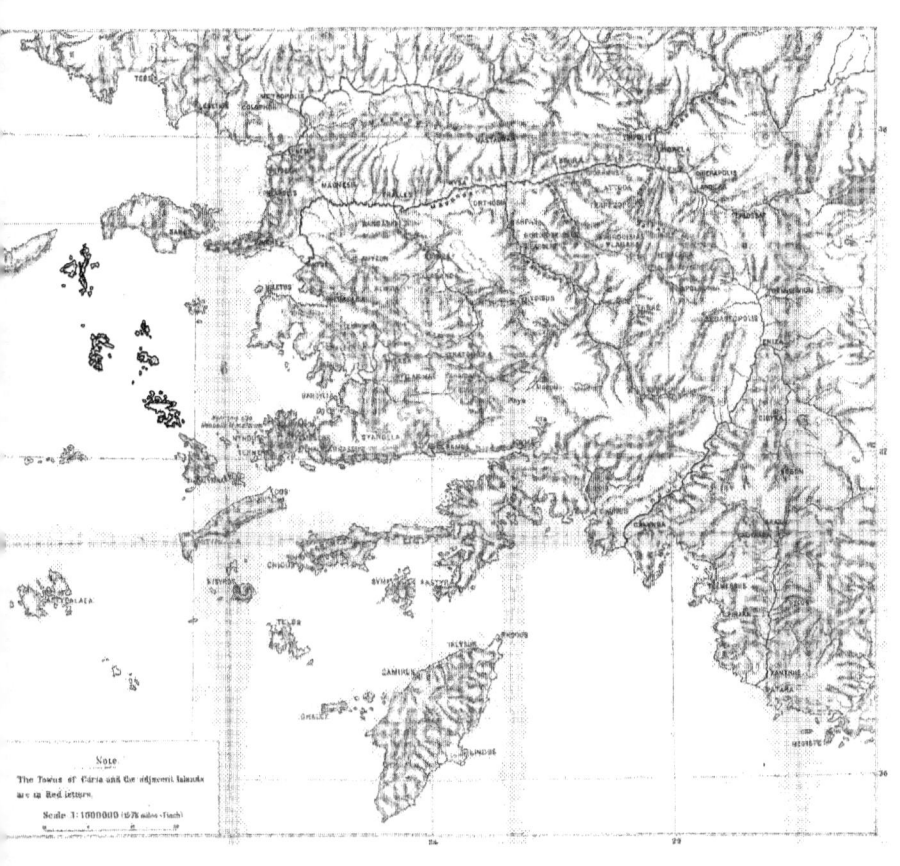

GREEK COINAGE OF CARIA AND THE ADJACENT ISLANDS.

INTRODUCTION.

§ I.—GEOGRAPHICAL LIMITS OF CARIA.

THE geographical limits assigned to Caria in the present volume correspond with those which have been adopted by Prof. W. M. Ramsay in his recent work *The Cities and Bishoprics of Phrygia* (Oxford, 1895). The northern boundary is the course of the Maeander; the eastern that of its tributary stream the Caprus, the north-eastern spurs of the Salbacus range, and, lastly, the river Indus from its source to the sea.

The towns of Trapezopolis, Attuda, and Cidramus, all situate on the northern lower slopes of the Salbacus, are thus included in Caria, and not in Phrygia, while those of Tralles, Nysa, Mastaura, Briula, &c., which lay north of the Maeander, will be dealt with in the volume describing the coinage of Lydia.

In Caria, properly so called, that is to say in the inland districts, there was no coinage whatever before Alexander's conquest; and, on the coast, Cnidus and Chersonesus, Idyma, Termera, and Astyra were the only mints before the commencement of the fine series of coins of the Hecatomnid dynasty. In the Greek islands, on the other hand, Calymna, Cos, Rhodes, &c., silver coins were in general use from very early times.

Speaking generally, it may be said that coined money did not come into common use as a medium of exchange in the towns and village communities of Central Caria until long after the age of Alexander the Great. The second century B.C., from the date of the victory of the Romans over Antiochus in B.C. 189, marks the beginning of a new state of things, and a rapid development of commercial activity accompanied by the introduction of autonomous coinages at all the principal centres of population. The quasi-regal issues of Alexandrine tetradrachms and of imitations of the gold Philippus were in the second and first centuries superseded by autonomous municipal silver coinages, some of which, *e.g.* those of Stratonicea, Tabae, &c., survived into early Imperial times. As a rule, however, the coinage, in Caria as elsewhere, from Augustus to Gallienus, was restricted to bronze.

For convenience of reference an alphabetical order has been followed in the Introduction as in the text, and under each city a sketch is given of its numismatic history.

§ II.—NUMISMATIC HISTORY OF THE GREEK AND CARIAN TOWNS OF S.W. ASIA MINOR.

ALABANDA. Alabanda was an ancient Carian town, said to have been founded by Kar, and named after Alabandos, his son, by Kallirrhoë, daughter of Maeandros. The name is thought by Steph. Byz.* to be the Carian equivalent of ἱππόνικος or εὔιππος.† Another tradition makes Alabandos a son of Euippos.‡ The town was situate on the Marsyas about twenty miles south of its confluence with the Maeander at the modern *Arab-Hissar*.§

---

* *s.v.* 'Αλάβανδα.   † Cf. Cic., *Nat. deor.*, 3, 15, 9.
‡ Steph. Byz., *l.c.*   Euippos was the eponymous hero of the Carian δῆμος Εὐίππη.
§ Waddington, *As. Min.*, 40.

No coins appear to have been struck at Alabanda before the beginning of the second century B.C., when it is mentioned among the allies of Rome in the war against Philip V of Macedon, *circ.* B.C. 197.* In this same year Antiochus III, after having made himself master of Ephesus, proceeded to plant colonies in various towns of Asia Minor, and in his honour these towns adopted for a time the name of Antioch. Among them was doubtless Alabanda, which bore the name of Antiochia for a short period between B.C. 197 and the defeat of Antiochus at the battle of Magnesia in B.C. 190.†

For the tetradrachms of Alabanda, reading ΑΛΑΒΑΝΔΕΩΝ, struck immediately before the change of the name, see Mionnet, iii., 305, nos. 4-7. Of these earliest issues of Alabanda there is as yet but one specimen in the British Museum (p. 271, no. 1). They bear the names of the local magistrates (according to Babelon, *Mél.*, i., p. 9, of the στρατηγοὶ ἐπὶ χώρας), ΔΙΟΓΕΝΗΣ, ΜΗΝΟ-ΔΟΤΟΣ, ΔΗΜΗΤΡΙΟΣ, [Ι]ΣΟΚΡΑΤΗΣ,‡ ΜΕΝΕΚΛΗΣ, and ΜΕΝΕΣΘΕΥΣ.§ Of these magistrates, the last four, Demetrius, Isokrates, Menekles, and Menestheus, would seem to have held office during the year in which the city first received its new name of Antiochia, for they re-appear in the list of magistrates' names on the coins reading ΑΝΤΙΟΧΕΩΝ.||

---

* Polyb., xvi. 24.
† Babelon, *Mélanges Num.*, i. 7.
‡ This name is misread ΣΟΚΡΑΤΗΣ by Mionnet, and ΣΩΚΡΑΤΗΣ by Babelon.
§ Mionnet also gives the name of ΤΙΜΟΚΛΗΣ, but although this name occurs on coins reading ΑΝΤΙΟΧΕΩΝ, there is no sufficient evidence that it also occurs on coins with the legend ΑΛΑΒΑΝΔΕΩΝ.
|| The list of names on the coins of Alabanda with the ethnic ΑΝΤΙΟΧΕΩΝ is, so far as I have been able to complete it, as follows:—

Tetradrachms:—ΑΡΙ]ΣΤΕΥΣ (Hunter, p. 26, no. 1), ΔΗΜΗΤΡΙΟΣ (Wadd., *Mél.*, ii., pl. i. 6), ΙΣΟΚΡΑΤΗΣ (Bab., *Mél.*, i., p. 14),

The fact that the silver coins of Alabanda reading ΑΝΤΙΟΧΕΩΝ are at present more commonly met with than those reading ΑΛΑΒΑΝΔΕΩΝ is probably only due to chance. After the defeat of Antiochus at the battle of Magnesia, B.C. 190, Alabanda resumed its original name.

The subsequent coinage consists partly of Alexandrine tetradrachms* bearing the dates (?) Α—ϿΙ (1-15), and partly of tridrachms, didrachms, and octobols, of the Rhodian Standard bearing the following dates (?) and the legend ΑΛΑΒΑΝΔΕΩΝ :— Ⳑ. Α (yr. 1), 177 grs. (Bab., *Mél.*, i., p. 12) ; ΙΑ (yr. 11), 175·4 grs. (B. M., *infra*, p. 2) ; ϿΙ and ΙϹ (yr. 15), 113 grs. (B.M., *infra*, p. 3), 110 grs. (Bab., *Mél.*, i., p. 12) ; ΚΑ (yr. 21), 187·5 grs. (Bab., *Mél.*, i., p. 11) ; no date, 74·8 grs. (B. M., *infra*, p. 3) ; and Æ with name ΠΑΜΦΙΛΟΣ (Im., *Gr. M.*, 661). From what era these dated tetradrachms, &c., are reckoned there is nothing to show, but it seems *primâ facie* probable that when western Asia Minor was re-organized by a Roman Commission presided over by the Consul Volso, B.C. 189, Alabanda may have been one of the towns which had their liberties confirmed, and which, in reward for having joined the Romans at Magnesia, were relieved from the payment of tribute. The year B.C. 189 may therefore have been the era

---

ΜΕΝΕΚΛΗΣ (Mion., iii., no. 53), ΜΕΝΕΣΘΕΥΣ (Mion., iii., no. 54, and *Sup.* vi., nos. 57, 67), ΣΥΜΜΑΧΟΣ (Bab., *Mél.*, i., p.14), ΤΙΜΟΚΛΗΣ (B. M., *infra*, p. 1, no. 1), ΦΙΛΤΟΓΕΝΗΣ (Wadd., *As. Min.*, p. 42), ΧΡΥΣΟΓΟΝΟΣ (Bab., *Mél.*, i., p. 13), Ⳇ (Bab., *Mél.*, i., p. 13), and Σ (Montagu Sale, Lot 595).
Drachms :—ΔΙΟΝΥΣΙΟΣ, Ε]ΡΜΑΓΟΡ[ΑΣ] ? ΙΣΟΚΡΑΤΗΣ, ΜΕΝΕΚΛΗΣ and ΜΕΝΕΣΘΕΥΣ (B. M., *infra*, p. 1, nos. 3—7).
Bronze :— ΑΡΙΣΤΕΥΣ (Im., *Gr. M.*, 662), and ΜΕΝΕΣΘΕΥΣ (Hunter, pl. v. 7).

* Müller, *Num. d'Alex.*, 1144-1150.

from which the Alabandian tetradrachms of the Alexandrine type and the silver coins of the Rhodian weight reading ΑΛΑΒΑΝ-ΔΕΩΝ are dated, though Babelon* prefers, chiefly on account of their style, to attribute them to the period after B.C. 168, when Caria and Lycia were declared free by the Roman Senate.† It is this last-mentioned date (B.C. 168) which I have adopted in the text (p. 2). It must not be forgotten, however, that as early as B.C. 170 the Alabandian legates pleaded at Rome that they had already built a temple to the goddess Roma, and instituted annual games in her honour;‡ but whether the privilege of *immunitas a tributis* (ἀτέλεια), of which Alabanda boasts on her coins of later Imperial times, dates from this early period, as Sterrett§ suggests, or from subsequent times, there is nothing whatever to show. The inscription ΘΕΑ [PΩ]MH accompanying the type of the goddess Roma seated on a cuirass and holding in her hand a figure of Nike (p. 4, no. 20) proves, however, that the worship of Roma lasted at Alabanda as long as it continued to coin money.

The coins of Alabanda struck between B.C. 168 (?) and Imperial times are rare, and it may be doubted whether any of them were issued after the constitution of the Roman province of Asia, B.C. 133, until the time of Augustus.

During the invasion of Asia Minor by Q. Labienus, B.C. 40-39, when nearly all the cities of the southern coast submitted to him, Alabanda, Mylasa, and Stratonicea offered a stubborn resistance. The two former were captured, and suffered much at the invader's hands.|| The accession of Augustus was therefore hailed by them as the commencement of a new era of liberty.

From this time until the reign of Philip the coinage of Alabanda

---

* *Mél.*, i., p. 12. † Polyb., xxx. 5; Livy, xlv. 25.
‡ Livy, xliii. 6. § *Inscr. of Assos*, p. 25.
|| Le Bas-Wadd., p. 193.

appears to have been plentiful. Only one or two specimens are known with magistrates' names, viz., ... A Ἀνδρωνος, Archon (p. 4), and Ἀριστογένης, Hipparch (Imhoof, *Gr. M.*, 661). Mionnet (Suppl., vi., 439, 27) also describes a coin of M. Aurelius on which the magistrate's name is preceded by ΕΠ.ϹΤΡ[ατηγοῦ], and on coins of Livia (S., vi., p. 436-7) he gives a magistrate's name with ΕΠΙ Γ[ραμματέως], but this is a very doubtful reading. The coins of Sept. Severus and Caracalla are usually countermarked with a head of Geta. The latest known coin of Alabanda is one of Otacilia reading ΑΛΑΒΑΝΔΕΩΝ ΛΑΚΕΔΑΙΜΟΝΙΩΝ (Mt. S., vi., 443, 42).

For types not included in the text, see Head, *H. N.*, p. 519.

ALINDA. Alinda is placed by Kiepert some 12 miles west of Alabanda, at the modern *Demirdjideressi*. It was situated on a rocky height commanding the plain of *Karpuzly-ova*, through which an affluent of the Marsyas flows in an easterly direction towards Alabanda.

The district called Hidrias, of which Alinda was the capital and a strong fortress, was ceded by Ada, the widow of Hidrieus, to Alexander the Great. No coins appear to have been struck at Alinda before the beginning of the second century B.C. The reverse type of the bronze coin (Pl. ii., no. 9) is evidently suggested by that of the contemporary half-cistophorus. The other second-century bronze coins resemble in style some of the coins of Philip V of Macedon, who wintered in Caria B.C. 201, and are also like those of the neighbouring Heraclea in Ionia, which likewise date from about the same time. Mionnet (Suppl., vi., 443) describes two silver drachms under Alinda, the first of which certainly belongs to Corcyra (cf. B. M. Cat., *Corcyra*, 366, 377), and it is doubtful whether the second is correctly described.

The Imperial coins range from Augustus to Caracalla and Plautilla, and from the time of Sept. Severus sometimes bear the name and title of the magistrates (archons) Μένιππος and Οὐλιάδης.

AMYZON Amyzon is a small town mentioned by Ptolemy* and Strabo.† It was situated on a height a few miles north-west of Alinda. Borrell‡ was the first to attribute coins to this town. I would assign the two specimens in the British Museum to the Imperial period, but I am at a loss to explain the type of p. 13, no. 1 (Pl. iii. 1), which is distinctly a negress's head. Whether the two coins bearing the magistrate's name ΔΗΜΗ-ΤΡΙΟC, published by Imhoof Blumer,§ belong to the Imperial period or to a somewhat earlier date is a doubtful point.

ANTIOCHIA AD MAEANDRUM Antiochia ad Maeandrum stood on high ground overlooking the plain of the Maeander at its confluence with the Morsynus. It was founded by one of the Seleucid kings, probably Antiochus Soter,|| though it does not seem to have struck any coins before B.C. 168 (except perhaps a few tetradrachms of the Alexandrine type [Müller, *Num. d'Alex.*, nos. 1176-7, there attributed to Antiochia Pisidiae]), when Caria received the gift of freedom from the Roman Senate.¶

In addition to the tetradrachm with the name of ΑΙΝΕΑΣ described in the text (p. 14, no. 1, Pl. iii. 3), a second and still more remarkable specimen has recently been acquired by the *Bibliothèque Nationale*, having on the obverse a head of Zeus, and on the reverse an eagle standing on a thunderbolt, the whole surrounded by a circular Maeander pattern. The magistrate's name on this coin is ΣΟΛ[ων?] (Pl. xlv. 10). To the drachms of the same period may also be added a specimen in the cabinet of Herr A. Loebbecke, of Brunswick, with the magistrate's name ΔΙΟ-

---

* v., 2, 19; Pliny, *N. H.*, v., 109. † p. 658.
‡ *Num. Chron.*, ix., 144. § *Mon. Gr.*, 304, and *Gr. M.*, p. 662.
|| Soter (B c. 281-261). Ramsay, *C. B. Phryg.*, p. 185.
¶ Polyb., xxx. 5; T. Liv., xlv., 25.

ΤΡΕΦΗΣ,* and to the series of bronze coins specimens bearing the names of ΔΙΟΝΥΣΙΟΣ,† ΛΥΚΩΝ, ΘΕΟΞΕ·, MENICKOY, and ΕΡΜΟΓΕ.‡

The earliest coins of the Imperial period (Augustus) were issued by the authority of the entire college of magistrates (Συναρχία), comprising in all probability members of the Δῆμος, Βουλή, and Γερουσία, under the presidency of the eponymous magistrate, whose name appears in the genitive case, e.g. CYNAPXIA ΑΝΤΙΟΧΕΩΝ, ΑΓΛΑΟΥ or ΠΑΙΩΝΙΟΥ. The term Συναρχία is not met with on the coins of any other city, though it occurs in inscriptions.§

A coin of Augustus, *Rev.* head of Tiberius, published by Imhoof Blumer,|| with the names ΙΕΡΣΗC ΕΥΓΕΝΕΤΩΡ ΑΠΟΛΛΟΔΟΤΟϹ, may be an instance of the custom of polyonymy which Waddington ¶ notices as prevalent at Aphrodisias; or, with greater probability, it may record the names of the three principal magistrates of the Synarchy. (Cf. coins of Plarasa and Aphrodisias with three names.)

After the time of Augustus, the only magistrate's name which I have met with on coins of Antioch is that of ΚΛ·ΑΓΛΑΟΥ ΦΡΟΥΓΙ (Cl. Aglaus Frugi) on coins of Domitian, accompanied by the title ἐπιμελη[τής] (concerning which see Head, *Hist. Num.*, Introd., lxvii.).**

In addition to the long list of divinities, whose busts or figures are described in the text of the Catalogue, Mionnet (iii., 814, no. 62) records a specimen reading ΖΕΥϹ ΟΛΥΜΠΙΟϹ; but I

---

* *Zeit. f. Num.*, xii., Pl. xiii. 3. † *Z. f. N.*, xii., 322.
‡ Imhoof, *Mon. Gr.*, 304.
§ Dittenberger, *Syll.*, 165, 33; 218, 1; 132, 20; 234, 2, 8.
|| *Gr. M.*, 662. ¶ *As. Min.*, 44.
** In *Hist. Num.*, p. 520, I have also cited the titles ΑΡΧ[ΩΝ] and ΓΡ[ΑΜΜΑΤΕΥϹ] on insufficient evidence.

suspect that this is a misreading of Sestini's (*Desc. Num. Vet.*, 367) for ΖΕΥC ΒΟΥΛΑΙΟC. Among the types of the Imperial coins that of ΖΕΥC ΚΑΠΕΤΩΛΙΟC (Pl. iv. 4) and the representation of the Bridge over the Maeander (Pl. iv. 7) are among the most noteworthy.

APHRODISIAS. Aphrodisias stood on a spur of Mount Salbacus about 1600 feet above the river Morsynus near its source, some 20 miles S.E. of Antiochia. A few miles to the east of the town the little river Timeles, an affluent of the Harpasus, took its rise. Personifications of both these streams (the Morsynus and the Timeles) occur on coins of the Imperial age.* Although according to Steph. Byz. (*s.v.* Μεγάλη πόλις) it was an ancient city, it does not seem to have coined much money before the latter part of the first century B.C. Its first important issue consists of silver drachms and bronze struck in conjunction with the town of Plarasa, which was probably situate also on the river Morsynus, in the immediate neighbourhood of Aphrodisias. The two places formed in fact one community, upon which the rights of ἐλευθερία and ἀτέλεια were conferred by a Senatusconsultum in the time of M. Antony, B.C. 39-35,† and this event may have been the occasion of the coinage of silver in the joint names of the two united municipalities.

At an earlier period (3rd or 2nd cent. B.C.) according to Imhoof-Blumer,‡ Plarasa seems to have struck some bronze coins independently of Aphrodisias. The only known specimen of this coinage bears a single magistrate's name, [Δ]ΑΜΟΝΙΚΟΣ. Im-

---

* The coins with the legend ΤΙΜΕΛΗC belong, according to Waddington, to the age of the Antonines. Ramsay (*C. B. Phr.*, p. 189) remarks that they commemorate the introduction of the water of the Timeles into Aphrodisias by means of an aqueduct constructed at the expense of Karminios Claudianus, the second of that name.

Boeckh, *C. I. G.*, 2737, 2845.   ‡ *Gr. M.*, 663.

hoof (*l.c.*) also describes a bronze coin of the autonomous class struck in the name of Aphrodisias alone, and another specimen with different types is described in the present volume (p. 25, no. 5, Pl. v. 4).

The silver issue of Plarasa and Aphrodisias can hardly have lasted much beyond the reign of Augustus, for all the known specimens are very uniform in style. About 17 varieties have been published. Of these one bears a single name in the nominative case, ΞΕΝΟΚΡΑΤΗΣ*; ten have a name in the nominative followed by a patronymic in the genitive; three give also the name of the grandfather as well as that of the father of the magistrate; and the remaining three bear the names of three magistrates all in the nominative case. One very remarkable specimen, published for the first time in the present work (p. 26, no. 6, Pl. v. 5), supplies, in addition, the official title of the magistrate, Ἱερεὺς Δήμου, a title as yet unrecorded on any other coin. Two specimens (Imhoof, *Mon. Gr.* 305 and *Gr. M.* 663), the latter now in the British Museum (*infra*, p. 271), bear the sign (✳) of the denarius, whence it may be inferred that these silver pieces, although of light weight (55 grs.), were tariffed as equivalent to Roman denarii.†

From the time of Augustus down to the reign of Gallienus the coinage consists of bronze only, and the name of Plarasa no longer appears. The magistrates' names are Ἀπολλώνιος, in the reign

---

* Imh., *Mon. Gr.*, 305.

† On the silver drachms of Plarasa and Aphrodisias I have noted the following magistrate's names in addition to those described in the text: ΑΝΔΡΩΝ ΦΑΝΙΟΥ (Mion., iii., 321, 101); ΜΗΝΟΔΟΤΟΣ ΑΓΕΛΑΟΥ (Imhoof, *Mon. gr.*, 305), ΑΡΤ. ΣΩ. ΙΗ. (Imhoof, *l.c.*), ΞΕΝΟΚΡΑΤΗΣ (Imhoof, *l.c.*), ΞΕΝΟΚΡΑΤΗΣ ΞΕΝΟΚΡΑΤΟΥ (Imhoof, *l.c.*), ΗΦΑΙΣΤΙΩΝ ΧΑΡΙΞΕΝΟΥ (Imhoof, *l.c.*), ΙΑΣΩΝ ΣΚΥΜΝΟΥ, ΠΥΘΙΩΝ ΠΟΛΥΚΡΑΤΟΥ (Mion., iii., 322, 104, incompletely read by M.), ΥΨΙΚΛΗΣ ✳ ΑΔΡΑΣΤΟΥ (Imhoof, *l.c.*). Concerning Hypsikles Adrasti f. see *C. I. G.*, 2752, and *Bull. Corr. Hell.*, xiv., 612.

of Augustus,* who is distinguished by the title Ύἱος Ἀφροδισιέων; Τ. Κλ. Ζῆλος (temp. M. Aurelii) Ἱερεύς; Τι. Κλ. Ζήνων; Μένιππος; and Μενεσθεὺς Ἰσόβουνος (temp. S. Severi). Of these magistrates Zenon is designated as Ἀρχιερεύς and Ἀρχινεοκόρος, Menippos has no title, and Menestheus appears as the chief of a college of Archons (pp. 43-45, nos. 112, 117-119); he was also ἀρχινεοποιὸς θεᾶς Ἀφροδίτης.† In the time of Philip we meet with the name of an Archon Πο. Αἰλ. Ἀπολλωνίανος, who is mentioned also in an inscription ‡ as a πρειμοπειλάριος, and in the reigns of Trajan Decius and Gallienus with the names of the Archons Στρατόνικος and Ἑρμογένης Ἀπελλᾶ. On other inscriptions of Aphrodisias there occur names which are identical with those on Imperial coins, but there is no evidence to show that they are the same individuals.

Many of the issues of bronze coins bear the inscription ΑΝЄ-ΘΗΚЄ, and were dedicated on special occasions by the chief magistrate to his native town (ΤΗ ΠΑΤΡΙΔΙ). The word ЄΠΙΝΙΚΙΟΝ on coins dedicated by Τ. Κ. ΖΗΛΟC in the time of M. Aurelius and Verus (p. 41, no. 106, p. 42, no. 110) shows that these issues were dedicated after a victory, probably in the eastern campaigns of L. Verus, or possibly in the games such as ΑΤΤΑΛΗΑ, ΓΟΡΔΙΑΝΗΑ, ΚΑΠЄΤΩΛΙΑ, ΟΙΚΟΥΜЄΝΙΚΟC, ΠΥΘΙΑ, the names of which are commemorated on coins of Aphrodisias. Of these agonistic festivals the ΚΑΠЄΤΩΛΙΑ are especially remarkable, as Aphrodisias seems to have been one of the few cities in the province of Asia in which they were celebrated. It is to be presumed that these games were instituted when Aphrodisias,

---

∗ Leake (Num. Hell., p. 25) suggests that this Apollonius may have been the author of the History of Caria (Καρικά) in no less than eighteen books; cf. Suidas, Lex., Ἀπολλώνιος Ἀφροδισιεὺς ἀρχιερεὺς καὶ ἱστορικός, γέγραφε Καρικά, Περὶ Τράλλεων, κ.τ.λ.

† Le Bas - Wadd., Inscr. d'As. Min., p. 377.

‡ Boeckh, C. I. G., 2792.

by the Senatusconsultum* above referred to, was constituted a *civitas immunis et libera*.† The Temple of Ζεὺς Καπετώλιος and the statue of the god which occurs on coins of Antiochia (p. 19, no. 32, p. 20, no. 43, p. 21, nos. 46, 47) date perhaps from the same period. The senate in this decree also confers rights of asylum upon the temple of Aphrodite and its precints, equivalent to those enjoyed by the temple of Artemis at Ephesus. The growth of Aphrodisias appears to have been in a large measure due to the increasing importance of its famous temple of Aphrodite, which probably obtained for it at a later time the title and status of Metropolis of Caria.

Apollonia Salbace, so called to distinguish it from other towns bearing the same name, was situated in the district **APOLLONIA SALBACE.** Salbace, probably at the modern village of *Medet* about 10 miles N.E. of Tabae, and S. of the range of mountains called Salbacus. According to Kiepert's Atlas the northern branch of the river Harpasus took its rise in the immediate neighbourhood of the city.

The Maeander symbol on the earliest coins (first century B.C.) which bear the name of Apollonia throws much doubt upon the attribution of these specimens, but, as the river Harpasus was an important tributary of the Maeander, it is just possible that this fact may have been held as a sufficient excuse for the usurpation by Apollonia of the symbol of the greater river (see note *infra*,

---

* *C. I. G.*, 2737.

† This decree runs as follows:—τὸν δῆμον τὸν Πλαρ[ασιέων καὶ 'Αφροδισιέ]ων τὴν ἐλευθερίαν καὶ τὴν ἀτέλειαν οὕτως πάντων τῶν πραγ[μάτων ἔχειν καθ]άπερ καὶ ἥτις πολιτεία τῷ καλλίστῳ τε νόμῳ ἐστίν, [ὑπὸ τοῦ δήμο]υ τοῦ 'Ρωμαίων, τὴν ἐλευθερίαν καὶ τὴν ἀτέλειαν ἔχει, φίλη τε καὶ σύ[μμαχος οὖσα]. More than 3000 bronze tablets of this kind were hung up in the Temple of Jupiter Capitolinus at Rome, duplicate copies being deposited in the temples of the various cities upon which the Romans had conferred privileges. (Marquardt and Mommsen, *Röm. Alterthümer*, Bd. iv., 2nd ed., p. 74, note 2.)

p. 54). Ramsay (*C. B. Phryg.*, p. 192) and Imhoof-Blumer would, however, assign the coins with the Maeander symbol to Tripolis, and if this attribution is, as I suspect, the correct one, it will prove that Tripolis bore the name of Apollonia in the first cent. B.C. The reverse type of these first century B.C. coins reading ΑΠΟΛ- ΛΩΝΙΑΤΩΝ is a figure on horseback with the double-axe or labrys over shoulder. This figure has been hitherto always taken for an Amazon, but Ramsay in his *Antiquities of Southern Phrygia*,* gives reasons for identifying it with the Phrygian god Sabazios or Saoazos, whose name was corrupted by the Greeks into Σώζων. (Cf. Antioch, no. 13, and Pl. iii. 7.) It is noteworthy, however, that the Rider on no. 2, p. 54 is certainly a woman. The long hair worn in a knot behind the head, and the chiton with apoptygma confined by a belt below the breast, show this quite distinctly, though these characteristic points are not clear on the specimen figured on Pl. ix. no. 1. The title of the magistrate whose name appears on the coins of Apollonia appears to have been always Στρατηγός. On the earlier Imperial coins his name is in the nominative usually followed by the patronymic, *i.e.* ΠΑΠΙΑΣ ΚΑΛΛΙΠΠΟΥ, ΚΑΛΛΙΠΠΟΣ ΑΡΤΕΜΙΔΩΡΟΥ, &c. On the later Imperial coins (Trajan to Gallienus) it is generally in the genitive, as ΠΑΠΙΟΥ ΚΑΛΛΙΠΠΟΥ, often accompanied by the title ΣΤΡΑ(τηγοῦ), and sometimes preceded by the preposition διά or ἐπί. The patronymic on the later Imperial coins is usually omitted. In addition to the names of the strategi recorded in the text the following have, up to the present, been published:—
ΚΑΛΛΙΠΠΟΥ ΣΤΡΑ. Γ. (Time of Trajan) (Wadd., *As. Min.*, p. 133); ΑΠΟΛΛΩΝΙΟΣ ΚΩΚΟΥ, Caligula (Imhoof, *Gr. M.* 609); ΕΠΙ Λ. ΤΕΙΜΟΘΕΟΥ ΣΤΡ. Hadrian (Wadd., *As. Min.* 136); ΚΛΑΥΔΙ. ΡΟΥ. ΣΤΡΑ M. Aur. (Wadd., *As. Min.* 137); ΚΑΛ-

---

* *American Journ. of Archæology*, vol. iii., p. 363.

ΛΙΠΠΟΥ CTPA., Faustina (Imhoof, *Mon. Gr.* 306); ΝΙΚΟ-CTPATOY CTPA., Caracalla (Imhoof, *Gr. M.* 669); ΕΠΙ ΝΙΚΟ-CTPATOY, Geta (Wadd., *As. Min.* 137); ΑΓΑΘΕΙΝΟΥ CTPA., Mamaea (Boutkowski).

Four places of the name of Astyra are mentioned by ancient writers:

ASTYRA. (i.) Astyra at or near the source of the river Rhodius, about 20 miles S.E. of Abydus in the Troad. Strabo (xiii. 23) says that in his time this town was in ruins, and dependent upon Abydus, but that in ancient times it had been autonomous and possessed of rich gold-mines, which, though almost exhausted, still produced a little gold. These mines doubtless supplied Lampsacus and Abydus with their gold coinage. (ii.) Astyra on the gulf of Adramyteum, formerly a little town, but in Strabo's time no more than a village. Here there was at one time a temple of Artemis Astyrene administered and cared for by the Antandrians.* (iii.) Astyra opposite Lesbos, mentioned by Pausanias (iv. 35, 10), seems to have been only a name of some hot springs in the territory of Atarneus. (iv.) Astyra πόλις Φοινίκης κατὰ ʽΡόδον, ἐν ᾗ ἐτιμᾶτο ἡ Ἀθηνᾶ Ἀστυρίς (Steph. Byz.). From the style and the types of the coins described in the text there can be no doubt that the last-mentioned city is the one to which they belong. Borrell,† misunderstanding the statement of Stephanus, and influenced by the fact that most of the above-mentioned specimens were found together at Rhodes, has assigned the town of Astyra to that island. Leake ‡ has, however, pointed out that the words used by Steph. Byz., πόλις Φοινίκης κατὰ ʽΡόδον, clearly mean a city in the peninsula of Phoenix opposite Rhodes. Here therefore, on the mainland, and not in the island of Rhodes, the site of Astyra must be sought. The fact that some of the fourth century coins of Astyra have on

---

* Strab., xiii. 65. † *Num. Chron.*, ix., 167.
‡ *Num. Hell.*, Asia, p. 26.

the obverse a full-face head of Helios (Pl. x. 5, 6) resembling the coins of the city of Rhodus is by no means a proof of their having been struck in that island, though it is doubtless an indication of Rhodian influence (as is also the similar head on the coins of Mausolus). After the foundation of Rhodus (B.C. 408) the coinage of the important Rhodian cities Lindus, Ialysus, and Camirus came to an end; and it is in the highest degree improbable that Astyra, had it been also a Rhodian town, would have been the only city in the island to retain the right of coining money in its own name after the centralization of the separate city coinages in the new capital.

If no coins of Astyra subsequent to archaic times had come to light, something might have been said in favour of Borrell's attribution of the town to Rhodes; but as there is not only bronze but also silver money of Astyra of the fourth century B.C.,[*] it is extremely unlikely that a small town like Astyra would have continued to strike coins after the closing of the mints of the more important cities of Camirus, Ialysus and Lindus.

ATTUDA or ATTUDDA. Attuda or Attudda was situate on the frontiers of Caria and Phrygia Pacatiana, according to Ramsay,[†] close to the modern village of *Assar*. Its territory was bounded on the north by the Maeander, on the north-east by the Lycus, on the east by the territory of Laodicea, and on the south and south-west by the Salbacus range of mountains and the territory of the neighbouring city of Trapezopolis (*Kadi Keui?*). There is some uncertainty as to whether Attuda should be included in Caria or Phrygia; but as its coins seem to be rather Carian than Phrygian in style, I have preferred to include this town in the present volume. The ethnological evidence is very scanty, but on the whole there seems to be a preponderance of evidence in favour

---

[*] Waddington, *Asie Mineure*, p. 58.   [†] *C. B. Phr.*, p. 165.

of a prevalence of the Carian over the Phrygian element in the population in the Roman Imperial period. Attuda, though it was not a large town, must have been of some importance, as the Roman high road along the Maeander and Lycus valleys, which ran almost in a straight line from Ephesus and Magnesia on the west to Laodicea and Apamea on the east, passed through its territory, though not actually through the city.* Though Attuda is not mentioned by any historian, nor even by Strabo, its name appears in the lists of Hierocles, and in the Notitiae Episcopatuum.† By far the oldest records of the town are however its coins, and the fact that it issued silver money which, judging by the style of the drachm (Pl. x. no. 9), cannot be later than the early part of the first century B.C., is a distinct proof that it must have been even then a place of some standing. From this time there appears to be a break in the coinage till the Imperial age. Of this period the most important coin is Pl. x. 15, bearing the bust and name of the god **MHN KAPOY**, whose temple was an object of veneration in Strabo's time, B.C. 64—A.D. 19. It was situate on the left or western bank of the river Kapros, at a place called in Byzantine times Caria, which may be identified with the modern *Gereli*. At the neighbouring village of Μηνὸς κώμη there was a spring of alkaline waters (Athen., 43), and in connection with this spring and with the Hieron of the god a famous school of medicine (Strab., 580), located apparently at Laodicea 13 miles distant.

The heads of this school in Strabo's time were Zeuxis and Alexander Philalethes, whose names appear on coins of Laodicea of the reign of Augustus.

If this establishment was dependent (as it seems to have been) upon the temple of Mên Karou, we may infer that among the

---

* Ramsay, *C. B. Phr.*, p. 167.
† Ramsay, *Cities and Bishoprics of Phrygia*, p. 207.

manifold aspects under which Mên was worshipped that of a healer of diseases must be included. The Cock and the Serpent, which are elsewhere conspicuous among the attributes of this god, also point to a partial assimilation of Mên to Asklepios; and the occurrence of Asklepios and Hygieia as coin-types at Attuda (nos. 3, 22, 32) is, to some extent, confirmatory of this hypothesis.* The exact signification of the epithet ΚΑΡΟΥ, as here applied to the god Mên, is doubtful. It appears to be an indeclinable word (not a genitive case)†; but it is sufficiently intelligible to show that Mên was a god worshipped by Carians, and furthermore that Attuda, when it struck coins with the bust of Mên Karou, must have been essentially a Carian town.

Next after Mên Karou the types of the mother-goddesses Leto and Kybele are especially noteworthy. The temple of Kybele (coin of Sept. Severus, no. 29, Pl. xi. 1) may have been chiefly frequented by the families of Phrygian origin resident in the town. The remaining coin-types, which are numerous, are not especially characteristic, except perhaps that of Sabazios on horseback (Pl. x. 12), concerning which see Ramsay (*Ant. of S. Phryg.*, p. 21).

Attuda is one of a small group of cities belonging, with one exception (Laodicea) to north-eastern Caria, and occupying the lower slopes of the Salbacus range of mountains, on the coins of which the preposition διά more or less frequently takes the place of ἐπί before the name of the magistrate. It is probable that this indicates that the coins were issued at the expense of the official whose name it precedes, and that it conveys a different meaning from ἐπί, which is merely the equivalent of a date. The towns in question are Laodicea ad Lycum, Attuda, Cidramus, and Trapezo-

---

* On this subject see W. H. Roscher, jun. (*Bericht. d. k. Sächs. Gesellsch. d. Wissensch.*, 1891).

† Le-Bas and Wadd., *Inscr. d'As. Min.*, p. 216.

polis. At Apollonia Salbace and at Tubae διά in place of ἐπί also occurs, but only exceptionally.

The only magistrates of Attuda whose titles are recorded are Menippos Υἱὸς πόλεως in the time of Trajan; Karminios Klaudianos *Asiarch* (Aurelius and Verus);* and the priestess Cl. Flavia Arri, ἱέρεια in the reign of Sept. Severus. The title υἱὸς πόλεως occurs elsewhere on coins only at Cotiaeum in Phrygia, though we have a similar title, υἱὸς Ἀφροδισιέων, at Aphrodisias.† The title ἱέρεια, though more frequent, is also rare; we meet with it on coins of Smyrna in Ionia and of Eucarpia and Prymnessus in Phrygia. Concerning an alliance coin of Attuda with Trapezopolis, see *Trapezopolis.*

BARGASA. The exact site of Bargasa is still doubtful. Strabo's (656) order is as follows: εἶτα μετὰ Κνίδον Κέραμος καὶ Βάργασα πολίχνια ὑπὲρ θαλάττης, whence Kiepert places it conjecturally about mid-way between Ceramus and Halicarnassus, on the northern coast of the Ceramic gulf, though he adds in a note that on the Ptolemaic map it is placed much farther north, inland, in the neighbourhood of Alabanda and Amyzon. The scanty coinage of this town (exclusively Imperial) seems to reveal a predominance of the worship of Asklepios. Mr. Paton thinks that, as the coins of Bargasa chiefly come from the interior of Caria, the site of the town must be looked for in the district indicated by Ptolemy.

BARGYLIA. On the ruins and inscriptions of Bargylia, see Le Bas-Wadd. (*Voy. arch. en As. Min.*, iii., 135). It stood on the southern shore of the gulf called after it, and nearly opposite Iasus. It is said to have been founded by Bellerophon in honour of his companion Bargylos, who had been killed by a kick from Pegasos (Steph. Byz., *s.v.*). It is quite possible

---

* Ramsay, *C. and B. Phryg.*, p. 166.
† The municipal adoption of distinguished citizens appears to have been purely honorary. (See *Bull. Corr. Hell.*, xii., 255.)

that some archaic coins of Asiatic style, and with Pegasos on the obverse, may have been struck at Bargylia. No inscribed coins have, however, been discovered which can be assigned to an earlier date than the first century B.C. The neighbouring town Cindya seems at one time to have been more important than Bargylia, for in the middle of the fifth century B.C. it paid two talents tribute to Athens, while Bargylia only paid 2000 drachms per annum. Subsequently Cindya ceased to exist as a πόλις, but the temple of Artemis Kindyas down to Imperial times continued to be an object of veneration. At Bargylia the head or the statue of this goddess is an almost constant coin-type. It was popularly believed concerning this statue, which stood in a temple open to the sky, that neither rain nor snow ever fell upon it.* No Imperial coins of Bargylia are known after the time of Geta.† None of them bear magistrates' names.

CALLIPOLIS. Imhoof‡ describes a bronze coin of Callipolis of the second or first century B.C. Obv. Head of Apollo; Rev. Quiver in shallow incuse square. Arrian§ mentions Callipolis with the citadel of Halicarnassus, Myndus, Caunus, and Thera, as held by Orontobates for a time against Alexander's generals Ptolemy and Asander. The place was probably situated somewhere on the southern coast.

CARYANDA. The site of Caryanda has been recently fixed by Myres and Paton at a few miles north of Telmessus. Imhoof-Blumer‖ assigns to it some small bronze coins of the fourth century B.C.

CAUNUS. Caunus stood on the banks of the river Calbis, between its mouth and a lake a little north of the town. Though Caunus was one of the chief ports on the south

---

* Polyb., xvi. 12; Strab., 658.   † Sestini, Lett. di cont., vi., 43.
‡ Mon. Gr., 307.   § Anab., ii. 5, 7.
‖ Mon. Gr., 307, Pl. F. 1.

coast of Caria, and, on account of its harbour, which could be closed, a naval station of some strength, we cannot confidently attribute to it any coins before the time of Alexander the Great, though it may be suspected that some of the uncertain Carian coins of the archaic period may have been struck there. There is especially one series of silver staters which seems likely to have been issued by the Caunians before the Persian conquest :—

Obv. Forepart of Lion, of archaic style and with mane indicated by dots or very short lines ; on the shoulder of the beast is sometimes the symbol ☥ and sometimes O.

Rev. Incuse square divided into two oblong halves, as on the early coins of Camirus and Lindus. Æ ·75 ; Wt. 172·2 grs.

The weight of these staters, which is intermediate between those of Camirus and those of Lycia, and the form of the incuse square, both point to the southern coast of Caria. It is noteworthy also that the symbol ☥ on the lion's shoulder also occurs in the field of a coin of Caunus dating from about B.C. 300 (p. 75, no. 11, Pl. xii. 4) ; but this may be only a chance coincidence.

For the later history of Caunus, see Holleaux (*Bull. Corr. Hell.*, 1893, p. 61 sqq.). After Alexander's death, Caunus, like the rest of Caria, was possessed in turn by the satrap Asander, by Eumenes, by Antigonus (B.C. 313), and lastly by Ptolemy Soter from B.C. 309. About B.C. 189 the Rhodians purchased Caunus, probably from Ptolemy Epiphanes, but in B.C. 167 it revolted from Rhodes, and obtained from the Roman Senate in the following year a recognition of its freedom. It is probable that when Caunus shook off Rhodian rule in B.C. 167, it may have begun to issue small silver coins of the Rhodian type, differentiated from the Rhodian issues by the addition of an eagle in front of the right cheek of the full-face head of Helios (Pl. xxxix. 12-14). These coins are described under Rhodes (p. 249, nos. 210-218); but they are without the letters P—O, and bear in the field various letters and monograms which were formerly taken to be the initials of Lycian allied towns, but which may be preferably explained as initials of magistrates' names.

CERAMUS. Ceramus was situate on the northern coast of the Ceramic gulf, about midway between Halicarnassus on the west and Idyma, at the head of the gulf, on the east. Strabo (660), speaking of the sanctuary of Zeus Chrysaoreus at Stratonicea, common to all the Carians, says that Ceramus was one of the most important towns of the Chrysaorian confederacy. This is confirmed by the Zeus-types of its coins and by traces of the old road which once connected Ceramus with Stratonicea, and which passed through Panamara (see J. L. Myres, *Athenæum*, 1895, p. 255). Its earliest issues in silver and bronze closely resemble the contemporary second or first century coins of Stratonicea, *obv.* Head of Zeus, *rev.* Eagle (*cf.* Pl. xii. nos. 8, 9 with Pl. xxiii. no. 11 sqq.). The coin of Antoninus Pius (Pl. xii. no. 12) shows a draped statue of the god, standing, holding patera and sceptre, and with an eagle at his feet. The remarkable figure on the reverse of the coin of Commodus (Pl. xii. 13) is probably Zeus Stratios or Labraundos; the animal at his feet has the appearance of a panther, but is perhaps meant for a goat (see note on p. 78 *infra*).

CHALCETOR? Chalcetor was a town of small importance,* the site of which has been fixed at *Kara-Koyoun*, a few miles south of Euromus, by Paton and Myres (*Athenæum*, 1895, p. 255). Whether the coins described in the text are correctly attributed to this place, or whether M. J. P. Six is right in assigning them to the small island of Chalcia off the western coast of Rhodes, is a doubtful point.†

---

* Strab., xiv. 636, 658.
† *Num. Chron.*, 1890, p. 246.

CHERSONESUS. Chersonesus, the narrow neck of land projecting some 50 miles westwards from the mainland towards the island of Cos, seems to have contained in early times, in addition to the important city of Cnidus at its western extremity, three other independent communities united in a Tripolis or league, which continued to exist under the name of the Κοινὸν Χερσονασίων down to the time of the Rhodian dominion in Caria. This κοινόν was assessed separately from Cnidus in the Athenian Tribute Lists,[*] under the name Χερρονήσιοι, at 3 talents per annum between B.C. 454 and 426, while Cnidus during the same years paid an equal sum, except between the years B.C. 450-447, when it was rated at 5 talents. On this subject see Six in *Zeit. f. Num.*, iii., 375, and Paton, *Class. Rev.*, 1889, p. 422. The coins of the Chersonesii, which seem to be all anterior to B.C. 500, are of the Aeginetic standard, like the contemporary coins of Cnidus.

CIDRAMUS. The site of Cidramus has not been identified, but Ramsay remarks (*American Journ. Arch.*, iii., p. 356) that the only ancient authorities (the *Notitiae*) in which its name appears assign it to Caria. The fact, however, that ΖΕΥC ΛΥΔΙΟC (p. 81, no. 2) occurs on its coins shows that it must have been near the Lydian frontier. Ramsay would expect to find traces of its remains somewhere between Antiochia and Attuda, a little to the west of Carura and about due south of the modern village of *Ortakche*, south of the Maeander, on a spur of the hills that fringe the valley.

No coins are known of Cidramus before the age of Augustus, and the latest are those of Julia Maesa. Down to Hadrian's time the magistrate's name is in the nominative, followed by that of his father in the genitive. From the reign of Hadrian to that of M. Aurelius the magistrate's name is in the genitive preceded by the

---

[*] *Corp. Inscr. Att.*, nos. 228-264.

GREEK AND CARIAN TOWNS. xlvii

preposition διά* in place of ἐπί and followed, as before, by the father's name. In addition to the magistrates' names recorded in the text the following have been elsewhere published:— ΠΟΛΕΜΩΝ ϹΕΛΕΥΚΟΥ (obv. ΡΩΜ?) Imp. Times, Nero (*Rev. Num.*, 1851, 167); ΜΟΥΣΑΙΟΣ ΚΑΛΛΙΚΡΑΤΟΥΣ ΠΡ[ύτανις] Imperial, Augustus (*Zeit. f. Num.*, xv. 52); ΠΑΜΦΙΛΟϹ ϹΕΛΕΥΚΟΥ, Vespasian (Imhoof, *Gr. M.* 732); ΔΙΑ ΠΑΝΦΙΛΟΥ ΚΑΙ Π... Hadrian (Imhoof, *Gr. M.* 732); ΔΙ ϹΕΛΕΥΚΟ ΠΟΛΕΜΩ, M. Aurelius (Imhoof, *Gr. M.* 732).† The frequent appearance of Aphrodite among the coin-types of Cidramus may be explained by the fact that Cidramus was situated within ten or a dozen miles of the famous temple of that goddess at the neighbouring city of Aphrodisias.

CNIDUS. The site of Cnidus has been so thoroughly explored that there is no need of further comment on it in this Catalogue. The cultus of Aphrodite at Cnidus probably points to an original Phœnician settlement. The introduction of the worship of the Triopian Apollo is later, and due to the Dorian colony which established itself on the Triopian peninsula and on the opposite coast of the mainland. Of the Triopian Apollo, whose sanctuary was the meeting-place of the members of the Dorian Hexapolis, consisting of the six cities Cnidus, Cos, Halicarnassus, Ialysus, Camirus, and Lindus, the symbol on the coins appears to have been the Lion.

B.C. 700—650. The uninscribed coin (Pl. xiii. 7) which I have ventured to assign to Cnidus, belongs certainly to the seventh century B.C. It is a very archaic silver stater, unfortunately in poor condition. Its present weight is only 158·1 grs., but it

---

* See *supra*, under Attuda.
† The *stemma* of the influential family in which the names Seleucus, Polemon and Pamphilus recur has been conjecturally restored by Ramsay (*C. and B. Phryg.*, p. 185).

may have lost by wear and in the process of cleaning both oxide and metal sufficient to bring it up to the Aeginetic standard, which prevailed at Cnidus from the earliest times. The obverse of this unique stater shows a female head of rude archaic style with a round earring. This is probably the earliest representation of the human head known on coins, and can only represent Aphrodite. The reverse, with its two roughly-executed incuse squares, large and small, proves that it belongs to the same period and region as the earliest coins of Cos and Chios (Pl. xxx. 1, and *Num. Chron.*, 1890, Pl. ii. 15, 16). The earliest staters of Cyme in Aeolis (B. M. Cat., *Troas, Aeolis, and Lesbos*, Pl. xix. 4-6), from the Santorin Find, exhibit the same curious double incuse square, although in this instance the incuse squares contain stars, and may be consequently of a somewhat later date.

Perhaps before the end of the seventh century the head of Aphrodite makes its first appearance within the incuse square on the reverse (Pl. xiii. nos. 8, 9). On the earliest examples the hair is confined in a saccos round which a band is twisted. Some of the later specimens are inscribed KΥ or ΥΟΙΔΙΥΚ. The Ο in this inscription is *omicron*, not *omega* (Pl. xiii. 10, 11).*

B.C. 650—550.

Towards the close of the sixth century a well-marked advance is noticeable in the style and execution of the Lion and of the head of Aphrodite, both, however, strongly archaic in character (Pl. xiv. nos. 1-4). A precisely similar improvement in the coinage of Athens took place at the same time, in the reign of Hippias, B.C. 527-510).†

B.C. 550—480.

The archaic issues of Cnidus come to an end about B.C. 480

---

* Imhoof, *Z. f. N.*, i., 142; and A. Kirchhoff, *Griech. Alphabet*, 2nd ed., p. 49-53 and Taf. i.
† B. M. Cat. *Attica*, Pl. iii.

(Pl. xiv. nos. 3, 4), and from this time down to the end of the Athenian hegemony Cnidus does not seem to have struck coins, or at any rate there are hardly any which can possibly be assigned to this period. The only two specimens which have come under my notice, and which I am inclined to attribute to the middle of the fifth century, are two small coins weighing 26 and 27 grs., bearing (for the first time at Cnidus) magistrates' names, HΠΆ and PΦVΆ ('Επήρατος and Εὔφρων? Imhoof, *Mon. Gr.*, 309). A similar diminution of the coinage, and in some cases apparently a complete cessation of currency, during the period in which Athens was collecting her tribute, is apparent at several other cities besides Cnidus.

In B.C. 412, when, after the disastrous failure of the Athenian campaign in Sicily, Cnidus revolted from Athens,
B.C. 412—400.
it appears to have begun again to coin money, for the specimen figured on Pl. xiv. no. 5, clearly belongs in style to the end of the fifth century.

About B.C. 400 Cnidus, following the example of Rhodes, adopted the so-called Rhodian standard.* The head of
B.C. 400—390.
Aphrodite henceforth occupies the obverse side of the coin (Pl. xiv. 6),† and is specialized as 'Ἀφροδίτη Εὔπλοια by the addition of her symbol, the Prow.

Between B.C. 394 and 390 must be placed the Federal coinage of Cnidus, Iasus, Rhodes, Samos, and Ephesus, of which Pl. xiv. no. 9 is the Cnidian example.

In the next period, which embraces nearly the whole of the fourth century (B.C. 390-300), the Cnidian mint seems to
B.C. 390—300.
have been again active, though very few tetradrachms were struck. The specimens in the British Museum (Pl. xv. no. 1, and Montagu Sale Cat., Pl. viii. 599) are the only two

---

* To the specimens described in the text may be added a didrachm with name ΑΓΑΘΙΝΟΣ (Imhoof, *Z. f. N.*, i, 143).
† Except in one instance (Pl. xiv. no. 8).

l INTRODUCTION.

which I have seen. It has been thought that the head of the goddess on this and other later tetradrachms of Cnidus (Pl. xlv. 7, 8) are memory copies from the famous statue by Praxiteles; but it may be doubted whether the divergencies do not counterbalance the points of resemblance.

The coinage of Cnidus throughout the third century B.C. is plentiful, and it may be consequently inferred that under Alexander's successors the port of Cnidus regained much of its ancient prosperity. Specially favoured by the Ptolemies,* it no doubt derived much profit from the commerce between Egypt and the West, as its harbour afforded a convenient station for vessels bound to and from Alexandria. As many as five beautiful tetradrachms of this period are known in addition to the drachms described in the text (nos. 40-47, Pl. xv. 9-11). They bear the following magistrates' names: [A]ΝΤΙΟΧΙΔΑ[Σ], De Luynes Coll., Wt. 230 grs. (Imhoof, *Gr. M.*, Pl. x. 5); [ΘΕΥ]ΜΕ-ΛΩΝ (Pl. xlv. 7), from Montagu Coll., Wt. 227·5 grs., helmet as adjunct symbol behind head of goddess; ΚΛΕΟΣΘΕΝΗΣ, Waddington Coll., Wt. 232 grs.; ΣΩΣΙΜΑΧ[ΟΣ], Berlin Coll., Wt. 217 grs. (Imhoof, *Mon. Gr.*, p. 309); ΤΕΛΕΣΙΦΡΩΝ, Weber Coll., Wt. 214·5 grs. (Pl. xlv. 8), Ɛ behind head.

On the smaller coins of this period (B.C. 300-190) the following names of magistrates may be added from trustworthy sources:—
Drachms: ΘΕΟΦΑΝΗΣ (Mion., Suppl., vi. 221); [Θϯ]ΕΥΔΩΡΟΣ Mion., iii. 207). *Tetrobols:* ΑΡΙΣΤΟΚΛΗΣ (*Z. f. N.*, i. 145); ΣΩΣΙΓΕΝΗΣ, Rev. Tripod (Imhoof, *Mon. Gr.*, 310). *Diobols:* ΑΓΗΤΩΡ, Rev. Bucranium (Imhoof, *Z. f. N.*, i. 146); ΑΝΤΙΠΑ-ΤΡΟΣ. *Bronze:* ΤΕΛΕΑΣ and Ɛ, Rev. Prow (Imhoof, *Mon. Gr.*, p. 310); ΤΕΛΕCΙΦΡΩΝ and Ɛ, Rev. Prow (*ibid*); ΑΚΡΟ..... (Mion., iii., p. 341); ΑΝΝΙΚΑ; ΔΑΜΟΚ... (Mion., Suppl., vi.,

---

* Theocr., *Idyl.*, xvii. 66.

p. 482, no. 280); **ΙΠΠΟΔΑ** (Imhoof, *Z.f.N.*, i., 146); ... **ΛΑΚΩΝ** (Imhoof, *Mon. Gr.*, 310); **ΜΟΡΦΙΩΝ** (*ibid*).

The monogram ⟨E⟩, which is of frequent occurrence on coins of this period, remains unexplained. As an artist's signature it is inadmissible at so late a date.

B.C. 190—167. After the defeat of Antiochus the Great by the Romans in B.C. 190, the character of the Cnidian coinage became assimilated to that of Rhodes. For the head of Aphrodite on the obverse was substituted that of the full-face Apollo. The rose, the badge of Rhodes, moreover appears on some specimens as a symbol in the field of the reverse (Pl. xvi. no. 1). The weight of these new semi-Rhodian silver coins corresponds with that of two of the light Rhodian drachms of the period. The magistrates' names on the coins of this class are **ΑΓΕΦΩΝ*** and **ΔΙΟΚΛΗΣ**; and it is noteworthy that the last-mentioned name occurs also on a drachm of the Rhodian type without **P O**, struck somewhere on the mainland (Pl. xxxix. no. 9), whence we may infer that Cnidus was for a time governed by the same Rhodian magistrate as the town at which the drachm was struck.

To this period (B.C. 190-167) belong also the Alexandrine tetradrachms assigned by Müller (nos. 1151-2) to Cnidus, with a tripod in the field as a distinctive mint-symbol.

After B.C. 167. From the time when Rhodes was deprived of her possessions on the mainland (B.C. 166), Cnidus, if we may draw an inference from its coinage, ceased to be of much account. Silver money was no longer issued from the Cnidian mint, and even bronze, as time goes on, becomes less and less plentiful, and after the time of Caracalla comes also to an end.

To the lists of magistrates whose names are recorded in the

---

*Wadd., *As. Min.*, 45.

present volume, on the bronze coins subsequent to B.C. 167, the following may be added:—

After B.C. 167. **EYN** (?) ... *Rev.* Lyre (Mion. *Suppl.* vi., p. 484).
  EYK (?) ... *Rev.* Nike („   „   „).
1st *cent.* B.C. **ΑΡΧΙΑΣ** *Rev.* Two bunches of grapes (Mion. iii., p. 342).
  ΕΚΑΤΑΙΟΣ *Rev.* „   „   „   „ (Mion. *Suppl.*, vi., p. 485).
  ΕΥΦΡΑ[ΝΩ]Ρ *Rev.* Bunch of grapes (Imh. *Mon. Gr.* p. 310).
  ΗΡΩΔΗΣ *Rev.* Bunch of grapes (Imh. *Mon. Gr.* 310.)
  ΘΕΟΓΝΩΤΟΣ (or **ΘΕΥΓΝΩΤΟΣ**?) *Rev.* Two bunches of grapes (Mion., iii., p. 342).
Imperial. Faustina Jun. **ΚΑΛΛΙΚΡΑΤΗΣ** (Mion. *Suppl.* vi., p. 486).
  Caracalla? **ΚΑΛΛΙΚΡΑΤΗΣ** *Rev.* Dionysos standing.

CYS.

The site of Cys is identified by Cousin and Deschamps* with the modern village of *Béli-Pouli*, in the mountainous country which separates the upper valleys of the Marsyas and Harpasus. For descriptions of the coins reading **ΚΥ, ΚΥΙ, ΚΥΙΤΩΝ** and **[Κ]ΥΕΙΤΩΝ** see *Hist. Num.*, 525. There are no specimens in the British Museum.

The name of the place in Steph. Byz. appears as Κύον, but the inscriptions prove the correct form to have been Κῦς.

EUIPPE.

The exact site of Euippe, probably close to Alabanda, *q.v.*, is not known. It is called by Steph. Byz. Δῆμος Καρίας. In addition to the two coins described in the text and figured (Pl. xvii. 1, 2) two others are published; one, an autonomous coin, *Obv.* Bust of Artemis r., *Rev.* **ΕΥΙΠΠΕΩ[Ν]** Pegasos r., Æ Size ·65 ;† the other, an Imperial coin of Commodus, *Rev.* Cultus-statue of Aphrodite or the Ephesian Artemis between star and crescent.‡

---

* *Bull. Corr. Hell.*, xi., 305.   † Fox, ii., Pl. v. 100.
‡ *Berl. Blätt.*, i., Pl. viii. 10.

GREEK AND CARIAN TOWNS. liii

Pliny* mentions, among other Carian towns in the vicinity of
Halicarnassus, a place of which the name Uranium
EURALIUM. has been, probably erroneously, corrected by Sillig
to Euralium on the evidence of a coin of Caracalla described by
Borrell,† reading ΕΥΡΑΛΕΩΝ. As Pliny's text is very corrupt,
the coin, which is supposed to be unique, may belong to some other
place.

Euromus was situate at the modern *Ayakly*, about 8 miles N.W.
of Mylasa, and the same distance S.W. of Labranda,
EUROMUS. where stood the sanctuary of Zeus Labraundos. It
cannot have been a place of any importance. It is doubtful whether
the Zeus worshipped at Euromus was altogether identical with Zeus
Labraundos, for the types of the coins of Euromus show a cultus-
statue of Zeus accompanied sometimes by the pilei of the Dioskuri,
sometimes by a stag, and sometimes by an eagle, while on one coin
of Caracalla, described by Mionnet (iii. 346, 254) after Vaillant
(*Num. Gr.*, p. 100), he is also specially designated as ΖΕΥC
ΕΥΡΩΜΕΥC. Nevertheless, the labrys or double-axe held by the
god of Euromus sufficiently indicates his close relation to the Zeus
of Labranda. On a coin of the second (?) century B.C. described by
Imhoof,‡ *Obv.* Head of Zeus, *Rev.* Labrys, the name of a magistrate
ΕΚΑΣ is recorded.

Gordiuteichos, another small Carian town, was perhaps situated
at the modern *Karasu*, about 10 miles below Aphro-
GORDIUTEICHOS. disias on the left bank of the Morsynus. It is
mentioned by Livy § as between Antioch and Tabae and two days'
march from the latter, and by Steph. Byz. Γορδίου τεῖχος πόλις
[Καρίας] Μίδου κτίσμα τοῦ παιδὸς Γορδίου, ὁ πολίτης Γορδιοτειχίτης.
The coins of this city are very rare. The only other published

---

* *N. H.*, V. xxix. † *Num. Chron.*, ix., 151.
‡ *Mon. Gr.*, 310. § xxxviii. 13.

specimen is in the Loebbecke Collection.* They belong apparently to the second century B.C. (see Pl. xvii. 9).

HALICARNASSUS. For the early history of Halicarnassus see Newton, *Halicarnassus, Cnidus and Branchidae*, vol. ii., pt. i. The fact that there are no coins of Halicarnassus which can be assigned to an earlier date than the beginning of the 5th cent. B.C.

Before B.C. 480. (Pl. xviii. 1, 2), and that during the next hundred years no large coins appear to have been struck there, is an indication that the trade-route between Egypt and the West, which touched and enriched the ports of Rhodes, Cnidus, Cos, Calymna, and Miletus, passed west of Halicarnassus, leaving it comparatively unaffected by the main stream of commerce. Had it been otherwise we can hardly suppose that Halicarnassus would not have had in these times a silver currency of greater importance.

Between circ. B.C. 480 and 400 there is an interval during which Halicarnassus apparently struck no money.

About B.C. 400 the coinage begins again with drachms (Pl. xviii. no. 3) bearing a full-face head of Apollo, the style

B.C. 400—377. and pose of which seem to be borrowed from the head of Helios on the contemporary coins of Rhodes. This type was adopted by the powerful Carian dynast Mausolus when (circ. B.C. 367) he transferred the seat of his government

Residence of the Satraps of Caria. from the inland stronghold at Mylasa, the ancestral home of his race, to the more conveniently situated coast town of Halicarnassus.

From this time down to that of Alexander's conquest Halicarnassus, as the capital of Caria, was the place of mintage of the splendid series of coins struck in the names of Mausolus, Hidrieus, Pixodarus and Orontobates (Pl. xxviii. and xlv. 4). (See below, p lxxx. *sqq.*)

---

* *Zeit. f. Num.*, xv., 45, Pl. iii. 14.

The destruction of Halicarnassus by Alexander the Great, B.C.
334, renders it highly improbable that Alexandrine
Destroyed by Alexander. tetradrachms were struck there, at any rate any of the earlier class.

The date of the rebuilding of the city after its destruction in
334 B.C. is uncertain, but inscriptions prove that
Rebuilt in 3rd cent. B.C. this must have taken place while it formed part of the dominions of the Ptolemies, and consequently in the course of the 3rd cent. B C.* The style of the bronze coins, nos. 14-19 (Pl. xviii. 9, 10), tallies with this date.

In B.C. 188 the Romans, after the defeat of Antiochus the Great,
handed over the greater part of Caria to the
B.C. 188—166, and later. Rhodians, but it is to a later period that we must assign the drachms bearing the head of the Rhodian Helios on the obverse (Pl. xviii. nos. 14, 15), and perhaps also some of the hemidrachms without the letters P—O (Pl. xxxix. nos. 9-11), two of which, with the magistrate's name ΔΙΟΚΛΗΣ, bear the mint-mark ⊟, possibly an archaistic survival of the aspirate, the initial letter of Halicarnassos (*cf.* the analogous use of Ϙ on the later coins of Corinth).

In Imperial times Halicarnassus was one of the least important
cities of Caria. Cicero (*Epist. ad Quint. frat.*, i. 1)
Imperial times. describes it as almost deserted until it was restored by his brother Quintus, and subsequently the scarcity of Imperial coins shows that, like Cnidus, it never recovered its ancient glory.

The Imperial issues cease altogether after the reign of Gordian. The most interesting type in this period is the radiate figure of Zeus Askraios ? standing between two trees in each of which sits a bird (no. 83, Pl. xix. 2). The head of the historian Herodotus (Pl. xix. 3) is also of considerable interest, and may be compared

---

* Newton, *Halic., Cnidus and Branchidae*, vol. ii., pt. ii., p. 688.

with the series of coins of Mytilene commemorating famous citizens.*

HARPASA. Of Harpasa, situate on the right bank of the Harpasus some 12 miles south of its junction with the Maeander, I know of only one coin (Pl. xix. no. 5) which can be attributed to præ-Imperial times. The Imperial coinage, with and without Emperors' heads, seems to range from Trajan's time to that of Gordian. Among the magistrates' names the most noteworthy is that of Candidus Celsus, supposed by M. Waddington† to be that of a son of Ti. Julius Candidus Marius Celsus, who belonged to a consular family of high rank in the second century of the Empire. There is, however, nothing to show that the Candidus Celsus of the Harpasa coins was a Proconsul of Asia, as Waddington surmises.

A coin of Caracalla‡ gives a magistrate's name, M.AV. ΕVAN-ΔPOC. B. APXIATPOC. The title 'Ἀρχίατρος occurs also on coins of Heraclea Salbace, under Ant. Pius and M. Aurelius (see *infra*, p. 120, nos. 25, 26), and in inscriptions of various Carian towns (Alabanda, Aphrodisias, and Euromus); see Marquardt, *Privatleben d. Römer*, p. 753, 8 ; 755, 4.

HERACLEA SALBACE. Heraclea Salbace was first correctly placed by Waddington (*As. Min.*, p. 51) at the modern *Makuf*.§ It stood at the foot of the Salbacus range of mountains, at the north-eastern end of the plain of Tabae. Its territory seems to have been bounded on the west by the small river Timeles, the name of which appears on a coin of Imperial times ‖ This river, rising in the hilly country which separates the high

---

* B. M. *Cat. Mys.*, Introd., p. lxx.
† *Fastes*, p. 209.
‡ Imhoof, *Gr. M.*, p. 671.
§ *Cf.* Le Bas-Waddington, *Inscr. d'As. Min.*, tom. iii., pt. i., p. 402.
‖ Leake, *Num. Hell. As.*, p. 65.

plains which formed the territory of Heraclea from the valley of Aphrodisias on their northern side, is also represented on coins of Aphrodisias, whose water-supply was derived from its sources (see *supra*, p. xxxiii.).

There are no coins of Heraclea earlier than the first century B.C. The series with Emperors' names closes with Macrinus. As a rule, they do not bear magistrates' names. The exceptions are the following: ΑΠΟΛΛΩΝΙΟΣ ΑΠΟΛΛΩΝΙΟΥ (Augustus), ΓΛΥΚΩΝ ΙΕΡΕΥΣ (Nero), and CT. ΑΤΤΑΛΟC ΑΡΧΙΑΤΡΟC ΝЄΟΙC* (Ant. Pius and M. Aurelius). In an inscription found at *Makuf*,† mention is made of a certain Glykon who had been twice Stephanephoros, Gymnasiarch, προγραφεὶς τῆς Βουλῆς, and priest of Herakles. This is probably the same Glykon whose name appears on the coins of Nero. The name of Statilios Attalos also occurs in an inscription, with his title Ἀρχίατρος.‡

The prevalent Herakles types show, as might be inferred from the name of the town, that the predominant cultus was that of Herakles. The head of this divinity on coins of Nero, signed by Glykon, the priest of Herakles, bears a striking resemblance to the head of Herakles on presumably contemporary silver coins of the city of Tabae (Pl. xxv. 6, 7). Among the numerous other types described in the text there are two of special interest : one is a temple containing a statue of a goddess resembling the Ephesian Artemis (Pl. xx. 10), but which may be intended for the Aphrodite of the neighbouring city of Aphrodisias; the other is a figure of Aphrodite, with her right arm extended behind her and holding a mirror before her face (Pl. xx. 11). As this type is also met with

---

* Supply ΑΝЄΘΗΚЄ. Statilios Attalos on this occasion evidently presented a sum of money to the gymnastic college of the Νέοι. Cf. Th. Reinach on Inscr. of Iasus in *Rev. des Etudes grecques*, vi., p. 163.

† *C. I. G.*, 3953, c.

‡ Le Bas-Waddington, iii. 402.

at Cidramus (Pl. xiii. 4), it is probable that it is a copy of a statue.

HYDISUS.

Hydisus was a small town in central Caria, about 25 miles E. of Alabanda. It is mentioned by Ptolemy[*] and by Pliny.[†] The correct form of the name is revealed by an inscription from Lagina[‡] (ΥΔΙΣΟΣ), and this is confirmed by the coin described in the text (Pl. xx. 12). The name of the town occurs in the Athenian Tribute lists,[§] but only the first letters Υ and ΥΔΙ are apparent.

HYLLARIMA.

Hyllarima is placed on Kiepert's map on the right bank of the river Harpasus, about 30 miles above Harpasa and half that distance above Neapolis. This site would agree well with the order of Hierocles,—"*Harpasa, Neapolis, Hylarema, Antiokheia, Aphrodisias.*" On the other hand, Steph. Byz. says that Hyllarima was ὕπερθε Στρατονικείας, a statement supported by the order of the *Notitiae;* and Prof. Ramsay is now inclined to look for the site of Hyllarima somewhere near the sources of the Marsyas, a little to the west or south-west of Stratonicea,[||] and between Mylasa and Mobolla (*Mughla*).

The style of the only two coins known of Hyllarima, both bearing the name of the Archon Teimotheos, and belonging to early Imperial times (Pl. xx. 13, and *Rev. Num.*, 1892, Pl. iv. 14), seems to accord more nearly with that of the coins of the north-eastern district of Caria than with that of the money of Mylasa and Stratonicea; but the arguments adduced by Ramsay in favour of some site on the road leading from Mylasa to Stratonicea are too strong to be upset by such doubtful evidence as is afforded by

---

[*] V. 2, 20.   [†] *N. H.*, v. 29, 29.
[‡] *Bull. Corr. Hell.*, ix. 444.   [§] *C. I. A.*, i., 231, 233.
[||] *Num. Chron.*, 1891, p. 139.

the coins, even though this evidence seems to be supported by the order of Hierocles.

IASUS. Iasus was an ancient Argive colony on the north side of the Bargylian gulf. It occupied a small island, which is now connected with the mainland. There are no archaic coins which can be with certainty attributed to Iasus, although it has been suggested that the following drachms of the Aeginetic Standard may have been struck there :—

Obv. Naked youth riding on dolphin.
Rev. Incuse square divided into eight triangular compartments, of which three are in relief. [Brit. Mus.] Æ 92·5 grs. Size ·7.
Obv. Similar type, but dolphin-rider holds uncertain object in extended right hand.
Rev. Rough incuse square quartered. [Brit. Mus.] Æ 92·3 grs. Size ·65.

As there is no evidence of any tradition of a dolphin-rider at Iasus before the age of Alexander the Great, it is safer for the present to leave these coins unattributed. In style and weight they resemble the coins of the Aegean islands, though the type (Arion ?) suggests the possibility of their attribution to Methymna.

Excluding these archaic specimens, the earliest coin struck at Iasus would be the beautiful silver tetradrachm in the British Museum (*Cat. Ionia*, p. 325, Pl. xxxi. 6), having on the obverse the head of a Persian Satrap, and on the reverse BAΞIΛ and a Lyre. The head of this Satrap is thought by M. Six and by M. Babelon to be that of Tissaphernes, and the reasons for the attribution of the coin to Iasus are set forth by the latter in *Rev. Num.*, 1892, p. 427. The date of the issue of this coin is, according to Babelon, B.C. 395 ; according to Six,* B.C. 412-408.

---

* *Num. Chron.*, 1888, p. 107.

The next coin, and the earliest which bears the name of Iasus,
belongs to the small series of alliance coins issued
circ. B.C. 394, by Cnidus, Samos, Ephesus, Rhodes,
and Iasus.* As this League seems to have been
dissolved in B.C. 390,† the federal coinage of the above-mentioned
towns was probably restricted to a single issue. Henceforth for more
than a hundred years Iasus has left us no numismatic record. It
would seem, therefore, that under the Carian dynasts, Mausolus and
his successors, and under Alexander the Great and his successors in
Asia Minor down to about the middle of the third century, its
autonomy was incomplete, and that it did not enjoy the right of
coinage. But, in common with many other towns in western Asia
Minor, Iasus appears to have recovered complete or almost complete autonomy from the Seleucidae, *circ.* B.C. 261-246,‡ and it is
doubtless to about this time that the beginning
of a purely Iasian coinage must be ascribed.
The drachms of this period, of the so-called Persic Standard
(82 grs.), may be compared with the contemporary issue at Miletus
(cf. *B. M. Cat. Ionia*, Pl. xxi.). They are signed by the eponymous
magistrate of the city, the Στεφανηφόρος of Apollo.§ The remarkable type of these coins, a youth swimming beside a dolphin,
is explained by Hicks (*Journ. Hell. Stud.*, viii. 93 sq.). The pretty
story of the boy and the dolphin is recorded by Athenaeus on the
authority of Duris of Samos, an historian of the age of Alexander.
There would even seem to be some sort of historical basis for this
strange incident, for Alexander the Great is said to have ordered
the boy to be sent to his court. The name of the youth, as given

---

* Waddington, *Rev. Num.*, 1863, Pl. x. 1-4; and Imhoof, *Mon. Gr.*, Pl. F. 6.
† Judeich, *Kleinasiat. Stud.*, p. 80.
‡ Hicks, *Gr. Hist. Inscr.*, no. 174.
§ Le Bas and Waddington, *Inscr. As. Min.*, Part v., p. 86 sq.

by Athenaeus (xiii. 606) is Dionysios, but Plutarch and Pliny (*N. H.*, ix. 8) call him Hermias, an Iasian name which occurs both on coins (Imhoof, *Mon. Gr.*, 311) and inscriptions.* The Boy and Dolphin as a coin-type of the Iasians is mentioned by three ancient writers, Aelian,† Plutarch,‡ and Pollux.§ The stele erected at Iasus in commemoration of this curious story is described by Aelian (*l.c.*) as representing a youth *riding* upon a dolphin, in which respect it must have differed from the coins.

From B.C. 190-168 Iasus, with the rest of Caria, was under the Rhodian dominion. From 168 until it was incorporated into the Roman Province of Asia it was again nominally free, but does not seem to have coined any money. The subsequent issues belong to Imperial times and range from Augustus to Gordian. The chief divinities of Iasus were Apollo, Artemis Astias, Zeus Megistos, and Iasos the eponymous hero and founder (Pl. xxi. 7).

Circ. B.C. 190-168.

Idyma stood at the head of the Ceramic gulf, where the little river Idymus‖ empties itself into what is now called Giova Bay. Idyma is several times mentioned in the Athenian Tribute Lists. It was rated at first at 4000 drachms, but after B.C. 447 its assessment was reduced to 2000 dr. Waddington¶ was the first to point out that in fragment VI of these lists mention is made of Πακτύης ʼΙδυμ[εύς], whence he concludes that in B.C. 445 the town was governed by a despot named Pactyes, and from the later fragments of the same lists, in which the name of Pactyes no longer occurs, he infers that his rule had come to an end before the year B.C. 437.

IDYMA.

The coinage of Idyma may have begun before B.C. 600, if I am

---

* Reinach, *Rev. des Etudes grecques*, vi. 195-200.
† *Hist. Anim.*, vi. 15.   ‡ *De Solert. Anim.*, 36.   § ix. 84.
‖ Steph. Byz., *s.v.*   ¶ *Rev. Num.*, 1856, p. 59; *C. I. A.*, i. 227.

right in assigning to it an archaic drachm of Aeginetic wt. (90·5 grs.) in the Montagu Coll. *Obv.* Head of Pan. *Rev.* Incuse square. There is also another specimen, weighing 88·4 grs., among the uncertain coins in the British Museum. The inscribed coins, however, consist chiefly of drachms of the Phœnician Standard (58·2 grs.) which seem to belong to the latter half of the 5th cent. B.C. (Pl. **xxi.** 8, 9). The head on the obverse of these coins, as Imhoof has shown (*Mon. Gr.*, p. 312), is that of Pan, while the reverse type, a fig-leaf, seems to have been suggested by the coins of Camirus in Rhodes, a fact which may point to commercial intercourse between the two cities.

There are only two known coins of Idyma which appear to be of later date than the end of the 5th cent. B.C.; one of these is the drachm (Pl. **xxi.** no. 10), and the other is a bronze coin published by Imhoof and figured in his *Mon. gr.* (Pl. F. 8).

For some inscriptions of Idyma of Imperial times, see Cousin and Diehl (*Bull. Corr. Hell.*, **x.** 428).

MYLASA.
Mylasa was situated at a distance of about 10 miles in a direct line from the coast on the upper course of the river Kyberses, which flows down from Mylasa through the 'Ομβιανὸν πεδίον, in a northerly direction past the town of Olymus, and then turns towards the south and discharges its waters into the Bargylian gulf near Iasus. According to Strabo (659), the town was built at the foot of a precipitous mountain containing rich quarries of a beautiful white marble, which yielded ample material for the erection of the numerous porticos and temples which adorned the town, the size of which was however dwarfed by the lofty superincumbent rocky heights.

Mylasa, originally a place of small importance (κώμη, Strab. 659), became, in the time of Hecatomnus, a royal residence, and the chief city of Caria. In Strabo's time there were two famous temples of Zeus within the territory of Mylasa, one of Zeus 'Οσογῶα or

'Οσογώς in the city itself, and the other of Zeus Λάβραυνδος or Στράτιος at the village of Labranda, about 10 miles north of Mylasa. Zeus Osogoa was a combination of the Greek gods Zeus and Poseidon (Ζηνοποσειδῶν). He is represented on coins as holding an eagle and resting upon a trident, and his symbol on some coins is the crab. The cultus-statue of Zeus Labraundos on Imperial coins is a terminal figure with a polos on his head, a bipennis (λάβρυς) in one hand and a spear in the other; but on the coins of Hecatomnus, the earliest coins struck at Mylasa, he is represented as walking, and clothed in a long chiton and himation, holding the labrys over his right shoulder and a long spear in his left hand. From the time when Mausolus removed the royal residence from Mylasa to Halicarnassus no coins were struck at Mylasa until after the age of Alexander the Great.

It seems probable that the bronze coins bearing the name of Eupolemus, the general of Cassander (Pl. xxi. nos. 11, 12) may have been struck at Mylasa in B.C. 314*; and early in the second century B.C., after the victory of the Romans over Antiochus at Magnesia, Mylasa, which may then have been made a free city by the Romans,† was the place of mintage of the Alexandrine tetradrachms with the monogram M and the characteristic symbol composed of the Labrys and Trident combined.‡ To this time I would also assign a very remarkable gold stater with the types and name of Philip; the symbol on the reverse, Labrys and Trident in one, shows that it must have been struck at Mylasa. It formed part of a small hoard of gold Philippi found in the Maeander valley, which belong in style to a period long subsequent to Philip's own time, and which are certainly of Asiatic origin (see *infra*, p. cviii.).

---

* See Wroth in *Num. Chron.*, 1891, p. 135.
† Marquardt and Mommsen, *Handbuch der römischen Alterthümer*, iv., p. 346.
‡ Müller, 1141-1143.

Some of the bronze coins of the second century B.C. have on the reverse this same combination of Labrys and Trident (Pl. xxi. no. 13); others have the Trident or the Labrys alone (nos. 14-17). The Imperial coins of Mylasa extend over the entire period from Augustus to Valerian. In the time of Augustus they bear the name of the Grammateus, but thenceforth they are without a magistrate's name. In Hadrian's time Mylasa was one of the mints which issued silver coins with Latin inscriptions, of the weight of 3 Roman denarii. Of these (so called) medallions of Asia there are some bearing figures of Zeus Labraundos and of Zeus Osogoa (Pinder, *Cistoph.*, Pl. vii. 2, 3, 7, 8).

MYNDUS. Myndus, though, like its near neighbour Halicarnassus, it was an ancient Dorian seaport, does not seem to have been a place of great importance, and there are no coins attributed to it before the second century B.C. The harbour of Myndus, where the remains of the city have been identified,[*] is now called *Gumishli*. Waddington[†] acquired eight bronze coins of the town in an adjacent village.

The earliest and certainly the most important coin of Myndus is the apparently unique tetradrachm in the Hague cabinet (Pl. xlv. 9), which belongs to the class of flat spread coins which came into fashion in western Asia Minor about B.C. 190. The obverse type is a head of Apollo, and on the reverse is a winged thunderbolt accompanied by the inscription ΜΥΝΔΙΩΝ and two monograms, the whole within a wreath.

The drachms etc. are numerous, and seem to extend over a considerable time, and to belong chiefly to the first century B.C. (Pl. xxii. 6, 7). For numerous names of magistrates not represented in the British Museum, see Imhoof (*Zeit. f. Num.*, iii., 326, sq.) and Waddington (*As. Min.*, 53).

---

[*] Leake, *Num. Hell. Asiatic Greece*, p. 85.   [†] *As. Min.*, p. 53.

The Imperial coinage of Myndus extends down to the time of Sept. Severus.

Neapolis near Myndus is only mentioned by Mela* and by Pliny.† Both these writers place it in the Dorian peninsula west of Halicarnassus. No coins have hitherto been assigned to this Neapolis, but, if I have correctly read the specimen described in the text, I think that it is very probable that it may belong to this town. In fabric and style it is much more like the second and first century coins of the towns of the western coast than those of an inland city such as Neapolis on the Harpasus, nor can it be attributed to Neapolis in Ionia, a town which seems to have owed its foundation to Antoninus Pius. It is, however, not quite certain that the characters on the right of the lyre are in reality **MYN**. The attribution is therefore still somewhat conjectural.

NEAPOLIS MYNDIORUM ?

Neapolis ad Harpasum. An inscription has been discovered at the modern *Ineboli*, in the lower valley of the Harpasus, about eight miles above Harpasa, on the eastern side of the river, which proves that the place called Neapolis by Ptolemy and Hierocles occupied this site.‡ There has been much confusion between the coins which belong to this town and those of Neapolis in Ionia. It would seem, however, that Neapolis in Ionia, a coast town a few miles south of Ephesus, was distinguished from other places of the same name by the addition of the title Aurelia or Hadriana Aurelia.§ As the British Museum has acquired several coins of the Ionian Neapolis Aurelia since the publication of the *Catalogue of the Coins of Ionia*, 1892, I append descriptions here; and if we add to these nos. 111 and

NEAPOLIS AD HARPASUM.

---

* I. 16.   † *N. H.*, v. 29.
‡ Kubitschek and Reichel, *Ueber eine Reise in Karien und Phrygien*, in the *Anzeiger der phil.-hist. Classe*. (*K. Akad. d. Wiss. zu Wien.*), 1893, no. xxiv.
§ See Imhoof, *Mon. Gr.*, p. 294, and Löbbecke, *Z. f. N.*, xv. 44.

112 described by Imhoof (*l.c.*), and nos. 1-3 of Löbbecke's list (*Z. f. N., l.c.*), a series of coins may be constructed which seems to be clearly separable from those of Neapolis near Myndus and Neapolis near Harpasa. The Museum specimens are the following :—

Antoninus Pius.

Obv. A·K·TI· A·AΔP·ANTΩNEI NOC KTICTHC Bust r. laur. and draped.

Rev. ΕΠΙΓ ΠΡΩΤΕΟΝ ΑΔ ΑΥΡΗ ΝΕΑΠΟΛΕΙΤΩ Apollo Kitharœdos standing r., clad in long chiton and himation, holding in r. plectrum, and in l. lyre. Æ 1·

Severus Alexander.

Obv. AYT·K·M·AYP CE YOYH ΑΛΕΞΑΝΔΡΟC Bust r. laur., wearing cuirass and paludamentum.

Rev. ΑΥΡ·ΔΙΟΝΥCΙΟC ΞΗΝΩΝΟC ΑΝ[Ε] ΘΗ ΚΑ and in ex. ΑΥΡ ΝΕΑΠΟΛ ΕΙΤΩΝ Tetrastyle temple containing statue of Apollo clad in long chiton, his r. raised above his head, his l. supporting lyre placed on tripod round which serpent coils. Æ 1·4

Maximinus.

Obv. AVT·K·Γ·I·OVH· ΜΑΞΙΜΕΙΝΟC Bust of Maximinus r. laur., wearing cuirass and paludamentum.

Rev. ΑΥΡ·ΝΕΑΠΟ ΛΕΙΤΩΝ Dionysos standing l., himation over legs, holding in r. kantharos, and in l. thyrsos. Æ ·9

The coins of Neapolis ad Harpasum begin apparently in the reign of Gordian and end with Trebonianus Gallus and Volusian. The name of a magistrate, Candidus (Grammateus), occurs twice in the series, once on a coin of Gordian, A.D. 238-244 (*Z. f. N.*, x.78), and once some ten years later on a coin of Volusian (*infra*, p. 142, no. 6), where he appears as Grammateus for the fourth time. The resemblance of the prevailing type (Athena with spear and shield) of the coins of this city to that of the coins of Harpasa renders it probable that the same cultus of Athena was predominant in the two neighbouring towns, and the recurrence of the name Candidus at a later period at Neapolis than at Harpasa tells against Waddington's opinion that the Candidus Celsus of the Harpasa coins of M. Aurelius was a Proconsul of Asia. The two men were probably local magistrates belonging to the same family.

ORTHOSIA. The site of Orthosia has been fixed near the modern *Ortas* close to *Jenibazar*, by Kubitschek and Reichel.* The town stood on high ground overlooking the valley of the Maeander, in the direction of Nysa, which occupied the opposite hills on the northern side of the river, at a distance of ten or twelve miles.

The coinage of Orthosia begins either in the third or early in the second century B.C., and extends through Imperial Times down to the reigns of Maximinus and Maximus. The cultus of Dionysos, and that of Hades and Persephone, which seem to have prevailed at Orthosia, may have been derived from the important town of Nysa, a centre of religious influence which extended over a wide region on both sides of the Maeander.†

The autonomous coins of Orthosia bear magistrates' names in the nominative case. See (in addition to those given in the text) Imhoof, *Mon. Gr.*, p. 313. The Imperial coins are without names of magistrates.

SEBASTOPOLIS. The position of Sebastopolis has been fixed by inscriptions at the modern *Kizilje*, on the road from Apollonia Salbace to Cibyra, at about eight miles S.E. of the former. The coins of Sebastopolis extend from the time of Vespasian to that of Sept. Severus (Domna). The magistrate's name Παπίας ’Απολλωνίου on p. 146, no. 1, occurs also on a coin of Vespasian in the French collection. The same name Παπίας is also met with

---

* *K. Akad. d. Wiss. zu Wien. Anzeiger d. phil.-hist. Cl.*, 1893, no. 24.
† Strabo, xi v. c. i. 46, 47

on Imperial coins of the neighbouring cities of Apollonia and Tabae.

STRATONICEA. Stratonicea, which ranks with Mylasa and Alabanda as one of the three chief inland towns of Caria, was situate at the modern *Eski-Hissar*, on the main road from Alabanda, and about 30 miles south of that town, on the left side of the upper valley of the Marsyas, not far from its sources. Strabo (xiv. 2, 25) says that it was a Macedonian colony; and according to Steph. Byz. it was named after Stratonice, wife of Antiochus I. It is probable, however, that an older town, variously called Hidrias, Chrysaoris, and Hecatesia, existed here long before the Macedonian settlement.*

Within the territory of Stratonicea there were three famous temples, one of Hekate at Lagina, a few miles north of the city, where a great festival called Hekatesia was celebrated every five years,† another of Zeus Chrysaoreus, or Karios, near the city itself. This last was a centre, both religious and political, for all communities of Carian race, and the head-quarters of a National League, called the Chrysaoric Systema, of which Stratonicea, although not itself a Carian city, was one of the members, in virtue of the numerous Carian κῶμαι situate within its territory. The third temple was that of Zeus Panamaros, or Panemerios, the site of which was discovered by MM. Cousin and Deschamps in 1886, at the modern *Bagh-yaka*, on a height difficult of access,‡ which Kiepert, on the authority of Benndorf, who visited it in 1892, places about 12 miles S.E. of Stratonicea. Zeus Panamaros and Hekate were, as the numerous inscriptions abundantly prove, the two special tutelary divinities of the Stratoniceans, and the coin-types serve to confirm the epigraphic evidence.

---

* Waddington, *As. Min.*, 57.
† *Bull. Corr. Hell.*, 1881, 236. Newton, *Essays*, 175.
‡ *Bull. Corr. Hell.*, xi. 373, xii. 82.

GREEK AND CARIAN TOWNS. lxix

There are no coins of Stratonicea which can be attributed to an earlier date than B.C. 168, unless perhaps some few coins of Alexander's types with the letters ΣΤΡΑ in monogram (Müller, *Num. d'Alex.*, 1134-6). Down to B.C. 168 the town was subject to Rhodes, and does not seem to have been in a position to strike its own coins. But when Caria was declared free and independent of Rhodes by the Romans at the conclusion of the third Macedonian war, Stratonicea obtained her freedom (Polyb., xxx. 19) and began to strike silver money.

The reintroduction of the incuse square on the reverses of their silver coins by the Rhodians (*circ.* B.C. 166) seems to have set a fashion for small silver money, which was immediately followed by Cos, the towns of the Lycian League, and by Ceramus and Stratonicea in Caria.

The types of the Stratonicean hemidrachms of Rhodian weight, which clearly belong to this period (Pl. xxiii. 11-12), are the head of Zeus on the obverse, and an eagle in the shallow incuse square of the reverse. Whether these types refer to Zeus Chrysaoreus or to Zeus Panamaros is doubtful, but the fact that the same types occur on the contemporary hemidrachms of Ceramus (Pl. xii. 8) seems to indicate Zeus Chrysaoreus, whose cultus was common to all Carians, as the divinity represented on the Stratonicean coinage of this period, the circulation of which was certainly not confined to the precincts of the city. These hemidrachms bear the names, in the nominative case, probably of the eponymous magistrate of Stratonicea, who, as in many other cities of Asia, was the Archon Stephanephoros. (Le Bas and Wadd., 517, 519, 525.)*

---

* In addition to the magistrates' names supplied by this Catalogue on the silver coins of this period, the following have been noted, ΑΡΙΣΤΕΑΣ 24 grs., *Rev.* Nike (Imhoof, *Mon. Gr.*, 315); ΑΤΤΑΛΟΣ Α *Rev.* Nike, and ΑΡ (Mion., *S.* vi. 535), ΓΑΙΟΣ, *Rev.* Nike (Waddington, *As. Min.*, 55), ΔΗΜΟΣΘΕΝΗΣ, *Rev.* Nike (Wadd., *l.c.*); ΔΙΟΚΛΗΣ ΚΙ., 29 grs. *Rev.*

INTRODUCTION.

Next in order of date follows a series of hemidrachms bearing on the obverse the head of the goddess Hekate (Pl. xxiii. 13), and on the reverse a figure of Nike in a shallow incuse square. One of these coins is signed by ʽΕκαταῖος Σωσάνδρου, who, as we learn from an inscription,* was a Priest of the temple of Hekate at Lagina; but Hekataios may have been either previously or subsequently Stephanephoros of Stratonicea, for there is no evidence to show that coins were struck by the Temple authorities independently of the municipal Boule.

The small bronze coins (Pl. xxiii. 14-16) with the shallow incuse square on the reverse belong to the same period as the silver coins above referred to. They are all apparently previous to the Mithradatic war (B.C. 88-84), during which Stratonicea remained faithful to Rome, and suffered much in consequence at the hands of Mithradates.† After Sulla's victory Stratonicea recovered, by a decree of the Senate (B.C. 81), all or more than all the privileges which had previously been enjoyed by her.‡ The city seems at this time to have been constituted a *civitas libera et immunis sine foedere*. The right of asylum of the temple of Hekate was also recognised and confirmed.

The coins which I propose to assign to this period of renewed prosperity after B.C. 81 are: (i.) the stater or tetradrachm weighing 166 grs. (*Z. f. N.*, xvi., Pl. i. 2) *Obv.* Head of Zeus, *Rev.* ΜΕΛΑΝΘΙΟΣ ΣΤΡΑΤΟΝΙΚΕΩΝ Hekate standing to front, holding

---

Nike (Imhoof, *Gr. M.*, 674); ΦΑΝΙΑC ΚΙΘΑ 18 grs., *Rev.* Nike (Imhoof, *op. cit.*, 674); ΑΡΙΣΤΕΑΣ and ΑΡΙCΤΕΑC, 21 and 19 grs., *Rev.* Eagle (Imhoof, *Mon. Gr.*, 315); ΑΡΤΕΜΙΔΩ *Rev.* Eagle, 17 grs. (Imhoof, *M. G.*, 315); ΠΥΘΕΑΣ, *Rev.* Eagle (Mion., *S.* vi., 535); ΧΡΥCΟΥ *Rev.* Eagle, 1½ grs. (Im., *M. Gr.*, 315). The last is the only one here attributed to this period which is not in the nominative case.

* *Bull. Corr. Hell.*, xi. 13.
† Appian, *De Bell. Mith.*, xxi.
‡ *Bull. Corr. Hell.*, ix. 462.

patera and torch, the whole within a laurel wreath; (ii.) the corresponding drachm, wt. 52·8 grs. (*infra*, p. 150 and Pl. xxiii. no. 17); and (iii.) the bronze coins with Pegasos or Nike on the reverse (Pl. xxiii. 18 and p. 150). The abandonment of the incuse square and the substitution on the reverse of a dotted circle is noticeable also on the Rhodian drachms of this period (Pl. xl. and xli. 1, 2).

During the invasion of Asia Minor by Labienus (B.C. 40), Alabanda, Mylasa and Stratonicea were the only three cities which offered any serious resistance to his attacks. The two former were taken, but Stratonicea was successful in repulsing the invaders, though her temples of Hekate at Lagina and of Zeus at Panamara were plundered by the foreign troops. They were, however, shortly afterwards restored, and all their ancient rights and privileges were confirmed by decrees of the Senate under Augustus, B.C. 39, and again under Tiberius, A.D. 22.*

The coinage of Stratonicea, with or without the head of the reigning emperor, extends from the time of Augustus to that of Gallienus. It was one of the few cities which, under the Empire, issued from time to time silver coins. Of these, two bearing the names respectively of ΣΩΠΥΡΟΣ and of ΑΡΙϹΤΕΑϹ [ΧΙΔ ?] are described by Imhoof (*Gr. M.*, 673, 674). The first (wt. 53 grs.) has on the *obv.* the head of Hekate, the second (wt. 47 grs.) that of Augustus. Two other specimens (99 grs. and 32·4 grs.) are described in the present Catalogue and figured (Pl. xxiv. 1 and 5); the first of these is probably of the time of Augustus, and the second was struck under Antoninus Pius.† A fourth silver coin of the Imperial time

---

* *Bull. Corr. Hell.*, ix. 472, and xi. 237. Cf. also Le Bas-Wadd., *Inscr. d'As. Min.*, 519.

† This coin bears the magistrate's name ΦΛ. ΑΡΙϹΤΟΛΑΟϹ which may serve to date approximately an inscription recently discovered by Hula and Szanto (*Bericht über eine Reise in Karien*, p. 35, in the *Sitzungsberichte d. K. Akad. d. Wissensch. in Wien. Phil.-Hist. Cl.* Bd., 132) at *Pisiköi* (Pisye), on the road

is described by Mionnet (iii. p. 378, no. 440). Like the British Museum specimen above referred to, it belongs to the reign of Antoninus Pius, but the magistrate's name is ΚΛΑΥ. ΑΡΙϹΤΕΑϹ. The reverse type of all these silver coins is the same, viz. a bearded equestrian figure, holding in one hand a circular object resembling a phiale, and in the other a sceptre. This type often recurs on the large bronze coins of Stratonicea throughout the Imperial series, and it may reasonably be conjectured that it is not the Emperor, but Zeus Panamaros. If so, this equestrian Zeus may be compared with the Phrygian, Pisidian, and Lydian god Sozon or Sabazios, who is also frequently represented on horseback carrying a club or double-axe, and sometimes radiate, or with the Phrygian god Mên, who, if not originally identical with Sabazios, as Ramsay supposes,* is certainly a divinity scarcely distinguishable from Sabazios in his attributes. On one of the Stratonicean coins probably struck in Hadrian's time (Pl. xxiv. 4), the equestrian figure seems to be radiate, a fact which leads one to infer that Zeus Panamaros was a solar god, and which may serve to explain the frequent substitution of Πανημέριος for Πανάμαρος in inscriptions. The following remarkable inscriptions on coins of the reigns of Trajan and Hadrian also claim attention, as they have hitherto been always thought to prove that Stratonicea bore for a short time the strange title 'Indica.' These are, no 46 rev. ϹΤΡΑΤΟΝΕΙ. ΙΝΔΕΙ type Nike; nos. 47, 48 rev. ϹΥΝΚΛΗΤΟϹ ΙΝΔΙ. ϹΤΡΑ. type, Bust of Senate: no. 89 ΙΕΡΑ ϹΥΝΚΛΗΤΟϹ Bust of Senate, rev. ΙΝΔΕΙ ΘΕΑ ΡΩΜΗ Head of Roma turreted. Eckhel (*Num. Vet.*, 213, and *D. N. V.*, ii., p. 590) mentions some other varieties, and gives it as his opinion that the epithet was derived from the part

---

from Stratonicea to Idyma, and about 16 miles W. of Panamara. On this stone we read the name of a priestess, Φλ. 'Αριστολαῒς Φλ. 'Αριστολάου θυγάτηρ. This Aristolaos is doubtless the same man who struck the coin of Stratonicea.

* *Antiquities of S. Phrygia*, p. 21.

of Caria watered by the river Indus. Granting, however, that the territory of Stratonicea may possibly have included the κῶμαι in this region, there is still a difficulty in explaining the legends CYNKΛHTOC INΔI. CTPA., INΔEI. ΘEA PΩMH, and INΔ. ΘEOC CYNKΛHTOC (Eckhel, D. N. V., 591). For my own part, I am convinced that these coins do not belong to the Carian Stratonicea, but to Stratonicea ad Caicum in Lydia. Both in style and types they are far more like Lydian or Mysian coins than Carian, and one of the Museum specimens (no. 48) was found in the Hermus plain.*

Another coin, which probably also belongs to the time of Trajan or Hadrian, bears the inscription ΨHΦICAMENOY ΦΛABIOY ΔIOMHΔOYC (Pl. xxiv. 4); whence we may infer that Fl. Diomedes was the Γραμματεὺς τοῦ Δήμου, who, as we learn from inscriptions, possessed considerable authority in the proposing of motions (*Gr. Inscr. in Brit. Mus.*, Part iii., p. 164), and that these coins were issued in pursuance of a ψήφισμα proposed by him.

In the time of Sept. Severus commences a series of bronze coins of large dimensions, of which the extant specimens are mostly in very poor preservation. They are frequently countermarked with a head of Athena and with the word ΘEOV, showing that they were guaranteed by the authorities of a Temple. These large bronze coins bear the names of magistrates, preceded almost always by ἐπί, and usually by their official titles ΠPV. (Πρύτανις); APX. ("Ἄρχων); ΓPA. (Γραμματεύς); CTPA (Στρατηγός); frequently followed by the name of the father, as ΕΠΙ ΠPV. ΛΕΟΝΤΟC AΛKAI[OV] (Pl. xxiv. 6), and exceptionally by the numeral B, which may indicate either that the father's name was identical

---

* These specimens will be redescribed in their proper place in the volume dealing with the coinage of Lydia. Since writing the above, I see that M. Imhoof-Blumer has expressed the same opinion (*Rev. Suisse de Numismatique*, vi., 1896).

k

with that of the magistrate, or that the latter was in office for the second time. In one instance (Pl. xxiv. 10), where we read [ΕΠΙ] ΠΡΥ ΖΩCIMOV ΠΟCΙΤΤΟV Β (for τὸ β'), it is certain that Zosimos must have been elected Πρύτανις for the second time.*

To Syangela, a few miles east of Halicarnassus, Imhoof-Blumer†

SYANGELA? is inclined to attribute the drachm of Attic weight (63 grs.) first published by Waddington,‡ and assigned by him to the island of Syme, between Rhodes and the mainland. Imhoof-Blumer publishes also a bronze coin§ of the same place. Notwithstanding the fact that the drachm was acquired at *Budrum* together with coins of Cos, Miletus, Samos, &c., it seems to me that both weight and style are against its being either of Syangela or of Syme. For my own part, I prefer to assign it conjecturally to Syros.

Tabae, the modern *Davas*, the name of which is identical

TABAE. with the Carian or Lydian word *Taba* (rock),‖ stood on the heights at the western end of a wide and fertile plain, extending for about sixteen miles in a north-easterly direction towards the lofty Salbacus range of mountains, which formed its boundary towards Phrygia. The Ταβηνὸν πεδίον was watered by the northern branch of the river Harpasus, into which flowed from the north the tributary stream called Timeles,

---

* I have noted the following magistrates' names in addition to those given in the text:—ΚΛΑΥ. ΑΡΙCΤΕΑC (Mion., iii. 378); ΕΠΙ ΚΛΑΥΔΙΟΥ ΑΡΙCΤΕΟΥ (Mion., *l.c.*); ΕΠΙ ΠΡΥ. ACENA(?) (Waddington Coll.); ΕΠΙΜΕΛΗ. ΤΙ. ΑΡΙCΤΕΑ (Mion., *S.*, vi. 538); ΕΠΙ ΑVΡ. ΔΙΟΝΥCΙΟΥ. (Mion., *S.*, vi. 539); ΕΠΙ ΛΕΟΝΙΔΟΥ (Imhoof, *Gr. M.*, 675); ΕΠΙ ΠΡΥ . . . . ΝΙΟC Γ. ΦΙΛΩΝΟC (Imhoof, *Gr. M.*, 677).

† *Mon. Gr.*, p. 323.
‡ *Num. d'As. Min.*, Pl. xi. 4.
§ *l.c.*, Pl. F. 13.
‖ Sayce, *Karian Language and Inscriptions*, London, 1837, p. 8.

which took its rise in the high pass between the plain of Tabae and the valley of Aphrodisias (q.v.). The towns of Apollonia Salbace (*Medet*) and Heraclea Salbace (*Makuf*) also overlooked the plain of Tabae from its south-eastern and north-eastern sides.

According to Strabo (xiii. 13), the population of the Tabenian plain was a mixed one, consisting of Carians, Phrygians, and Pisidians, and although in course of time it necessarily became hellenized, there is no reason to suppose that there was any Greek settlement there, at any rate before the second century B.C., when we first hear of Tabae as a town whose inhabitants (B.C. 189) opposed the march of Cn. Manlius Vulso. They were, however, overpowered by the Roman troops, and subjected to a heavy fine, in consequence of this hostile demonstration.[*] From this time until B.C. 166, Tabae, with the rest of Caria, was more or less directly subject to Rhodes, and it would seem that during this period, and perhaps previously, Tabae was a member, and probably the predominant one, of the '*Systema*' of allied κῶμαι called the Κοινὸν Ταρμιανῶν,[†] just as Stratonicea, which was sometimes called πόλις Χρυσαορέων, was the headquarters of the Chrysaoric '*systema.*' Subsequently, as we gather from an inscription dating from about B.C. 82,[‡] Tabae took the side of the Romans in the war against Mithradates, and, like Stratonicea, was recompensed by Sulla for its loyalty, receiving from him, and afterwards probably from the Roman Senate, the rights and privileges of αὐτονομία and of a *civitas sine foedere libera et immunis.*

The first series of Tabenian coins may possibly belong to the latter half of the second century (after B.C. 166), when Caria was declared free by the Romans, but I am more inclined to assign them to the first century, after B.C. 81, when, at the close of the

---

[*] Livy, xxxviii. 13 ; *cf.* Ramsay, *Amer. Journ. Arch.*, 1888, p. 272.
[†] *Bull. Corr. Hell.*, x. 488.   [‡] *Bull. Corr. Hell.*, xiii. 504.

Mithradatic war, Tabae appears to have received the gift of autonomy. In either case no experienced eye can fail to perceive that there must have been a considerable interval of time between the issue of the drachm (p. 160, no. 1, Pl. xxv. no. 1) and that of the other silver (p. 162, nos. 17-30, Pl. xxv. nos. 6-11) and bronze coins, which by reason of their style, their types, and the name of one of the magistrates (Καλλικράτης), which recurs on a coin of Nero, must necessarily belong to early Imperial times.

The issue of silver coins at Tabae under the earlier Emperors indicates clearly (although there is no corroborative evidence) that privileges similar to those conferred upon Stratonicea by the Senatusconsultum of B.C. 39 (see Introd. Stratonicea, p. lxxi.) may have been also acquired by Tabae. This inference is further strengthened by the fact that the neighbouring city of Aphrodisias was constituted ἐλευθέρα and ἀτελής through the instrumentality of M. Antony,* and that it also began to strike silver drachms, &c., in conjunction with Plarasa at about the same time as Tabae. These considerations all point to some special privileges, including the right of coining silver, which were conferred by the Romans upon Stratonicea, Plarasa and Aphrodisias, Tabae, Attuda, and perhaps upon other Carian towns. This right continued to be exercised at Stratonicea as late as the reign of Ant. Pius, at Tabae down perhaps to the time of Nero, and at Aphrodisias at least during the reign of Augustus. Of Attuda only one silver coin is at present known (Pl. x. no. 9), which seems to belong to the earlier half of the first century B.C., in which case it would be contemporary with the earliest issue at Tabae.

The coins of Tabae of Imperial times in bronze extend down to the time of Gallienus and Saloninus. It is noteworthy that in the

---

* Mommsen and Marquardt, *Handbuch d. röm. Alterthümer*, Bd. iv., p. 346, 2nd ed.; Boeckh, *C. I. G.*, 2737, 2845.

time of Domitian the preposition διά takes the place of the usual ἐπί (see *supra*, under Attuda), but this usage is limited at Tabae to coins of Domitian's reign.

The only magistrate's title on Tabenian coins is that of Archon, which, from the time of Caracalla to the end of the series, is never omitted. To the names recorded in this volume must be added that of the Archon Statilius Apollonius on coins of Caracalla and Geta (*Zeit. f. Num.*, i, 149).

The Imperial coinage of Tabae is plentiful, showing that it must have been in this period one of the most flourishing inland cities of Asia Minor. The reverse types prove that, in addition to the divinities which we meet with in almost every series of Imperial coins, the following were especially honoured at Tabae. These are Aphrodite, the Dioskuri, Poseidon, Homonoia(?), a goddess wearing a kalathos and holding grapes and corn (Demeter?), a male Pantheistic divinity, Artemis, Mên, Dionysos, Pan, and Nemesis.

TELMESSUS. Telmessus, a few miles N.W. of Halicarnassus, was a place hardly likely to have issued coins. The bronze pieces reading ΤΕ, ΤΕΛ and ΤΕΛΜΗΣΣ belong to the Lycian town of the same name. See *Zeit. f. Num.*, i. 151.

TERMERA. Strabo* places Termera correctly in the Termerian peninsula, just opposite Cos, and about 12 miles west of Halicarnassus and somewhat less than that south of Myndus.

In old times it must have been a place of considerable importance, and we learn from Herodotus (v. 37) that in the time of Darius Hystaspes it was governed by a Tyrant named Tymnes, whose son Histiaeus held high rank as a Commander of the Carian contingent of the fleet in the expedition of Xerxes against Hellas in B.C. 480 (Herod., vii. 98), when he had probably succeeded his father as despot. Waddington † conjectures that the Tymnes whose name

---

* xiv. 657.   † *Mél. de Num.*, p. 7.

appears on the coin described in the present volume (p. 176, Pl. xxvii. 2) was a son of this Histiaeus and a grandson of the Tymnes mentioned by Herodotus. If so, he must have succeeded his father Histiaeus not long after B.C. 480. In the middle of the fifth century the name of Termera occurs several times in the Athenian Tribute-lists, and it was then assessed at a higher rate than either Myndus or Halicarnassus, its nearest neighbours. Presumably, it was at this time not under the rule of a despot, but there is no evidence that it was in a position to strike money in its own name. This cessation of autonomous issues during the period of the Athenian supremacy is very noticeable at several other much more important towns, Cnidus, for instance, where the absence of a coinage during this time is surprising. Termera henceforth appears to have been eclipsed by the neighbouring city of Halicarnassus, and *circ.* B.C. 367 its inhabitants were transported by Mausolus to his new capital. It is true that Pliny (v. 107) mentions Termera as still in existence in his time, and he seems to call it a *civitas libera;* but, as Waddington (*Rev. Num.*, 1856, 55) points out, the word *libera* perhaps applies to Bargylia, which stands next in Pliny's lists, for it is quite conceivable that the words *Bargylia* and *libera* may have been transposed by a copyist. If Termera had been a *civitas libera* in Roman times, it would almost certainly have coined money.

TRAPEZOPOLIS. Ptolemy and Pliny both class Trapezopolis to Caria, and, although it was situated on the north-eastern or Phrygian side of the Salbacus range, near the modern *Assar* and *Kadi Keui*,[*] it was included in the conventus of Alabanda. The coins, which are wholly of the Imperial period and which extend, so far as we know, only to the time of Severus and Domna, are Carian rather than Phrygian in appearance. The prevalent use of

---

[*] Ramsay, *Ant. of S. Phryg.*, A. v.

διά in place of ἐπί before the magistrate's name serves to connect Trapezopolis with the small group of towns in north-east Caria, Attuda, Cidramus, Apollonia Salbace, Tabae, and with Laodicea ad Lycum, where the same custom has been noticed. In the time of Augustus the magistrate's name in the nominative case is accompanied by a monogram. Next in order of time follow the coins on which the name in the genitive is preceded by διά. These seem to belong to the period between the reigns of Domitian and M. Aurelius, but they are without the heads or names of the Emperors (Pl. xxvii. 5-6). In the time of Sept. Severus the magistrate's name is preceded by his title Ἀρχ[οντος] or by ἐπὶ Ἄρχοντος. In one instance the name of the father is added (p. 179, no. 11), and in another that of a colleague in office (no. 13). The types Dionysos, Mên, Asklepios, Nemesis, Apollo, Kybele, may be compared with the similar types at the neighbouring and more important city Attuda, which I also include in Caria rather than in Phrygia.

An alliance coin between Attuda and Trapezopolis is published by Sestini (*Mus. Hederv.*, ii. 339, Tab. xxvi. 8). The inclusion in this alliance of Eumenia in Phrygia with Attuda and Trapezopolis is probably due to a wrong reading of a magistrate's name. This coin, as Ramsay remarks (*C. B. Phr.*, 166), indicates more than a mere alliance, it marks the two cities as conterminous, and united in the worship of the same goddess, whose name, as we learn from inscriptions, was Μήτηρ Ἀδραστος.

§ III.—SATRAPS OF CARIA.

FROM the beginning of the hegemony of Athens, B.C. 469, down to the time of her Sicilian losses during the Peloponnesian war, the Greek towns on the Carian coasts were for the most part attached to the Athenian League, and, with the exception perhaps of Cos, struck few coins. Nor was there any coinage as yet in the interior of Caria. On the break up of the League, *circ.* B.C. 412, the Greek cities, together with the whole of Caria, were assigned to the satrapy of Tissaphernes, after the suppression of the revolt of the rebellious Satraps Pissuthnes and his son Amorges. It is to Tissaphernes and to the mint of Iasus that M. Six* and M. Babelon† have recently attributed the fine and unique tetradrachm of Rhodian weight, *obv.* Head of Satrap, *rev.* ΒΑΣΙΛ Lyre.‡ The date of the issue of this coin, according to M. Six, was B.C. 411, according to M. Babelon, B.C. 395. After the death of Tissaphernes the Satrapy of Caria south of the Maeander was bestowed by the Great King upon Hecatomnus of Mylasa, in whose family it remained down to the capture of Halicarnassus by Alexander, B.C. 334. The policy consistently adhered to by the Hecatomnids from first to last was the aggrandizement of their own family at the expense, on the one hand, of the independent Carian communities and of the semi-autonomous Greek cities and islands, and, on the other hand, of the King of Persia.

The following brief historical and chronological notes will perhaps suffice for numismatic purposes.

---

* *Num. Chron.*, 1888, p. 107 *sq.*   † *Rev. Num.*, 1892, p. 424 *sq.*
‡ B. M. *Cat. Ion.*, Pl. xxxi. 6.

SATRAPS OF CARIA. lxxxi

HECATOMNUS.
B.C. 395 ?
Hecatomnus, as Satrap of Caria, dominates the ancient Carian League, and threatens the independence of the Greek cities on the coast. He strikes drachms of Attic weight, probably at Mylasa: *Obv.* EKA Forepart of Lion looking back; *Rev.* Star in incuse circle.* The types of these coins are imitated from those of Miletus.

B.C. 390—386.
Hecatomnus and Autophradates of Lydia commissioned by Artaxerxes Mnemon to suppress the revolt of Evagoras I, king of Salamis in Cyprus. Evagoras maintains his position, secretly supported by Hecatomnus.

B.C. 387.
Peace of Antalcidas. Greek towns in Caria assigned to Hécatomnus.

B.C. 386.
Probable date of issue of Tetradrachms of Phoenician weight: *Obv.* Zeus Labraundos; *Rev.* EKATOM Lion (Pl. xxviii. 1).

Halicarnassus assigned by Hecatomnus to his eldest son Mausolus.

Probable date of issue of coins by Mausolus of the Samian(?) Standard and Milesian types: *Obv.* MA Lion's head and fore-leg; *Rev.* Star.†

MAUSOLUS.
B.C. 377.
Mausolus succeeds to the Satrapy of Caria.

B.C. 367(1).
Synoikismos of six Lelegian towns with Halicarnassus, and removal of the satrapal residence from Mylasa to that city.

B.C. 366.
Opposition to Mausolus on the part of the old Carian League, and accusation of disloyalty to the Persian King preferred against him by Arlissus of Mylasa. The city of Mylasa confiscates property of Arlissus, and bestows it upon Mausolus.

---

* B. M. *Cat. Ion.*, Pl. xxi. 5.
† B. M. *Cat. Ion.*, Pl. xxi. 6.

Iasus also exiles opponents of Mausolus and confiscates their property.*

Probable date of the first issue by Mausolus of Tetradrachms and
B.C. 366. Drachms of the Rhodian standard: *Obv.* Head of Apollo laur., facing, as on previous autonomous coins of Halicarnassus (Pl. xviii. 3); *Rev.* ΜΑΥΣΣΩΛΛΟ Zeus Labraundos (Pl. xxviii. 2-4). A comparison of this figure with that on the coin of Hecatomnus (Pl. xxviii. 1) shows that it is a mere copy, quite devoid of the life and spirit of the original conception.

Mausolus commissioned to quell with his fleet the rebellious
B.C. 364. Satrap Ariobarzanes at Assus and Adramyteum. He all the while secretly fosters the rebellion and allies himself with Agesilaus.

Collapse of the Rebellion. Mausolus reverts to his allegiance to
B.C. 361. the Great King. Destruction of Hecatomnus's statue at Mylasa by adherents of the old Carian party. The Demos of Mylasa confiscates their property.

Rhodes, Chios, and Cos revolt from Athens and form a separate
B.C. 357. alliance with Mausolus. Decree of Erythrae in his honour.

Athens makes peace with the separate League. Mausolus suc-
B.C. 355. cessfully supports the Aristocrats against the Democratic party at Rhodus. Cos subject to Mausolus.

Unsuccessful attempt upon the life of Mausolus by Manitas and
B.C. 353. Thyssus of Mylasa, members of the Carian Nationalist party.

B.C. 353. Death of Mausolus.

The Carian Κοινόν still issues independent decrees and sends

---

* *Bull. Corr. Hell.*, v., 493.

SATRAPS OF CARIA.   lxxxiii

its own envoys to Persia. The Carian towns, though tributary to the Satraps, continue to retain their autonomy.

Artemisia, widow of Mausolus, succeeds him, and may have con-
tinued to coin in his name. The Democratic party
ARTEMISIA.
B.C. 353—351. again ascendent in Rhodes. Rhodian attack upon
Halicarnassus repulsed. Rhodes and Heraclea ad Latmum, both free after the death of Mausolus, regained by stratagems of Artemisia.

B.C. 352.   Building of the Mausoleum.
B.C. 351.   Death of Artemisia.

HIDRIEUS. Hidrieus second son of Hecatomnus, succeeds to
the Satrapy of Caria, and marries his younger sister Ada.

He is commissioned to suppress the revolt in Cyprus. Chios and Tralles subject to him.

Coins of Hidrieus similar to those of Mausolus. The reverse type of his ¼ Drachm a Milesian star (Pl. xxviii. 8).* ¼ Drachms of Mausolus are unknown.

ADA.   Hidrieus dies, and Ada, his sister and widow,
B.C. 344. succeeds him in the Satrapy, and may also have
continued to issue coins in his name.

Pixodarus, the youngest son of Hecatomnus, seizes the Carian
Satrapy. His sister Ada retires to the inland
PIXODARUS.
B.C. 340. fortress of Alinda, which she continues to hold
till Alexander's invasion.

B.C. 340. Pixodarus with other Satraps sent to oppose
Philip of Macedon during his attacks upon Perinthus and Byzantium.

Chios, Cos, and Rhodes, dependent upon Caria, send contingents.†

---

* Cf. *Cat. Ion.*, Pl. xxi. 5-7.   † Diod., xvi. 77.

Influence of Pixodarus in Lycia. His gifts to Xanthus, Tlos, and Pinara.*

B.C. 337. Artaxerxes Ochos murdered. Arses King of Persia, B.C. 337-335.

Ada the younger, daughter of Pixodarus, offered in marriage (i) to Arrhidaeus son of Philip of Macedon, (ii) to Alexander, and (iii) finally married to Orontobates, a Persian of exalted rank.

B.C. 337.

Pixodarus' silver coinage consists of Didrachms, Drachms and Quarter Drachms similar to those of Hidrieus, but no Tetradrachms bearing his name have yet been found.

Pixodarus also initiates a gold coinage (Pl. xxviii. 9-12) : *Obv.* Head of Apollo in profile, as on contemporary coins of Miletus †; *Rev.* Zeus Labraundos, as on the silver coins of himself and his predecessors. The fact that Pixodarus issued gold coins, a prerogative of the Great King which he never delegated to his satraps, is a sign rather of a general relaxation of direct Persian control than of any special claim of absolute independence on the part of Pixodarus.

It must also be borne in mind that Philip's gold mines and his new mints were now in active operation, and that gold money of various kings and cities was about this time being introduced into general circulation in the West.

B.C. 335. Arses killed. Darius III, King of Persia.

ORONTOBATES. Pixodarus dies, and his Satrapy is inherited by Orontobates, the husband of his daughter Ada.

B.C. 334.

Orontobates strikes tetradrachms of the usual type, but reading POONTOΓATO, the Carian form of the name which was Graecized by Arrian ‡ as Ὀροντοβάτης.§ Eckhel's and Mionnet's reading OΘONTOΓATO is erroneous.

---

* Pertsch, in M. Schmidt's *Neue Lykische Studien*, 1869, p. 1 sqq.
† B. M. *Cat. Ion.*, Pl. xxi. 9-11.   ‡ *Anab.*, ii. 5, 7.
§ *Rev. Num.*, 1887, p. 94.

Alexander takes Halicarnassus, but Orontobates continues to hold
B.C. 334. the fortresses in Salmacis and on the island, as well as Myndus, Caunus and other towns, till B.C. 333.
B.C. 323. On Alexander's death Asander receives the Carian satrapy.

§ IV.—ISLANDS OF CARIA.

ASTYPALAEA, one of the Sporades midway between Cos and Amorgos,
ASTYPALAEA. was said to have been named after Astypalaea, daughter of Phoenix and Perimede, sister of Europa. Astypalaea was mother of Ancaeus, king of the Leleges* and of Samos, also of Eurypylus, king of Cos.

The geographical position of the island, which lay on the direct trade-route between Phoenicia, Cyprus, Rhodes, Cnidus, Cos, on the east, and European Greece on the west, gave it no doubt a commercial importance. Its name occurs in the Athenian quota list† B.C. 440 and in the assessment list of 425, but the amount of its assessment is wanting. In B.C. 436 it is rated at 200 drachms ‡ as the sum payable to Athena, which at the rate of 1 mina per talent gives 12000 dr. (about £480) as the yearly tribute.

Astypalaea struck no coins before the third century, and subsequently only small bronze coins, in its own name.

The foundation of Alexandria must have largely added to the value of Astypalaea as a station on the route to Egypt.

The prevailing types of the coins point to a special cultus of Perseus, and they bear a remarkably close resemblance to those of

---

* Paus., vii. 4.   † Dittenberger, *Sylloge*, p. 34.
‡ Hicks, *Gk. Hist. Inscr.*, p. 48.

Seriphos, which it is difficult to account for, as Seriphos, the special home of the cult of Perseus, though on the same trade-route, was not a very near neighbour of Astypalaea.

In the second century B.C. the port of Astypalaea, owing doubtless to the convenience of its harbour for vessels trading between Alexandria and the West, rose so much in commercial importance that, like Rhodes, Cnidus, Nisyros, Cos, &c. (all stations on the same trade-route), it was constituted (perhaps by the Ptolemies then predominant in the Aegean Sea) a mint for the issue of tetradrachms and even of gold staters of the Alexandrine type,* bearing the harpa of Perseus as a distinctive symbol.

This prosperity would seem to have been undiminished in the year B.C. 105, when Astypalaea by a Senatusconsultum received the rights of a Civitas Foederata. One copy of this decree was ordered to be deposited in the Capitol and a second in the temple of Athena and Asklepios at Astypalaea.†

Of Calymna, which lay off the coast of Caria, about ten miles west of Myndus and the same distance north of Cos, ancient silver staters are extant (Pl. xxix. 8), which seem from their rude archaic style to belong to the earlier half of the sixth century B.C. In weight these coins correspond with the silver coins of Croesus of Lydia, B.C. 568-554.‡ In style the helmeted head on the obverse resembles in its primitive rudeness and coarseness some of the earliest Athenian tetradrachms.§ These Calymnian staters are, with those of Athens, among the earliest examples known of coins bearing a type in the incuse of the reverse. The adaptation of the form of the incuse to the shape of the lyre which

CALYMNA.

---

* Müller, *Num. d'Alex.*, nos. 1170-1172.
† ..... ἐν δὲ Ἀστυπαλαιέων ἐν τῷ ἱερῷ τῆς Ἀθηνᾶς καὶ τοῦ Ἀσκληπιοῦ καὶ πρὸς τῷ βωμῷ [τοῦ Διὸς(?) καὶ] τῆς Ῥώμης. Hicks, *Gk. Hist. Inscr.*, p. 349; Boeckh, *C. I. G.*, 2485.
‡ Head, *Hist. Num.*, p. 546.   § Cf. B. M. *Cat. Attica*, Pl. ii.

it contains is also an indication of high antiquity, and, so far as I remember, only found on early electrum staters of the seventh or sixth century B.C. attributed to Parium(?)* and to Miletus(?),† and on archaic silver coins of Eretria in Euboea ‡ and Apollonia ad Rhyndacum.§ The head of the bearded warrior may be that of Ares or of some legendary hero.‖ The chelys on the reverse is presumably the symbol of the Delian Apollo, the ruins of whose temple are still to be seen at Calymna. In fabric there is a very remarkable difference between these Calymnian coins and the earliest issues of Cos, Cnidus, Ialysus, Camirus, Lindus, Posidium Carpathi, &c., which are as a rule thick and bean-shaped, while those of Calymna are thin, flat and spread, in the style of most of the coins of Eretria in Euboea.

From the sixth century B.C. down to *circ*. 300 B.C. Calymna does not appear to have coined any money, but early in the third century its coinage became plentiful.

Paton and Hicks¶ are of opinion that Calymna (probably early in the third century) became a dependency of Cos. The Calymnian silver coins seem, however, to indicate that the island must have retained its independence at least down to the middle of the third century, for a comparison of the style, fabric, and weight of the later Calymnian silver coins (Pl. xxix. 9) with those of Cos (Pl. xxxi. 2, &c.) shows so close a resemblance between them that it is impossible to attribute them to different periods, and the Coan specimens cannot be placed earlier than B.C. 300.

The fact that in the large hoard of nearly 10,000 Calymnian coins found in the island in 1823,** mixed with coins of Rhodes, Cos, and of the Carian Satraps, Mausolus, Hidrieus, and Pixodarus, no coins

---

* B. M. *Cat. Ion.*, Pl. ii. 14.   † *Ibid.*, Pl. iii. 5, 6.
‡ B. M. *Cat. Cent. Gr.*, Pl. xxiii. 4.   § B. M. *Cat. Mys.*, Pl. ii. 1.
‖ Cf. early coins of Aeneia in Macedon; B. M. *Cat. Mac.*, p. 41.
¶ *Inscr. of Cos*, p. 353.   ** *Num. Chron*, ix., 166.

of Alexander the Great were present is perhaps remarkable, but it cannot weigh against the clear evidence afforded by the style of the Coan specimens (Pl. xxxi. 2 sqq.).

It is worthy of note that while all the coins of Cos bear magistrates' names in addition to the ethnic KΩION, those of Calymna have only KAΛYMNION. Whether this absence of the name of the eponymous magistrate may be significant of dependence upon Cos is a doubtful point.

CARPATHOS.

All that is known concerning Carpathos, which gave its name to the sea between Crete and Rhodes, and which in early times must have been of considerable importance, owing to its intermediate position between those great islands, is to be found in Imhoof-Blumer's valuable article in the *Zeitschrift für Numismatik*,* where all previous notices are collected.

The attribution to the city of Posidium of the sixth century silver staters (Pl. xxix. 14, 15) similar in style to those of Camirus (Pl. xxxiv. 7) and in weight to those of Lindus (Pl. xxxiv. 12) is due to Imhoof-Blumer, in whose collection is a specimen on which the letters ΓΟϟ are clearly legible.† Thirds of the stater are likewise known, weighing about 67 grs.‡

Posidium (the modern *Posin*), on the eastern coast of the island, faced the southern end of Rhodes, and was equally accessible from either Camirus or Lindus. Its name is mentioned only by Ptolemy.§ In addition to that of Posidium, the names are recorded of four other towns in the island, Brykus, Carpathus, Arkeseia, and Nisyrus, but no coins have been found of any of these places. Posidium, therefore, seems to have been the

---

* Bd. i., p. 153.
† *Zeit. f. Num.*, i., Pl. iii. 20; *Mon. Gr.*, Pl. F. 9; and *Choix*, Pl. iv. 143.
‡ Imhoof-Blumer, *Mon. Gr.*, Pl. F. 10.   § *Geog.*, v. 2.

principal port so long as Carpathos retained its autonomy. It was probably the chief city of the original Carpathians ('Ετεοκαρπάθιοι ἐκ Καρπάθου), who appear separately in the Athenian Quota Lists as paying 1,000 drachms, the same amount at which the people of 'Αρκέσεια Καρπάθου are rated in contemporary lists.

Chalce or Chalcia, a small island off the west coast of Rhodes.

CHALCE or CHALCIA. The little bronze coins attributed to it by M. Six (*Num. Chron.*, 1890, p. 246) are in the present volume assigned conjecturally to Chalcetor (p. 79 and xlv. *supra*).

The history, epigraphy, and numismatics of Cos have been so

COS. thoroughly investigated by Paton and Hicks,* that it is hardly possible to add much in this catalogue to that which has been already fully discussed by them.

Since the publication of the above-mentioned exhaustive treatise there have, however, come to light some archaic silver coins (Pl. xxx. 1, 2) which call for a few additional comments. There is also, unnoticed by Paton and Hicks, a small electrum coin (wt. 1·9 grs.),† (*Obv.* Crab; *Rev.* Incuse square quartered), which is the 96th part of a stater, dating from the seventh century B.C., either of the Phoenician standard, or, perhaps more probably, of the Aeginetic standard, according to which the earliest Coan silver coins, like those of Cnidus (Pl. xiii. 7), of Chios,‡ and of Cyme (?)§ were adjusted.

These seventh century silver staters are all characterized by the

VIIth cent. Staters of Aeginetic wt. addition of a small incuse square (probably as a countermark) beside the larger square. The fact that all the earliest coins of Cyme, Teos, Chios, Cos, Chersonesus, Idyma(?), Camirus, are of Aeginetic weight, as are also those of the Cretan cities, seems to show that the com-

---

* *Inscrr. of Cos.*, Oxford, 1891. † B. M. *Cat. Ion.*, p. 6, no. 29.
‡ *Num. Chron.*, 1890, Pl. ii. 15. § B. M. *Cat. Troas*, &c., Pl. xix. 4-7.

mercial activity of all these places was in the seventh and sixth centuries B.C. chiefly directed towards the Aegean islands and the Peloponnesus, while, on the other hand, Lindus, Ialysus, Poseidium in Carpathos, Miletus, and most of the towns on the mainland of Asia Minor traded principally with the East, if the Phoenician standard of their earliest coins warrants such an inference.

The chief city of Cos, which originally bore the same name as the island, was situated in or near the bay now called *Kastri*, towards the western extremity of Cos, and exactly opposite Cnidus and the Triopian promontory, from which it was distant only about thirty English miles in a direct line.

At the temple of Apollo on this promontory the members of the Dorian pentapolis, Cnidus, Cos, Ialysus, Camirus and Lindus, met from time to time, perhaps annually, to celebrate the Triopian Festivals. It was probably on these occasions that the several cities of the League struck their early coins.

The precise signification of the crab as the special emblem of Cos is very doubtful, but that it was a symbol intimately connected with the cult of Herakles seems quite certain from the fact that from the fourth century downwards it is constantly accompanied by the Heraklean Club, while on certain coins of Imperial times (Pl. xxxiii. 4, 5) it is seen at the feet of Herakles himself. The myth, as related by Hyginus[*] and Apollodorus,[†] tells how a crab bit the foot of Herakles while he was struggling with the Lernaean Hydra, and this may be cited in illustration of the connection of the crab with Herakles, though in the Coan tradition it would appear from the coin-types that the crab must have been regarded rather as an ally than as an enemy of Herakles.

---

[*] 2 *Astron.*, 23.
[†] *Bibl.*, l. ii., c. 5, § 2.

In the fifth century, to which the next issue of Coan coins belongs,

Vth cent. Tetradrachms of Attic wt. we find that tetradrachms of Attic weight have replaced the Aeginetic coins of the seventh and sixth centuries. The Heraklean Crab now occupies the reverse, while the obverse is devoted to an agonistic type, a naked Discobolus before a prize tripod, which clearly alludes to the Triopian games (Pl. xxx. 3-5).

It is a noteworthy fact, though one which is hard to explain, that although Cnidus and Cos were both tributary allies of Athens during the greater part of the fifth century B.C. (each paying three Talents yearly), Cnidus does not appear to have coined any money, for there is an interval between *circ.* B.C. 479 and 412 in the series of the coins of Cnidus, while, on the other hand, Cos during this very period issued tetradrachms of Attic weight, inscribed at first KOΣ, later KΩΣ, and finally KΩION.

After these fifth century issues of Attic tetradrachms there follows a considerable interval, during which no coins seem to have been struck in Cos.

Various influences were at work in the fourth century tending to divert the trade-route from the western to the eastern extremity of the island. Among these influences the most powerful was doubtless the synoikismos of six Lelegian towns in the neighbourhood of Halicarnassus with that city, effected by Mausolus in B.C. 367.

The removal of the Carian capital from Mylasa to so favourable a site as Halicarnassus was immediately followed by an influx of commercial prosperity, which is attested by the rich series of coins which Mausolus began at once to pour forth from his mint at Halicarnassus.

Foundation of New City. B.C. 366. The towns and demes of Cos, in order to attract to their own island some share of the new trade just beginning to flow in increased volume through the narrow strait which divided Cos from the mainland, now found themselves impelled to transfer the chief emporium of their commerce from the western to the eastern extremity of the island. Here, at the eastern point of Cos, there had existed from of old a small and comparatively unimportant town, by name Κῶς ἡ Μεροπίς,[*] and on the sea-shore near this old town the new capital was built, and a closed harbour constructed, the older capital being henceforth known as 'Αστυπάλαια or Κῶς ἡ 'Αστυπάλαια. This synoikismos of the Coans, following shortly after that of the Rhodians and that of the Lelegian towns round Halicarnassus, forms part of a general movement of previously scattered populations towards the shores of the trade-route from Egypt and Syria through Cyprus to the west.

The failure of Athens to maintain her ascendency and to continue to levy tribute, the incompetence of Sparta to uphold the rule of the oligarchical minorities, and the utter impotence of Persia, all contributed to the independent growth of a few of the most favourably situated Greek cities on the coasts of Asia Minor and the adjacent islands, and to the increasing prosperity of such commercial centres as Rhodus, Halicarnassus, Cos, Ephesus, &c. This is clearly manifest from the renewed activity in the mints of all these places which is noticeable in the fourth century B.C.

Of the rise and growth of the new city of Cos, Diodorus Siculus (xv. 76) gives the following account :—"Ἅμα δὲ τούτοις πραττομένοις Κῷοι μετῴκησαν εἰς τὴν νῦν οἰκουμένην πόλιν, καὶ κατεσκεύασαν αὐτὴν ἀξιόλογον· πλῆθός τε γὰρ ἀνδρῶν εἰς ταύτην ἠθροίσθη, καὶ τείχη πολυτελῆ κατεσκευάσθη, καὶ λιμὴν ἀξιόλογος. Ἀπὸ δὲ τούτων τῶν χρόνων ἀεὶ μᾶλλον ηὐξήθη προσόδοις τε δημοσίαις καὶ τοῖς τῶν ἰδιωτῶν πλούτοις, καὶ τὸ σύνολον ἐνάμιλλος ἐγένετο ταῖς πρωτευούσαις πόλεσιν.[†]

---

[*] Paton and Hicks, Inscrr. of Cos, Introd., p. xlix.
[†] Cf. Strabo, xiv., ii. 19.

ISLANDS OF CARIA.   xciii

The new capital of the island of Cos, founded in B.C. 366, began at once to issue silver and bronze coins. The tetradrachms of Attic weight issued by the old city of Cos (ἡ Ἀστυπάλαια) during the latter half of the previous century were now discarded. The weight standard of the coinage of the new city was assimilated to that which already prevailed at Chios, Rhodus, Cnidus, Ephesus, Samos, Halicarnassus (under Mausolus), &c. (Tetradrachm 240-230 grs. (max.), Didrachm 122-110 grs., Drachm 60-55 grs.). This standard is for convenience sake, though erroneously, called 'Rhodian'; for it is certain that it was already in use at some cities (e.g. Chios) long before the foundation of Rhodus, B.C. 408. It is, I am inclined to think, merely a reduced form of the Attic standard (Tetradrachm 270-260 grs.), notwithstanding the fact that, at some places (e.g. Ephesus), it replaces a previous coinage not of the Attic but of the so-called Phoenician weight (Tetradrachm circ. 220 grs.). At Cos, however, and at some other towns, it replaces an older currency of Attic weight.

Coinage after B.C. 366 on the Rhodian Standard

The types of the new Coan issues (B.C. 366-300, Pl. xxx. 6-15) are, on the obverses, Heads of Herakles, always bearded on the tetradrachms, and either bearded or youthful on the didrachms. The reverse types are the Heraklean Crab and Club, or a veiled female head, perhaps Demeter, on the didrachms* with the bearded head and on the obverses of the bronze coins. The legend is always ΚΩΙΟΝ for ΚΩΙΩΝ, a survival of the old spelling which was maintained on the coins down to the second century B.C.

From B.C. 366 onwards the coins of Cos bear the name in the nominative case of a magistrate, perhaps of the Μόναρχος, the

---

* The same veiled head is also, though very rarely, met with on tetradrachms; cf. the specimen (Pl. xlv. 5) in Dr. Weber's cabinet.

eponymous magistrate of the town, or not improbably of one of the Προστάται, as on the drachms of a later date (B.C. 166-88).*

After the capture of Halicarnassus by Alexander's general Ptolemy, B.C. 333, all the Carian coast towns submitted to the Macedonian rule, but there is nothing to show that any Macedonian coins were issued at this time from the Coan mint.

After the death of Alexander the island fell to the share of the kings of Egypt, and in B.C. 309 Ptolemy Soter, with his Queen Berenice, passed the winter at Cos, where their son Philadelphus was born. It is to this period of the Ptolemaic rule that I would assign the next issue of Coan coins.

B.C. 300—190. The tetradrachms and didrachms of this series bear a head of young Herakles, the unmistakeable Lysippean treatment of which distinguishes it from that on the coins of the preceding age, in spite of the fact that the incuse square is still retained on some of the earlier specimens of the period. On the drachms of this time the head of the bearded Herakles still survives (Pl. xxxi. 7, 8); but the recurrence on these coins of the names of several magistrates, e.g., ΕΜΓΡΕΓΩΝ, ΜΟΣΧΙΩΝ, ΠΟΛΥΑΡΧΟΣ on drachms, and ΔΗΜΗΤΡΙΟC, CΤΕΦΑΝΟC, &c., on hemidrachms (Pl. xxxi. 9, 10), the latter with the youthful head of Herakles, compel us to assign these to the same period as the didrachms. The bronze coins of this time, like the larger silver coins, bear a head of the youthful Herakles. (Pl. xxxi. 11, 12).

B.C. 190—166. In the second Macedonian War (B.C 200-196) and in the war against Antiochus (B.C. 191-188) Cos, like Rhodes, had remained faithful to the Romans, and after the decisive victory at Magnesia (B.C. 190) was rewarded for her

---

* See *infra*, p. 206, nos. 125-131.

fidelity by the grant of αὐτονομία.* To this period I would assign the Coan tetradrachms of the Alexandrine type with crab, club, and sometimes magistrate's name in front of the seated figure of Zeus on the reverse.† The Attic standard, which was gaining ground about this time all along the west coast of Asia Minor, was thus adopted at Cos for the tetradrachms, but the Coan or Rhodian weight was retained for the didrachms and drachms. The head of Herakles on the didrachms and bronze coins is represented for the first time nearly facing (Pl. xxxi. 13), like the head of Helios on the contemporary gold coins of Rhodes (Pl. xxxix. 19). The drachms still show the bearded head of Herakles in profile (Pl. xxxi. 15), and are only distinguishable from those of an earlier date by their flatter fabric and the omission of the dotted square on the reverse.

At the close of this period the more modern spelling ΚΩΙΩΝ begins for the first time to replace the older form ΚΩΙΟΝ on some of the smaller denominations in silver and bronze (Pl. xxxi. 16, &c.).

In the next period, B.C. 166-88, a complete change takes place in the coinage both of Cos and Rhodes, and at Cos the change is even more apparent than it is at Rhodes,

B.C. 166—88.

for the time-honoured Heraklean types of Dorian origin were now generally abandoned in favour of types relating to Asklepios, whose worship had gradually eclipsed that of Herakles, and who had come to be the representative divinity of the island.

The most remarkable coin of this time is, however, the unique tetradrachm of light Attic weight (256¼ grs.) in the Hunter Collection :‡ *Obv.* Head of Aphrodite, wearing myrtle-wreath, diadem and necklace; *Rev.* ΚΩΙΩΝ ΝΙΚΟΣΤΡΑΤΟΣ Asklepios, with

---

* Cf. Plin., *N. H.*, v., 104.
† Müller, *Num. d'Alex.*, no. 1153; Paton and Hicks, *Inscr. of Cos*, p. 311.
‡ Combe, *Desc. Num. vet. in. Mus. Hunter*, p. 112, no. 1; cf. Dutens, Tab. iv. fig. 4.

himation over lower limbs and left shoulder, standing r., and leaning with left arm on serpent-staff (Pl. xlv. 6). The head of Aphrodite on this coin reminds us that the most famous among the works of Apelles was his Aphrodite anadyomene (rising from the sea), which he painted for the Coans, and that Praxiteles also had executed for the city of Cos a half-draped statue of Aphrodite, which the Coans chose in preference to his more widely renowned naked figure of the same goddess, which was purchased by the Cnidians (cf. Pl. xlv. 11).

Whether the Attic standard was, from B.C. 166 onwards, also adopted for the smaller denominations is a doubtful point, as these small coins might have passed equally well either as Attic tetrobols and triobols or as drachms and tetrobols of Rhodian weight. It is perhaps preferable to call them Rhodian. They are characterized by the restoration of the incuse square in a shallow form, on the reverses, an archaistic fashion, introduced in the first instance at the Rhodian mint and imitated on the mainland by the Lycians, &c. The drachms(?) of this period bear the ancient types: *Obv.* Head of young Herakles; *Rev.* Crab and club (Pl. xxxii. 1). The tetrobols(?), on the other hand, have on the *obv.* a head of Asklepios, and on the *rev.* a coiled serpent (Pl. xxxii. 2-5). These may be divided into the following classes:—

(α) *Rev.* ΚΩΙΩΝ and one magistrate's name.
(β) *Rev.* ΚΩΝ and one magistrate's name.
(γ) *Rev.* ΚΩΙ or ΚΩ and one magistrate's name accompanied by his title ΠΡΟΣΤΑ[της].
(δ) *Rev.* ΚΩΙ, ΚΩ, or ΚΩΝ and names of two magistrates (Προστάται ?).

Nearly all these coins have unexplained letters or mint-marks, A, Δ, E, H or ΔP, outside the incuse square. These letters are perhaps the initials of the officinae of the mint, or, less probably, numerals.

ISLANDS OF CARIA.   xcvii

The bronze coins of this period, with the head of the youthful Herakles three-quarter face towards r. (Pl. xxxii. 6), closely resemble the issues of the previous period (Pl. xxxi. 17, 18), though they are distinctly later in style and are inscribed ΚΩΙΩΝ in place of the earlier form ΚΩΙΟΝ.

There is no possibility of fixing any exact chronological lower limit to the long series of silver coins above described, bearing the names of two magistrates, but it can hardly have continued after the time of the Mithradatic war.

Circ. B.C. 88—50.   The silver coins which seem to fall into the next period, which extends from the time of Sulla to the Tyranny of Nikias, whose date may be assumed to be *circ.* B.C. 50, are few in number, and divisible into three classes:—

(α) Head of Apollo.   *Rev.* Lyre.   Wt. 24-16 grs.   (Pl. xxxii. 7.)
(β) Head of Asklepios.   *Rev.* Serpent staff.   Wt. 39 grs.   (Pl. xxxii. 9.)
(γ) Head of Asklepios.   *Rev.* Coiled serpent.   Wt. 36-33 grs.   (Pl. xxxii. 11.)

There are also bronze coins of each of these three classes of larger size than any previously struck in Cos.   (Pl. xxxii. 8, 10, 12.)

Circ. B.C. 50— Augustus.   These lead up to the still larger bronze pieces which bear the name and portrait of Nikias (Pl. xxxii. 13), a tyrant of the island concerning whom we know scarcely anything.*

Imperial Times.   This brings us down to Imperial times, during which the coinage consists exclusively of bronze. It ranges from Augustus to Philip Jun.

The most interesting types occur on coins without emperors' heads; nos. 209 and 210, having on the reverse the seated Herakles with an infant on his arm and a crab at his feet, are especially noteworthy.†

---

* Strab., xiv. p. 658.   Paton and Hicks, *Introd.*, p. xl.
† (See *supra*, p. xc.)

The coins bearing portraits of the famous Coan physicians, Hippokrates and Xenophon (nos. 212—216), with Asklepian reverse types, are also remarkable, especially no. 215, on which Xenophon has the title Ἱερεύς.

The small island of Megiste, though geographically attached to the coast of Lycia, seems from the Doric dialect of the few inscriptions which have been copied in the island,* and from the types and weight of its rare silver drachms, to have been colonized from Rhodes. As, however, it struck money in its own name, and as the head of Helios as represented on the obverse of its coins is purposely differentiated from that on the contemporary coins of Rhodes, it may be safely inferred that at the time of their issue, in the latter part of the fourth century B.C., Megiste was an autonomous city.

MEGISTE.

The head of the god on these drachms (Pl. xxxiv. 1-3) is in profile and surrounded by a radiate disk. It is apparently copied from a gold stater of Lampsacus in the Waddington Collection,† the date of which seems to be *circ.* B.C. 350.

There are also small bronze coins of Megiste, similar to the silver drachms (p. 221, no. 4). As no later coins of Megiste are known, it is presumable that when, with the Rhodian Peraea, it fell under the direct rule of Rhodes, it was deprived of the right of coinage (*circ.* B.C. 300), and that when the Rhodians lost their possessions on the mainland (B.C. 168), Megiste may have been attached to Lycia.

Of the small volcanic island of Nisyros, which lies midway between the Triopian promontory and the southern point of Cos, from which it was said to have been torn off

NISYROS.

---

* Boeckh, *C. I. G.*, iii., 4301; Le Bas-Wadd., 1268; *Bull. Corr. Hell.*, xvi., 304
† *Hist. Num.*, p. 456, fig. 281.

by Poseidon with his trident and hurled upon the Giant Polybotes, there is a good account in Ross's Travels.*

The two following rare silver drachms, neither of which is in the British Museum, must be here described:—

Obv. Young male head bare, within wreath.

Rev. N—I Rose with tendril and bud on either side. Æ 47 grs.
(Millingen, *Syll.*, Pl. ii. 50.)

Obv. Head of Artemis? r., wearing stephane, earring and necklace.

Rev. ΝΙΣΥΡΙΟΝ Poseidon facing, seated towards l. on rock, his
ΙΜΕΡΑΙΟΣ right hand resting on his trident, his left on the rock; himation over lower limbs. Æ 35 grs.
(Imhoof Coll. *Zeit. f. Num.*, i., Pl. iv. 18.)

The first of these pieces shows that Nisyros, like Megiste, struck coins with the Rhodian rose on the reverse. The difference of the obverse type from that of the Rhodian coins is, however, sufficient to prove that Nisyros was independent of Rhodes. The other coin, with the seated Poseidon on the reverse, is also clearly autonomous and contemporary with the bronze coins, nos. 1-7, in the present catalogue (Pl. xxxiv. 4, 5).

The coinage of Nisyros thus falls altogether into the latter half of the fourth century B.C. The seated figure of Poseidon on the drachm, and the dolphin and trident on the bronze coins, point to the predominance of the cult of Poseidon in the island.†

Müller ‡ ascribes to the town of Nisyros some second century tetradrachms of the Alexandrine types. This attribution is, however, certainly erroneous, as it rests upon a false basis. The tetradrachms in question bear as an adjunct symbol a bucranium, which is the reverse type of certain bronze coins § formerly assigned

---

* Ross, *Reisen auf den Griech. Ins.*, ii., 67.
† Strab., x., p. 488. "Εχει δὲ καὶ πόλιν ὁμώνυμον καὶ λιμένα καὶ θερμὰ καὶ Ποσειδῶνος ἱερόν.
‡ *Num. d'Alex.*, nos. 1168-9.
§ Mion., iii., p. 412, no. 102, and *Suppl.*, vi., p. 584, nos. 144-147.

INTRODUCTION.

to Nisyros, but which belong in reality to Aegina.* Thus, with the disappearance of the bucranium as a coin-type of Nisyros, there is no longer any reason for attributing to so small and unimportant a town the Alexandrine tetradrachms in question.

The admirable situation and climate of Rhodes, and the commercial genius of its population, contributed to make it a great maritime power, and the wise and just laws, which the merchants of Rhodes strove to apply in their dealings with the other sea-faring peoples, soon raised the island to a position of influence unsurpassed by that of any other Greek state.

RHODES.

Of the three ancient cities of Rhodes, Lindus on the eastern coats, Camirus on the western, and Ialysus near the northern extremity of the island, it would seem that the two former alone coined money in the earliest times (6th cent. B.C.). The coinage of Ialysus is distinctly later in style, and belongs to the 5th cent. (Pl. xxxv. 1-6). Camirus, like Cos and Cnidus, made use of the Aeginetic standard, whence it may be inferred that her trade was chiefly in the direction of the Aegean islands, Crete, and Peloponnesus, where the Aeginetic standard prevailed. The recent discovery of small electrum coins of Camirus (Pl. xxxiv. 6) shows, however, that the trading vessels of Camirus had also dealings with the Ionian coast towns where in early times electrum was the standard currency.

LINDUS, IALYSUS and CAMIRUS.

The fig-leaf may have been selected as a coin-type for no other reason than that the fruit of this tree was one of the chief natural products of the island.† It must, however, not be forgotten that the fig may have also been a religious symbol, possibly of some local Dionysos (cf. the Dionysos συκίτης or συκάτης at Lacedaemon‡) or Zeus (cf. Ζεὺς συκάσιος §).

---

* B. M. Cat. *Attica*, &c., p. 144, nos. 224-227.
† Torr, *Rhodes in anc. times*, p. 69.
‡ Ath., 78. C.
§ Eust., 1572, 58.

Lindus on the eastern coast struck coins on the Phoenician standard, an indication that her commercial relations were mainly in the direction of Phoenicia and Egypt.

The Lion's head, the prevailing type of the Lindian coinage, may be merely a copy of the widely circulating Cnidian coins, in which case it probably possesses no local religious significance.

The peculiar form of the incuse reverses of the coins of Camirus and Lindus, consisting of a square divided into two oblong parts by a broad band, sometimes, as on Pl. xxxv. 8, inscribed ΛΙΝΔΙ, is original, and hardly ever met with outside Rhodes, except at Posidium in the neighbouring island of Carpathos (Pl. xxix. 14).

The coins of Ialysus, which does not seem to have issued money before the early part of the 5th cent. B.C., differ essentially from those of the other two cities of the island. In weight they follow the Phoenician standard.

The types—Fore-part of winged Boar and Eagle's head—may be original; but it is noteworthy that the winged Boar is also found on contemporary coins of Clazomenae (*Cat. Ion.*, Pl. iii. 18 and Pl. vi. 1-4), Lycia, and Cyrene (*Num. Chron.*, 1891, Pl. i. 8, 9), while the Eagle's head, accompanied by a floral scroll in the corner of the incuse square, occurs also at Cyrene (*N. C.*, 1891, Pl. i. 7) and on coins of Cyprus.* The fabric of the coins of Ialysus is also like that of coins of Cyprus, Lycia, and Cyrene, and has little in common with that of the coins of Camirus and Lindus. Whether these remarkable divergences in type, style and fabric between the coins of Ialysus and those of Lindus and Camirus are due to the fact that her commercial activity was chiefly directed towards Lycia, Cyprus, and Cyrene, or whether they are to be explained on the supposition that the two other Rhodian cities had ceased to coin money, and that Ialysus superseded them and remained from this time until

---

* Babelon, *Perses Achém.*, Pl. xx., 13, 14.

the foundation of Rhodes the only place of mintage during the fifth century, is a doubtful point.

On the foundation of the new capital of the island in B.C. 408,

Foundation of Rhodus. B.C. 408. the independent coinage of Ialysus came to an end; Camirus and Lindus, as we have already seen, having probably ceased to strike money at an earlier date.

The new city, which is said by Strabo * to have been unequalled in splendour by any other town which he had seen, seems to have lost no time in inaugurating a coinage on a scale worthy of such an occasion.

The types of the new Rhodian coins were evidently deliberately

Coin types. chosen as national emblems, the head of Helios, the patron god of the whole island, and the Rose, ῥόδον, the flower from which it took its name, and which still blooms in great abundance in the southern part of the island.†

The facing head of Helios is in the colossal style, for which the Rhodians had always so great a predilection.‡

In the year of the foundation of the city B.C. 408, full-face or rather three-quarter-face heads on coins were a novelty, of which the best examples were the unrivalled masterpieces executed by Kimon at Syracuse in B.C. 409, and perhaps some years earlier at Neapolis.§ The engraver of the new Rhodian coin-dies, no doubt inspired by the exquisite *chef d'œuvre* of the Sicilian artist, asserted at the same time his individuality by avoiding a mere slavish reproduction of the Syracusan type, such for instance as that on the coins of Larissa in Thessaly.|| The result is a worthy

---

* Strab., xiv. 2, 5.
† Sir C. Wilson, in Murray's *Handbook of Asia Minor*, 1895, p. 371.
‡ Holm, *Griech. Gesch.*, iv., 625, 632.
§ A. J. Evans in *Num. Chron.*, 1891, Pl. xi.
|| *Num. Chron.*, 1891, Pl. xi., 13-15.

ISLANDS OF CARIA.   ciii

and characteristic rendering of the Sun-god in his noon-day glory, with rounded face and ample locks of hair blown back as if by a strong wind, and thus delicately suggesting his rapid course. The crown of rays, which artists of a later age preferred to emphasize in more materialistic form, is, on these earliest coins, merely hinted at by a skilful adaptation of the locks of hair (compare *e.g.* Pl. xxxvi. 5 with Pl. xxxviii. 1).

The coins which belong to the period before Alexander (B.C. 408-333) fall into three classes, of which the first

RHODUS.
B.C. 408—333. consists of tetradrachms and hemidrachms of reduced Attic weight (Pl. xxxvi. 1-4, and Pl. xlv. 1), struck probably before the ascendency of the Democratic party (B.C. 396), when Rhodes reverted to the Athenian alliance, from which she had fallen away after the Sicilian campaign of B.C. 412. The issue of tetradrachms of reduced Attic weight may have been regarded at Athens as damaging to her interests, for it has been already remarked * that, wherever she had the power to interfere, she seems to have put an end to the silver coinage of her subject allies, probably because all such silver coinages tended to diminish the rich profits which she derived from the mines of Laurium and from the export of her famous 'Owl' tetradrachms.

Next in order of time follows the coinage of the League between

Federal Coinage.
Rhodus, Cnidus, Rhodes, Cnidus, Iasus, Samos and Ephesus: *Obv.*
Iasus, Samos, Infant Herakles strangling the two serpents; *Rev.*
Ephesus, B.C. 394. The emblem of the issuing city, in the case of Rhodus, the Rose (Pl. xlv. 2). This Federal coinage, as Waddington pointed out,† dates from Conon's victory at Cnidus, B.C. 394. The type, which is borrowed from coins of Thebes,‡ shows that Rhodes and the other cities above mentioned now

---

* Cnidus, *supra*, p. xlix.   † *Rev. Num.*, 1863, p. 223 *ff.*
‡ B. M. *Cat. Cent. Gr.*, Pl. xii. 7, 8, and xiv. 1, 2, 7, 8.

adhered to the anti-Spartan alliance formed under the leadership of Thebes in B.C. 395.* In weight the coins of this Asiatic 'Symmachy' consist of Aeginetic didrachms of very light weight (178 grs.). This weight is foreign, at this period, to Asia Minor, and must therefore have been adopted to facilitate exchange, the new didrachms being also tridrachms of the standard adopted about the same time at Rhodes, of which the Drachm weighed 60, the Didrachm 120, and the Tetradrachm 240 grs. (maximum).

Origin of the Rhodian Standard.

Holm † goes so far as to seek here an explanation of the origin of the so-called 'Rhodian standard' on the hypothesis that it was an attempt to harmonize the Phoenician and Aeginetic standards by raising the Phoenician drachm from 55 to 60 grs., and reducing the Aeginetic from about 95 to 90 grs., so that an Aeginetic didrachm reduced to about 180 grs. might be equivalent to a Rhodian tridrachm of the same weight. It is possible that some such motive may account for the introduction of a 60-grain drachm; but Holm forgets that this weight, which for convenience sake we call 'Rhodian,' did not originate at Rhodes, but at Chios, where it came into use in quite the early part of the 5th century. ‡ The standard in question may therefore have been originally a reduction of the Attic.

Of the splendid series of coins issued from the Rhodian mint between B.C. 408 and the time of Alexander the *chef d'œuvre* is the gold stater (Pl. xxxvi. 5) which, on account of the well-marked incuse square on the reverse, must be assigned to the early part of the 4th cent. It is probably one of the earliest pure gold coins struck by any Greek

Gold coinage of the 4th cent. B.C.

---

* B. M. *Cat. Cent. Gr.*, Introd. xl.; and Holm, *Gr. Gesch.*, iii., 54.
† *Griech. Gesch.*, iii., 55.
‡ B. M. *Cat. Ion.*. p. 328 seq.

town, and perhaps anterior to the commencement of the series of Lampsacene gold staters.*

The single letters on the 4th cent. coins of Rhodes give place first to double letters, and, later on, to magistrates' names at full length in the nominative case (p. 235).

Silver coinage of the 4th cent. B.C. and later. The long series of Rhodian silver coins which extends from B.C. 408 down to the occupation of the city by Cassius, B.C. 43, is very difficult to arrange in chronological order, owing to the repetitions, at sometimes long intervals of time, of the various types of the head of Helios, unradiate, radiate, full-face, or side-face. These types are in the main as follows:—

(a) Three-quarter face, head *unradiate* :—Pl. xxxvi. 5-11; Pl. xxxvii. 1, 2, 4-6 ; Pl. xxxix. 1-7.

(β) The same head *radiate*:—Pl. xxxvii. 8 ; Pl. xxxviii. 1-8 ; Pl. xxxix. 19 ; Pl. xl. 12-15 ; Pl. xli. 1-4.

(γ) The same head *radiate in profile* :—Pl. xxxvi. 12, 13 ; Pl. xxxvii. 7, 8 ; Pl. xl. 1-11, &c.

These three types are not strictly consecutive, but are contemporary on coins of different denominations ; but it may be taken as certain that there are on the *tetradrachms* no unradiate heads after the age of Alexander the Great (Pl. xxxvi.). The unradiate head survived, however, on the *didrachm* down to the end of the 4th cent., for to this period must be assigned the specimens with magistrates' names at full length (Pl. xxxvii. 1, 2), none of which occur on unradiate tetradrachms. On the *drachms*, etc., the unradiate full or three-quarter face head continued to be used down, apparently, to the middle of the 2nd cent. (*circ.* B.C. 166) and perhaps even later (Pl. xxxix. 1-7). The Rhodian drachm of this type would seem also to have been frequently imitated in the Rhodian Peraea, and

---

* B. M. *Cat. Mys.*, p. 80.

perhaps beyond its limits in southern Caria, for some long time after they had ceased to be issued at Rhodes itself (Pl. xxxix. 8-14).

The radiate head of Helios appears for the first time *in profile* on didrachms (Pl. xxxvi. 12), on diobols (Pl. xxxvi. 13), and on trihemiobols (Pl. xxxvii. 7, 8), which clearly belong to the latter part of the 4th cent. B.C. After an interval of more than a century the radiate head in profile again appears on drachms and bronze coins which I have assigned conjecturally to the 2nd cent. B.C. (Pl. xl.).

The clearly defined shallow incuse square, which is such a marked Re-introduction of feature on the reverses of the coins of this class, the incuse square must not be mistaken for a sign of antiquity. It in the 2nd cent. B.C. is merely a revival of a process of minting which had long fallen into disuse. The re-introduction of the incuse square seems to have been first adopted at the Rhodian mint for the gold money issued *circ.* B.C. 189 (Pl. xxxix. 19), when, after the defeat of Antiochus, Asia was re-organized and the whole of Caria assigned by the Romans to Rhodes. The fashion subsequently came into general use in Caria (cf. Aphrodisias Pl. v. 1, Stratonicea Pl. xxiii. 11-16, Cos Pl. xxxii. 1-5), in Lycia on the coins of the League from B.C. 168, and even in Peloponnesus on the latest silver coins of Sicyon and Argos.*

The date at which the new issue of Rhodian drachms, with the head Later drachms of Helios in profile and incuse square on the reverse, with head of replaced the series with the head of the same god Helios in profile. seen from the front, cannot be precisely fixed. Many of the same magistrates' names are met with on coins of both classes (full-face and side-face), but this fact by no means proves that the two series are contemporary, for it must not be assumed that the same names are necessarily those of the same individuals,

---

* B. M. Cat. *Pelop.*, Pl. ix. 12.

or, even if they are, that the same men may not have been from time to time re-appointed as responsible magistrates.

In the absence of any exact data for fixing the chronological sequence of the two distinct series of Rhodian drachms, (α) full-face and (β) side-face, we may infer from the far more frequent occurrence on the full-face drachms (Pl. xxxvii. 4, 5, and Pl. xxxix. 1-11) of names which are also met with on the larger coins of the 3rd cent. B.C. (Pl. xxxviii.), that these drachms are anterior in date to the series with the heads in profile (Pl. xl.) on which fewer identical names recur.

The date of the change from type (α) to type (β) may perhaps be fixed approximately by a comparison of the names on both these series with those which are found on the series of Rhodian coins with regal types, which seem to have been issued chiefly for circulation in the Rhodian possessions on the mainland of Asia between B.C. 189 and 166, the period during which Rhodes was at the height of her prosperity and mistress of the whole of Caria and Lycia from the Maeander to the sea.

The reorganization of Asia, B.C. 189, ushered in a time of peace and a revival of commerce, which may account for the contemporaneous issue at so many Asiatic cities of tetradrachms bearing the name and types of Alexander, and even occasionally of Lysimachus. These restorations of extinct regal types were especially prevalent in the Ionian coast towns and the adjacent islands, Chios, Cos, and Rhodes.*

Reorganization of Asia, and restoration of the Alexandrine tetradrachm, B.C. 189.

The decisive victory of Rome over Antiochus had put an end to the long struggle of rival kings for supremacy in western Asia Minor. The Greek cities of Caria, now either free or tributary to Rhodes,

---

* B. M. *Cat. Ion.*, Introd., p. xlviii.

were at last in a position to strike money in their own names. For the most part, however, and perhaps to avoid giving offence to the rival monarchs of Syria, Egypt, Pergamum, and Macedon, they prudently preferred to revert to the types of the coinage of Alexander, equally acceptable to all the rival kings, and (what was of still more importance) familiar to traders in every Mediterranean port, and even as far east as India.

Reissue of gold Philippi in the 2nd cent. B.C. The tide of commercial prosperity which swept over Western Asia in the earlier half of the 2nd century, and which is indicated by the reintroduction of the Alexandrine tetradrachm, is still further made evident by a recent discovery (last year) of a small hoard of gold Philippi, unearthed in the Maeander valley. These interesting specimens, as yet unpublished, have been acquired by the British Museum. The style of the laureate heads on the obverses of these gold coins differs so remarkably from that of the gold staters of Philip's own time that there can be no doubt that they belong to a later age. Some of the heads resemble regal portraits, but are not sufficiently characteristic to enable us, if they are portraits, to identify them with any approach to certainty. The adjunct symbols on the reverses are, however, quite sufficient to prove that these gold Philippi were issued at various mints in S.W. Asia Minor, and that they belong to the same period as the silver Alexandrine tetradrachms. Among them the following are the most remarkable :—

(i.) Clazomenae ? m.m. Half winged-Boar, and spear-head.
(ii.) Mylasa. m.m. Trident and Labrys combined, and mon. Ω
(iii.) Magnesia. m.m. Maeander symbol and monograms ⋈ E .
(iv.) Alabanda or Antiochia ad Maeandrum. Letters AN.

These gold Philippi seem to belong to the same period, B.C. 189-166, as the two very rare gold staters of Rhodian mintage bearing the names and types respectively of Philip and of Lysimachus, and on

their reverses those of the Rhodian magistrates, ΜΝΑΣΙΜΑΧΟΣ on the Philippus,* and ΑΡΙΣΤΟΒΟΥΛΟΣ on the Lysimachus.†
Both names occur on Rhodian didrachms of the period ending B.C. 166 (pp. 243-244, nos. 137 and 143-146).

The attribution of the Alexandrine tetradrachms to the period B.C. 189-166 being almost certain, it follows that the coins with Rhodian types which bear the same magistrates' names must belong, within reasonable limits, to about the same period. The names which occur both on Alexandrine tetradrachms and on the full-face coins (Types a and β) are ΑΙΝΗΤΩΡ, ΑΡΙΣΤΟΒΟΥΛΟΣ, ΔΑΜΟΚΡΙΝΗΣ,‡ ΣΤΑΣΙΩΝ, and ΤΕΙΣΥΛΟΣ. Those which are common to the Alexandrines and the side-faced drachms (p. cv., type γ) are ΑΙΝΗΤΩΡ, ΑΡΙΣΤΟΒΟΥΛΟΣ, ΔΑΜΑΤΡΙοΣ and ΣΤΑΣΙΩΝ. From the recurrence of these names we may safely infer that the change in the type of the Rhodian drachms from full-face to side-face took place between B.C. 189 and 166, and, as many of the full-face drachms are of late style and very light weight, it is not likely that this type can have been abandoned much, if at all, earlier than B.C. 166.

The introduction of the new type of drachm with the head of
Monetary reforms after B.C. 166. Helios radiate *in profile* and shallow incuse square on the reverse, and of a weight appreciably heavier than that of the degraded specimens of the later issues of the full-face series, points to a reform and entire renovation of the drachm coinage. If I am right in dating this reform from B.C. 166, I would suggest that it may have been due in a great measure to the disastrous losses incurred by the Rhodian merchants when the previously tributary cities on the mainland were declared free by the Romans.

---

* Ashburnham Sale Cat., Lot 76.   † Montagu Sale Cat., Lot 619.
‡ Wrongly read in the text as ΔΑΜΟΚΡΙΤΟΣ

INTRODUCTION.

The erection of Delos into a free port was also a severe blow to Rhodian commerce, and the stoppage of the issue of tetradrachms from the Rhodian mint (itself perhaps a sign of a financial crisis) may have been the immediate result of this sudden collapse. Rhodes, however, though crippled, was by no means left without resources, and it was all the more important to maintain her credit now that she no longer issued large coins of full weight, by restoring the drachm and by devoting greater attention to its weight.

The later issues of the full-face drachms, which were of much debased weight, had doubtless come to be regarded merely as a sort of token currency, but, so long as they were readily exchangeable at a fixed rate for tetradrachms and didrachms of recognized value, they served their purpose as small change. As soon, however, as this ceased to be the case, it became necessary to increase the weight of the drachm to something more nearly approaching its nominal value, and, for the sake of distinguishing the new drachms of heavier weight from the debased tokens still widely current, a new type was obviously required. The substitution of the profile head for the facing head may be thus easily accounted for, and the re-introduction of the incuse square on the reverse may also be explained as an indication of a deliberate intention to restore the credit of the Rhodian currency, by issuing a new drachm approximating in value to the higher standard which had prevailed in former times before the incuse square had been abandoned. (Cf. the drachm, Pl. xxxvi. 11, wt. 56 grs., struck in the 4th cent., before the abandonment of the archaic incuse square, with the drachms figured on Pl. xxxix. 1-4, of debased weight, and finally with the restored drachm, Pl. xl. 1-11.)

The drachm raised in weight. The average weight of 35 full-face drachms in the British Museum (nos. 153-187) is only 38·43 grs., while that of the 56 restored drachms (nos. 235-290) is 41·23 grs.

ISLANDS OF CARIA.   cxi

If these last-mentioned coins are to be looked upon as tetrobols of the Attic standard, they would be equivalent, at 6 to 1, to Attic tetradrachms of 247·38 grs. If, however, as is more probable, they passed as drachms of reduced Rhodian weight, they would be exchangeable at 4 to 1 for tetradrachms weighing about 168 grs., of which the unique silver coin of Stratonicea,* weighing 166 grs., is a contemporary example. It is thus open to question whether this Stratonicean coin ought to be regarded as a tridrachm or as a tetradrachm, that is to say, as equivalent to 3 drachms of 56 grs., or to 4 drachms of 42 grs. Though the *average* weight of the drachms of the 'profile' series does not exceed 42 grs., it must be borne in mind that many specimens are considerably heavier than Attic tetrobols of 45 grs., the heaviest of those in the British Museum (Pl. xl. 7) weighing as much as 50·4 grs., and yielding a tetradrachm of 201·6 grs. This is fully up to the average weight of the Rhodian tetradrachms of the period previous to B.C. 166. (Nos. 118—128, Pl. xxxviii. 1-3.)

The probability therefore is that all these coins are Rhodian drachms, though it is also quite possible that the later issues may have been purposely reduced in weight in order to facilitate exchange at 6 to 1 with the Attic tetradrachm, which in the course of the 2nd century took the place of tetradrachms of Rhodian weight.

Rhodes faithful to the Romans, during the Mithradatic war, B.C. 87—84.

The great revolt of the Greek cities of Asia Minor against the Roman rule, B.C. 87-84, when Mithradates was almost everywhere hailed as a liberator, marks an epoch in the coinage of many cities of western Asia Minor.†

Rhodes, at this time almost alone among the Greek States,

---

* *Zeit. f. Num.*, 1888, p. 5, Pl. i. 2.
† *e. g.* Ephesus, which struck gold staters in this period only.

INTRODUCTION.

remained faithful to the Roman alliance, and successfully repelled the attacks of Mithradates upon the city, and when Sulla with the help of the Rhodian fleet passed over into Asia and quelled the revolt, the Rhodians were rewarded for their loyalty to Rome by the gift of Freedom and by the restoration of a portion of their ancient possessions on the mainland.*

Restoration of the Peraea to Rhodes. Latest Rhodian silver coins.
It is to this period of renewed prosperity that we may attribute the last issue of Rhodian silver coins. These pieces (Pl. xli. 1-2, and Pl. xlv. 3) weigh from 68·4 grs. to 61·7 grs., yielding an average of 64·27 grs. I have called some of these coins (nos. 335-341) Attic drachms, as the coins struck at Athens at this late period are of about the same average weight, but some of the Rhodian specimens (*e.g.* no. 334, 68·4 grs., and Pl. xlv. 3, 68·25 grs.) are in excess of the maximum weight of Attic drachms. It is therefore quite possible that the coins of this class may have been issued to pass as trihemi-drachms of the *cistophoric* standard, which prevailed at this time in the Province of Asia. The cistophoric drachm weighs about 49 grs., and a trihemidrachm of full weight should therefore weigh about 73 grs. In any case, at Rhodes itself, these new heavier coins would have been called drachms.

Valuations of the Rhodian drachm in Roman money.
The cistophorus was tariffed by the Romans as equivalent to 3 denarii,† and the light Rhodian drachms, which, as we know from inscriptions of Caria,‡ continued to circulate in enormous quantities in Asia Minor long after they had ceased to be struck in Rhodes, and which were reckoned as equivalent to the cistophoric drachm, were tariffed by

---

* *e.g.* Caunus, &c.
† Hultsch, *Griech. und Röm. Metrologie*, p. 581.
‡ ἀργυρίου λεπτοῦ 'Ροδίου δραχμή. *C. I. G.*, 2693, *e. f.* passim.

ISLANDS OF CARIA.   cxiii

Festus,* in the 1st century B.C., at 12 assaria or $\frac{12}{8}$ of a denarius. At a later period, as we learn from an inscription of Cibyra,† A.D. 71, the Rhodian drachms then current were only reckoned as equivalent to 10 assaria, or $\frac{10}{8}$ of the denarius.

·It is therefore possible that the heavy Rhodian drachms issued after B.C. 88 (Pl. xli. 1, 2), weighing 70·65 grs., may have been issued of that weight with the intention of making them practically equivalent to Roman denarii of 16 assaria, but, as the Roman denarius at this time weighed only about 60 grs., the exchange (as in the case of the cistophorus = 3 denarii) must have been distinctly in favour of the Romans. The comparative rarity of the Rhodian drachms of this heavy weight shows that this issue must have been limited to a very few years.

The exact date of the cessation of the issue of silver coins from the Rhodian mint cannot be absolutely fixed. The remarkable similarity in the obverse and reverse types of the bronze coins (Pl. xli. 3-4) to the latest silver drachms (Pl. xli. 1-2) shows that they are nearly contemporary.

The large size and heavy weight of these bronze pieces is also an indication that they were intended to supersede a silver coinage, and that they cannot have been simply tokens of mere nominal value.

Silver drachms superseded by large bronze pieces.

Perhaps these large bronze coins may have been locally current as *drachms* and tariffed, like the light Rhodian silver drachms (still widely current though no longer minted),‡ at 10 assaria or $\frac{10}{8}$ of the denarius.

There is, however, another valuation, dating from about the same

---

* P. 359: Talentorum non unum genus. Atticum est sex milium denarium, Rhodium et Cistophorum quatuor milium et quingentorum denarium (*i.e.* $\frac{10}{6 0}=\frac{1 2}{1 0}$).
† *C. I. G.*, 4380, *a.* Vol. iii., p. 1167. Τοῦ Ῥωμαϊκοῦ δηναρίου ἰσχύοντος ἀσσάρια δεκαέξ, ἡ Ῥοδία δραχμὴ τούτου τοῦ δηναρίου ἰσχύει ἐν Κιβύρᾳ ἀσσάρια δέκα.
‡ *C. I. G.*, 4380, *a.* Inscr. of Cibyra, above cited.

p

cxiv . INTRODUCTION.

period as the Cibyra inscription (*circ.* A.D. 71), of the Rhodian drachm, which seems at first sight irreconcilable with it. The anonymous metrological writer of Alexandria* says οὐ λανθάνει δέ με καὶ τῶν δραχμῶν εἶναι πλείους διαφοράς· τήν τε γὰρ Αἰγιναίαν καὶ τὴν Ῥοδίαν μνᾶν τῆς Πτολεμαϊκῆς εἶναι πενταπλάσιον. The Ptolemaic (*i.e.* the Alexandrian) drachm of the 1st cent. A.D. is by the same writer valued at ¼ of the denarius.

The Aeginetic and Rhodian drachms, which he here estimates at 5/4 or 1¼ denarii, must have been therefore exactly double the weight of the *light* Rhodian drachms, estimated in the Cibyra inscription at ⅝ of the denarius.

It would seem therefore that this writer designates as '*drachms*' the Rhodian *didrachms*, such as those figured on Pl. xxxviii. 4-8, and it is quite probable that a similar loose use of the word δραχμή for all silver coins of about the size of the Roman denarius, great numbers of which must have remained in circulation for a century, or perhaps two, after they had ceased to be issued, was very general at this time. This indefinite application of the term 'drachm' to various coins of about the same size, though differing from one another very considerably in weight, accounts for the expression ἀργυρίου λεπτοῦ Ῥοδίου δραχμή† in Carian inscriptions, in which sums of money are calculated on the basis of the Rhodian drachm of 50-35 grs.

Indefinite use of the term 'drachm.'

This implies that there were heavier Rhodian coins still current (δραχμαὶ παχεῖαι).‡ Some of these may have been in reality

---

* Hultsch, *Metrol. Script. reliq.*, i., 301.

† *C. I. G.*, 2693, ⊎. *f.*

‡ Hultsch, *Metrolog. Script. rel.*, 321, *Excerpt. ex Hesychio:* Λεπτὰς καὶ παχείας, Ζάλευκος ἐν Νόμοις τὰς δραχμάς, λεπτὰς μὲν τὰς ἐξωβόλους, παχείας δὲ τὰς πλέον ἐχούσας.

drachms of full weight, 60-55 grs., issued in the fourth century B.C. (nos. 38-40, p. 234), but the majority were doubtless light or worn didrachms of the 3rd and 2nd centuries, averaging in weight about 100 grs., and possibly also the latest silver coins (Pl. xli. 1-2) weighing 70-65 grs. The fact that these early drachms of full weight, later didrachms of reduced weight, and the still later issues of 'Cistophoric' weight (trihemidrachms of 73 grs. max.) continued to circulate in Caria, side by side with the full-face drachms of debased weight, down to Imperial times, is quite sufficient to account for the various valuations above cited from Festus, from the inscription of Cibyra, and from the Alexandrian metrologist, which are respectively at $\frac{12}{16}$, $\frac{10}{16}$ and $\frac{20}{16}$ of the Roman denarius (*i.e.*, 12, 10, and 20 assaria).

There can be little doubt that the very large bronze coins (Pl. xli. 3, 4), which are almost identical both on obverse and reverse with the latest Rhodian silver drachms of 70·65 grs. (Pl. xli. 1, 2), superseded these silver drachms between B.C. 88 and B.C. 43; and, moreover, that they tend to show that during this period Rhodes was probably deprived by the Romans of the right of striking silver money, and that she was consequently driven to strike bronze pieces of extraordinarily large dimensions in order to render them more generally acceptable as apparent equivalents in bronze to the silver drachms.

Date of the introduction of heavy bronze money.

In the civil war between Pompey and Caesar, B.C. 48-43, Rhodes sided at first with Pompey, but afterwards, B.C. 47-46, supported Caesar, and after his death, B.C. 44, still remained faithful to his party. In B.C. 43 C. Cassius captured the town and imposed heavy fines upon the Rhodian merchants, amounting to 8,500 talents.

Policy of Rhodes during the Civil War between Pompey and Caesar. Capture of the city by Cassius. His extortions, B.C. 43.

In the following year, B.C. 42, Cassius Parmensis, after the death
of C. Cassius, came to Rhodes, and, after manning
thirty Rhodian ships with his own crews, burned the
whole of the remainder of the Rhodian fleet, thus
destroying for ever the power of Rhodes at sea.

Final ruin of Rhodian commercial prosperity B.C. 42.

From the extortions of C. Cassius and from the subsequent utter destruction of her maritime influence the city of Rhodes never recovered, notwithstanding the fact that in B.C. 41 Antony made some futile endeavours to reward her for her fidelity to the cause of Caesar.

Under Augustus and Tiberius Rhodes still retained her freedom, but Claudius withdrew this privilege, though at a later period he nominally restored it.

Under Vespasian Rhodes was united with the Roman province of Lycia, etc., and the city was selected for the residence of the Roman Prefect.

The Imperial coinage of Rhodes does not extend beyond the reign of Commodus, and it is scarcely likely that the island ever recovered from the effects of the terrible earthquake, A.D. 155, in the reign of Antoninus Pius.

Rhodian coinage under the Empire.

The large bronze coins of the early imperial period are especially interesting. The prevalent obverse types are heads of Dionysos,* unradiate or radiate, and heads of Helios radiate in profile (Pls. xlii. and xliii.). The reverse type is usually Nike standing on a prow, rose, or globe, or crowning a trophy (Pl. xliii. 1), doubtless intended to commemorate Rhodian victories at sea.

The magistrate's name on these large bronze coins is no longer in the nominative, but always in the genitive case, preceded by ἐπί and often accompanied by his title Ταμίας, the Treasurer or Comptroller of the public

Magistrates in autonomous and Imperial times.

---

* Concerning the cult of Dionysos at Rhodes, see Torr, *Rhodes in ancient times*, p. 76.

finances, and not a Roman Provincial Quaestor. It must not, however, be inferred from the fact that the coins of Imperial times were issued in the name of the Ταμίας that the magistrates' names in the nominative case on the earlier Rhodian coins are also those of Ταμίαι.* It is more likely that down to B.C. 48 the magistrate whose name appears on the coins was the president for the time being of the board of Prytaneis. The adjunct symbols,

Adjunct Symbols.
which are far fewer in number than the magistrates' names, but which almost always accompany them, must be the signets of some other official, for the same signet is frequently found in combination with different names.

Early in Imperial times a final reduction in the value of the Rhodian currency seems to have taken place. The

Final Reduction of the Rhodian bronze coinage.
large bronze pieces which supplanted the heavy silver drachm, and which probably inherited from it the popular appellation of 'Drachm,' were now in their turn superseded by coins of about the same size, but distinguished by the addition of the nominal current value at full length, POΔIΩN ΔIΔPAXMON [Pl. xliii. 1, 2, 7, 8]. The prominent position given to the name of the denomination shows clearly that it was now necessary to call special attention to the fact that the large bronze coins were henceforth to pass as Didrachms, and no longer as Drachms.

When this reduction took place can only be inferred from the unusual inscription on the obverse of the earliest examples (Pl. xliii. 1) POΔIOI YΠEP TΩN CEBACTΩN. Such an inscription can only refer to Augustus or Tiberius and Livia, to whose time we may therefore safely ascribe the supposed depreciation of the Rhodian bronze drachm. There is no evidence that any subsequent change took place after this time in the value of the

---

* Lenormant, *La Monnaie dans l'antiquité*, iii., 59, expresses a different opinion.

Rhodian coins, but from the reign of Nerva onwards it seems to have been obligatory to place the head of the Emperor on the obverses.

SYME. Concerning the coins assigned by Waddington to this island and by Imhoof-Blumer to Syangela (see *supra*, p. lxxiv.).

TELOS. For the coins attributed to Telos by Imhoof-Blumer see *Zeit f. Num.*, i. 151. They belong to the 4th cent. B.C.

BARCLAY V. HEAD.

CARIA.

CARIA.

No.	Wt.	Metal, Size.	Obverse.		Reverse.
			ALABANDA.		
			Under name of Antioch, B.C. 197—189.*		
			SILVER.		
			Attic Standard.		
			Tetradrachms.		
			Head of Apollo l., laur.	ΑΝΤΙΟΧΕΩΝ	Pegasos flying r.
1	250·	Æ 1·20		ΤΙΜΟΚΛΗΣ	
				[Pl. I. 1.]	
2	245·8	Æ 1·15	border of dots.	,,	
			Drachms.		
			Head of Apollo r., laur.	ΑΝΤΙΟΧΕΩΝ	Pegasos flying r.
3	63·9	Æ ·75		ΔΙΟΝΥΣΙΟΣ	[Bank coll.]
				[Pl. I. 2.]	
4	61·2	Æ ·7		ΙΣΟΚΡΑΤΗΣ	[,,]

* The dates are those suggested by Babelon (*Rev. Num.*, 1890, p. 417, *sqq.*).

CARIA.

No.	Wt.	Metal. Size.	Obverse.	Reverse.
5	59·5	AR ·75		ΜΕΝΕΚΛΗΣ
6	60·	AR ·75		ΜΕΝΕΣΘΕΥΣ [Pl. i. 8.]
7	65·9	AR ·7	type 1.	[..ΜΑΓΟΡ.. ?] type 1. [Pl. i. 4.]

BRONZE.

8		Æ ·65	Head of Apollo l., laur.	ΑΝΤΙΟ ΧΕΩΝ . Humped bull butting r. beneath bull, M [Pl. i. 5.]
9		Æ ·4	Head of Apollo r., laur.; border of dots.	ΑΝΤΙΟ ΙΧΕΩΝ (sic) Raven? with closed wings r. in front, caduceus. [Pl. i. 6.]

ALABANDA.

After B.C. 168?

SILVER.

Rhodian Standard.*

Tridrachm.

10	175·4	AR 1	Head of Apollo r., laur., hair rolled, with two curls hanging down neck, ends of diadem seen behind neck.	ΑΛΑ [ΒΑΝ] ΔΕΩΝ Pegasos galloping r.; the whole in laurel-wreath. beneath, ΙΑ [Pl. i. 7.]

* Babelon (*Rev. Num.*, 1890, p. 428) calls these coins Tridrachms and Didrachms of the Attic standard. They seem to me to approach more nearly to the Rhodian weight.

ALABANDA. 3

No.	Wt.	Metal. Size.	Obverse.	Reverse.
			Didrachm.	
11	113·	R 1·	Similar. [Pl. I. 8.]	ΑΛΑΒΑΝ Tripod with taenia ΔΕΩΝ hanging over it; in field l., helmet and ƎΙ : the whole in laurel-wreath.
			Octobol.	
12	74·8	R ·8	Similar type, diadem not apparent. [Pl. I. 9.]	ΑΛΑΒΑ ΝΔΕΩΝ Tripod; the whole in laurel-wreath.
			BRONZE.	
13		Æ ·65	Similar.	ΑΛΑΒΑΝ Tripod bound with ΔΕΩΝ taenia.
14		Æ ·6	Similar type: border of dots. [Pl. I. 10.]	ΑΛΑΒ ΑΝ Cultus-statue of ΔΕ ΩΝ goddess facing, arms extended; she wears long chiton with falling fold (apoptygma), modius, and veil: the whole in laurel-wreath.
15		Æ ·7	Similar type.	ΑΛΑΒΑΝ Lyre (kithara). ΔΕΩΝ
16		Æ ·5	Similar type l.	Inscr. obscure. Raven? standing l., wings open: the whole in laurel-wreath?

CARIA.

No.	Metal. Size.	Obverse.	Reverse.
17	Æ ·35	Similar type r.	ΑΛΑ ΒΑΝ Raven ? standing r., wings closed.
18	Æ ·45	Similar type r.	ΑΛΑΒΑΝ ΔΕΩΝ Fore-part of humped bull r.

[Pl. I. 11.]

Imperial Times.

(a) Without heads of Emperors.

Time of Vespasian ?

19	Æ ·85	ΑΛΑΒΑΝΔΕΩΝ Bust of Demos ? r., bearded; neck draped: border of dots.	CVNKΛ HTOC Female figure, the Senate, seated l.; holding in r. lituus, and resting with l. on sceptre.

[Pl. II. 1.]

Later Imperial Times.

20	Æ ·9	ΘΕΑ [ΡΩ]ΜΗ Roma helmeted, seated l. on cuirass; holds Nike on r. and sword in l.; behind her, shield: border of dots. (Countermark, Head of Geta r.; in front, Γ)	ΑΤΕ ΛΕΙΑC ΑΛΑΒΑ ΝΔΕΩ Ν Within a laurel-wreath.

[Pl. II. 2.]

21	Æ ·9	Similar, but Roma rests on spear with l.	ΑΤΕ ΛΕΙ ΟC Within laurel-wreath.
22	Æ 1·2	ΑΛΑ ΒΑΝΔΕΩΝ Bust of Tyche of City r., turreted and with cornucopiae at shoulder: border of dots.	ΕΠΙ[......]ΑΑ ΝΔΡΩΝΟCΑΡΧ Asklepios standing l., resting on serpent-staff: border of dots. (double-struck.) [Bank Coll.]

[Pl. II. 3.]

ALABANDA. 5

No.	Metal. Size.	Obverse.	Reverse.
23	Æ ·85	ΑΛΑΒΑΝ ΔΕΩΝ Female bust r., veiled: border of dots.	ΑΛΑΒΑ ΝΔΕΩΝ Hermes naked but for chlamys standing l., holding in r. caduceus, l. extended behind him: border of dots.
24	Æ ·65	ΑΛΑΒΑ ΝΔΕ Ω Ν Raven? r., wings open and head reverted.	Laurel-branch with fillet attached: border of dots.

(β) With heads of Emperors.

Augustus.

| 25 | Æ ·8 | ΣΕΒΑΣΤΟΣ? Head of Augustus r., beneath which, Capricorn r. | ΑΛΑΒΑΝ ΔΕΩΝ Female bust r. (Alabanda?), wearing wreath. |
| 26 | Æ ·7 | ΣΕΒΑΣ] ΤΟΣ Head of Augustus r., laur. | ΑΛΑ[Β]ΑΝΔΕ ΩΝ Bust of Apollo r., laur., with lyre in front. |

Livia?

| 27 | Æ ·85 | Bust of Livia? r., veiled. | ΑΛΑΒΑΝΔΕΩΝ Female bust r., wearing wreath, and with small laurel-branch at her breast (Alabanda?). |

[Pl. II. 4.]

Augustus and Livia.

Agrippa, Caius, and Lucius.

| 28 | Æ ·8 | ΣΕΒΑΣΤΟΙ Heads of Augustus r., laur., and of Livia l., face to face. | ΑΛΑΒΑΝΔΕ ΩΝ Head of Agrippa l., laur., and of Caius and Lucius jugate r., laur., and surmounted by stars. |

No.	Metal. Size.	Obverse.	Reverse.
		Agrippina Junior.	
29	Æ 1·35	ΑΓΡΙΠΠΙΝΑϹΕΒΑϹ [TH] Bust of Agrippina r., hair in queue.	ΑΛΑΒΑΝΔΕΩΝ Female bust r., turreted (Tyche of City?).
		Nero.	
30	Æ 1·4	ΝΕΡΩΝΚΛΑΥΔΙΟϹ ΚΑΙϹΑΡ Head of young Nero r., bare.	ΑΛΑΒΑΝΔΕΩΝ Bust of young Dionysos r., wearing wreath of ivy.
		Vespasian.	
31	Æ 1·25	ΑΥΤΟΚΡΑΤΩΡ ΟΥΕ ϹΠΑϹΙΑΝΟϹ ΚΑΙϹ ΑΡ Head of Vespasian r., laur.; beneath neck, lituus. [Pl. II. 5.]	ΑΛΑΒΑΝΔΕΩΝ Zeus seated r., naked to waist, resting with r. on sceptre, and holding in l. a thunderbolt upon his knee.
		Septimius Severus.	
32	Æ 1·15	AV·K·Λ·C CEV.....OC Bust of Severus r., laur. (Two countermarks containing respectively the head of an emperor (Geta?) and the numeral Ϛ)	Α ΛΑΒΑ ΝΔΕΩΝ Athena standing l, holding in r. patera, and resting with l. on spear.
33	Æ 1·1	AV·K·Λ·CE· CEVHPO C.. Bust of Severus r., laur., wearing cuirass. (Countermark, Head of Emperor (Geta?)	ΑΛΑΒΑΝ ΔΕΩΝ Zeus naked, standing l., holding on r. eagle, and resting with l. on sceptre.

ALABANDA.

No.	Metal. Size.	Obverse.	Reverse.
		Julia Domna.	
34	Æ 1·4	IOVΛIAΔ OMNA· AVΓ·C Bust of Julia Domna r. (Countermark, Head of Emperor r. (Geta?), in front of which Γ)	AΛABA NΔEΩN Tyche standing l. in chiton and peplos, wearing modius, and holding rudder and cornucopiae.
35	Æ 1·4	(Same countermark.)	
		(same dies.)	
36	Æ 1·	IOVΛIA· ΔOMNA·C Similar bust and countermark.	AΛA BA NΔ EΩN Laurel-branch with three sprays, filleted.
37	Æ 1·05		(Countermark, radiate head of an emperor (Geta?)
		Caracalla.	
38	Æ 1·45	AKMAV PANTΩNI NOC C Bust of Caracalla r., laur., wearing cuirass and paludamentum. (Countermark, Head of Emperor r. (Geta?), in front of which Γ)	AΛABANΔ E ΩN Apollo wearing long chiton and himation standing to front, head l., holding on r. raven, and in l. laurel-branch ; to r. cippus, on which, lyre (kithara). [Pl. II. 6.]
39	Æ 1·05	AVKMA ANTΩNI NOC C Similar.	AΛABAN ΔEΩN Similar.
40	Æ 1·05	AVKM ANTΩNIN OC Similar.	AΛAB A N ΔEΩN Laurel-branch with three sprays, filleted. [Pl. II. 7.]
41	Æ 1·1		
42	Æ 1·15	(Countermark, Head of Emperor (Geta?)	AΛ[A] BA N ΔEΩN (pierced.)

No.	Metal. Size.	Obverse.	Reverse.
43	Æ 1·05	AVKMA ANTΩNIN OC Similar.	AΛABA N ΔEΩN Lyre (kithara).
44	Æ 1·		
45	Æ 1·1	AVKMAVP ANTΩN [IN]OC C. (Countermark, as above.)	
46	Æ 1·	AVKMAVA NTΩNI .... (Countermark, as above.)	[AΛ]ABANΔEΩN
47	Æ 1·15	M·AV· ANTΩNEIN OC Bust of Caracalla r., laur., wears cuirass and paludamentum. (Countermark, ΓE, Head of Geta r.)	AΛA R ANΔEΩN Athena helmeted standing l., holds Nike and rests on spear; on ground beside her, shield. [Pl. II. 8.]
48	Æ 1·15	(same dies.)	
49	Æ 1·3	AVKMAV PANTΩNI NO C Bust of Caracalla r., laur., wearing cuirass and paludamentum. (Countermark, Head of Geta r., in front of which Γ)	AΛARA NΔEΩN Tyche standing l., wearing modius, holding with r. patera over flaming altar, and on l. arm cornucopiae. [Bank Coll.]
50	Æ 1·35	(same die and countermark.)	AΛARAN Δ EΩN

ALABANDA. 9

No.	Metal. Size.	Obverse.	Reverse.
51	Æ 1·3	AV KMAVP ANTΩ NEINOC Bust of Caracalla r., laur., wearing cuirass and paludamentum.	AΛAB AN ΔEΩN The Emperor standing to the front, head r., in military attire, spearing with r. a kneeling captive, and holding on extended l. Nike(?) and Lion's skin.
52	Æ 1·3		

CARIA.

No.	Metal. Size.	Obverse.	Reverse.
		ALINDA.	
		BRONZE.	
		Early Second Century B.C.	
1	Æ ·75	Head of young Herakles r., wearing lion's skin. [Pl. II. 9.]	ΑΛΙΝ ΔΕΩΝ Lion's skin hanging over club : the whole in oak-wreath.*
2	Æ ·55	Head of bearded Herakles r., laur.	Inscr. obscure, similar type.
3	Æ ·65	Young male head r. (Herakles ?), laur.	ΑΛΙΝΔΕΩΝ Club r.; beneath magistrate's name, obscure (ΔΙΟΝ?): the whole in oak-wreath.
4	Æ ·7	Similar.	ΑΛΙΝΔΕΩΝ Club l.; beneath, ΔΙΟΝΥ: the whole in oak-wreath.
5	Æ ·5	Similar.	ΑΛΙΝ ΔΕΩΝ Club r., in oak-wreath.
6	Æ ·35		
7	Æ ·35		type 1.
8	Æ ·7	Young male head r., laur. [Pl. II. 10.]	Λ ΙΝ ΔΕ ΩΝ Winged thunderbolt in in laurel-wreath.

* This reverse type may have been suggested by that of the half-cistophorus current in the 2nd century B.C.

ALINDA. 11

No.	Metal. Size.	Obverse.	Reverse.
9	Æ ·5	Young male head r., laur. ?	ΑΛΙΝ ΔΕΩΝ Bow in case: the whole in oak-wreath.
10	Æ ·85	Similar.	ΑΛΙΝ ΔΕ ΩΝ Bipennis (labrys).
11	Æ ·55	Similar.	ΑΛΙΝΔΕ[ΩΝ Pegasos springing r.

Imperial Coinage.

Augustus.

| 12 | Æ ·65 | ΣΕΒ..... Head of Augustus r., bare. | ΑΛΙΝ ΔΕΩΝ within oak-wreath. |

Nero.

| 13 | Æ ·7 | ΣΕΒΑΣΤ[ΟΣ Head of Nero r., laur. | ΑΛΙΝ ΔΕΩΝ Club and Bow-case, crossed; the whole in oak-wreath. |

Trajan.

| 14 | Æ ·95 | ΑΥΝΕΡ·ΤΡΑΙ ΑΝΟ ΟΚΑΙΓΕΡΔΑΚ Head of Trajan r., laur. | ΑΛΙΝ ΔΕ ΩΝ The Dioskuri standing facing one another, each armed with cuirass, spear, and sword; above their heads stars. |

[Pl. II. 11.]

Aelius Caesar ?

| 15 | Æ ·8 | ... ΑΙΛ............... Head of Aelius (?) r., laur. | Α ΛΙΝ ΔΕΩΝ Sarapis and Isis standing face to face, each wearing modius; Isis r. holds sistrum and situla; Sarapis, l., rests on sceptre. |

No.	Metal. Size.	Obverse.	Reverse.
		Sept. Severus.	
16	Æ 1·35	AVT KAIC CЄV HPO C ΠЄPTAΓ Head of Sept. Severus r., laur.	ЄΠIAPXONMЄN ΙΠ ΠOVA ΛINΔЄΩN Male figure clad in chiton and himation standing l., his r. arm raised, his l. wrapped in himation.
		Caracalla and Plautilla.	
17	Æ 1·55	........ANTΩNINOC NΘH... (N(ϵa)Θ(ϵa) H(ρa)) (rest illegible). Busts of Caracalla r., and Plautilla l., face to face.	APX·M·OVΛ .... ToC A ΛIN ΔЄ ΩN Apollo Kitharoedos standing to front, holding lyre on l. arm and plectrum in r. hand. [Pl. II. 12.]
18	Æ 1·45	Same die. (Countermark, Head r.)	... APX·M· OVΛ· OVΛIAΔ..., and (in ex.) AΛINΔЄΩN Herakles r., clad in lion's skin, pulling down the Keryneian stag.
		Plautilla.	
19	Æ 1·1	NЄA ΘЄA HPA ΠΛA VTIΛΛA Bust of Plautilla, r. (Countermark, Head of Geta r., in front Γ)	APX·M ...... OVΛI AΔoVAΛ INΔЄΩN Herakles naked standing to front, head r.; he holds club in r., and lion's skin in l., and is crowned by a little Nike who stands upon his r. shoulder.

No.	Metal. Size.	Obverse.	Reverse.
		## AMYZON. BRONZE. *Period of Roman Dominion.*	
1	Æ ·65	Young male head r., laur., and diademed : border of dots. | AMVZOΩ ΩΩƎ [Pl. III. 1.]	Bust of Negress? r., two long tresses of hair hanging down neck : border of dots.
2	Æ ·45	Bust of Artemis r., with quiver at shoulder. | AMYSO NEΩ N [Pl. III. 2.]	Flaming torch.

14 CARIA.

No.	Wt.	Metal. Size.	Obverse.	Reverse.
			ANTIOCHIA AD MAEANDRUM. SILVER. *Second Century (after* B.C. 168?). Attic Standard. **Tetradrachms.**	
1	236·5	ΑR 1·05	Head of Apollo r., laur., long curls hanging down neck; behind neck, bow in case or bow and quiver. [Pl. III. 3.]	ANTIOXEΩN Humped bull standing l., within circular Maeander pattern issuing above from pilei of Dioskuri. Beneath bull, ΑΙΝΕΑΣ.
			Drachms.	
2	62·	ΑR ·7	Head of Apollo r., laur., with long curls hanging down neck. [Pl. III. 4.]	ANTIOXEΩN Humped bull recumbent l. upon Maeander pattern; in front, cornucopiae: the whole within laurel-wreath. in ex., MENEΦPΩN
3	61·	ΑR ·65	(border of dots.)	(ANTIOXE), in ex. MEΛE
			BRONZE.	
4		Æ ·7	Head of Zeus r., laur.	ANTIOXEΩN Humped bull recumbent l. upon Maeander pattern.

ANTIOCHIA AD MAEANDRUM. 15

No.	Metal. Size.	Obverse.	Reverse.
		Bust of Mên r., wearing Phrygian cap laur.; behind shoulders, crescent: border of dots.	**ANTIOX** Humped bull standing r.; in ex., magistrate's name :—
5	Æ ·9		**EYΔH** (?) (Εὔδημος ?)
6	Æ ·8	(Countermark, male head r., radiate ?)	**MⱵNAN** [Pl. III. 5.]
7	Æ ·75		· **PIΛOX** · · (?)
8	Æ ·7		illegible.
9	Æ ·75	Head of Apollo l., laur.	**ANTIOX[EΩN TΩNΠPOΣ] MAIANΔPΩ** Eagle with open wings standing l. on Maeander pattern. [Pl. III. 6.]

Imperial Times.

(a) Without heads of Emperors.

Circ. Time of Sept. Severus.

10	Æ 1·0	**IЄPA] BOVΛH** Bust of Boule r., veiled: border of dots.	**ANTI OXЄΩN** Demeter veiled, wearing long chiton with falling fold and peplos, standing l., holding in r. ears of corn, and resting with l. on long torch : border of dots.
11	Æ ·7	**BOV ΛH** Bust of Boule r., veiled: border of dots.	**ANTI O XЄΩN** Nike standing l., holding wreath and palm: border of dots.

No.	Metal. Size.	Obverse.	Reverse.
12	Æ ·8	Bust of Athena (or Roma?) r., wearing crested helmet: border of dots.	AN TIO XEΩN Hermes naked standing l., holding purse and caduceus: border of dots.
13	Æ 1·1	Z[EVC] BOVΛAIOC Head of Zeus Boulaios l., laur.: border of dots.	ANTIOX EΩN M OPCVNOC River-god Morsynos clad in himation standing l., holding in r. patera? and in l. reed: border of dots.
14	Æ ·95	ΔHMOC ANTI O XE ΩN Head of youthful Demos r., bare: border of dots.	C Ω Z ΩN Youthful male figure standing l., clad in short chiton; r. extended; l. holding branch; himation wrapped round l. arm: border of dots.

[Pl. III. 7.]

| 15 | Æ ·9 | ΔH MOC Bust of youthful Demos r., bare: border of dots. | ANTIOXEΩN River-god Maeandros recumbent l., holding reed and cornucopiae; behind him, urn from which water flows; in ex., MAIAN ΔPOC: border of dots. |
| 16 | Æ ·9 | ΔHM OC Head of youthful Demos r., diademed: border of dots. | Similar, but of later style; in ex., MAIANΔP OC |

[Pl. III. 8.]

Circ. Gordian to Gallienus.

| 17 | Æ 1·05 | ANTI O XEΩN Bust of bearded Demos r., diademed: border of dots. | ANTIO XEΩN Zeus seated l., himation over legs, r. arm extended, l. resting on sceptre: border of dots. |

No.	Metal. Size.	Obverse.	Reverse.
18	Æ ·8	ΙЄΡΑΓЄ ΡΟVΣΙΑ Female bust of the Gerousia r.: border of dots.	ΑΝΤΙΟ ΧЄΩΝ Athena standing l., holding patera in r., and shield and spear in l.: border of dots.
19	Æ 1·0	ΙЄΡΑ ΣVΝΚΛΗΤΟΣ Female bust of the Senate r.: border of dots.	ΑΝ ΤΙΟ ΧЄΩΝ Female figure standing l., clad in long chiton and peplos, holding patera and resting on sceptre: border of dots.
20	Æ ·95		
21	Æ ·95	ΙЄΡΑ ΣVΝΚΛΗΤΟΣ Similar.	ΑΝΤΙΟ Χ ЄΩΝ Tyche wearing modius standing l., holding rudder and cornucopiae: border of dots.
22	Æ ·9	Ι]ЄΡΑ ΒΟVΛΗ Bust of Boule r., veiled: border of dots.	ΑΝΤΙΟ ΧЄΩΝ Similar type.
23	Æ ·85	ΙЄΡΑ ΒΟVΛΗ Bust of Boule r.: border of dots.	ΑΝ ΤΙ Ο ΧЄ ΩΝ Tetrastyle temple containing statue of Athena, holding patera, and armed with helmet, shield and spear: border of dots.
24	Æ ·8	ΙЄΡΑΣVΝ ΚΛΗΤΟ[Σ Female bust of the Senate r.: border of dots.	ΑΝ ΤΙ Ο ΧЄ ΩΝ Tetrastyle temple of Tyche: border of dots.

[Pl. III. 9.]

CARIA.

No.	Metal. Size.	Obverse.	Reverse.
25	Æ ·85	ΙЄΡΑΓ ЄΡΟVCΙΑ Female bust of the Gerousia r.: border of dots.	ΑΝ ΤΙ ΟΧ ЄΩ Ν Tetrastyle temple of Tyche: border of dots.
26	Æ ·9		ΑΝ ΤΙΟ ΧЄ ΩΝ [Bank Coll.]

(β) With heads or names of Emperors.

Augustus.

| 27 | Æ ·6 | ΑΝΤΙΟΧЄѠΝ Nike r., CЄΒΑC carrying ΤΟΥ wreath. | CΥΝΑΡΧΙΑΑΝ[ΤΙΟΧЄѠΝ] ΑΓ ΛΑΟΥ? Altar. |
| 28 | Æ ·6 | CЄΒ Α CΤΟC Head of Augustus r., bare. | ΟΧЄΩΝ CΥΝΑΡΧΙΑΑ[ΝΤΙ] ΠΑΙΩΝΙ ΟΥ Athena standing l., armed with helmet, spear, and round shield. [Pl. IV. 1.] |

Domitian.

29	Æ ·7	ΔΟΜΙΤΙΑΝΟC ΚΑΙ CΑΡ Head of Domitian r., laur.	ΑΝΤΙΟΧЄ ΙΑ City of Antioch seated l., turreted; r. hand extended; around, ЄΠΙ ΜЄΛΗ ΚΛ ΑΓΛ ΛΟ Υ ΦΡ ΟΥΓΙ [Pl. IV. 2.]
30	Æ ·7		
31	Æ ·7	Similar.	ΑΝΤΙΟ ΧЄΩΝ Liknophoros r., clad in short chiton, supporting basket on his head; around, ЄΠΙΜЄ ΛΗΚΛΑ ΓΛΑΟΥΦΡΟΥΓΙ (cf. Imhoof, *Gr. M.*, 615). [Pl. IV. 3.]

No.	Metal. Size.	Obverse.	Reverse.
		Trajan.	
32	Æ 1·3	·AVT·NEPB·TPAIA NOC·KAI·CE·ΓEP· ΔAK· Head of Trajan r., laur.	ANTIOX ZEVC KAΠETΩΛI OC Jupiter Capitolinus seated l., holding Nike and resting on sceptre. [Pl. IV. 4.]
		Antoninus Pius.	
33	Æ 1·3	.... AΔPIA .... Head of Antoninus Pius r., laur.	ANTIOXEΩN River-god Macandros recumbent l., holding reed and cornucopiae; behind him, urn from which water flows: in ex., MAIANΔ POC
34	Æ ·75	AVKAI AIΛ ANTΩ NEINOC Head of Antoninus Pius r., laur.	ANTI OXEΩN Nike r., holding wreath and palm.
35	Æ ·75		
		M. Aurelius.	
36	Æ ·95	MAVPH ΛIOC·KAI CAP Head of M. Aurelius Caesar r., bare.	ANTIOX EΩN Dionysos standing l., holding grapes and resting on thyrsos. [Bank Collection.]
37	Æ 1·05	AVKAIM AANTΩNI NO C Bust of M. Aurelius l., laur., in cuirass and paludamentum.	ANTI OXEΩN Demeter clad in long chiton and himation standing l., holding in r. poppy and ear of corn, and resting with l. on long torch.
38	Æ 1·	(Countermark, Bearded head r.)	

20 CARIA.

No.	Metal. Size.	Obverse.	Reverse.
		Faustina Junior.	
39	Æ ·95	ΦΑVCTEI ΝΑCEBA CT Bust of Faustina r.	H[P]AANTI OXEΩN Hera veiled standing to front, head r.; she is clad in chiton with himation over legs, her r. arm is bent and raised to her neck, and her l. holds sceptre. [Pl. IV. 5.]
40	Æ ·75	ΦΑVCTIN Α CEBAC Bust of Faustina r.	ΑΝΤΙΟ ΧΕΩΝ Cultus-statue of Ephesian Artemis; on either side, a stag looking up to the goddess.
		L. Verus.	
41	Æ 6	AV·KAI· Λ·BHPOC Head of L. Verus r., laur.	ΑΝΤΙΟ ΧΕΩΝ Winged Nemesis standing r., her l. arm bent and plucking chiton at her breast; her r. holds cubit-rule.
42	Æ ·6		inscr. blundered.
		Commodus.	
43	Æ 1·5	AVKAIMAVP KOM ΜΟΔΟC Bust of Commodus r., laur., wearing cuirass and paludamentum.	ΑΝΤΙΟΧΕ ΩΝ (in ex.) [ΖΕVC ΚΑΠ] ΕΤΩ ΛΙΟC Tetrastyle temple, within which, statue of Jupiter Capitolinus seated l., holding eagle and resting on sceptre. [Bank Collection.]
44	Æ 1·2	Similar.	ΑΝΤΙΟ ΧΕΩΝ Athena standing l., wearing helmet and resting on spear; she holds in r. patera over a flaming altar; behind her on the ground, a shield.

ANTIOCHIA AD MAEANDRUM. 21

No.	Metal. Size.	Obverse.	Reverse.
		Caracalla.	
45	Æ 1·0	M·AYP·ANTΩ. KAI CA[P Head of young Caracalla r., bare, wearing cuirass and paludamentum.	ANTI OXE Tetrastyle temple of ΩN Tyche.
		Severus Alexander.	
46	Æ 1·4	AVTKMAVP HAΛE ΞANΔPO[C Bust of Sev. Alexander r., laur., wears cuirass and paludamentum.	Z[E]VC KAΠET Ω ΛIOC ANTIOXE ΩN (in ex.) Jupiter Capitolinus seated r., resting on sceptre, and holding on extended l. Nike carrying palm and wreath, with which she crowns Tyche, who stands l. before Jupiter. Tyche wears modius (or turrets) and holds rudder and cornucopiae.
		Gordian III.	
47	Æ 1·35	AVT]KMANTΩ ΓOP ΔIANOC Bust of Gordian r., laur., wearing cuirass and paludamentum.	AN TIO Tetrastyle temple containing seated statue XEΩN of Jupiter Capitolinus l., holding Nike and resting on sceptre.
48	Æ 1·15	AVTKMANT ΓOPΔI ANOC Bust of Gordian r., laur., wearing cuirass and paludamentum.	ANTIO XEΩN Athena helmeted standing to front, head l.; she rests on spear with r., and on shield with l.

CARIA.

No.	Metal. Size.	Obverse.	Reverse.

Philip Junior.

49	Æ 1·1	ΜΙΟΥ·ΦΙΛΙΠΠΟϹ·ΚΑ ΙϹΑΡ Bust of young Philip r., bare, wearing cuirass and paludamentum.	ΑΝΤΙΟ ΧΕΩΝ Hekate triformis, holding in her six hands torches, key, serpent, dagger, etc.; to l., lighted altar; to r., dog looking up. [Pl. iv. 6.]
50	Æ 1·1	Same die.	ΑΝΤΙΟΧΕΩ Ν River-god Maeandros recumbent l., holding reed and resting on inverted vase from which water flows.
51	Æ ·85	ΜΙΟΥ·ΦΙΛΙΠΠΟϹ·ΚΑ ΙϹΑΡ Similar.	ΑΝΤΙΟ ΧΕ ΩΝ Tyche standing l., with usual attributes. [Bank Coll.]

Trajan Decius.

52	Æ 1·4	ΑΥΤ·Κ·ΤΡΑΙΑ ΝΟϹ ΔΕΚΙΟϹ Bust of Trajan Decius r., laur., wearing cuirass and paludamentum.	ΑΝΤΙΟΧΕ ΩΝ ΜΕΑΝΔΡΟϹ (in ex.) Bridge of six arches spanning the river. On the l. is the bridge-gateway, resembling a triumphal arch; on the parapet of the bridge is a recumbent statue of Maeandros l., holding reed and cornucopiae, and behind him, also on parapet, two standing figures or statues l.
53	Æ ·8	ΑΥΤΚΤΡΑΙΑΝΟϹΔΕ ΚΙϹ (sic) Bust of Trajan Decius r., laur., wearing cuirass and paludamentum.	ΑΝΤΙΟ ΧΕΩΝ Dionysos standing l., holding kantharos and resting on thyrsos; at his feet, panther.
54	Æ ·8	Same die.	ΑΝΤΙΟ Χ ΕΩΝ Tyche standing l., with usual attributes.

ANTIOCHIA AD MAEANDRUM.   23

No.	Metal. Size.	Obverse.	Reverse.
		Etruscilla.	
55	Æ 1·15	ЄPЄNIAAITPVCKIΛ ΛACЄB Bust of Herennia Etruscilla r.	ANTIOX River-god Maeandros ЄΩN recumbent l., holding reed and cornucopiae, and resting against vase from which water flows; above head of god a star.
		Valerian.	
56	Æ 1·4	AVKAIΠOΛIKINNIOC OVAΛЄPIANOC Bust of Valerian r., laur., wearing cuirass and paludamentum.	ANTIOXЄΩN Bridge over Maeandros similar to no. 52, but on top of gateway a stork, and behind the statue of Maeandros a figure r.; in waves, below bridge, two fishes.
		Gallienus.	
57	Æ 1·5	AVKΠOΓAΛΛI HNO[C Bust of Gallienus l., armed with cuirass, helmet, shield and spear.	ANTIOXЄ Bridge over Maeander, ΩN similar to no. 52, but stork perched on top of gateway, and no figures behind statue of Maeandros.
		[Pl. iv. 7.]	
58	Æ 1·4	AVKΠΓA ΛΛI HNOC Similar armed bust of Gallienus.	ANT IOX ЄΩN Male figure (Jupiter Capitolinus) seated l., holding Nike and resting on sceptre. Before him an agonistic table on which urn containing palm; beneath table, oenochoë.
59	Æ 1·0	AVKΠΛIKINNIOCΓA ΛΛIHNOC Bust of Gallienus r., laur.	KTICTHCAN TIOXЄΩN Male figure (the Founder) standing towards l., clad in short chiton and himation; he holds in extended r. uncertain object.
		[Pl. iv. 8.]	

CARIA.

No.	Metal. Size.	Obverse.	Reverse.
		Salonina.	
60	Æ 1·	IOVKOP CAΛΩNIN Bust of Salonina r., with crescent behind shoulders.	ANTIO XEΩN Tyche standing l., wearing modius, and holding rudder and cornucopiae.
61	Æ 1·0	Same die.	ANTIO XEΩN Altar bound with garland, on it stands an eagle l., with open wings.

PLARASA AND APHRODISIAS.

After B.C. 166.

BRONZE.

No.	Metal. Size.	Obverse.	Reverse.
1	Æ ·5	ΠΛΑΡΑ ΑΦ ΡΟ	Double-axe (Labrys).*	Cuirass on trophy-stand: the whole in incuse square. [Pl. v. 1.]
2	Æ ·45		
3	Æ ·45		border of dots. (no incuse square.) [Pl. v. 2.]
4	Æ ·4	Bust of Eros r., winged, hair in Erotic plait.	ΠΛΑ ΑΦΡΟ Rose. [Pl. v. 3.]
5	Æ ·35		ΑΦΡΟΔ[Ι] ΣΙΕΩΝ [Pl. v. 4.]

* The double axe, or Labrys, as Leake points out (*Num. Hell.*, *Asia*, p. 20), is a symbol especially characteristic of Carian divinites (see also Preller, *Gr. Myth.*, 4th ed., vol. i., p. 141). According to Appian (*De Bell. Civ.*, i., 97), Sulla dedicated to the goddess Aphrodite at Aphrodisias a golden wreath and an axe. This type is met with in Caria on coins of Plarasa and Aphrodisias, Euromus, Iasus, Mylasa and Myndus.

No.	Wt.	Metal. Size.	Obverse.	Reverse.
			First Century B.C. (*temp. Augusti*). Attic or Roman Standard reduced. Drachm.	
			Bust of Aphrodite* r., veiled, wearing stephane, earring, and necklace: border of dots.	ΠΛΑΡΑΣΕΩΝ ΚΑΙ ΑΦΡΟΔΕ ΙΣΙΕΩΝ Eagle with closed wings standing l. on winged thunderbolt. Magistrate's name:—

6	54·	ΑR ·7		(Eagle r.; behind neck, caduceus.)
				ΙΕΡΕΥ Ε
				ΣΔΗ ΠΙ
				ΜΟΥ ΚΡΑ
				   ΤΗΣΞ[Ε]
				   ΝΟΚΡΑ
				   ΤΟΥ[Σ
				[Pl. v. 5.]

7	50·8	ΑR ·7		(Eagle l., without caduceus.) Α Α ΠΟΛ ΓΕ ΛΩΝΙ ΛΑ ΟΣ ΟΥ
8	49·3	ΑR ·75		ΑΡ Α ΤΕ ΠΟΛ ΜΙ ΛΩΝ ΔΩ ΟΣ ΡΟΣ
9	51·5	ΑR ·65		ΑΡΤΕ (wreath behind eagle's head.) ΜΙ ΔΩ ΤΟΥ ΡΟΣ ΑΝ ΑΡΤΕ ΔΡΩ ΜΙΔΩ ΝοΣ ΡΟΥ [Pl. v. 6.]

* It is possible that the veiled bust on the silver coins of Aphrodisias may have been copied from the Roman coins of the Cassia family, which bear on the obverse a veiled bust of **LEIBERTAS** (Babelon, *Mon. de la Rép. Rom.*, i., p. 336). This fact is, however, not inconsistent with an assimilation of Ἐλευθερία to Aphrodite (cf. *infra*, no. 24, note).

No.	Wt.	Metal. Size.	Obverse.	Reverse.
10	52·	Æ ·65		ΚΑΛ (no wreath.) ΛΙΠ ⋮ ⋅ ⋅ ΠΟΣ ΠΕΙ ΛΕΟΝ ΤΟΥ ΤΕΩ Σ
11	51·5	Æ ·65	Type r. ΜΥ ΩΝ	ΔΙ[Ο] ΓΕ ΝΗΣ ΑΝΤΙ ΠΑΤΡ ΟΣ
12	48·9	Æ ·7	ΜΥ ΩΝ	ΔΙΟ ΓΕ ΝΗΣ ΑΝΤΙ ΠΑΤΡ ΟΣ
13	53·2	Æ ·65		(Cornucopiae behind neck.) ΜΥ ΩΝ ΚΑΛ ΛΙΠ ΠΟΥ
14	52·	Æ ·65	Similar.	Inscr. obscure. Eagle with open wings standing r. on thunderbolt. No magistrates' names legible.

No.	Metal. Size.	Obverse.	Reverse.
		BRONZE.	
15	Æ ·75	Head of Aphrodite r., wearing stephane, neck draped: border of dots. [Pl. v. 7.]	ΠΛΑΡΑ ΑΦΡΟΔΙ Eagle with closed wings standing r. on thunderbolt.
16	Æ ·7		
17	Æ ·75	(Two countermarks, Grapes, and Female head.)	

APHRODISIAS.

First Century B.C.

No.	Metal. Size.	Obverse.	Reverse.
18	Æ ·7	Head of veiled Aphrodite r.: border of dots. [Pl. v. 8.]	ΑΦΡΟΔ . . . . . . on thunderbolt. Eagle standing r.
19	Æ ·65	Head of Zeus r., laur. [Pl. v. 9.]	Α ΦΡΟΔ[Ι] ΣΙΕΩΝ Cultus-statue of Aphrodite r., veiled.
20	Æ ·75	Head of Aphrodite r., bound with wreath: border of dots. [Pl. v. 10.]	ΑΦΡΟΔΙ . . . . . . Bipennis (Labrys) with two filleted palm-branches crossed over its handle: border of dots.

APHRODISIAS.   29

No.	Metal. Size.	Obverse.	Reverse.

Imperial Times.

(a) Without heads of Emperors.

21	Æ ·9	ΑΦΡΟΔΙCΙΕ ΩΝ Bust of Athena r., wearing crested Corinthian helmet and aegis: border of dots.	Α]ΠΟΛΛΩΝΙΟC ΥΙΟC ΑΦΡ ΟΔ..... Distyle temple with Ionic columns containing cultus-statue of Aphrodite facing, veiled and wearing kalathos or modius; above her extended hands, to l., star; to r., crescent. The statue stands between a small seated figure of a Priestess r., and an altar? in the form of an Ionic capital surmounted by an uncertain object: border of dots.*

[Pl. v. 11.]

22	Æ ·8	ΔΗΜΟC? (obliterated): Young male head r., laur. (Demos?): border of dots. (Countermark, ΑΚΜ, Eagle with open wings.)	ΑΦΡΟΔΙCΙΕΩΝ (almost obliterated). River-god Timeles recumbent l.; beneath, ΤΙΜΕΛΗC (almost obliterated).
23	Æ ·95	ΔΗΜΟC Head of Demos r., bearded, and laur.: border of dots.	ΑΦΡΟΔΙ CΙΕΩΝ Zeus? bearded, wearing himation over legs, seated l.; his r. extended, his l. resting on seat: border of dots. (Cf. for type coin of Hadrian, no. 103.)

* The seated figure on the left and the object on the right of the statue are described from a comparison of all the coins of this type in the British Museum. The identification of the seated figure on the left as Eros (Imhoof, *Gr. M.*, p. 141) does not seem to be borne out by the specimens in the British Museum, nor is the object in front of the statue a rose. This coin is of the time of Augustus; cf. magistrate's name on nos. 85—89, *infra*.

No.	Metal. Size.	Obverse.	Reverse.
24	Æ 1·0	Same die.	ΑΦΡΟΔΕΙCΙΕΩΝ ΕΛΕΥΘΕΡ ΙΑ* Aphrodite Eleutheria, wearing chiton, and peplos (over legs and l. shoulder), standing l., holding patera and resting on sceptre : border of dots. [Pl. v. 12.]
25	Æ ·95	ΔΗΜΟC Youthful head of Demos r., laur : border of dots.	ΑΦΡΟΔΕΙ CΙΕΩΝ Similar type, but the goddess holds apple instead of patera : border of dots.
26	Æ 1·0		
27	Æ ·9	head wears diadem.	ΑΦΡ ΟΔ ΕΙCΙΕΩΝ
28	Æ 1·05	ΙΕΡΑCVΝ ΚΛΗΤΟC Youthful bust of Senate r.: border of dots.	·Τ·Κ· ΖΗΛΟ C·ΑΝ ΕΘ· ΑΦ ΡΟΔ ΕΙCΙ ΕΩΝ Aphrodite clad in long chiton and peplos standing to front, head l., carrying infant Eros and resting with l. on sceptre : border of dots. [Pl. v. 13.]
29	Æ 1·05	ΙΕΡΑCV ΝΚΛΗΤΟC Head of the Senate r., diademed : border of dots.	ΑΦΡΟΔΕΙC ΙΕΩΝ Aphrodite standing l., clad in long chiton and peplos, holds in r. patera, and rests with l. on sceptre : border of dots. [Bank Coll.]

* The goddess Eleutheria on this coin is clearly Aphrodite; cf. the specimens which follow, on which a figure in precisely the same attitude holds an apple. The name Eleuthera in an inscription of Cyane in Lycia (*C. I. G.*, Add. 4303, b. 1. Θεῷ μεγάλῳ Ἄρει καὶ Ἐλευθέρᾳ ἀρχηγέτιδι ἐπιφανεῖ θεᾷ), although the goddess is coupled with Ares, refers to Artemis and not to Aphrodite.

APHRODISIAS. 31

No.	Metal. Size.	Obverse.	Reverse.
30	Æ 1·	(Countermark, B) (same dies.)	
31	Æ ·95		ΑΦΡΟΔΕΙ ϹΙΕΩΝ holds patera?
32	Æ ·95	ϹVΝΚΛΗΤΟϹ	,, holds apple.
33	Æ 1·0	ΙΕΡΟϹ ΔΗΜΟϹ Youthful bust of Demos r., laur.: border of dots.	ΑΦΡΟΔΕΙ ϹΙΕΩΝ Cultus-statue of Aphrodite r., veiled and wearing kalathos between star and crescent; behind her, a small veiled figure of a priestess seated r., and, in front, an altar in the form of the capital of a column surmounted by a conical cover : border of dots.
34	Æ ·95	ΔΗΜΟϹ Youthful head of Demos r., laur.: border of dots.	ΑΦΡΟΔ Ε Ι ϹΙΕΩΝ Similar type; form of altar varied : border of dots.
35	Æ ·95	ΙΕΡΑ ΒΟV[ΛΗ] Bust of Boule r., veiled: border of dots.	ΑΦΡΟΔΕ ΙϹΙΕΩΝ Aphrodite naked r., holding her l. foot with her r. hand (untying her sandal?), and with her left hand a wreath; before her a little Eros extracting thorn? from her foot; border of dots.
36	Æ ·85	(Countermark, B) [Pl. v. 14.]	
37	Æ ·85	ΕΙΕΡΑ ΒΟVΛΗ Bust of Boule r., veiled: border of dots.	ΑΦΡΟΔΕ ΙϹΙΕΩΝ Eros winged, naked but for chlamys, stands to front, head l., holding long torch in both hands : border of dots.

No.	Metal. Size.	Obverse.	Reverse.
38	Æ ·75	IEPA BOVΛH Similar.	Similar, but without chlamys.
39	Æ ·8	Similar.	AΦPOΔ EILIEΩN Similar type, towards r. : border of dots.
40	Æ ·8		AΦPOΔ I CIEΩN [Pl. vi. 1.]
41	Æ ·75	IEPA BOVΛH Similar.	AΦPO[ΔI] LIEΩN Eros winged, naked, standing to front, head l., holding in r. long torch downwards, and in l. strung bow: border of dots.
42	Æ ·8	EIEPA BOVΛH Similar. (Same die as no. 37.)	AΦPOΔ EI[CI]EΩN Eros in attitude of Thanatos winged, naked, standing towards r. with legs crossed, and leaning upon inverted torch which rests on low altar : border of dots. [Pl. vi. 2.]
43	Æ ·75	IEPA BOVΛH Similar.	[AΦPO]Δ ICIEΩN Eros winged, naked, standing towards r., shooting with bow and arrow : border of dots.
44	Æ ·8	IEPA BOVΛH Similar.	AΦPOΔEI Two Erotes seated on CIEΩN ground face to face, playing with astragali : border of dots. [Pl. vi. 3.]
45	Æ ·75	IE PABOVΛH	AΦPOΔI C IEΩN
46	Æ ·75	,,	,,

APHRODISIAS.

No.	Metal. Size.	Obverse.	Reverse.
47	Æ ·9	ΔΗ ΜΟC Youthful bust of Demos r., laur.: border of dots. (Countermark, B) [Pl. vi. 4.]	ΑΦΡΟΔΕ ΙCΙΕΩΝ Dionysos, wearing himation over legs, standing l. beside column, on which he rests his l. arm; he holds in r. grapes, and in l. thyrsos; in front, panther looking back: border of dots.
48	Æ ·9	ΔΗΜΟC	Α ΦΡΟΔΙCΙΕ ΤΙ ΚΖΗΝΩΝ*
49	Æ ·75	ΔΗΜΟC Youthful bust of Demos r., laur.: border of dots.	ΑΦΡΟΔ ΕΙCΙΕΩΝ Dionysos naked, standing to front, head l., resting with l. on thyrsos, and holding in r. kantharos: in front, panther looking back; border of dots.
50	Æ ·85	Bust of young Dionysos, or of a Bacchante r.: border of dots.	ΑΦΡΟΔΕΙ CΙΕΩΝ Asklepios standing to front, head l., wearing himation over legs and l. shoulder, and resting with r. on serpent staff: border of dots.
51	Æ ·85	ΙΕΡΑ CVΝΚΛΗΤΟC Youthful bust of Senate r.: border of dots.	Similar.

* Ti. Cl. Zeno was Archiereus and Archineocoros. See coins of Julia Domna.

CARIA.

No.	Metal. Size.	Obverse.	Reverse.
52	Æ 1·0	ΙΕΡΑϹΥΝΚ ΛΗΤΟϹ Youthful bust of the Senate r. : border of dots. [Pl. vi. 5.]	ΑΦΡΟΔΕΙ ϹΙΕΩΝ Mên* standing l., wearing Phrygian cap, short chiton and cloak, crescent behind shoulders, his r. foot on bucranium; he holds in r. patera, and rests with l. on sceptre : border of dots.
53	Æ 1·0	ΙΕΡΑϹΥ ΝΚΛΗΤΟϹ Similar.	ΑΦΡΟΔΕΙ ϹΙΕΩΝ Similar.
54	Æ ·85	ΒΟΥΛΗΑΦΡΟΔΕΙ ϹΙ ΕΩΝ Bust of Boule r., wearing stephane; hair rolled: border of dots. [Pl. vi. 6.]	[ΕΠ]ΙΜΕΛΗΘΕΝΤΟϹΦΛ Α· ΜΥΩΝΟΣ ΑΡ . . . . . Winged Nemesis standing l., wearing long chiton, her r. raised in usual gesture, her l. hanging down and holding bridle : border of dots.
55	Æ ·95	ΙΕΡΑϹΥ ΝΚΛΗΤΟϹ Youthful bust of the Senate r., diademed: border of dots. [Pl. vi. 7.]	ΤΙ ΚΑΖΗΝΩΝ ΑΝΕ ΑΦΡΟΔ ΙϹΙΕΩΝ Leafless trunk of tree with three branches; on either side of it a naked man wearing a Phrygian cap; the one on the left wields an axe, the one on the right kneels on one knee, or runs away, turning his back to the tree†: border of dots.

* Probably Μὴν Ἀσκαινός. See Le Bas and Waddington, iii. p. 873, no. 1601 B.

† Cf. the myth of the birth of Adonis, Apollod., iii. 14, 3; Hyginus, Fab. 58 and 161; and the coins of Myra Lyciae, where a similar though not identical type occurs.

APHRODISIAS. 35

No.	Metal. Size.	Obverse.	Reverse.
56	Æ 1·5	IEPACV NKΛHTOC Similar.	KΛZHNΩAPX AΦPOΔICIEΩN Similar tree, but the three branches spring separately from an enclosure, apparently of trellis-work, and there are no men present: border of dots. [Pl. vi. 8.]
57	Æ 1·05	CVNKΛHTOC Similar.	AΦPOΔ E I CIEΩN Similar, but figure on each side as on no. 55.
58	Æ ·95	IEPACVNK ΛHTOC Similar.	AΦPOΔ E I CIEΩN Similar, but a lighted altar on either side of tree; no men present.
59	Æ ·95	IEPA CVNKΛHTOC Similar.	AΦPOΔ EICIEΩ N Similar, without men or altars.
60	Æ 1·0	IEPACY[N] KΛHTOC Head l.	TK[ZHΛO]C ANE ☉ and across field, AΦPO ΔEI CI EΩN Similar, but with altars at sides of tree.
61	Æ ·8	Inscr. obscure. Youthful head of Demos r., laur. (?): border of dots.	AΦPOΔ .... ΩN Leafless trunk of tree with three branches, flanked by two men, as on no. 55.
62	Æ ·75	IEPA BOVΛH Bust of Boule r., veiled: border of dots.	AΦPOΔEIC I EΩN Three leafless trunks in trellis enclosure.
63	Æ ·75		

OARIA.

No.	Metal. Size.	Obverse.	Reverse.
64	Æ ·8	ЄІЄРА ВОVΛΗ Similar.	ΑΦΡΟ ΔЄ ΙCΙЄΩΝ Zeus, wearing himation over legs, seated l. on throne with back; he holds Nike on r., and rests with l. on sceptre: border of dots.
65	Æ ·8	ЄІЄРА ВОVΛΗ Similar.	ΑΦΡΟΔЄ ΙCΙЄΩΝ Hermes* naked, standing to front, head l., chlamys round l. arm; he holds in r. purse, and in l. caduceus: border of dots.
66	Æ ·75	ΙЄΡΑ ВОVΛΗ	ΑΦΡΟΔЄΙ CΙЄΩΝ
67	Æ ·75	Bust of Sarapis r., wearing modius: border of dots.	ΑΦΡΟΔЄ ΙCΙЄΩΝ Isis, wearing long chiton with falling fold, standing to front, head l., holds sistrum and situla; behind her shoulders, crescent: border of dots.
68	Æ ·7		ΑΦΡΟΔ Ι CΙЄΩΝ
69	Æ ·75	Bust of Sarapis r., wearing modius: border of dots.	ΑΦΡΟΔЄΙCΙ ЄΩΝ Harpokrates naked, standing l., placing the forefinger of his r. hand on his lips; cornucopiae and chlamys on l. arm: border of dots. [Pl. VI. 9.]
70	Æ ·65		ΑΦΡΟΔЄ Ι CΙЄΩΝ
71	Æ ·7		,,

* Probably statue of Hermes Agoraios; cf. Le Bas and Waddington, iii., p. 373, no. 1601, B.

APHRODISIAS. 37

No.	Metal. Size.	Obverse.	Reverse.
72	Æ ·75	Bust of Athena r., wearing close-fitting crested helmet : border of dots.	ΑΦΡΟΔ Ε ΙϹΙΕΩΝ Nike standing l., holding wreath and palm : border of dots.
73	Æ ·7	Similar.	ΑΦΡΟΔΕΙ ϹΙΕΩΝ Eros winged, standing to front, head l. ; holds in r. short torch, and in l. bow : border of dots.
74	Æ 1·25	ΙΕΡΑ ϹⅤΝΚΛΗΤΟϹ Youthful bust of the Senate r., laur. : border of dots. (Countermark uncertain.)	ΑΦΡ Ο ΔΕΙϹΙ ΕΩ Ν Agonistic table, on which two prize urns ; beneath, amphora and two palms : border of dots.
75	Æ ·95	ΙΕΡΑ ϹⅤΝΚΛΗΤΟϹ Similar type, but head diademed.	ΑΦΡΟΔ ΕΙϹΙΕΩΝ Agonistic table, on which prize urn containing palm, inscribed ΓΟΡΔΙ ΑΝΗΑ beneath table, ΑΤΤ ΑΛ ΗΑ border of dots.
76	Æ ·95		
77	Æ 1·1	ΙΕΡΑ ϹⅤΝΚΛΗΤ[ΟϹ] Similar type, but head laur.	ΑΦΡΟ ΔΕΙϹΙ Tetrastyle temple ΕΩΝ containing cultus-statue of Aphrodite r. on plinth : border of dots.

No	Metal Size.	Obverse.	Reverse.
78	Æ ·95	ΕΛΕVΘ[ΕΡΟC] ΔΗΜOC Youthful bust of Demos diademed, r. (Countermark, Ɓ)	ΑΦΡΟΔ ΕΙ CΙΕΩΝ Agonistic table, on which prize urn containing palm, inscribed ΓΟΡΔΙ ΑΝΗΑ beneath table, ΑΤΤ ΑΛΗ Α border of dots.
79	Æ ·75	Bust of youthful Dionysos l., wearing ivy-wreath; in front, thyrsos: border of dots.	ΑΦΡΟΔΕ ΙCΙ Lioness or panther [Ε]ΩΝ walking r.: border of dots.
80	Æ ·75	)	ΑΦΡΟΔΕ Ι Similar. CΙΕΩΝ
81	Æ ·8	ΔΗΜ ΟC Youthful bust of Demos r., laur.: border of dots.	ΑΦΡΟΔΕΙCΙΕ ΩΝ Eagle with open wings to the front, head l., holding serpent in claws: border of dots.
82	Æ ·7	Bust of Helios r., radiate: border of dots.	ΑΦΡΟΔΕΙ CΙΕΩΝ Eagle with open wings to the front, head r.: border of dots.
83	Æ ·7	Humped bull to r., head lowered: border of dots.	Α ΦΡ Ο ΔΕΙCΙΕΩΝ Similar type, but eagle's head l.: border of dots.
84	Æ ·55	Similar type: border of dots	ΑΦΡΟΔΙCΙΕΩΝ Bipennis (Labrys) bound with fillet: border of dots.

APHRODISIAS. 39

Imperial Coinage.

(β) With heads or names of Emperors.

Augustus.

No.	Metal. Size.	Obverse.	Reverse.
85	Æ ·8	ϹΕΒΑ ϹΤΟϹ Head of Augustus r., laur.	ΑΠΟΛΛѠΝΙΟϹ ΑΦΡΟΔΙϹΙΕѠ Ν ΥΙΟϹ Cultus-statue of Aphrodite facing, veiled, and wearing kalathos or modius; above her extended hands to l., star; to r., crescent.
86	Æ ·75		
87	Æ ·8		[Pl. VII. 1.]
88	Æ ·75	(ϹΕΒ ΑϹΤΟϹ)	(ΑΠΟΛΛΝΙΟ Ϲ *sic* κ.τ.λ.)
89	Æ ·75	(illegible.)	(... ΛΛΩΝΙΟ Ϲ κ.τ.λ.)
90	Æ ·55	ϹΕΒΑ ϹΤΟϹ Head of Augustus r., laur.	ΑΦΡΟΔΙϹ ΙΕ ΩΝϹΩΖΩΝ Bipennis (labrys) bound with fillet.
91	Æ ·55		(ΑΦΡΟΔΙϹ ΙΕΩΝϹΩΖ ΩΝ) [Pl. VII. 2.]
92	Æ ·6		(,,)
93	Æ ·65		(ΑΦΡΟΔΙ ϹΙΕ ΩΝϹΩΖ ΩΝ)

No.	Metal. Size.	Obverse.	Reverse.
		Augustus and Livia.	
94	Æ ·75	CЄBACT OI Heads of Augustus laur., and of Livia, jugate, r.	AΠOΛΛΩNIOC AΦPOΔICIЄ ΩN YIOC Cultus-statue of Aphrodite facing, as on no. 85.
		Livia.	
95	Æ ·85	C Є BACTH Bust of Livia r., draped.	AΠOΛΛΩNI[OCYIOC]AΦPOΔ ИΩƎIƆI Distyle temple containing cultus-statue of Aphrodite, as on no. 21, between a small seated figure of a Priestess? on the left, and an Ionic capital surmounted by an uncertain object on the right.
			[Pl. VII. 3.]
96	Æ 1·05	(CEBA CTH)	
		Caius Caesar.	
97	Æ ·65	ΓΑΙΟΣ Head of Caius ΚΑΙΣΑΡ Caesar r., bare.	AΦPOΔI ΣIEΩN Head of Aphrodite r., wearing stephane and necklace.
98	Æ ·55		
		Tiberius.	
99	Æ ·8	ΘΕΟΣ ΣΕΒΑΣΤΟΣ Head of Augustus r., laur.	AΦP OΔI ΣIEΩN Cultus-statue of Aphrodite facing, veiled, and wearing kalathos; her arms extended.
100	Æ ·75		
101	Æ ·75		
102	Æ ·75		

APHRODISIAS. 41

No.	Metal. Size.	Obverse.	Reverse.
		Hadrian.	
103	Æ 1·2	AV·KAI·TPA AΔPIA NOCCE Bust of Hadrian r., laur., wearing cuirass with aegis and paludamentum.	AΦPOΔEI CIEΩN Zeus? naked to waist, seated l. on throne without back, himation over legs and l. shoulder; his r. arm is extended, his l. rests on throne.*
104	Æ 1·15	AV·KAI·TPA AΔPIA NOC CE Bust of Hadrian r., laur., wearing cuirass with aegis and paludamentum.	AΦPOΔEI CIEΩN Cultus-statue of Aphrodite r., veiled, and wearing kalathos or modius, round which serpent coils; in field l. crescent, r. star; in front, Eros stands r. aiming with bow and arrow.

[Pl. VII. 4.]

105	Æ 1·1	Same die.	AΦPOΔEI CIEΩN Tetrastyle temple, within which cultus-statue of Aphrodite facing, veiled, and wearing kalathos or modius.
		M. Aurelius.	
106	Æ 1·5	AVT AVP[ANTΩ] NINOC Bust of M. Aurelius l., laur., wearing cuirass and paludamentum.	T·K·ZHΛOCIE PEYCEΠINIKI ON ANE(θηκε); and in ex., AΦPOΔEICI EΩN Cultus-statue of Aphrodite l., before which stand M. Aurelius and L. Verus l., each clad in paludamentum and raising his r. hand in act of adoration.

* This type may be compared with that of no. 23, *supra*.

G

42   CARIA.

No.	Metal. Size.	Obverse.	Reverse.

Faustina Jun.

		ΦAVCTEINA CEBAC TH Bust of Faustina, r., draped.	T·K·ZHΛOC AN̄E Θ HKE· AΦPOΔICI Aphrodite standing l., wearing long chiton and peplos, resting with l. on sceptre, and holding on outstretched r. a figure of Eros l., with bow and arrow.
107	Æ 1·25		
		ΦAVCTEINA CEBAC TH Bust of Faustina r., draped.	T K Σ HΛOC ANEΘ HKE AΦPO ΔEICI E ΩN Cultus-statue of Aphrodite r., veiled, and wearing kalathos or modius; behind her, a small veiled figure of a priestess? seated r. on a throne, and in front an altar in the form of a tripod, or of a Corinthian capital, surmounted by a conical cover (cf. Daremberg et Saglio, Dict. des Ant., s.v. ara, fig. 428; and Schreiber, Die Hell. Reliefbilder, no. 71; also coin of Aperlae in Lycia).
108	Æ 1·2		
		ΦAVCTEINA CEBAC TH Bust of Faustina r., draped.	TKΣHΛOCAN EAΦPOΔEICI EΩ Tyche standing l., wearing modius, and holding rudder and cornucopiae.
109	Æ 1·2		

L. Verus.

| | | [AVT]KAICAP ΛAV P[OVHPOC] Bust of L. Verus r., laur.; wears cuirass and paludamentum. | T KΣHΛOC[IEPEYC EΠINIKI ONANE] AΦPOΔ[EI]C IEΩN (in ex.) Octastyle temple, in the central intercolumniation of which is a cultus-statue(?) of Aphrodite; flanking the temple on either side is a statue on a pedestal. |
| 110 | Æ 1·3 | | |

No.	Metal. Size.	Obverse.	Reverse.
		Sept. Severus.	
111	Æ 1·5	AV·KAI·Λ· CEΠ·CEO VHPOC ΠЄ PT·A VΓ (double struck). Bust of Sept. Severus r., laur., wearing cuirass and paludamentum.	MENI ΠΠO CK AIZHNΩNTH ΠATPIΔ AΦPOΔICIЄΩN (in ex.) (double struck). Severus in military costume, and wielding short javelin, on horseback, galloping r. over two prostrate foes.
		[Pl. vii. 5.]	
112	Æ 1·4	AVKAIΛCEΠT CEOV HPO[CΠЄ] Bust of Sept. Severus r., laur.	EΠIAPXTΩNΠЄ(ρι) [MENEC ΘЄA] ICOB OVNON (in field); AΦPOΔЄICI (in ex.) ЄΩN Cultus-statue of Aphrodite r., veiled; behind her, a small veiled figure of a Priestess? seated r. on throne, and in front altar, as on nos. 108, 114.
		Julia Domna.	
113	Æ 1·2	IOVΛIAΔO MИ[ACE BAC]TH Bust of Julia Domna r., draped.	[MENIΠΠO]CAN ЄΘH AΦPO ΔICIЄΩN Aphrodite and Ares standing facing one another; Aphrodite r., clad in long chiton with peplos over legs, embraces Ares round the right shoulder with her two arms; Ares l., naked, but armed with helmet, shield and spear, places his right hand on the peplos of the goddess; behind the two figures hangs the golden net in the form of a curtain.
		[Pl. vii. 6.]	

CARIA.

No.	Metal. Size.	Obverse.	Reverse.
114	Æ 1·6	ΙΟΥΛΙΑΔΟ ΜΝΑCΕΒΑCΤ Bust of Julia Domna r., draped.	ΜΕΝΙΠΠΟC ΚΑΙ ΣΗΝΩΝ ΑΝΕΘΕC ΑΦΡΟΔΙCΙ ΕΩΝ Cultus-statue of Aphrodite r., veiled and wearing modius; in field l. and r. star and crescent: behind her, a small veiled figure of a Priestess? seated r. on throne, and before her an altar, as on nos. 108, 112. [Pl. VII. 7.]
115	Æ 1·2	ΙΟΥΛΙΑΔΟ ΜΝΑCΕ ΒΑCΤ Η Bust of Julia Domna r., draped.	ΤΙΚΛΣΗΝΩΝΑΡΧΙΕ ΑΡΧΙΝΕ ΟΚΑΝΕΘ ΑΦΡ ΟΔΙ CΙΕ ΩΝ Cultus-statue of Aphrodite facing, wearing modius, and veil and long robes, fillets hanging from her extended hands; on either side a goose with head turned back towards goddess.
116	Æ 1·25		
117	Æ 1·2	ΙΟΥΛΙΑΔΟΜ ΝΑΑΥ ΓΟΥCΤΑ Bust of Julia Domna r., draped.	[ΕΠΙ ΑΡΧΤ]ΩΝΠΕΡΙΜΕΝΕC ΘΕΑΙCΟ ΒΟΥ ΝΟΝ ΑΦΡΟΔΕΙCΙ ΕΩΝ (in ex.) The three Charites, naked, in usual attitudes; the outer ones hold respectively, an ear of corn? and a flower.
118	Æ 1·15		[Pl. VII. 8.]

APHRODISIAS.   45

No.	Metal. Size.	Obverse.	Reverse.
119	Æ 1·2	ΙΟΥΛΙΑΔΟΜ ΝΑΑΥ ΓΟΥϹΤΑ Bust of Julia Domna r., draped.	ΕΠΙΑΡΧΟΤΩΝ ΠΕΜΕΝΕϹΘ ΕΑΙϹΟΒ ΟΥΝΟΝ ΑΦΡΟΔΕΙϹΙ ΕΩΝ (in ex.) Tyche standing l., wearing modius, and holding rudder and cornucopiae. (The inscr. in full would be ἐπὶ ἀρχό[ντων] τῶν πε[ρὶ] Μενεσθέα, κ.τ.λ.)

Caracalla.

120	Æ 1·45	ΑΥΚΑΙΜ ΑΥΑΝΤΩΝ ΕΙΝΟϹ Bust of Caracalla r., beardless and bare-headed; wears cuirass and paludamentum.	ΑΦΡΟ ΔΕΙ ϹΙΕΩΝ Tetrastyle temple, within which cultus-statue of Aphrodite r., between small seated Priestess? and a low altar in the form of a capital of a column surmounted by a conical cover.

Elagabalus.

121	Æ 1·35	ΑΥ ΚΑΙ ΜΑΥΡ ΑΝΤ ΩΝΕΙΝΟ Ϲ ϹΕΒ Bust of Elagabalus r., laur.; wearing cuirass and paludamentum.	ΑΦΡΟ ΔΕΙ ϹΙΕ ΩΝ Elagabalus, crowned by Demos. The Emperor stands r., resting on spear, and holding on extended l. small cultus-image of Aphrodite; before him Demos stands l., naked but for himation round waist and l. shoulder; in his raised r. a wreath, and in his l. a sceptre.
122	Æ ·45	Similar. (Countermark, Ζ or Ν in circle.)	ΑΦΡ ΟΔΕΙ ϹΙ ΕΩ Ν Emperor in military costume and wielding lance on horseback, galloping r. over prostrate foe.

No.	Metal. Size.	Obverse.	Reverse.
		Julia Mamaea.	
123	Æ 1·3	ΙΟΥΛΙΑ ΜΑΜΕΑϹΕΒ Bust of Julia Mamaea r.	ΑΦΡΟ ΔΕΙϹΙΕ ΩΝ Zeus, with himation over legs, seated l. on throne; holding Nike on extended r., and resting with l. on sceptre.
		Maximinus.	
124	Æ 1·4	Α[ΥΤΚ]ΓΙΟΥ ΜΑΞΙΜ ... Bust of Maximinus r., laur., wearing cuirass and paludamentum.	ΑΦΡ ΟΔΕ ΙϹΙΕΩΝ Aphrodite, naked but for peplos over legs, seated r. on throne; three Erotes playing around her, two behind and one in front. [Pl. VIII. 1.]
		Gordianus III.	
125	Æ 1·4	ΑΥΚΜΑΝ ΓΟΡΔΙΑ ΝΟϹ (sic) Bust of Gordian r., radiate, wearing cuirass and paludamentum.	ΑΦΡΟ ΔΕΙϹΙ ΕΩΝ Tetrastyle temple containing cultus-statue of Aphrodite r., between small figure of seated Priestess? and low altar? Aphrodite wears modius, flanked by crescent and star.
126	Æ 1·35	Inscr. obliterated.	ΑΦΡ Ο ΔΕΙ ϹΙΕΩΝ Cultus-statue of Aphrodite r., wearing modius, between small figure of seated Priestess? and low altar with conical cover? To r. and l. of central group is a cippus, on each of which an Eros, poised on one leg, points a torch towards the head of Aphrodite.

APHRODISIAS. 47

No.	Métal. Size.	Obverse.	Reverse.
127	Æ 1·4	AVKMAPAN ΓΟΡ ΔΙΑΝΟССЄ Bust of Gordian r., radiate, wearing cuirass and paludamentum.	ΑΦΡΟΔЄΙСΙЄΩΝ Centaur r., holding in l. strung bow?
128	Æ 1·2	AV·K·M ΑΝΓΟΡ ΔΙΑΝΟС Bust of Gordian r., laur., wearing cuirass and paludamentum.	ΓΟΡΔΙΑ ΝΗΑ ΑΤΤΑΛΗΑ ΑΦΡΟΔΙСΙЄ ΩΝ Three naked athletes, standing round a vase (hydria? for drawing lots?); two of them raise their right hands to their faces, the third points with r. hand, and holds palm in l. [Pl. viii. 2.]
129	Æ 1·35	AV·KA·MA· ΑΝΓΟΡ ΔΙΑΝΟС Bust of Gordian r., radiate, wearing cuirass and paludamentum.	ΑΦΡ ΟΔЄΙ СΙЄ ΩΝ Agonistic table inscribed ΚΑΠЄΤΩΛΙΑ; on the table is an urn inscribed ΓΟΡΔΙΑΝΗΑ, ΑΤΤΑΛΗΑ; on either side of the urn is a purse: beneath the table, which is supported by legs with lions' heads and feet, are two palms, and an amphora for drawing lots. [Pl. viii. 3.]
		Philippus Jun.	
130	Æ 1·15	ΜΑΡ ΙΟVΛΙ ΦΙΛΙΠ ΠΟСΚΑΙ·СЄ Bust of Philip Jun. r., bareheaded, wearing cuirass and paludamentum.	ЄΠΙΑΡΧΠΟΑΙΑ ΑΠΟΛΛΩΝ ΙΑΝΟV* ΑΦΡΟΔЄΙ СΙЄΩΝ Tyche standing l., wearing modius, and holding rudder and cornucopiae.

* P. Aelius Apollonianus is mentioned in an inscr. in Boeckh, C. I. G. 2792, as a Πρειμοπειλάριος.

No.	Metal. Size.	Obverse.	Reverse.
		Trajan Decius.	
131	Æ 1·3	AVKAIΓA .... ΔЄΚΙΟC Bust of Trajan Decius r., laur., wearing cuirass and paludamentum.	ЄΠΙΑΡΧCΤΡ ΑΤΟΝΙ ΚΟV ΑΦΡΟΔЄΙCΙЄ ΩΝ Emperor in quadriga r., his r. raised.
		Gallienus.	
132	Æ ·95	AV ΚΑΙ ΠΟΓΑΛ ΛΙΗΝ ΟC Bust of Gallienus l., radiate, wearing cuirass.	ΑΦΡΟ ΔЄΙ CΙЄΩΝ Zeus seated l., holding Nike on extended r., and resting with l. on sceptre.
133	Æ 1·05	AV ΚΑΙ ΠΟΓΑΛ ΛΙΗ ΝΟC Bust of Gallienus l., radiate, wearing cuirass and paludamentum.	Α ΦΡ ΟΔ ЄΙCΙ Tetrastyle ЄΩΝ temple, within which cultus-statue of Aphrodite r.
134	Æ 1·0	AVΚΑΙΠΟΓΑΛ ΛΙΗΝ ΟC Bust of Gallienus l., radiate, wearing cuirass and paludamentum.	Α Φ Similar type. Ρ Ο Δ]ЄΙCΙЄΩΝ
135	Æ 1·15	AVΚΑΙΠΟΓΑΛ ΛΙΗ ΝΟC Bust of Gallienus l., radiate, wearing cuirass and paludamentum.	ΑΦΡΟΔЄ Ι Emperor? in quadriga CΙЄΩΝ l., his r. extended, and holding sceptre in l.

APHRODISIAS. 49

No.	Metal. Size.	Obverse.	Reverse.
136	Æ 1·3	AV KΠO ΓΑΛΛΙΗ NO C Bust of Gallienus r., wearing helmet encircled by radiate crown, and armed with cuirass, shield and spear.	A ΦP O ΔEI Gallienus on CIEΩN horseback, galloping r., wielding lance.
137	Æ 1·05	AV KAIΠOΓAΛ ΛIH NOC Bust of Gallienus l., radiate, wearing cuirass and paludamentum.	EΠIA P AΠEΛ ΛA Similar ΑΦΡΟΔΙ type. CIEΩN
138	Æ 1·1	Same die.	EPMOΓENOVCAΠEΛΛA ΑΦΡΟΔΕΙ CIEΩN Similar type.
139	Æ 1·1	AVKAIΠOΛΓA ΛΛIH NOC Bust of Gallienus l., radiate, wearing cuirass and paludamentum.	A Φ P O Δ Similar type. I]CI EΩ И
140	Æ 1·1	Similar.	A Φ P O Δ I Similar type. C I E Ω N
141	Æ 1·05	Similar (AVKAIΠOΛI ΓA ΛΛIHNOC)	A Φ PO Δ I Similar type l. CIEΩN
142	Æ 1·	AV KAIΠOΓAΛ ΛIH NOC Similar type.	ΑΦΡ OΔ EI Similar type r.; CIEΩN beneath horse, two prostrate foes.

H

50   CARIA.

No.	Metal. Size.	Obverse.	Reverse.
143	Æ ·8	[Inscr. off *flan*. Head of Gallienus l., radiate.	A ΦP OΔICIE Gallienus on ΩN horseback, galloping l., wielding lance.
144	Æ ·95	AVKAITTOΛIΓA ΛΛI HNOC Similar type.	AΦPO [ΔEI] CIE Adonis, naked ΩN but for chlamys, charging r. at a wild boar l.; between them a plant (anemone ?) springs from the ground. [Pl. VIII. 4.]
145	Æ ·95	AVKAITTOΛI ΓAΛΛI HNOC Bust of Gallienus r., laur., wearing cuirass and paludamentum.	AΦPOΔ EI CIEΩN Tyche standing l., wearing modius, holding rudder and cornucopiae.
146	Æ ·95	AVKAITTOΛI ΓAΛΛI HNOC Bust of Gallienus l., radiate, wearing cuirass and paludamentum.	AΦPO Agonistic table, on which are ΔICIE two urns containing palms, ΩN and inscribed respectively, ΓOPΔIA[νηα] and TTV ΘIA [Bank Coll.]
147	Æ 1·05	AVKAITTOΛIΓA ΛΛI HNOC Similar.	AΦPOΔI Similar type, but the urns CIEΩN stand between two purses, and the table is apparently inscribed OIKOVMENIKOC
148	Æ 1·05	AVKAITTOΛI [ΓAΛΛ IHNOC] Similar.	AΦP Similar type, but no purses; OΔI urns inscribed KATTET CIE [ωλια], TTVΘIA, and table [ΩN] OIKOVMENIKOC

APHRODISIAS. 51

No.	Metal. Size.	Obverse.	Reverse.
149	Æ ·95	Inscr. obscure. Similar type.	A [Φ] Ⴖ Similar type; urns inscribed ΟΔΙC ΚΑΠΕΤΩΛ[ια], ΠVΘ ΙΕΩΝ ΙΑ; table uninscribed.
150	Æ 1·05	ΑVΚΑΙΠΟΛΓΑΛ ΛΙΗ ΝΟC Bust of Gallienus l., wearing helmet encircled by radiate crown, and armed with cuirass, shield and spear.	ΑΦΡΟΔΕΙCΙ Similar type; urns ΕΩΝ inscribed ΚΑΠΕ ΤΩΛΙ[Α], ΠV ΘΙΑ, and table ΟΙΚΟVΜΕΝΙΚΟC; beneath table, amphora between two purses.
151	Æ 1·15	ΑV ΚΠΟ ΓΑΛΛΙΗ ΝΟ C Similar type. Same die as no. 136.	ΑΦΡΟ ΔΕΙC ΙΕΩΝ Similar type, but purses not apparent beneath table.

Salonina.

152	Æ ·95	ΚΟΡΝCΑ ΛΩΝΙΝΑ Bust of Salonina r., wearing stephane; behind her shoulders, crescent.	Α]ΦΡΟΔ Ε Ι CΙΕΩΝ Cultus-statue of Aphrodite r., wearing modius, between small figure of seated Priestess? and low altar with conical cover?; in field l. and r., star and crescent.
153	Æ ·8	ΚΟΡ CΑΛΩΝΙΝΑ Similar.	ΑΦΡΟΔ ΙCΙΕΩΝ Similar; shape of altar? varied.
154	Æ ·8	ΙΟVΚΟΡ CΑΛΩΝΙ ΝΑ Similar.	ΑΦΡΟΔ Ι CΙΕΩΝ Similar; shape of altar? varied.

52   CARIA.

No.	Metal. Size.	Obverse.	Reverse.
155	Æ ·85	IOVKOPN CAΛΩNINA Similar.	AΦPOΔEI CIEΩN Hermes (Agoraios ?),* naked but for petasos and chlamys on l. arm, standing to front, head l.; he holds in r. purse, and in l. caduceus. [Pl. VIII. 5.]
156	Æ ·85	Similar.	AΦP OΔI CIEΩN Hermes, naked but for petasos, chlamys and winged pedilia, running r., looking back at ram, which he drags by the horn, and holding in l. caduceus. [Pl. VIII. 6.]
157	Æ ·95		(AΦP O ΔICIEΩN)
158	Æ 1·0	KOPNCA ΛΩNINA Same die as no. 152.	AΦPOΔEI CI [E]ΩN Tyche standing l., with usual attributes.
159	Æ ·95	ΠOΛIKOP CAΛΩNINAC Similar.	AΦPOΔIC I EΩN Similar.
160	Æ ·85	ΛIΠOKOP CAΛΩNINA Similar.	AΦPOΔI C IEΩN Similar.

* That Hermes Agoraios was worshipped at Aphrodisias we know from inscriptions (see Le Bas-Waddington, *As. Min. Inscr.*, iii. 373, no. 1601).

APHRODISIAS.

No.	Metal. Size.	Obverse.	Reverse.

ALLIANCE COINS.

APHRODISIAS AND EPHESUS.

Sept. Severus.

| | | ·ΑΥ·Κ·Λ·CЄΠ· ·CЄΟΥ
ΗΡΟC·Π Bust of
Sept. Severus r., laur.,
wearing cuirass and paludamentum. | ΑΦΡΟΔ ЄΙCΙΑC ЄΦ ЄCOC
and in *ex.* OMONOIA
Aphrodisias and Ephesos seated face
to face. Aphrodisias r., wears
modius, chiton and peplos, rests on
sceptre with her l., and supports on
extended r. cultus-statue of Aphrodite; Ephesos l., bare-headed and
naked to waist, rests on sceptre with
his l., and supports on his extended
r. cultus-statue of Artemis Ephesia.
Between the figures APX
ΦΛ
ΠЄ
Ρ |
| 161 | Æ 1·35 | | |

[Pl. XLIV. 1.]

APHRODISIAS AND ANTIOCHIA.

Severus Alexander.

| | | ΑΚΜΑΥ CЄΑΛЄΞΑΝ
ΔΡΟ Bust of Severus
Alexander r., laur., wearing cuirass and paludamentum. | ΑΦΡΟΔЄΙCΙ Α Ν ΤΙΟΧЄΩΝ
ЄΩΝ ΔΗ
ΜΟ
Ι
OMONOIA
The Demoi of Aphrodisias and Antiochia standing face to face, each wearing chlamys over shoulder, and supporting on their joined r. hands cultus-statue of Aphrodite; the Demos of Antioch carries a sceptre in his r. |
| 162 | Æ 1·4 | | |

[Pl. XLIV. 2.]

[See also Hierapolis Phrygiae in alliance with Aphrodisias.]

No.	Metal. Size.	Obverse.	Reverse.
		APOLLONIA SALBACE. BRONZE. *First Century* B.C.	
1	Æ ·75	Head of Zeus r., laur., two stiff curls hanging down back of neck. [Pl. ix. 1.]	ΑΠΟΛΛΩ ΝΙΑΤΩΝ Amazon (or Sabazios?) on horseback r., double-axe (labrys) over shoulder; beneath horse, Maeander pattern.*
2	Æ ·7		The Rider on this specimen is distinctly feminine (*see Introduction*).
3	Æ ·65	Head of Zeus r., laur. [Pl. ix. 2.]	ΑΠΟΛΛ[Ω] ΝΙΑΤΩ[Ν] to l., ΠΑΙ? Winged thunderbolt.
4	Æ ·85	Head of Apollo r., laur.	ΑΠΟΛΛΩΝΙΑΤΩΝ ΜΕΝΑΝΔΡΟC Eagle with spread wings standing r. on laurel-branch.
5	Æ ·55	Head of Apollo r., laur.	ΑΠΟΛΛΩ ΝΙΑΤΩΝ Lyre (kithara) with four strings.
6	Æ ·65	Head of Apollo r., laur.	Similar.

* The Maeander symbol on this coin and on two others published by Imhoof (*Gr. M.*, 667) makes it very doubtful whether their attribution to Apollonia Salbace is correct. The female(?) rider with the bipennis over shoulder and Maeander symbol beneath horse, occurs also on coins of Tripolis on the Maeander of the time of Augustus, and were it not for the fact that we have no evidence that Tripolis was ever called Apollonia, the attribution of these coins to that city would seem almost certain.

APOLLONIA. 55

No.	Metal. Size.	Obverse.	Reverse.
		Imperial Times. (a) Without heads of Emperors. Hadrian to the Antonines.	
7	Æ ·8	ΑΠΛΟΛΩΝΙΑ (sic) Bust of Athena r., helmeted and wearing aegis: border of dots. [Cf. similar bust on coin of Miletopolis Mysiae, struck under Hadrian; Cat. Mys., pl. xxi. 5.]	ΠΑΠΙΑC ΚΑΛΛΙΠΠΟV Zeus wearing chiton and himation seated l., on seat without back; holding on extended r. Nike, and resting with l. on sceptre: border of dots.
8	Æ ·75	[Pl. ix. 3.]	
9	Æ ·9	ΑΠΟΛΛΩ ΝΙΑΤΩΝ Female bust r., veiled: border of dots.	ΔΙΑ[Κ]ΑΛ ΛΙΠ ΟΥ Two uncertain draped figures standing face to face (Apollo and Artemis?): border of dots.
10	Æ ·95	Same die.	ΠΑΠΙ ΟV ΚΑΛΛ ΙΠΟV Similar type; Apollo has laurel-branch, Artemis, quiver, behind shoulder.
11	Æ ·95	ΑΠΟΛΛΩΝΙΑ CΑΛ ΒΑΚΗ Bust of Apollonia r.; hair rolled and looped up at back of neck: border of dots.	ΚΑΛΛΙΠ Π ΟV · CΤΡΑ· Δ· Asklepios and Hygieia standing to the front, face to face, with their usual attributes: border of dots.
12	Æ ·95	(Same dies.) [Pl. ix. 4.]	

No.	Metal. Size.	Obverse.	Reverse.
13	Æ ·95	ΙΕΡΑ ϹΥΝΚΛΗΤΟϹ Bust of the Senate r., diademed : border of dots.	ΧΑΡΜΙΔΗϹ ΝΕΙΚΟϹΤΡΑΤΑ ΠΟΛΛΩΝΙΑΤ ΩΝ ϹΤΡΑΤ ΗΓΩΝ Tyche standing l., wearing modius, and holding rudder and cornucopiae : border of dots. [Pl. ix. 5.]

Time of Sept. Severus or later.

14	Æ ·8	ΙΕΡΑ ΒΟΥΛΗ Bust of Boule r.: border of dots.	ΑΠΟΛΛΩ ΝΙ ΑΤΩΝ Asklepios and Hygieia, as on no. 11: border of dots.
15	Æ ·8	ΔΗΜΟϹ Head of youthful Demos r., bare : border of dots.	ΑΠΟΛΛΩΝ ΙΑΤΩΝ Dionysos, wearing short chiton, standing to front, head l., holding grapes and thyrsos : border of dots.
16	Æ ·65	Bust of Apollo r., laur. ; a laurel-branch in front : border of dots.	ΑΠΟΛΛΩ ΝΙΑΤΩΝ Winged caduceus.

Imperial Coinage.

(β) With heads of Emperors.

Augustus.

17	Æ ·7	ϹΕΒΑ ϹΤΟϹ Head of Augustus r., bare.	ΑΠΟΛΛΩΝΙ ΑΤΩΝ ΚΑΛ ΛΙΠΠΟϹ ΑΡΤΕΜΙ ΔΩΡΟΥ Apollo clad in long chiton and himation, standing to front, head l. ; holding on r. hand raven, and in l. laurel-branch. [Pl. ix. 6.]
18	Æ ·75		
19	Æ ·7	ϹΕΒΑϹ ΤΟϹ	

APOLLONIA. 57

No.	Metal. Size.	Obverse.	Reverse.
		Livia.	
20	Æ ·65	ΣΕΒ ΑΣΤΗ Bust of Livia r.	ΚΑΛΛΙΠΠΟΣ ΑΡΤΕΜΙΔΩΡ Ο Υ ΑΠΟΛ ΛΩΝΙΑΤ ΩΝ Dionysos, wearing short chiton, standing l., holding kantharos and resting on thyrsos. [Pl. ix. 7.]
		Nero.	
21	Æ ·6	ϹΕΒΑϹΤ[ΟϹ] Head of Nero r., laur.	ΑΠΟΛΛΩΝΙ Apollo, wearing long . . . . chiton, standing to front, his r. extended, holding uncertain object; l. resting on lyre placed on ground beside him.
		M. Aurelius.	
22	Æ 1·25	Μ ΑΥΡ ΑΝΤΩΝΕΙ ΝΟϹ Bust of M. Aurelius r., laur.; wearing paludamentum.	ΑΠΟΛΛ Ω ΝΙΑΤΩΝ Male (?) figure clad in chiton and with chlamys flying behind him, running r. with head turned back; he holds in raised r. uncertain object, and in l. spear. [Pl. ix. 8.]
23	Æ 1·45	·ΑΥΤ· ΚΑΙ·Μ·ΑΥΡΗΛ ΑΝΤΩΝΕΙΝΟϹ Bust of M. Aurelius r., laur.; wearing paludamentum.	ΕΠΙ ΚΑΛΙϹΠΟΥ (?) ΚΕΚΙΝΕ ΑΠΟΛΛΩΝΙ ΟΥΔ ΑΤΩΝ (inex.) Tetrastyle temple containing three figures; in the centre a female figure (Tyche?) l., holding patera? and cornucopiae?; on either side a smaller female figure (Nemeses?), one r. holding bridle?, and the other l. cubit-rule? (Tooled and perhaps altered.) [Pl. ix. 9.]

I

No.	Metal. Size.	Obverse.	Reverse.
		Caracalla.	
24	Æ ·95	ΑΝΤΩΝΙΝΟC ΑΥΓ ΟVCTOC Bust of Caracalla r., laur.	ΑΠΟΛΛΩΝΙ ΑΤΩΝ Tyche standing l., holding rudder and cornucopiae.
		Gallienus.	
25	Æ 1·55	ΑVΤΟ ΚΑΙ ΠΟVΛΙΚΙ ΓΑΛΛΗΝΟC Bust of Gallienus r., radiate; wearing cuirass and paludamentum.	CΤΡΑ ΜΕ ΝΑΝΔΡΟVΠΗΛΙ ΑΠΟΛΛΩ ΝΙΑΤΩΝ (in ex.) Emperor on galloping horse r., thrusting downwards with spear; beneath his horse, two lions.
26	Æ 1·3		
27	Æ ·95	. . . . ΛΛΙΗ ΝΟC Bust of Gallienus l., laur., wearing paludamentum.	CΤΡΑ ΜΕΝ . . . . ΑΠΟΛΛΩ ΝΙΑΤΩΝ Apollo Kitharoedos advancing r., naked but for chlamys.
		Salonina.	
28	Æ 1·2	ΚΟΡC ΑΛΩΝΙΝ Α Bust of Salonina r.; in field l., ℞	CΤΡΑΜΕΝ ΑΝΔΡΟ ΑΠΟΛΛ ΩΝΙΑ (in ex.) Τ Ω Ν (in field) Zeus, wearing himation over lower limbs, seated l., holding Nike on outstretched r. hand, and resting with l. on sceptre.

No.	Wt.	Metal. Size.	Obverse.	Reverse.
			ASTYRA. *Before circ.* B.C. 480. SILVER. Babylonic Standard. Stater.	
1	149·5	R ·75	Amphora. [Pl. x. 1.] [Borrell, *Num. Chron.*, ix. 166.]	A ⋛ T V Oenochoë and lyre ('chelys'), beneath which tendril with bud projecting to r.: traces of incuse square. [Bank Coll.]
			Smaller denominations.	
2	9·8	R ·3	Oenochoë within circle. [Pl. x. 2.]	Incuse square, quartered diagonally.
3	16·8	R ·4	A Vase with one handle, 'hemikotylion': border of dots. [Pl. x. 3.]	A Oenochoë without foot: the whole in incuse square in two planes.
4	14·2	R ·35		
5	12·3	R ·3		

CARIA.

No.	Wt.	Metal. Size.	Obverse.	Reverse.
6	7·4	AR ·25	Similar.	Incuse squares in three planes, superposed in form of inverted pyramid, shaped like a lacunar.
7	3·2	AR ·2	Rose.	A in incuse square. [Pl. x. 4.]

BRONZE.

Fourth Century B.C.

8		Æ ·8	Head of Helios or Apollo laur.? facing, as on coins of Mausolus, &c.	AΣTY Amphora containing branch of ivy or vine; in field r., oenochoë.
9		Æ ·75		[Pl. x. 5.]
10		Æ ·55		in field r., uncertain symbol (labrys, astragalus, or hemikotylion ?)
11		Æ ·5	Head of Helios (or Apollo?) three-quarter-face towards r., without rays, as on earliest gold coins of Rhodos.	A T Amphora, above which, Σ Y bunch of grapes; in field r., oenochoë. [Pl. x. 6.]

ASTYRA. 61

No.	Metal. Size.	Obverse.			Reverse.
12	Æ ·5	Female head, Aphrodite (?) r., wearing earring and necklace; hair in sphendone; loose locks escaping at crown of head.	A ᚴ T Y		Amphora; in field l., bunch of grapes.
13	Æ ·5				
		[Pl. x. 7.]			
		Similar head r.	A T	ᚴ Y	Amphora
14	Æ ·4				
15	Æ ·45		AᚴTY		(amphora contains branch).
		Female head r., Aphrodite (?) wearing necklace; hair bound with plain diadem and gathered into a knot behind.	A T	ᚴ Y	Amphora, in field r., oenochoë.
16	Æ ·4				
		[Pl. x. 8.]			
17	Æ ·35				
18	Æ ·35				
19	Æ ·35				

CARIA.

No.	Wt.	Metal. Size.	Obverse.	Reverse.
			ATTUDA.	
			First Century B.C.	
			SILVER.	
			Drachm.	
1	53·1	AR ·7	Head of the City r., turreted, two long locks of hair hanging down neck. [Pl. x. 9.]	ΑΤΤΟΥΔΔΕΩΝ Apollo naked, standing l., resting l. elbow on Corinthian column, and holding in extended r. uncertain object; in front [ΣΩ]Σ (?) [ΙΠ]Ο ΛΙΣ ΧΑΡ ΜΙ ΔΗΣ ΛΕ Ω]Ν?
			BRONZE.	
			Imperial Times.	
			(a) Without heads of Emperors.	
			Time of Trajan.	
2		Æ ·75	Bust of Athena r., wearing crested helmet and aegis, spear projecting in front of bust: border of dots.	ΑΤΤΟΥ ΔΕΩΝ Tyche standing l., wearing modius, and holding rudder and cornucopiae: border of dots.
3		Æ ·75	ΑΤΤΟΥ ΔΕΩΝ Bust of Asklepios r.; in front, serpent-staff: border of dots. [Pl. x. 10.]	ΔΙ ΑΜΕ ΝΙΠΠΟΥ Hygieia standing r., feeding serpent from patera: border of dots.

ATTUDA. 63

No.	Metal. Size.	Obverse.	Reverse.
4	Æ ·75	ΔΗΜΟCΑΤΤΟVΔΕ ΩΝ Bust of Demos r., bearded, shoulders bare, hair bound with taenia: border of dots.	ΔΙΑΜΕΝΙΠΟV ΑΠΟΛΩΝΟV (sic) Apollo naked, standing facing, holding branch and bow: border of dots.
5	Æ ·75		[Pl. x. 11.]
6	Æ ·85	ΔΗΜΟC ΑΤΤΟVΔΕ ΩΝ Head of youthful Demos r.: border of dots.	ΔΙΑΜΕΝΙΠΠΟV Sabazios on horseback r., with chlamys flying behind him, holding labrys over shoulder: border of dots.
			[Pl. x. 12.]
7	Æ 1·0	ΠΟΛΙC ΑΤΤΟVΔΕ ΩΝ Bust of City r., turreted: border of dots.	ΔΙΑ Μ·ΑΙΛΙ [ΜΕΝΙΠΠΟΥ] Dionysos standing l., wearing himation, holding kantharos and resting on thyrsos; at his feet, panther: border of dots.
8	Æ ·6	ΑΤΤΟVΔΕ ΩΝ Bust of City r., turreted: border of dots.	ΔΙΑ ΜΕ ΝΙΠΠΟV Nemesis clad in long chiton, standing l., her r. arm bent at elbow, and plucking chiton at neck; l. hanging down holding bridle: border of dots.
9	Æ ·65	ΑΤΤ Ο VΔΕΩΝ Head of City r., turreted: border of dots.	ΔΙΑΜΕΝΙΠΟV (sic) Three ears of corn: border of dots.

CARIA.

No.	Metal. Size.	Obverse.	Reverse.
		Time of Sept. Severus.	
10	Æ ·85	ΑΤΤΟV ΔΑ Bust of City r., turreted : border of dots.	ΔΙΑΦΛΑΒΙ ΑCΙЄΡΙΑC Cultus-statue of goddess wearing long chiton with falling fold and belt, modius, and veil, standing to front; fillets hanging from her hands : border of dots. [Pl. x. 13.]
11	Æ ·75	(Same die.)	(Same die.)
12	Æ ·95	ΔΗΜΟC Bust of youthful Demos r., laur.: border of dots. Two countermarks (emperors heads).	ΑΤΤΟVΔЄΩΝ ΔΙΑ ΦΛΑΒΙ CΙ ЄΡΙΑC Apollo naked, standing to front, head l., holding branch and resting l. elbow on column.
13	Æ 1·0	ΔΗΜΟC Bust of youthful Demos r., laur. : border of dots.	ΑΤΤΟV ΔЄΩΝ Dionysos, naked but for himation, standing to front, head l., holding kantharos and resting on thyrsos : border of dots. [Pl. x. 14.]
14	Æ ·95	ΔΗΜΟC Same type and border. Two countermarks, (i) head of emperor r., (ii) letters ΔΡ.	ΑΤΤΟV [ΔЄΩΝ] Leto clad in long chiton and flying peplos, running r., carrying her two children.
15	Æ ·9	ΔΗΜΟC Same type and border. (Countermark, Γ)	ΑΤΤΟ V ΔЄΩΝ Sabazios on horseback r., holding labrys over shoulder : border of dots.

ATTUDA. 65

No.	Metal. Size.	Obverse.	Reverse.
16	Æ ·85	ΔΗΜΟC Same type and border.	ΑΤΤΟVΔΕΩΝ Large altar of Mên garlanded ; on it, three pine-cones, between which two small flaming altars (?) : border of dots.
17	Æ ·65	ΔΗΜ OC Same type and border.	ΑΤΤΟVΔΕΩΝ Large altar of Mên : on it, three pine-cones, between which two altars in the form of short columns : border of dots.
18	Æ ·9	ΜΗΝ ΚΑΡΟV Bust of Mên Karou r., wearing Phrygian cap ; behind shoulders, crescent : border of dots. (Countermark, Emperor's head.)	ΑΤΤΟV Δ ΕΩΝ Similar to no. 16.
19	Æ ·85	(no countermark.)	[Pl. x. 15.]
20	Æ ·95	ΙΕΡΑ CVΝΚΛΗΤΟC Bust of youthful Senate r., diademed : border of dots.	ΑΤΤΟ V ΔΕΩΝ Zeus naked, striding r., hurling thunderbolt with r., and holding eagle on extended l. : border of dots.
21	Æ ·95		[Pl. x. 16.]
22	Æ ·95	ΙΕΡΑCVΝ ΚΛΗΤΟC Similar type : border of dots.	ΑΤΤΟ VΔΕΩΝ Asklepios and Hygieia standing face to face, with usual attributes : border of dots.

K

66　　　　　　　　　　　　　　　CARIA.

No.	Metal. Size.	Obverse.	Reverse.
23	Æ ·75	IЄPA BOVΛH Bust of Boule r., voiled: border of dots.	ATTOV ΔЄΩ N Nemesis standing l., clad in long chiton, r. arm bent at elbow, plucking chiton at neck; l. holding bridle ? [Bank Coll.]
24	Æ ·8	IЄPA BOVΛH Similar.	ATTOV ΔЄΩN Tree, in front of which a lighted altar.
25	Æ ·85		[Pl. x. 17.]
26	Æ ·85	(Countermark, B)	

(β) With Emperors' heads.

Trajan.

27	Æ 1·15	AY KAI . . . . CЄΓЄPΔAKIKOC Bust of Trajan r., laur., in cuirass and paludamentum.	ΔIA MЄNIΠΠO YYIOY ΠO ΛЄOC ATTOY ΔЄΩN Kybele, wearing long chiton and modius, standing to the front between two lions, on whose heads she places her extended hands.

Commodus.

28	Æ 1·1	AVT·KAI·M·AVP KO MMOΔOC Bust of Commodus r., bearded and laur., in cuirass and paludamentum.	ATTOV ΔЄΩN Kybele enthroned between two lions, her r. extended, l. elbow resting on tympanum.

ATTUDA. 67

No.	Metal. Size.	Obverse.	Reverse.
		Sept. Severus.	
29	Æ 1·65	ΑΥΚΑΙΛCΕ ΠCΕΥΗΡΟCΠΕ[Ρ] ΑΥΚΑΙΑΝΤΟΝΕΙ ΝΟCΛCΕΠΓΕΤ ΑCΚΑΙ Bust of Sept. Severus r., laur., in cuirass and paludamentum, between busts of Caracalla and Geta r. and l., bare, each in cuirass and paludamentum.	ΕΠΙΜΕΡΟ ΥΦΟΥ ΠΟΛΥΔ ΑΝ ΤΩΝΙ ΑΤΤΟΥΔΕ ΩΝ Tetrastyle temple, within which Kybele standing between two lions, on whose heads she lays her extended hands.[*]

[Pl. xi. 1.]

| 30 | Æ 1·4 | ΑΥ·ΚΑΙ· ·Λ·CΕΠ·CΕ ΟΥΗ ΡΟC Bust of Sept. Severus r., laur., in cuirass and paludamentum. | ΔΙΑΚΛΦΛΑΒΙ AC ΑΡΡΙ ΙΕΡ ΕΙΑC ΑΤ ΤΟΥ ΔΕ ΩΝ Kybele standing to front between two lions, on whose heads she lays her extended hands. [Pl. xi. 2.] |

| 31 | Æ 1·45 | ΑΥΚΑΙΛΟ ΥCΕΠCΕΥ ΗΡΟC ΠΕΡ Bust of Sept. Severus r., laur., in cuirass and paludamentum. | ΑΥ ΤΟΚ Κ ΑΙ·Α ΝΤ....... ΑΤΤΟΥΔΕ [ΩΝ] Caracalla on galloping horse r., brandishing spear: beneath horse, two prostrate enemies. |

Julia Domna.

| 32 | Æ 1·15 | ΙΟΥΛΙΑ ΔΟ ΜΝΑC ΕΒ Bust of Julia Domna r. | ΑΤΤΟΥ ΔΕΩΝ Asklepios standing facing, head l., holding serpent-staff; beside him, Telesphoros. |

[*] ΕΠΙΜΕ may probably be completed as ἐπιμεληθέντος (cf. *Hist. Num.*, Introd., p. lxvii.).

CARIA.

No.	Metal. Size.	Obverse.	Reverse.
		Gallienus.	
33	Æ 1·15	AVK .... ΓΑΛΛΙΗΝΟ C Bust of Gallienus r., radiate, in cuirass and paludamentum.	ATTO VΔΕΩΝΝ (sic) Kybele, wearing long chiton, standing to the front between two lions, on whose heads she places her extended hands.
34	Æ 1·2		
35	Æ 1·15	ΠΟΛΙ ΓΑΛΛΙΗΝΟC Bust of Gallienus r., radiate; in cuirass and paludamentum.	A T T OYΔ Kybele, wearing ΕΩΝ long chiton, seated on lion l.; over her shoulder, long sceptre.
36	Æ ·95	.. ΚΑΙ Π .. ΓΑΛΛΙΗ NOC Similar.	ΑΤΤ OVΔΕΩΝ Tyche standing l., with usual attributes.
		Salonina.	
37	Æ ·95	KOPN CΑΛΩΝΙΝΑ Bust of Salonina r., behind shoulders, crescent.	ATTOY ΔΕΩΝ Herakles naked, standing to front, head l., resting with r. on club, and holding in l. lion's skin.
38	Æ ·85		
39	Æ ·9	ΙΟΥ KOP CΑΛΩΝΙ NA Similar.	ATTOY Δ Large altar of Mên ΕΩΝ garlanded; on it, three pine-cones, between which two small flaming altars.
40	Æ ·9		A TTOY Δ . ΕΩΝ

ATTUDA.

No.	Metal. Size.	Obverse.	Reverse.
		Valerian Junior.	
41	Æ 1·1	.... CA ΛΩNIN[OC] ΟΥΑΛΕ ΡΙΑΝΟC Bust of Valerian Jun., r. laur., in cuirass and paludamentum.	ATT ΟΥΔΕΩΝ Athena, clad in long chiton with aegis, standing to front, her r. resting on shield, her l. on spear.

No.	Metal. Size.	Obverse.	Reverse.
		BARGASA.	
		BRONZE.	
		Imperial Time.	
1	Æ ·8	ΙΕΡΑ ΒΟΥΛΗ Bust of Boule r., veiled: border of dots. [Pl. xi. 3.]	ΒΑΡΓΑ CΗΝΩΝ Telesphoros, in usual costume, standing to front: border of dots.
		Commodus.	
2	Æ 1·1	Λ·ΑΥΡΗ ΚΟΜΟΔΟC Bust of Commodus r., laur.	ΒΑΡΓΑCΗ ΝΩΝ Asklepios l., and Hygieia r., standing face to face, with their usual attributes.
		Gallienus.	
3	Æ 1·0	ΑΥ ΚΑΙΠΟ ΛΙΓΑΛΛΙ ΗΝΟC Bust of Gallienus r., radiate, wearing cuirass and paludamentum. [Pl. xi. 4.]	ΕΠΙ ΑΥ ΕΡ ΜѠΝΟC ΒΑΡ ΓΑCΗ ΝΩΝ The Emperor on horseback r.
4	Æ 1·05		

BARGYLIA.

BARGYLI A.

First Century B.C.

SILVER.

Drachm.

No.	Wt.	Metal. Size.	Obverse.	Reverse.
1	46·	AR ·65	Head of Artemis Kindyas r., hair in knot behind, and covered with veil: the whole within laurel-wreath. [Pl. xi. 5.]	BAPΓ VΛIHTωN Pegasos flying r.; behind, star: border of dots.

BRONZE.

No.	Wt.	Metal. Size.	Obverse.	Reverse.
2		Æ ·75	Similar.	BA PΓV ΛIHTΩ[N] Pegasos flying r. [Pl. xi. 6.]
3		Æ ·75	(without veil.)	
4		Æ ·65	(border of dots in place of laurel-wreath.)	BAP ΓYΛI TΩN H Same type varied.
5		Æ ·55	Similar head: border of dots.	BAPΓYΛI H TΩN Quiver with strap and strung bow: border of dots.
6		Æ ·6		B A P ΓY

CARIA.

No.	Metal. Size.	Obverse.	Reverse.
7	Æ .85	Bust facing of Artemis Kindyas, veiled and wearing stephanos (?): border of dots.	[BAPΓ]YΛ[IH] Bellerophon riding TΩN on flying Pegasos r.: border of dots.
8	Æ .75		(ω in inscr.)
9	Æ .7	Pegasos flying r.: border of dots.	BAPΓYΛI Statue of Artemis Kindyas standing on basis, HTΩN facing and veiled.
10	Æ .7	Stag standing r.: border of dots.	BAPΓY Similar. ΛIHTΩN [Pl. XI. 7.]
11	Æ .75	Pegasos flying r.: border of dots.	[B]APΓYΛ[I Stag standing r.: HTΩN border of dots. [Pl. XI. 8.]
12	Æ .55	Forepart of Pegasos r.: border of dots.	Same inscr. Forepart of stag r.

Imperial.

Titus.

13	Æ .75	TITOC KAICAP CEBACTOC Head of Titus r., laur.	BAPΓY ΛIHTωN Statue of Artemis Kindyas, facing and veiled, and with hands crossed over her breast; before statue, flaming altar; and on r., stag, looking up. [Pl. XI. 9.]

BARGYLIA. 73

No.	Metal. Size.	Obverse.	Reverse.
		Sept. Severus and Julia Domna.	
14	Æ 1·4	AVKAC CEYHPOC [ΠЄ?] IOV ΔOMNA AVΓ Busts face to face of S. Severus r., laur., wearing cuirass and paludamentum, and of J. Domna l. [Pl. xi. 10.]	BAPΓYΛ IHTΩN Asklepios standing to front, head r., wearing himation over lower limbs and l. shoulder, and leaning with l. on serpent-staff.
		Julia Domna.	
15	Æ ·85	. . . . . . ΔOMNA . . Bust of Julia Domna r., (behind, uncertain countermark).	BAP ΓVΛIH TΩN within laurel-wreath.

L

CARIA.

No	Metal. Size.	Obverse.	Reverse.
		CAUNUS.	
		BRONZE.	
		Before circ. B.C. 309.*	
1	Æ ·45	Forepart of bull r. K A Sphinx seated r. [Pl. xii. 1.]	
2	Æ ·4		
3	Æ ·45	Bull butting r. K A Sphinx seated r. [Pl. xii. 2.]	
4	Æ ·5		
5	Æ ·5		
6	Æ ·5		
7	Æ ·5	Bull butting r.; above, wreath. K A Sphinx seated r. Y [Pl. xii. 3.]	
8	Æ ·45		
9	Æ ·45		
10	Æ ·4		

* As Borrell (*Num. Chron.*, ix. 149) states that he acquired some of these coins from a Greek merchant captain trading between Rhodes and the coast of the mainland, there is every reason to suppose that the attribution to Caunus is correct, for this town was situated on the southern coast of Caria, opposite Rhodes. Dr. Imhoof-Blumer's suggestion that they may perhaps belong to Caryanda (*Num. Zeit.*, 1884, p. 269) on the gulf of Bargylia seems to me to be a less probable attribution, as not one of the specimens in the British Museum shows any trace of the letter P behind the tail of the Sphinx.

CAUNUS. 75

No.	Wt.	Metal. Size.	Obverse.		Reverse.
			Under the Ptolemies.		
			Circ. B.C. 309—189.		
			SILVER.		
			Rhodian Standard.		
			Hemidrachm.		
11	14·1	𝐀 ·4	Head of Alexander the Great r., diademed. [Pl. XII. 4.]	K ⳩	Cornucopiae bound with fillet; in field r., crux ansata ♀: border of dots.
			BRONZE.		
12		Æ ·45	Head of Alexander the Great r. [Pl. XII. 5.]	K ⳩	Cornucopiae bound with fillet.
13		Æ ·6	Head of Athena r., wearing crested Corinthian helmet: her hair arranged in formal curls, as on many of the gold staters of Alexander.	K ⳩	Cornucopiae bound with fillet.
			After B.C. 166.		
			SILVER.		
			Rhodian Standard.		
			Hemidrachms.		
14	17·4	𝐀 ·4	Head of Athena r., wearing crested helmet.	K ⳩	Sword in sheath with strap.
				above, KTH ΤΟΣ in field l., Bull's head facing.	[Bank Coll.]
15	13·6	𝐀 ·4		above, KTH ΤΟΣ in field r., Caduceus.	
16	17·2	𝐀 ·5		above, ΦΑ ΡΟΣ in field r., Bunch of grapes. [Pl. XII. 6.]	

No.	Metal. Size.	Obverse.	Reverse.
		BRONZE.	
17	Æ ·4	Head of Apollo? r., laur.? hair in formal curls. K [Pl. xii. 7.]	Х Sword in sheath with strap.
18	Æ ·35		
19	Æ ·35		[Bank Coll.]
20	Æ ·4		
21	Æ ·5		(the whole in shallow incuse square as on contemporary coins of Rhodes.)

CERAMUS.

SILVER.

After B.C. 166.

Rhodian Standard.

Drachm.

No.	Wt.	Metal. Size.	Obverse	Reverse
1	38·6	AR ·55	Head of Zeus r., laur.	KEPAMIH ΠΟΛΙΤΗC which, eagle l., with head turned back.* Shallow incuse square, within [Pl. XII. 8.]

BRONZE.

No.	Wt.	Metal. Size.	Obverse	Reverse
2		Æ ·5	Head of Zeus r., laur.	KEPAM ΑΠΟΛ which, eagle r. Shallow incuse square, within [Pl. XII. 9.]
3		Æ ·9	Head of Zeus r., laur., hair in formal curls; border of dots.	KEPAMIH ΕΡΜΟΦΑΝΤΟC Eagle l., with head turned back.† [Pl. XII. 10.]

* ΠΟΛΙΤΗC is probably the name of the magistrate, but cf. Sestini (*Hedervar*, ii., p. 218, 6), a re-struck coin read by him, doubtless wrongly, ΚΕΡΑΜΙΗΠΟΛΙΤΩΝ

† The name Μ·ΚΛ·ΕΡΜΟΦΑΝΤΟC recurs at a later period on a coin of Commodus, with the addition of a title, ΑΡΞΑC ΚΕΡΑΜΙΗΤΩΝ (*Z. f. N.*, ii. 111).

No.	Metal. Size.	Obverse.	Reverse.
4	Æ ·65	Head of City r., turreted: border of dots. [Pl. xii. 11.]	K E Caduceus; the whole in laurel-wreath.
5	Æ ·65		
6	Æ ·5		(K E not visible.)

Imperial.

Antoninus Pius.

7	Æ 1·3	ΑΥΤΟΚ ΚΑΙC ΑΝΤΩ .... Head of Antoninus Pius l., laur. [Pl. xii. 12.]	ΑΙΛΙ ΘЄΜΙCΤΟΚΛΗC ΠΡΩ ΤΟΝ ΑΡΞ ΚΕΡΑΜΙΗΤΩΝ Zeus standing l., clad in himation, holding patera and resting on sceptre surmounted by eagle: at his feet an eagle l., looking back.*

Commodus.

8	Æ 1·4	[ΑΥ ΚΑΙ Λ ΑΥ (?)] ΚΟ ΜΟΔΟC Bust of Commodus r., laur., wearing cuirass and paludamentum. [Pl. xii. 13.]	ЄΠΙ ΔΙ ΟΔΟΑΡΞ ΚΕΡΑ ΜΙΗ ΤΩΝ Male figure (Zeus Stratios, or Labraundos?) standing r., clad in short chiton, holding spear in r. and labrys in l.; behind him an animal resembling a goat recumbent with fore-foot raised.†

* Cf. Friedlaender's reading of the reverse inscription in *Z. f. N.*, ii. 109, Π·ΑΙΛΙ·ΘЄΜΙCΤΟΚΛΗC ΠΡΟΤΟΛЄΟΝΔΙC ΚЄΡΑ ΜΙ which is almost certainly wrong. On the present specimen the words ΠΡΩΤΟΝ and ΑΡΞ, though very indistinct, are decipherable.

† The divinity here represented is the same as the one on a coin of Commodus figured in *Zeit. f. Num.*, ii., p. 111. On that coin he stands with a lion at his feet, facing a figure of Zeus Chrysaoreus with eagle at feet. It is probably an archaic statue of Zeus Stratios or Labraundos. The animal at the feet of the god on this coin resembles a goat or stag (cf. coin of Mylasa, Pl. xxii. 4).

CHALCETOR (?) *

Fourth Century B.C.

BRONZE.

No.	Metal. Size.	Obverse.	Reverse.
1	Æ ·35	Female head r., wearing ear-ring and necklace: hair rolled.	Spear-head.
2	Æ ·35		
3	Æ ·35		
4	Æ ·35		

* See Introduction.

No.	Wt.	Metal. Size.	Obverse.	Reverse.
			CHERSONESUS CNIDIA.	
			SILVER.	
			Circ. B.C. 550—500.	
			Aeginetic Standard.	
			Stater.	
1	183·4	AR ·85	+ Forepart of lion r. [Pl. XIII. 1.]	Incuse square, within which ΚΝΙ+ head and neck of bull r. [Bank Coll.]
			Drachm.	
2	90·4	AR ·65	Forepart of lion r. [Pl. XIII. 2.]	Incuse square, within which +ED and bull's head facing.
			Obol?	
3	13·5	AR ·4	Lion's head r. [Pl. XIII. 3.]	Incuse square, within which +ED head and neck of bull r.

No.	Metal. Size.	Obverse.	Reverse.
		CIDRAMUS. *Imperial Times.* (α) Without heads of Emperors.	
1	Æ 1·45	ΙЄΡΑC VΝΚΛΗΤΟ C Bust of the Senate r., diademed: border of dots.	ΚΙΔΡΑΜΗ ΝΩΝ Zeus seated l., naked to waist, himation over lower limbs, holds patera and rests on sceptre: border of dots.
2	Æ ·65	Ζ ЄΥCΛ VΔΙΟC Bust of Zeus r., laur.: border of dots.	ΚΙΔ ΡΑ ΜΗΝΩΝ Hermes, naked but for chlamys, standing to front, head l., holds purse and caduceus.
		(β) With heads of Emperors. Nero.	
3	Æ ·75	ΝЄ ΡΩΝ Bust of youthful Nero r., radiate.	ΠΟ ΛЄΜΩ ΝCЄΛЄΥ ΚΟΥΚΙ ΔΡΑ within a laurel-wreath.
4	Æ ·75		
		Nero (?) *	
5	Æ 1·	ΣΕΒΑΣΤΟΣ Head of Nero? r., laur.	ΠΟΛЄΜΩΝΣΕ ΛΕΥΚΟΥΚΙΔΡ Α Μ Η ΝΩ Ν Cultus-statue of Aphrodite† to front, wearing modius and veil, her forearms extended at right angles from her body.

* The head on this coin has been described as that of Augustus, but to me at least, it seems rather to resemble Nero. This attribution is further strengthened by the magistrate's name on the reverse ΠΟΛЄΜΩΝ ΣΕΛΕΥΚΟΥ, as on nos. 3 and 4.

† This Asiatic goddess is without doubt the famous Aphrodite of the neighbouring city of Aphrodisias.

CARIA.

No.	Metal. Size.	Obverse.	Reverse.
		Antoninus Pius.	
6	Æ ·95	AV KAI AΔPIA AN TΩNEINOC Head of Antoninus Pius r., laur.	ΔIA......... ΠΟΛΕΜΩΝΟC KIΔPAMH NΩ N Cultus-statue of Aphrodite, as on previous coin.
		Elagabalus.	
7	Æ 1·3	AV K MA ANTΩNEI NOC Bust of Elagabalus r., laur.; wears cuirass and paludamentum.	K IΔϘA M H NΩN Aphrodite, clad in long chiton and peplos, standing r., her r. arm extended behind her, and her l. arm bent and holding mirror (?); behind her, two or more Erotes.* [Pl. XIII. 4.]
8	Æ 1·15	Same die.	KIΔPA MHNΩN Veiled goddess standing to front, supporting with her right hand a kalathos upon her head, and with her left upon her breast holding the folds of her veil.† [Pl. XIII. 5.]
		Julia Maesa.	
9	Æ ·8	IOVΛIAM AICACEB Bust of Julia Maesa r.	KIΔPAM HNΩN Dionysos naked to waist, but with himation over lower limbs, standing l., resting on column; holds in r. grapes, and in l. thyrsos; at his feet, panther.

* This type of Aphrodite and Erotes may be compared with somewhat similar subjects on a coin of Maximinus at Aphrodisias (Pl. VIII. 1), and on a coin of Etruscilla at Antioch (Mion., iii., 320, 94).

† This type may be compared with that of some of the coins of Cibyra in Phrygia, on which a goddess is also represented holding a basket upon her head.

No.	Metal. Size.	Obverse.	Reverse.
10	Æ ·75	ΙΟVΛΙΑΜ ΑΙCΑCΕΒ Bust of Julia Maesa r. (Same die as no. 9.)	ΚΙΔΡΑΜΗ ΝΩΝ Mên standing l., with r. foot on bull's head; he wears Phrygian cap and short chiton, and holds in r. pine-cone, and in l. spear; behind his shoulders, crescent. [Pl. XIII. 6.]

84   CARIA.

No.	Wt.	Metal. Size.	Obverse.	Reverse.
			## CNIDUS.	
			Circ. B.C. 700—650.	
			SILVER.	
			Aeginetic Standard?	
			Stater.	
1	153·1 (much worn)	AR ·8	Head of Aphrodite? l., of the rudest archaic style, wearing round earring. [Pl. XIII. 7.] [Lawson, Smyrna.]	Two rough incuse squares, large and small; the larger one is perhaps of the mill-sail type badly struck.
			Circ. B.C. 650—550.	
			Aeginetic Standard.	
			Drachms.	
2	95·	AR ·6	Forepart of lion r. (foreleg not visible.) [Pl. XIII. 8.]	Incuse square, within which head of Aphrodite r., wearing round earring and saccos bound with riband passed three times round it: hair indicated by dots.
3	96·	AR ·65	(,,) [Pl. XIII. 9.]	(head l.)
4	99·5	AR ·6	[Pl. XIII. 10.]	|K Ⱶ (reverse re-struck).
5	94·7	AR ·65		K Ⱶ (reverse re-struck).
6	95·	AR ·65	[Pl. XIII. 11.]	ꓦꓳIΔIꓦꓘ Incuse square, within which head of Aphrodite r.; hair bound with taenia, back hair in formal curls down neck."

No.	Wt.	Metal. Size.	Obverse.	Reverse.
7	95·	Æ ·65	Head (or fore-part) of lion l.	Incuse square, within which head of Aphrodite l., without earring; hair indicated by lines; the ends of the queue turned up beneath a broad diadema. [Pl. xiii. 12.]

Diobols.

8	26·8	Æ ·45	Head of lion r.	Incuse square, within which head of Aphrodite r., wearing round earring; hair bound with taenia, and falling in formal curls down neck.
9	27·3	Æ ·45		Similar but dotted square within incuse square. [Pl. xiii. 13.]
10	26·	Æ ·45		Linear square within incuse square; floral ornament in r. top corner: within, head of Aphrodite r., hair in queue.

Circ. B.C. 550—500.

Drachms.

11	95·7	Æ ·65	Forepart of lion r.	Incuse square, within which head of Aphrodite r., of fine archaic style, wearing pendent earring and necklace; hair indicated by dots, in queue and bound with diadema of beads.
12	96·7	Æ ·65		(Same dies.) [Pl. xiv. 1.]

CARIA.

No.	Wt.	Metal. Size.	Obverse.	Reverse.
13	95·7	AR ·65		K N I earring round; necklace with ornament in front; diadema plain. [Pl. xiv. 2.]
14	94·9	AR ·65		(Same dies.)
15	98·3	AR ·65		
16	93·2	AR ·7		

Circ. B.C. 500—480.

Drachms.

17	98·5	AR ·65	Forepart of lion r.	Incuse square, within which, head of Aphrodite r., of fine archaic style, wearing necklace but no earring; hair in lines (not dots) worn in queue, and bound with sphendone. [Pl. xiv. 3.]
18	97·2	AR ·65	Similar.	Similar, but hair bound with myrtle wreath.
19	93·3	AR ·65		(Same dies.) [Pl. xiv. 4.]

Circ. B.C. 412—400.

Drachms.

20	93·7	AR ·7	Forepart of lion r.	Incuse square, within which K N around head of Aphrodite r., of transitional style, wearing sphendone. [Pl. xiv. 5.]
21	91·4	AR ·7		

CNIDUS.   87

No.	Wt.	Metal. Size.	Obverse.	Reverse.
			Obols.	
			Forepart of lion r.	Incuse square, within which head of Aphrodite r., hair in bunch behind.
22	13·5	R ·35		
23	11·6	R ·35	*	(hair rolled)
			Circ. B.C. 400—390. Rhodian Standard. **Tetradrachm.**	
24	233·	R ·95	[K] N[I] Head of Aphrodite Euploia l., wearing earring and necklace of beads; above forehead, ampyx, on which monogram ⧢ : in field, behind, prow.	Incuse square, within which forepart of lion l. beneath EOBΩΛO[ϟ] [Pl. xiv. 6.]
			(R.P.K. Found by Gell on the site of Cnidus in 1812.)	
			Didrachm.	
25	110·7	R ·8	K NI Head of Aphrodite Euploia r., wearing earring and necklace; hair in sphendone; in field, behind, prow.	Traces of incuse square, within which forepart of lion r. in front, ΛΑΜΓΩΝ [Pl. xiv. 7.]

* The style of this coin seems to be later than that of no. 22.

CARIA.

No.	Wt.	Metal. Size.	Obverse.	Reverse.

Drachm.

26	57·6	AR ·6	Forepart of lion r.	Incuse square, within which head of Aphrodite Euploia r.; hair in sphendone: behind, prow upwards. [Pl. xiv. 8.]

Circ. B.C. 394—390.

Rhodian Standard.

Tridrachm.

Federal Coinage. (Cnidus, Rhodes, Iasus, Ephesus and Samos.)

27	164·8	AR ·9	[ΣΥ]Ν Infant Herakles r., strangling two serpents; around his body, crepundia?	[Κ]ΝΙΔΙΩΝ Head of Aphrodite Euploia r., wearing earring and necklace; hair in sphendone. behind, prow r. [Pl. xiv. 9.]

Circ. B.C. 390—300.

Tetradrachm.

28	223·4	AR ·9	Head of Aphrodite Euploia l., wearing earring and necklace; hair gathered into a knot behind; ampyx across forehead: behind, prow l.	Forepart of lion r. [Pl. xv. 1.]

No.	Wt.	Metal. Size.	Obverse.	Reverse.
			Drachms.	
29	50·	ℛ ·6	Head of Aphrodite r., wearing earring : hair rolled in front and confined at the back in a sphendone.	KNI Forepart of lion r. above, APXEKP[ATHΣ] [Pl. xv. 2.]
30	54·	ℛ ·55		| above, EYΦP[ΩN]* [Pl. xv. 3.]
31	49·	ℛ ·55		above, [T]EΛECIΦ[PΩN]*
32	48·1	ℛ ·55		,, ,, (?)
33	49·5	ℛ ·55		Magistrate's name illegible.
34	47·4	ℛ ·6	Head of Aphrodite l., wearing earring; hair in sphendone.	KNI Forepart of lion r. above, KAΛΛIΦPΩN [Pl. xv. 4.]
			Hemidrachms.	
35	25·1	ℛ ·45	Head of Aphrodite r., wearing earring; hair rolled in front and confined at the back in a sphendone.	Forepart of lion r. above, KΛEIN[IΓΓOΣ] [Pl. xv. 5.]
36	25·2	ℛ ·5		above, KΛEINIΓΓOΣ beneath, caduceus. [Pl. xv. 6.]

* Although these magistrates' names recur on coins of the next period, it is not certain that they are the same individuals, as the style of these specimens shows that they are decidedly of an earlier date.

90   CARIA.

No.	Wt.	Metal. Size.	Obverse.	Reverse.
37	21·3 [pierced]	AR ·5	Head of Aphrodite r., wearing earring; hair rolled.	KNI Bull's head facing. in field r., ΑΡΙΦ[ΡΩ]Ν
38	21·3	AR ·45		,, ΠΑΝΘΑΛΗΣ [Pl. xv. 7.]
39	19·2	AR ·45	Head of Aphrodite r., wearing earring; hair bound with diadema.	KNI Head and neck of bull r., (head almost facing). in field r., ΒΑΙΩΝ [Pl. xv. 8.]

Circ. B.C. 300—190.
Rhodian Standard.
Drachms.

40	43·2	AR ·65	Head of Aphrodite r., wearing stephane, earring and necklace: border of dots.	KNI Forepart of lion r. above, ΑΥΤΟΚΡΑΤΗΣ
41	45·7	AR ·65		,, ,, [Pl. xv. 9.]
42	49·2	AR ·65		above, ,,
43	42·5	AR ·65	Head of Aphrodite r., wearing earring and necklace; hair in sphendone: border of dots. behind neck, helmet.	KNI Forepart of lion r. above, ΘΕΥΜΕΛΩΝ* [Pl. xv. 10.]
44	47·3	AR ·6	(Same die.)	above, ,,

* A tetradrachm of this issue was in the late Mr. Montagu's collection, see *Num. Chron.* 1892, Pl. iii. 7. Its weight is 227·5 grs.

CNIDUS.   91

No.	Wt.	Metal. Size.	Obverse.	Reverse.
			Head of Aphrodite r., wearing earring and necklace; hair gathered up and tied at the back of head; ends loose: border of dots?	KNI Forepart of lion r.
45	48·6	Æ ·6	behind Ɛ (?)	above, ΑΓΑΘΟΦ[ΑΝΗΣ]
46	52·2	Æ ·55	,, Ɛ	,, ΤΕΛΕΑΣ [Pl. xv. 11.]
47	51·3	Æ ·65	,, ,,	above, ,,

Tetrobols.

			Head of Artemis r., wearing stephane; quiver at shoulder.	[KN]ΙΔΙΩ[N] Tripod. ΚΑΡΝΕΙΣ ΚΟΣ
48	37·7	Æ ·55		[Pl. xv. 12.]
49	35·6	Æ ·5	(with round earring and necklace.)	ΚΑΛΛΙΠΠΟΣ [Pl. xv. 13.]

Hemidrachms.

			Bust of Artemis r., wearing stephane; quiver at shoulder; shoulders draped: border of dots?	ΝΩΙΔΙΝΚ ΝΩ٩ΦΥƷ Tripod.
50	26·4	Æ ·6		
51	25·9	Æ ·55		ΚΝΙΔΙΩΝ ΚΥΔΟΚΛΗ[Σ]

92 CARIA.

No.	Metal. Size.	Obverse.	Reverse.
		BRONZE.	
52	Æ ·65	Head of City l., turreted. [Pl. xv. 14.]	ΚΝΙΔΙΩΝ Forepart of lion l.
53	Æ ·65		
54	Æ ·7		
55	Æ ·65	ΔΑΜ[Ο ΚΡΑΤΙΑΣ] Head of Aphrodite r.; or of the Democracy, wearing earring and necklace; hair in sphendone: behind, Ε	ΚΝΙ Prow r.; beneath, club. above, ΑΝ ΤΙ ? in front, grapes.
56	Æ ·6	[ΔΑΜ]ΟΚΡΑΤΙ[ΑΣ]	„ ΑΡΙΣΤΑΓΟΡ ΑΣ
57	Æ ·55	Inscr. obscure. No monogram.	ΚΝΙΔΙΩΝ (beneath); around, ΚΛΕΙΤΟΦΩ[Ν]
58	Æ ·5	Inscr. obscure. Ε (?)	ΚΝΙ (above); beneath, ΑΣ ......
59	Æ ·5	„ „ (?)	„ magistrate's name illegible.
60	Æ ·55	„ „ (?)	[ΚΝΙ]ΔΙΩΝ ? (beneath); magistrate's name not visible; in front, uncertain symbol.
61	Æ ·55	Head of Aphrodite r., hair rolled.	ΚΝΙ Prow r.; beneath, club. around, ΠΥΘΩΝ.

CNIDUS. 93

No.	Metal. Size.	Obverse.	Reverse.
62	Æ ·55	Female head r., wearing stephane.	KNI Prow r.; below, club: beneath, ΚΑΡΝΕΙΣ[ΚΟΣ].
63	Æ ·5	Female head r., wearing diadema.	KNI Prow r.; below, club. behind, caduceus; beneath, ΜΟΙ ΡΙ[ΧΟΣ] [Pl. xv. 15.]
64	Æ ·5		behind, serpent coiled round omphalos; beneath, ΜΟΙΡΙΧ . .
65	Æ ·4	Head of Apollo l., laur.	KNI Prow r. beneath, [ΛΑ]ΧΑΡΤΟΣ [Pl. xv. 16.]
66	Æ ·4		
67	Æ ·35	Head of Apollo r., laur.	KNI Prow r. beneath,]ΟΚΡΑΤ[(Φιλοκρατίδας ?) [Pl. xv. 17.]
68	Æ ·45		KNI beneath; above,]ΚΡΑΤΛΑC (sic)
69	Æ ·45		KN above; magistrate's name not visible.
70	Æ ·45		,, ; beneath, ΤΡΑ
71	Æ ·45		KNI Prow l., magistrate's name invisible.

No.	Wt.	Metal. Size.	Obverse.	Reverse.
72		Æ .8	Head of Artemis r., wearing stephane; at her shoulder, quiver.	KNIΔIΩN Tripod: border of dots. ΦIΛOKPATIΔAC [Pl. xv. 18.]
73		Æ .5	Similar head r.	KNI Bull's head facing. beneath, API[ΣTAΓ]OPA[Σ] [Pl. xv. 19.]

Circ. B.C. 190—167.

(For Alexandrine tetradrachms of this period (symbol tripod) see Müller (*Num. d'Alex.*) Nos. 151-2.)

Rhodian Standard reduced.

Didrachms.

74	76·6	AR .75	Head of Rhodian Helios facing without rays: border of dots.	KNI Forepart of lion r. behind, rose; beneath, ΔIOKΛHΣ
75	72·5	AR .8		[Pl. xvi. 1.
76	78·	AR .75		symbol and name obscure.
77	65·1	AR .75		behind, altar; magistrate's name invisible.

CNIDUS. 95

No.	Metal. Size.	Obverse.	Reverse.
		After B.C. 167.	
		BRONZE.	
		Head of Apollo r., laur.; hair in formal curls. (Cf. contemporary coins of the later Lycian League.)	Head and neck of Bull l.: border of dots.
78	Æ ·65		KNEI KAΦICO
79	Æ ·6	(hair varied.)	MOΣXO[Σ] KNIΔIΩN
80	Æ ·75		ΠA NTAΛEUN KNIΔIΩ
81	Æ ·75		
82	Æ ·7		ΠAN T AΛE KNIΔIΩ [Pl. xvi. 2.]
83	Æ ·65	Head of Apollo r., laur.; hair in formal curls.	[KNIΔ]IΩN Head and neck of bull l. : border of dots. beneath, AΦI (? [K]AΦI)
84	Æ ·55		type r.; name illegible.
85	Æ ·75	Head of Apollo r., laur.; hair in formal curls. [Pl. xvi. 3.]	KNIΔIΩN APIΣTOΠO ΛIΣ Between lines of inscription, bunch of grapes.
86	Æ ·75		

No.	Metal. Size.	Obverse.	Reverse.
		BRONZE.	
		First Century B.C.	
87	Æ 1·1	Large head of young Dionysos l., crowned with ivy. (Countermark, female head r. (Aphrodite ?)	KN[IΔI]ΩN Vine-branch with two bunches of grapes : border of dots. above, ΕΠΑ ΓΑΘΟΣ
88	Æ 1·1	[Pl. XVI. 4.]	
89	Æ 1·05	Large head of young Dionysos r., crowned with ivy : border of dots. (Countermark, Female head r. (Aphrodite ?) [Pl. XVI. 5.]	KNIΔIΩN Vine-branch with bunch of grapes between tendril and leaf. beneath, ///ΑΛΕΩΝ [or ///ΑΝΩΝ]
90	Æ ·75	Head of Athena r., wearing crested helmet.	KNIΔIΩN ΕΥΒΟΥΛ[ΟC] Nike advancing l., carrying wreath and palm.
91	Æ ·75		KNIΔIΩN ΤΕΛΕΣΙΠΠΟΣ
92	Æ 1·3	Head of the Aphrodite of Praxiteles r. : border of dots.	KNIΔIΩN ΔΙΟΚΛΗΣ Dionysos robed in long chiton and himation standing l., holding kantharos and thyrsos : border of dots.
93	Æ 1·15	Head of the Aphrodite of Praxiteles r. : border of dots.	KNI Δ ΙΩΝ Dionysos robed in long chiton and himation, standing l., holding kantharos and thyrsos : border of dots.
94	Æ ·95		ΝΩΙΔ ΙΝΧ

CNIDUS. 97

No.	Metal. Size.	Obverse.	Reverse.
95	Æ 1·1	ΚΝΙ Δ ΙΩΝ (?) Head of the Aphrodite of Praxiteles r.: border of dots.	ΝΩΙΔ Ι Ж Tyche standing l., turreted ; holds rudder and cornucopiae : border of dots.
96	Æ 1·05		

Imperial Time.

(α) Without heads of Emperors.

97	Æ ·85	Τ·Κ·Τ· ΕΠΙΕΥ ΠΟΛΕ ΙΤΑ* Bearded head r. : border of dots.	ΚΝΙ ΔΙΩΝ Lighted altar between two bunches of grapes : border of dots.
		[Pl. XVI. 6.]	
98	Æ ·75		

(β) With heads of Emperors.

Caracalla ?

99	Æ 1·25	ΑΥ·Κ·ΜΑΡΑV .... Bust of Caracalla? r., laur.; wears cuirass and paludamentum.	ΚΝΙΔΙ.. Homonoia? standing r., holding cornucopiae and patera over altar.
		(Broken in half.)	

Caracalla and Plautilla.

100	Æ 1·3	... ΤΩΝΙΝΟC ΦΟΥΡΒΙΑ ΠΛΑΥΤΙΛΛΑ Busts of Caracalla and Plautilla face to face.	ΚΝΙ ΔΙΩΝ The Cnidian Aphrodite of Praxiteles standing r., with amphora beside her; Asklepios stands l., facing the goddess.
		[Pl. XVI. 7.]	

* Eckhel's suggestion (*D.N.V.* iii. 580), that the unexplained obverse inscription of this coin may be understood as Τύχη Κνιδίων Τριώπας, is absurd.

O

No.	Metal. Size.	Obverse.	Reverse.
1	Æ ·45	EUIPPE. BRONZE. *Second Century* B.C. ? Bust of Artemis r., at her shoulder, bow and quiver. (Countermark, star.)	. . ΙΠΠΕΩΝ Quiver with strap. . . ΔΕΟΟΤ . . [Μόδεστος?] [Pl. XVII. 1.] (H. P. Borrell, *N. C.*, ix. 151.)
2	Æ ·85	*Imperial.* Lucilla. ΛΟΥΚΙΛΛ ΑΟΕΒΑ ΟΤΗ Bust of Lucilla r.	ΕVΙΠΠΤ Ε ΩΝ Hygieia standing r., feeding serpent. [Pl. XVII. 2.]

EUROMUS.

BRONZE.

Early Second Century B.C.

No.	Metal. Size.	Obverse.		Reverse.
1	Æ ·65	Head of Zeus r., laur. [Pl. xvii. 3.]	EYPΩ MEΩN	Double axe (Labrys) r.: the whole in laurel-wreath.
2	Æ ·6	Head of Zeus r., laur.	E Y P Ω	Double axe (Labrys): the whole in laurel-wreath.

First Century B.C.

3	Æ ·75	Head of young Dionysos r., wearing band across forehead and ivy-wreath. [Pl. xvii. 4.]	EVPΩ M[EΩN]	Cultus-statue of Zeus Labraundos, facing; holding in r. double axe (labrys), and in l. spear: the statue stands between the pilei of the Dioskuri surmounted by stars.
4	Æ ·7	EVPΩM EΩN	Stag standing r.; beneath, ΠΟΛΕ; in front, double axe (labrys). [Pl. xvii. 5.]	No inscr. Same type.

No.	Metal. Size.	Obverse.	Reverse.
		Early Imperial Times.	
		(α) Without heads of Emperors.	
5	Æ ·55	Cultus-statue of Zeus Labraundos as on previous coins, but no pilei: border of dots. [Pl. xvii. 6.]	ΕΥΡѠΜΕѠΝ Eagle r., wings open: border of dots.
6	Æ ·6	Terminal cultus-statue of Zeus Labraundos, holding double axe (labrys) and spear: at his side, stag looking up: border of dots.	ΕΥΡΩΜΕΩΝ Eagle to front on thunderbolt, wings open: border of dots.
		(β) With heads of Emperors.	
		Augustus.	
7	Æ ·75	ϹΕΒΑ ϹΤΟϹ Head of Augustus r., bare. [Pl. xvii. 7.]	ΕΥΡΩ Μ[Ε] Ω[Ν] Stag standing r.
		Augustus and Livia.	
8	Æ ·95	ϹΕΒΑϹΤΟΙ Heads of Augustus r. and Livia l., face to face. [Pl. xvii. 8.]	ΕΥ [ΡΩ]ΜΕΩΝ Terminal cultus-statue of Zeus Labraundos facing; wielding in raised r. double axe (labrys), and resting on spear: at his feet, eagle.

No.	Metal. Size.	Obverse.	Reverse.
		GORDIUTEICHOS. BRONZE. *Second Century* B.C.	
1	Æ ·65	Head of Zeus r., laur. [Pl. XVII. 9.]	ΓΟ ΡΔΙΟ Cultus-statue of TEIXITΩ[N] Aphrodite r., wearing long robes and veil; her arms extended before her.
2	Æ ·6		

No.	Wt.	Metal. Size.	Obverse.	Reverse.
			HALICARNASSUS. *Before* B.C. 480. SILVER. Phœnician Standard (?) **Obols.**	
1	10·5	AR ·35	Forepart of winged horse r. [Pl. xviii. 1.]	Incuse square, within which goat's head and foreleg (?) r. (Borrell.)
2	9·	AR ·3	[Pl. xviii. 2.]	(Borrell.)
			Circ. B.C. 400—377. Rhodian Standard. **Drachms.**	
3	52·8	AR ·55	Head of Apollo, laur., facing.	AAI Eagle (?) with wings open r.; in front, olive spray: the whole in incuse square. (Borrell.)
4	48·8	AR ·5	[Pl. xviii. 3.]	(R.P.K.)
			Obols.	
5	10·3	AR ·35	Forepart of winged horse r. [Pl. xviii. 4.]	A Forepart of running goat r., in incuse circle. (Petrides.)
6	9·4	AR ·35	| AAI [Pl. xviii. 5.]	(Borrell.)

HALICARNASSUS.

No.	Metal. Size.	Obverse.	Reverse.
		BRONZE.	
7	Æ ·85	ΑΛΙ Forepart of winged horse l. ; plain border.	Lyre between two straight laurel-branches. Straight line beneath [and above] lyre, forming, with branches, linear square.
8	Æ ·85	[Pl. xviii. 6.]	(Newton.)
9	Æ ·35		(,,)
10	Æ ·35		(,,)
11	Æ ·35		(traces of incuse circle.)
12	Æ ·4	Forepart of winged horse r. : border of dots. [Pl. xviii. 7.]	Lyre between two laurel-branches, with a straight line above and beneath, forming a linear square. (Borrell.)
13	Æ ·35	Head of Athena r., wearing crested Athenian helmet. [Pl. xviii. 8.]	Lyre between two laurel-branches.
		BRONZE.	
		Early Second Century B.C. ?	
		Head of Poseidon (?) r. : border of dots.	ΑΛΙΚΑΡ ΝΑΣΣΕΩΝ Tripod with three handles and ὅλμος.
14	Æ ·7		above ΕΠΙ (?) beneath, Σ Ο
15	Æ ·7		,, (?) ,, ,,
16	Æ ·6		(Border of dots.)
17	Æ ·55	[Pl. xviii. 9.]	

No.	Metal. Size.	Obverse.	Reverse.
18	Æ ·5	Head of Apollo l., laur.	ΑΛΙ Eagle l., wings open; in front, lyre.
			[Pl. xviii. 10.]
19	Æ ·45		

Later Second or First Century B.C.

No.	Metal. Size.	Obverse.	Reverse.
		Head of Poseidon r.	Trident, ornamented with a volute on each side of handle, and dolphins between prongs.
20	Æ ·7		ΑΛΙΚΑ (Caduceus in place of volute ΑΠΟΛ in field, l.)
21	Æ ·65		ΑΛΙΚΑ ΕϹΤΙ
22	Æ ·65		,,
			[Pl. xviii. 11.]
23	Æ ·65		ΑΛΙΚΑΡ ΕϹΤ
24	Æ ·65		,,
25	Æ ·65		ΑΛΚΑΙ (sic) ΕϹΤΙ
26	Æ ·65		ΑΛΙΚ ΙΑϹШΝ
27	Æ ·7		ΑΛΙΚΑΡ ΙΕΡΟΚΛ[Η] in field l., star.
28	Æ ·65		ΑΛΙΚ ΚΛΕΙ

No.	Metal. Size.	Obverse.	Reverse.
29	Æ ·65		ΑΛΙΚΑΡ ΚΛΕ.
30	Æ ·7	[Re-struck on coin of ....? (*obv.* Head of Apollo r., laur. ; *Rev.* type not apparent.)]	ΑΛΙΚΑ ΛΑΜΠΙ
31	Æ ·65		ΑΛΙΚ ΜΕΛΑΝ
32	Æ ·65		ΑΛΙΚ ΜΕΛΑΝ
33	Æ ·65		ΑΛΙΚΑΡ ΜΕΛΑ
34	Æ ·7		ΑΛΙΚΑ ΜΕΛΑ
35	Æ ·75		ΑΛΙΚ ΧΑΡΜ
36	Æ ·65		ΑΛΙΚ ΧΑΡΜ
37	Æ ·7		ΑΛΙΚΑ ———? [Pl. xviii. 12.]

No.	Wt.	Metal. Size.	Obverse.	Reverse.
38		Æ ·45	Head of young Herakles r., wearing lion's skin: border of dots.	ΑΛΙ Bow in case and club: border of dots. beneath, ΚΛΕΙ
39		Æ ·45		
40		Æ ·45		
41		Æ ·45		beneath, ΔΡΑΚΩ[Ν]? [Pl. xviii. 13.]
42		Æ ·45		above, ΟΛΥΜ ..?

First Century B.C.

SILVER.

Attic Standard.

Drachms.

No.	Wt.	Metal. Size.	Obverse.	Reverse.
43	60·6	Æ ·7	Head of Rhodian Helios facing, without rays: border of dots.	Bust of Athena r., wearing crested helmet and aegis. ΑΛΙΚΑΡ [Δ]ΡΑΚ[ΩΝ] [Pl. xviii. 14.]
44	65·0	Æ ·7		ΕΡΜΩΝ ΑΛΙΚΑΡΝ (R.P.K.)
45	64·9	Æ ·75		ΜΟΣΧ ΟΣ [ΑΛΙ]ΚΑΡΝΑΣΣΕΩΝ (Bank Coll.)
46	56·2	Æ ·7		ΑΛΙΚΑΡΝΑC ΜΟCΧΟC (Borrell.) [Pl. xviii. 15.]
47	60·3	Æ ·65		ΜΟCΧ ΑΛΙΚΑΡΝΑC (Paton.)

HALICARNASSUS.

No.	Wt.	Metal. Size.	Obverse.	Reverse.	
			Hemidrachm.		
48	27·1	AR ·6	Head of Apollo r., laur.	ΑΛΙΚΑΡ ΝΑΣΣΕΩΝ [Pl. xviii. 16.]	Lyre (kithara).
			Trihemiobols.		
49	14·8	AR ·5	Bust of Athena r., wearing crested helmet and aegis.	Owl r., wings closed. ΑΛΙ ΟΙΔ [Pl. xviii. 17.]	
50	13·4	AR ·5		ΑΛΙΚ ΧΑΡΜΗΝ ?	(Lawson.)
51	13·7	AR ·45		ΑΛΙΚ (owl l.) ΧΑΡΜ ? [Pl. xviii. 18.]	(Borrell.)
52	13·8	AR ·35		ΑΛΙΚ ΧΑΡΜ ?	
53	13·2	AR ·45		[ΑΛΙ] ΚΑΡΝ	
			BRONZE.		
			Head of Helios facing: border of dots.	ΑΛΙΚΑΡΝ Bust of Athena r., wearing crested helmet and aegis: border of dots.	
54		Æ ·8		ΑΙΘΩΝ [Pl. xviii. 19.]	
55		Æ ·8		ΑΙΘΩΝ	
56		Æ ·85		ΑΡΤΕ ..?	
57		Æ ·85		ΝΕΟΚΛΗ	

108   CARIA.

No.	Metal. Size.	Obverse.	Reverse.
58	Æ ·7	Head of Helios r., radiate.	ΑΛΙΚΑ Lyre (kithara) and magistrate's name: border of dots. ΑΝΔΡΟΜΕ? [Pl. XVIII. 20.]
59	Æ ·7		ΑΡΤΕ
60	Æ ·7		[ΔΙ]ΟΝΥ ?
61	Æ ·7		ΔΙΟСΚ
62	Æ ·85	Head of Apollo r., laur.	ΑΛΙΚΑΡ Lyre (kithara) and magistrate's name: border of dots. ΑΝΤΙΓ ?
63	Æ ·85	(Countermark, Star of eight rays.)	,, ?
64	Æ ·5	Head of Apollo r., laur.: border of dots.	ΑΛΙΚΑΡ Lyre (chelys): border ΝΑΣΣΕΩΝ of dots.
65	Æ ·45		
66	Æ ·4	Head of Athena r., wearing crested helmet: border of dots.	Α ΛΙ Ornamented trident: border of dots.
67	Æ ·35		

No.	Metal. Size.	Obverse.	Reverse.
68	Æ ·45	Head of Athena r., wearing crested helmet: border of dots.	ΑΛΙ Owl r., wings closed: border of dots.
69	Æ ·45		
70	Æ ·45		
71	Æ ·35		ΑΛΙΚΑ
72	Æ ·45	Youthful male head r. (Hermes?)	ΑΛΙΚ Winged caduceus and magistrate's name: border of dots. ΑCΠΑ
73	Æ ·6	Head of Zeus r., laur.	ΑΛΙΚ Head-dress of Isis as on ΑΡΝΑ drachms of Myndus: border of dots.
74	Æ ·7	Head of Apollo ? r., laur.	ΑΛΙΚ Figure standing l., clad in long chiton; r. extended, and resting with l. on sceptre ?; behind, CΩΔ?: the whole in incuse square.
		(Cf. Mion., vi. 640, no. 189, and vii. 112.)	
		Head of Poseidon r., diademed.	ΑΛΙΚΑΡ Veiled female figure standing facing, holding in r. patera ?, and in l. cornucopiae ?; border of dots.
75	Æ ·75		in field r., ΑΠΟΛΛΟ
		[Pl. xviii. 21.]	
76	Æ ·75		in field r., ΑΡΙCΤΟ
77	Æ ·7	,,	ΙΕΡΟ
78	Æ ·7	,,	ΜΕΝ ΕΚ
79	Æ ·85	(type enclosed in wreath.)	,, l., ΜΟCΧΙ
80	Æ ·85	(,,)	,, ,,

CARIA.

No.	Metal. Size.	Obverse.	Reverse.
		Imperial Coinage.	
		Nero.	
81	Æ ·8	ΝΕΡΩΝΣΕ ΒΑΣΣ ΤΟΣ (sic). Head of Nero r., laur.	ΑΛΙΚΑΡ ΝΑΣΣΕΩΝ Terminal figure of Athena facing, armed with shield and spear.
		Trajan.	
82	Æ ·95	ΑVΤΟΚΑΙΝΕΡΒΑC .. .. Head of Trajan r., laur.	ΑΛΙΚΑΡΝΑ ... ΩΝ Bust of Athena l., wearing crested helmet and aegis; beneath bust, ΑΡΠ ΑΛ [Pl. xix. 1.]
83	Æ 1·2	ΑVΤΟΚΑΙΝΕΡΒΑCΤ ΡΑ ..... CΕΒΑCΓΕΡ ΔΑΚΙ Head of Trajan r., laur.	ΑΛΙΚΑΡ ΝΑ CCΕΩΝ Bearded figure standing to front (Zeus Askraios?).* He is radiate and wears long chiton and himation; on either side of him, a tree, in the branches of which sits a bird. [Pl. xix. 2.]
		Hadrian.	
84	Æ ·8	Inscr. obscure. Head of Hadrian r., laur.	ΑΛΙΚΑΡΝΑCCΕΩΝ ΗΡΟΔΟ ΤΟC Bust of Herodotus r., bald and bearded. [Pl. xix. 3.]
		Antoninus Pius.	
85	Æ 1·2	///////////// ΑΝΤΩΝ ////// Head of Antoninus Pius r., laur.	[Α]ΛΙΚ ΑΡΝ Α[C]CΕΩΝ Zeus Askraios (?) between two trees, on each of which, a bird, as on no. 83.

* With regard to Zeus 'Ασκραῖος (?) see Overbeck, *Kunstmyth.*, ii. 210.

HALICARNASSUS.   111

No.	Metal. Size.	Obverse.	Reverse.
		Faustina Junior.	
86	Æ ·7	... CTEINACEBAC .. Bust of Faustina r.	ΑΛΙΚΑ P N ACEΩ Distyle N temple, star in pediment, columns with spiral fluting; between them, terminal figure of Athena, armed with shield and spear. [Pl. xix. 4.]
		Commodus.	
87	Æ 1·05	AYT ... C·MAY PKO MOΔOC Bust of Commodus r., laur.: wearing cuirass and paludamentum.	ΑΛΙ[Κ A P] NACCEΩ N Distyle temple, within which, Homonoia wearing modius and holding patera and cornucopiae stands l. before a flaming altar.
		Sept. Severus.	
88	Æ 1·15	///////////// HPOCCEB Bust of Severus r., laur., wearing cuirass and paludamentum.	AP]ΧΕΥ♀♁ΚΑΜΫC ΤΡΑ♁ΚΛ [ΕΟΥC] (?) [Α]ΛΙΚΑΡΝ (in ex.) Zeus Askraios (?) as on nos. 83, 85, supra.
		Gordianus III.	
89	Æ 1·05	AYTKMAN TΓOPΔ IANO[C] Bust of Gordian III r., laur., wearing cuirass and paludamentum.	ΑΛΙΚΑ PNACC ΕΩΝ Tetrastyle temple, within which, statue of Homonoia standing l., before altar; she wears modius, and holds patera and cornucopiae.

No.	Metal. Size.	Obverse.	Reverse.
		ALLIANCE COINS.	
		HALICARNASSUS AND SAMOS.	
		Sept. Severus and Julia Domna.	
90	Æ 1·5	Inscr. illegible. Busts of Sept. Severus and Julia Domna face to face: Severus r., laur., wearing cuirass and paludamentum ; that of Domna l., draped. [Pl. xliv. 3.]	ΑΛΙΚΑΡΝΑϹϹΕ [/////////////////// ///////] and, in ex., name of archon, illegible. Zeus Askraios ? and Hera : Zeus standing to front, radiate, and clad in long chiton with himation, his arms hanging at his sides ; before him, Hera standing L. in biga of peacocks ; holding patera and long sceptre.
		HALICARNASSUS AND COS.	
		Caracalla and Geta.	
91	Æ 1·3	..... ΑΝΤΩ ΝΕΙ ΝΟϹ.............. Busts, face to face, of Caracalla r., laur., and Geta l., bare-headed, each wearing cuirass and paludamentum. [Pl. xliv. 4.]	ΑΛΙΚΑΡΝΑϹϹ ΕΩΝ ΚΚΩΩ ΝΟΜΟΝΟ, and, in ex., ΑΡΧ·Τ·ΦΛ·ΔΗΜ ΗΤΡΙΟΥ ΙΟΥΛ Apollo Kitharoedos standing r., holding lyre (kithara) in l., and patera (or plectrum ?) in r. ; before him, Asklepios stands l., resting on serpent-staff.

No.	Metal. Size.	Obverse.	Reverse.
		HARPASA. *Second Century* B.C. BRONZE.	
1	Æ ·75	Head of Zeus r., laur.	ΑΡΠΑΞΗ ΝΩΝ Apollo Kitharoedos, clad in long chiton, standing r., holding lyre under l. arm, and plectrum in r. hand; before him, a laurel-branch. [Pl. xix. 5.]
		Imperial Times. (a) Without heads of Emperors.	
2	Æ ·6	Α ΘΗΝΑΓΟ ΡΟΥ Bust of Athena r., wearing crested helmet and aegis: border of dots.	ΑΡΠΑCΗ ΝΩΝ Cultus-statue, facing, of Asiatic goddess resembling Artemis Ephesia.
3	Æ ·6	(no inscr.)	(ΑΡΠΑ CΗΝΩΝ)
4	Æ ·85	ΔΗΜΟC ΑΡΠΑCΗ ΝωΝ Head of youthful Demos r.: border of dots.	ΕΠΙΚΑΝΔΙΔΟΥ ΚΕΛCΟΥ* Athena advancing r., armed with helmet and round shield, and striking downwards with spear: border of dots. [Pl. xix. 6.]

* Candidus Celsus is supposed by Waddington (*Fastes*, p. 209) to have been Proconsul of Asia. His name recurs on a coin of M. Aurelius Caesar (see no. 10). A grammateus of the name of Candidus is also met with on coins of the neighbouring town of Neapolis (see infra, Neap. no. 6) dating from the time of Volusian.

No.	Metal. Size.	Obverse.	Reverse.
5	Æ ·8	ΔΗ ΜΟC Head of Demos r. : border of dots.	ΑΡΠΑ CΗΝΩΝ Similar.
6	Æ ·85	Head of Sarapis r., wearing modius : border of dots.	ΑΡΠΑC ΗΝΩΝ Dionysos standing l., naked to waist, himation over legs ; he rests l. arm on column, and holds in l. grapes and in r. kantharos; at his feet, panther : border of dots.

(β) With heads of Emperors.

Hadrian.

7	Æ ·9	ΑVΚΑΙΤΡΑ [ΑΔ]ΡΙΑ ΝΟC Head of Hadrian r., laur.	ΑΡΠΑ CΗΝΩ[Ν] River-god, Harpasos, recumbent l., holding cornucopiae, behind which, vase, reversed.

Sabina.

8	Æ ·8	CΑΒΕΙΝΑ CΕΒΑC ΤΗ Bust of Sabina r.	ΑΡΠΑ CΗΝΩ[Ν] Athena advancing r., as on no. 4.
9	Æ ·8	(same dies.)	

M. Aurelius.

10	Æ 1·0	ΜΑΥΡΗΛΙΟC ΟΥΗΡ ΟCΚΑΙCΑΡ Head of Aurelius Caesar r., bare. [Pl. xix. 7.]	ΕΠΙΚΑΝΔΙΔΟV ΚΕΛ COV ; (in ex.) ΑΡΠΑCΗΝΩΝ. River-god Harpasos recumbent l., holding reed and cornucopiae ; behind, vase, reversed.

No.	Metal. Size.	Obverse.	Reverse.
		Caracalla.	
11	Æ 1·35	ΑΥΚΜΑΥ ΑΝΤΩΝΕ ΙΝΟC Bust of Caracalla r., laur., wearing cuirass and aegis.	ΑΡΠ A C HNΩN (the letters HN in this inscr. have been altered by tooling into CE). Zeus, wearing himation over lower limbs, seated l., holding Nike on extended r., and resting with l. on sceptre.
		Julia Mamaea.	
12	Æ 1·2	ΙΟΥΛΙΑ ΜΑΜΕΑCΕ Bust of Julia Mamaea r.; crescent behind shoulders.	ΑΡΠΑ CHИΩИ Athena standing r., armed with helmet and round shield, and striking downwards with spear.
		Gordianus Pius.	
13	Æ 1·2	ΑΥΤ Κ Μ ΑΝ ΓΟΡΔΙΑΝΟC CE Bust of Gordian III r., laur., wearing cuirass and paludamentum.	ΑΡΠ A CHNΩN Zeus, wearing himation over lower limbs, seated l., holding Nike and resting on sceptre.
		[Pl. xix. 8.]	
14	Æ ·85	A K MAN ΓΟΡΔΙΑΝΟC Bust of Gordian III r., radiate, wearing cuirass and paludamentum.	ΑΡΠΑC HNΩN River-god Harpasos recumbent l., holding reed and cornucopiae; beneath him, flowing water.

[For alliance coin of Harpasa with Neapolis Cariae see Sestini, *Descr. Num. Vet.*, p. 345. Sestini takes the alliance to be between Harpasa and Neapolis Ioniae.]

CARIA.

No.	Metal. Size.	Obverse.	Reverse.
		### HERACLEA SALBACE. BRONZE. *First Century* B.C.	
		Head of Artemis r., quiver at shoulder.	HPAKΛE ΩTΩN Herakles naked, standing to front, resting on club with r., and carrying lion's skin on l. arm.
1	Æ ·65		(A in inscr.)
2	Æ ·6		(,,)
3	Æ ·55		(,,)
		[Pl. xix. 9.]	
		Imperial Times. (a) Without heads of Emperors.	
		Cornucopiae containing two bunches of grapes, between two ears of corn : border of dots.	HPAKΛ EΩTΩN Double axe (Labrys) bound with fillet : border of dots.
4	Æ ·7		
		[Pl. xix. 10.]	
		IEPA BOVΛH Bust of Boule r., veiled and laureate : border of dots.	HPAKΛ EΩ TΩN Asklepios naked to waist, himation over l. arm and legs, seated l. on chair, holding in r. patera over a serpent coiled and erect before him, and in l. crooked staff : border of dots.
5	Æ ·9		
6	Æ ·9		(same dies.)
		[These coins belong to the time of Caracalla. Cf. Fox, ii., pl. iv. 77.]	

No.	Metal. Size.	Obverse.	Reverse.
7	Æ ·95	ΙΕΡ ΑΒΟVΛΗ Bust of Boule r., veiled and laur. : border of dots.	ΗΡΑΚΛΕ Ω ΤΩΝ Tyche standing l., wearing modius, and holding rudder and cornucopiae.
8	Æ 1·25	ΙΕΡΑCVΝ ΚΛΗΤΟC Youthful bust of the Senate l. : border of dots.	ΗΡΑΚΛΕ ΩΤΩΝ Tyche standing l., turreted, and holding rudder and cornucopiae: border of dots.

[Pl. xix. 11.]

| 9 | Æ 1·0 | ΙΕΡΑCVΝ ΚΛΗΤΟC Youthful bust of the Senate r.: border of dots. | ΗΡΑΚΛΕΩ Τ ΩΝ Similar type : border of dots. |

[These two coins, though bearing the same types, belong to different periods; no. 8 seems to be of the time of the Antonines, no. 9 of the time of Gallienus ?]

| 10 | Æ ·8 | ΔΗΜΟC Bust of youthful Demos r., laur. : border of dots. | ΗΡΑΚΛΕ ΩΤΩΝ Hygieia wearing modius, standing l. before altar, and feeding serpent which she holds in her arms. |
| 11 | Æ ·75 | Bust of Sarapis r., bound with taenia, and wearing modius : border of dots. | ΗΡΑΚΛ ΕΩΤΩΝ Isis standing to front, head l. ; she wears usual head dress and long chiton. She holds in r. sistrum, and in l. situla ; behind her shoulders, crescent: border of dots. |

[Pl. xx. 1.]

| 12 | Æ ·7 | | |
| 13 | Æ ·75 | | |

118   CARIA.

No.	Metal. Size.	Obverse.	Reverse.
14	Æ ·75	ΗΡΑΚΛΙ Α Bust of Tyche of City, turreted, l., holding in raised r. aplustre, and on l. arm cornucopiae: border of dots. [Pl. xx. 2.]	ΗΡΑΚΛΕΩ ΤΩΝ Hermes naked, standing to front, head l., holding purse in r., and chlamys and caduceus on l. arm: border of dots.

(β) With heads of Emperors.

Augustus.

15	Æ ·75	ΣΕΒΑΣΤΟΣ Head of Augustus r., bare. [Pl. xx. 3.]	ΟΣ ΑΠΟΛΛΩΝΙ ΑΠΟΛΛΩΝΙΟΥ ΗΡΑ ΚΛΕΩΤ ΩΝ — Bearded Herakles, naked, standing l., his r. arm extended and holding club on l. arm.
16	Æ ·75		
17	Æ ·8		
18	Æ ·75	ΣΕΒΑΣΤΟΣ Head of Augustus r., laur.	ΗΡΑΚΛΕ ΩΤΩΝ Head of Asklepios or Zeus r., laur.
19	Æ ·85	ϹΕΒ ΑϹΤΟϹ Head of Augustus(?) r., laur.	ΗΡΑΚΛ ΕΩΤΩΝ Distyle Temple, containing cultus-statue of goddess facing (Aphrodite? or Artemis Ephesia?) [Bank Coll.]

No.	Metal. Size.	Obverse.	Reverse.
		Nero.	
20	Æ ·65	**ΚΑΙ ΣΑΡ** Bust of youthful Nero r., bare. [Pl. xx. 4.]	**ΓΛΥΚΩΝ** Sabazios or Sozon standing l., clad in short chiton and with chlamys over shoulders: he holds in r. patera, and in l. double-axe (labrys).
21	Æ ·75	**ΝΕΡΩΝ ΚΑΙΣΑΡ** Head of Nero r., bare.	**ΩΝ** **ΓΛΥΚΩΝΙΕΡ ... ΗΡΑΚΛΕΩΤ** Bearded Herakles naked, standing l., his r. arm extended; club and lion's skin on l. arm.
22	Æ ·75	**ΝΕΡΩΝ ΚΑΙΣΑΡ** Bust of Nero r., bare-headed, wearing cuirass. [Pl. xx. 5.]	**ΓΛΥΚΩΝΙΕΡΕΥΣ ΗΡΑΚΛΕΩΤ ΩΝ** Head of bearded Herakles r.*
		Vespasian.	
23	Æ ·95	**ϹΕΒΑϹΤΟϹ** Head of Vespasian r., laur.	**ΗΡΑΚΛΕΩΤΩΝ** Athena standing r., turreted,† with spear in raised r., and shield on l. arm: behind, owl. Countermark ⋈ [Pl. xx. 6.]

* Cf. Head of same style on Æ coins of Tabae. Concerning Glykon see Introduction.

† As to mural crown worn by goddesses see Furtwängler (*Coll. Sabouroff*, i., pl. xxv.)

No.	Metal. Size.	Obverse.	Reverse.
		Domitian.	
24	Æ ·8	ΔΟ..... ΝΟCΚΑ.... Head of Domitian r., laur.	ΗΡΑ .... ΤΩΝ Bearded Herakles naked, standing l., his r. arm extended; club and lion's skin on l. arm. [Pl. xx. 7.]
		Antoninus Pius.	
25	Æ 1·45	ΑΥΚΑΙΤΙΑΙΑΔΡΙ ΑΝ ΤΩΝΕΙΝΟC CEB Bust of Antoninus Pius r., laur., wearing paludamentum.	CTATTAΛΟC* ΑΡΧΙΑΤΡΟC ΗΡΑΚΛΕΩ ΤΩΝ, and across field, ΝΕ ΟΙC Herakles naked, standing to front, holding club downwards in r., and strung bow in extended l. [Pl. xx. 8.]
		M. Aurelius.	
26	Æ 1·3	ΜΑΥΡΗΛΙΟC ΟΥΗ ΡΟC ΚΑΙCΑΡ Head of M. Aurelius r., bare.	CT ΑΤΤΑΛΟC ΑΡΧΙΑ ΤΡΟC ΗΡΑΚΛΕΩΤΩΝ, and in ex., ΝΕΟΙC Asklepios naked to waist, himation over l. shoulder and legs, seated l. on chair, holding in his r. a patera over a serpent coiled and erect before him; in his l. hand is a crooked staff.
27	Æ 1·5	ΑΥΚΑΙ ΑΝΤΩΝΕΙΝ ΟC Bust of M. Aurelius r., laur., wearing cuirass and paludamentum. [Pl. xx. 9.]	ΗΡΑΚΛ[Ε] ΩΤΩΝ Similar type.

* The letters CT on this coin stand for Statilios not for Στρατηγός. (See Introduction.)

No.	Metal. Size.	Obverse.	Reverse.
		Sept. Severus.	
		...... ЄПСЄ ...... Bust of Sept. Severus r., laur., wearing cuirass and paludamentum.	HPAKΛЄ ΩTΩN Herakles standing to front, head l.; on l. arm, club and lion's skin which also covers his head; with his r., he pours libation upon flaming altar.
28	Æ 1·45	(Countermark, wreath containing letter A)	
		Julia Domna.	
		IOVΛIAΔO MNACЄ BACT Bust of Julia Domna r., draped.	HPA K Λ ЄΩT Ω N Tetrastyle temple containing cultus-statue of goddess (Aphrodite facing): in front of statue, small altar with semicircular cover: in ex., altar garlanded. [Pl. xx. 10.]
29	Æ 1·15		
30	Æ 1·1		
		Macrinus.	
		M·OΠ·C ЄBH MAK PЄIN O C Bust of Macrinus r., laur., wearing cuirass and paludamentum.	HPAK Λ Є ΩTΩN Aphrodite clad in long chiton standing to front, head r.; her r. arm is extended, her l. holds mirror.*
31	Æ 1·0		
		[Pl. xx. 11.]	

* A similar figure of Aphrodite occurs on a coin of Cidramus (p. 82, no. 7, *supra*, Pl. xiii. 4).

CARIA.

No.	Metal. Size.	Obverse.	Reverse.
		HYDISUS. BRONZE. *First Century* B.C.	
1	Æ ·75	Bust of Athena r., wearing crested helmet and aegis: plain border.	ΥΔΙ Bearded figure standing ΣΕΩ [N] to front, head to r. He is armed with helmet and cuirass, rests with r. on spear, and carries shield on l. arm. [Pl. xx. 12.]
2	Æ ·75		

* The armed figure is perhaps a local form of Zeus.

HYLLARIMA.

BRONZE.

Early Imperial Time.

No.	Metal. Size.	Obverse.	Reverse.
1	Æ ·8	ЄΠΙΤЄΙΜΟΘЄΟΥ ΑΡΧΟΝΤΟC Female bust r., hair rolled: border of dots.	ΥΛΛΑΡΙΜЄ ѠΝ Athena standing to front, head l., holding olive-branch in lowered r., and shield and spear in l. : border of dots.
2	Æ ·75		

[Pl. xx. 13.]

IASUS.

Circ. B.C. 250—190.

SILVER.

Persic Standard.

Drachms.

No.	Wt.	Metal. Size.	Obverse.	Reverse.
1	82·0 (pierced)	AR ·75	Head of Apollo r., laur.	IA Youth, Hermias, and dolphin swimming r., l. arm of Hermias over dolphin's back. beneath, ΛΑΜΠΙΤοΣ [Bank Coll.]
2	75·3	AR ·7		,, ,, [Pl. xxi. 1.]
3	76·6	AR ·75		beneath, ΜΕΝΕΣΘΕΥ[Σ] [Pl. xxi. 2.]

Hemidrachms.

No.	Wt.	Metal. Size.	Obverse.	Reverse.
4	42·5	AR ·7	Head of Apollo r., laur.	IA Hermias and dolphin, as above: border of dots. beneath, ΠΑΝΤΑ[Ι]ΝΟΣ
5	37·6	AR ·6	Head of Apollo r., laur.: border of dots.	ΙΑΣΕΩΝ Hermias and dolphin, as above. [Pl. xxi. 3.]

No.	Metal. Size.	Obverse.	Reverse.
		BRONZE.	
6	Æ ·7	Head of Apollo r., laur.	IA Hermias and dolphin, as above. beneath, ΑΝΑΞΙΠΠΟΣ [Pl. xxi. 4.]
7	Æ ·65		beneath, „
8	Æ ·6		„ [Κ]ΤΗΣΙΑΣ
9	Æ ·65		„ ΠΑΥΣΑΝΙΑΣ
10	Æ ·6	Head of Apollo r., laur., hair in formal curls : border of dots.	IA Hermias and dolphin, as above. beneath, ΣΤΗΣΙΟΧΟΣ: the whole within wreath.
11	Æ ·45	Head of Artemis ? r. : border of dots.	IA Hermias and dolphin, as above. beneath, ΠΟ ...: the whole in wreath.
12	Æ ·45	Head of Apollo r., laur.	ΙΑΣ within ivy-wreath. ΕΩΝ [Pl. xxi. 5.]
13	Æ ·5	Lyre within laurel-wreath.	ΙΑϹΕШ Ν Hermias and dolphin, as above. beneath, magistrate's name illegible. [Pl. xxi. 6.]

126 CARIA

No.	Metal. Size.	Obverse.	Reverse.
14	Æ ·65	Apollo naked, standing to front, head r., holding arrow in r.	IAΣEΩN Artemis in short chiton standing to front, drawing arrow from quiver at shoulder, and holding bow in r.: in field r., star: the whole in laurel-wreath.

Imperial Times.

15	Æ ·85	IACOCKT IC TH C Head of Iasos bearded r., wearing diadem; sceptre (?) behind neck: border of dots.	IA CEΩN Hermias and dolphin as on preceding coins: border of dots.

Imperial Coinage.

Caracalla.

16	Æ 1·4	AYKM.. .... Bust of Caracalla r., laur., bearded, wearing cuirass and paludamentum.	IACE ΩN Zeus Sarapis enthroned l., wearing modius and himation; extending r. hand over Kerberos at his feet, and resting with l. on sceptre.

No.	Wt.	Metal. Size.	Obverse.	Reverse.
			IDYMA.	
			Circ. B.C. 437—400.	
			SILVER.	
			Phœnician Standard.	
			Drachm.	
			Head of Pan, full face with pointed ears and horns.	Incuse square, within which, I Δ V M I O N written round a fig-leaf.
1	58·2	Ɍ ·6		
			[Pl. xxi. 8.]	
2	54·6	Ɍ ·65		
3	50·3	Ɍ ·55		
4	56·	Ɍ ·6		
			[Pl. xxi. 9.]	
			Similar head of later style and of feminine appearance.	Similar, but of incuse square traces only remain.
5	58·	Ɍ ·55		
			[Pl. xxi. 10.]	

CARIA.

No.	Metal. Size.	Obverse.	Reverse.
		MYLASA.	
		Eupolemus, General of Cassander.	
		Campaign in Caria B.C. 314.	
		BRONZE.	
		Three Macedonian shields thrown together so that each is partially hidden: the central device of the shields consists of a spear-head: border of dots.	EYΓO ΛEMOY Sword in sheath with strap.
1	Æ ·75		in field l., double axe (labrys).
2	Æ ·65		,, ,, . [Pl. xxi. 11.]
3	Æ ·65		in field l., double axe (labrys).
4	Æ ·65		no symbol, in field, ⋈ [Pl. xxi. 12.]
5	Æ ·7		no symbol, ,, ,,
6	Æ ·65		
		Second Century B.C. *and later.*	
		[For the tetradrachms bearing the types and name of Alexander together with the monogram M and the symbol of Mylasa, Trident and Labrys combined, see Müller, *Num. d'Alex.*, nos. 1141-43. Gold Philippi were also struck at Mylasa in this period, see *Introduction*.]	
		BRONZE.	
7	Æ ·7	Free horse trotting r.	Ornamented trident and labrys combined. [Pl. xxi. 13.]

MYLASA.   129

No.	Metal. Size.	Obverse.	Reverse.
8	Æ ·65	Free horse trotting r.	MTΛA (sic) Ornamented trident.
9	Æ ·65	Similar.	MYΛA Similar. ΣEΩN
10	Æ ·6		
11	Æ ·45	Similar.	M Y Similar. [Pl. xxi. 14.]
12	Æ ·5	type l.	
13	Æ ·45	Forepart of galloping horse r.	MYΛA Similar. ΣEΩN [Pl. xxi. 15.]
14	Æ ·45	Double axe (labrys).	MYΛA Ornamented trident. ΣEΩN [Pl. xxi. 16.]
15	Æ ·3		
16	Æ ·35		

Imperial Times.

17	Æ ·65	Free horse trotting l. : border of dots.	MVΛA CEΩN Double axe (labrys), handle encircled by laurel-wreath : border of dots. [Pl. xxi. 17.]
18	Æ ·55		

s

130　　　　　　　　　CARIA.

No.	Metal, Size.	Obverse.	Reverse.
		Imperial Coinage.	
		Augustus.	
19	Æ ·8	Head of Augustus r., bare: plain border.	ΜΥΛΑ ΣΕΩΝ Head of Zeus Labraundos r., wearing polos.
20	Æ ·8	Head of Augustus r., bare. [Pl. xxii. 1.]	ΜΥΛΑ ϹΕΩΝ Head of Zeus Labraundos r., wearing laureate polos and laurel-wreath, with diadem, ends hanging behind neck.
21	Æ ·85	ΜΥΛΑΣΕΩΝ ΣΕΒΑΣ ΤΟΣ Head of Augustus r., laur.: plain border. [Pl. xxii. 2.]	ΘΛΑΣ ΤΟΣΑ ΝΕΘΗ ΚΕΝ in four lines occupying the whole field: plain border.
22	Æ ·85	ΜΥΛΑ ϹΕΩΝ Head of Augustus r., bare.	ΓΡΑΜ ΜΑΤΕΥ ΟΝΤΟϹ ΥΒΡΕ ΟΥ* in five lines, within a laurel-wreath.
23	Æ ·85	[ΜΥΛΑ] Similar type. ΣΕΩΝ	ΓΡΑΜ ΜΑΤΕΥ ΟΝΤΟΣ ΥΒΡΕΟΥ in four lines, within laurel-wreath.

* This is very probably Hybreas, the orator. See Strabo, 659, 660.

MYLASA. 131

No.	Metal. Size.	Obverse.	Reverse.
24	Æ ·65	Head of Augustus r., bare : plain border.	MVΛΑ ΣΕΩΝ Ornamented trident and labrys combined ; handle encircled by laurel-wreath and standing on the back of a crab.

Hadrian.

25	Æ ·9	//////// ΑΔΡΙΑΝΟΝ //// Head of Hadrian r., laur.	MVΛΑ CEΩN within a wreath of palm ?
26	Æ ·7	ΑVΤΟΚΡΑΤΟΡΑ ΑΔ ΡΙΑΝΟΝ CEBACT ON Bust of Hadrian r., laur., in cuirass and paludamentum.	MVΛΑ CEΩN Ornamented trident.
27	Æ ·75	Same die.	MVΛΑ CEΩN Stag standing r.

Antoninus Pius and Faustina.

28	Æ ·8	ΑΝΤΩΝΙΝ[ΟC] ΚΑΙ CAP Head of Antoninus Pius r., laur.	MVΛΑ [C]EΩN Bust of Faustina r., wearing stephane.

Antoninus Pius and M. Aurelius.

29	Æ 1·0	ΑΙΛΙΟC ΚΑΙCΑΡ ΑΝ ΤΩΝΕΙΝΟC Bust of Antoninus Pius r., laur.	MVΛΑ CEΩN Head of M. Aurelius r., bare.

CARIA.

No.	Metal. Size.	Obverse.	Reverse.
		Sept. Severus.	
30	Æ 1·0	AY KΛC CEYHPOC Π Bust of Severus r., laur., wearing cuirass and paludamentum.	M Y Trident and 'Labrys' ΛΑ CE combined, the handle Ω N standing on a crab: the whole within laurel-wreath. [Pl. xxII. 3.]
31	Æ ·75	AV KΛ·CEΠ·CEB H .... Head of Severus r., laur.	MVΛ ACE Tetrastyle temple containing statue of Zeus ωN Osogos resting on trident with r., and holding eagle in l.
32	Æ ·85		(Ω in inscr.)
		Caracalla.	
33	Æ 1·2	...... AVANTΩNINOC Bust of Caracalla r., laureate, in cuirass and paludamentum.	MYΛΑ CEΩN Zeus standing to front, looking l.; wears himation over l. shoulder and lower limbs; holds in r. patera, and leans with l. on sceptre; at his feet, stag l., looking up. [Pl. xxII. 4.]
34	Æ 1·2	AVKMAP AVAN.... N OC Bust of Caracalla r., bare, wearing cuirass and paludamentum.	MYΛΑ River-god (Kybersos?) CEΩN recumbent l., wearing himation over lower limbs and l. shoulder, holding in r. hand poppy and two ears of corn, and in l. arm cornucopiae.
35	Æ ·8	AVKMAV PANTΩNI Bust of Caracalla r., laur., wearing cuirass and paludamentum.	MVΛ ACE ΩN Tetrastyle temple containing cultus-statue of Zeus Labraundos, wearing polos, and holding in r. bipennis (labrys).

No.	Metal. Size.	Obverse.	Reverse.
36	Æ ·8	AVKMAVPA NTΩNI NOC Bust of Caracalla r., laur., wearing cuirass and paludamentum.	MYΛ A CEΩN Nike advancing r., holding wreath and palm.
		Caracalla and Geta.	
37	Æ 1·5	///////// ΓETAC KAI CAP Busts face to face of Caracalla r. and Geta l., each wearing cuirass and paludamentum.	MV Statues standing [Λ] A face to face of [C] [E] Zeus Osogos and ΩN Zeus Labraundos; Zeus Osogos r., clad in long chiton and himation, rests with r. on trident and holds eagle in l. ; Zeus Labraundos, in terminal form, wears polos, and holds in r. double axe (labrys), and in l. spear.
		Geta.	
38	Æ 1·45	ΠΟ CEΠTI MIOC ΓETAC Bust of Geta r., bare-headed, wearing cuirass and paludamentum.	MVΛΑ CEΩN Tetrastyle temple, within which cultus-statue of Zeus Labraundos facing, wearing polos; from his extended fore-arms hang fillets; he holds in his r. the labrys, and in his l. spear. [Pl. xxii. 5.]
39	Æ 1·35	ΠΟCEΠTIMIO CΓE TAC KAI Bust of Geta, r., bare, wearing cuirass and paludamentum.	Similar.
		Tranquillina.	
40		ΦCABTPA NKYΛΛE NA (sic) Bust of Tranquillina r.	MYΛΑ CE ΩN Zeus Osogos, clad in long chiton and· himation, standing r., holding eagle ?

MYNDUS.

Second and First Centuries B.C.

SILVER.

Attic Standard.

Tetradrachm.

[See Imhoof-Blumer, *Zeit. f. Num.*, iii. 326, Pl. ix. 1.]

Drachms.

No.	Wt.	Metal. Size.	Obverse.	Reverse.
			Head of Zeus r., laur.	ΜΥΝΔΙΩΝ Head-dress of Isis (horns, globe, and plumes, on two ears of corn); in field, magistrate's name; beneath, symbol: border of dots.
1	57·6	AR ·65		Μ ΥΝΔΙΩΝ beneath, star. Ε ΠΙΓΟΝΟΣ
2	48·1	AR ·7		Μ ΥΝΔΙΩ[Ν] ,, thunderbolt (or harpa ?) ΕΡ ΜΟΛΥΚ[ΟΣ]
3	61·5	AR ·75		ΜΥΝΔΙΩΝ beneath, grapes. ΗΡΟΔѠΡΟΣ [Pl. xxii. 6.]
4	51·2	AR ·65		Μ ΥΝΔΙΩΝ ,, star. ΘΕ ΟΔΟΤΟΣ
5	64·3	AR ·7	(Same die as last.)	Μ ΥΝΔΙΩΝ ,, ,, ΘΕΟΔΟΤΟC
6	65·3	AR ·7		ΜΥΝΔΙΩΝ ,, thunderbolt. ΘΕΟΔΩΡΟΣ [Pl. xxii. 7.]

MYNDUS.   135

No.	Wt.	Metal. Size.	Obverse.	Reverse.
7	57·2	AR ·7		M YNΔIΩN beneath, winged KAΛΛICTOΣ thunderbolt.
8	56·2	AR ·65		MYNΔIΩN MHNOΔOTO[Σ]

Hemidrachms.

Head of Dionysos r., wearing ivy-wreath; behind neck, thyrsos. | MYNΔIΩN Winged thunderbolt; in field, magistrate's name: border of dots.

9	33·5	AR ·6		MYNΔIΩN IEPOKΛHΣ
10	29·6	AR ·6		MYNΔIΩN beneath, branch ? MHNOΔO[TOC] [Pl. xxii. 8.]
11	28·	AR ·55		MYNΔIΩN CVMMAXOC
12	30·2	AR ·5		MYNΔIΩN ....

Trihemiobols.

Head of Dionysos r., wearing ivy-wreath. | MYNΔIΩN or MYNΔI Bunch of grapes and magistrate's name: border of dots.

13	11·4	AR ·45		MYNΔI EΞHKEC [Bank Coll.] [Pl. xxii. 9.]
14	15·2	AR ·45		MYNΔI ΘEOΔO
15	16·	AR ·5		MYNΔIΩN ....
16	18·6	AR ·45		illegible.

CARIA.

No.	Metal. Size.	Obverse.	Reverse.
		BRONZE.	
17	Æ 1·0	Head of Zeus r., laur.	ΜΥΝΔΙΩΝ Eagle with open wings standing r., on thunderbolt: border of dots. in front, ΙΣΙΔΩΡΟΣ [Pl. xxii. 10.] [Bank Coll.]
18	Æ ·65	Head of Zeus r., laur.	ΜΥΝΔΙΩΝ Winged thunderbolt, and magistrate's name: border of dots. ΜΗΝΟΔΟ ΤΟC
19	Æ ·6		,,
20	Æ ·6		,, [Pl. xxii. 11.]
21	Æ ·65		ΜΗΝΟΔ[Ο ΤΟC]
22	Æ ·55		,,
23	Æ ·55		ΣΥΜΜΑΧ [ΟΣ]
24	Æ ·7	Head of Apollo r., laur.	ΜΥΝΔΙΩΝ (usually abbreviated). Owl seated to front on filleted olive-branch. beneath, ЄΡ ΜΙΑΣ [Pl. xxii. 12.]
25	Æ ·7		beneath, ΕΡΜ Ι

MYNDUS. 137

No.	Metal. Size.	Obverse.	Reverse.
26	Æ ·75		beneath, ΜΕΛΑ
27	Æ ·75		,, ,,
28	Æ ·7		,, ? ΩϘΠ
29	Æ ·75		,, ,,
30	Æ ·75		,, CΩCT
31	Æ ·7		,, ,,
32	Æ ·7		,, CωƆT
33	Æ ·5	ΜΥΝΔΙΩΝ Pyramidal structure of three stages with a flight of steps on the right. (Fire-altar*) : border of dots.	ΘΕΟ ΚΛ ΗΣ Eagle r., with open wings : border of dots.
34	Æ ·5	Head of Apollo ? r., laur. : border of dots.	ΜΥΝ Portable fire-altar, with ΔΙΩΝ conical top, two handles, narrow waist, broad base, and three feet : border of dots.
35	Æ ·5		
36	Æ ·45		(no inscr. visible).
37	Æ ·45		

[Pl. xxii. 13.]

* This type seems to represent a Persian fire-altar (Atesh-gah). Cf. Perrot and Chipiez, v., 644. The ground-plan of a similar altar occurs on a small bronze coin, which may be also Carian, described in *Cat. Ion.*, p. 324.

T

138   CARIA.

No.	Metal. Size.	Obverse.		Reverse.
38	Æ ·45	Head of Artemis r.: bow and quiver at shoulder: border of dots. [Pl. xxii. 14.]	MYN ΔIΩN	Two dolphins swimming r.: border of dots.
39	Æ ·35			
40	Æ ·35		(MYN ΔIΩN)	
41	Æ ·45		[M] YN Δ	; above dolphins, flower?
42	Æ ·4	Head of Apollo ? r., laur.	MYN ΔIΩN	Tripod.
43	Æ ·35			
44	Æ ·4			
45	Æ ·55	Bearded head r.: border of dots. [Pl. xxii. 15.]	MYNΔI ΩN	Bearded ithyphallic term l.: border of dots.

Imperial.

Nero.

46	Æ ·65	NEPΩN ΣEBAΣTOΣ Bust of Nero r., bareheaded.	MYN ΔIΩN	Branch r.

MYNDUS. 139

No.	Metal. Size.	Obverse.	Reverse.
		Faustina Senior.	
47	Æ 1·15	ΦΑVCTEINA ΘЄΑ CЄ BACTH Head of Faustina r.	MVNΔIΩN Small fire-altar, with semicircular or conical cover and encircled with wreath, placed on the top of a larger square altar, apparently also wreathed: on either side a branch of olive?
		Sept. Severus and Julia Domna.	
48	Æ 1·3	AVK...... VHP..... [I O V Λ I)A ΔOMN A C Busts face to face of Sept. Severus r., and Domna l.	APXΔIΩNOCT OVΔIO ΦA NT OV (obscure) and (in ex.) MVNΔIΩN Apollo and Artemis standing; between them, tripod, around which serpent coils, and beside Artemis a fire-altar. Apollo, head r., clad in long chiton and himation, holds plectrum and lyre; Artemis, veiled, facing, clad in shorter chiton and peplos, holds in each hand a branch.
		[Pl. XXII. 16.]	
49	Æ 1·3	AVΛOV /////// VH PO C KAIOVΛIA Δ O M NAC Similar.	Similar.

No.	Metal. Size.	Obverse.	Reverse.
		NEAPOLIS MYNDIORUM?* BRONZE. *Second or First Century* B.C.	
1	Æ ·6	Head of Apollo r., laur., hair rolled : border of dots.	NE ΑΠ ΟΛΙ ΜΥΝ (?) Lyre; on the left, ΚΟΛΒΑ
		[Pl. xxiii. 1.]	
		* See Introduction.	

NEAPOLIS AD HARPASUM.

BRONZE.

Imperial.

Gordianus Pius.

No.	Metal, Size.	Obverse.	Reverse.
1	Æ ·85	AVTKMAN ΓΟΡΔIA NOC Bust of Gordian III r., laur., wearing cuirass and paludamentum.	NEAΠO ΛEITΩN Athena standing to front, head l., resting on spear with r., and on shield with l. [Pl. xxiii. 2.]
2	Æ ·85	(AVTKMANΓ ΟΡΔIANOC)	
3	Æ ·9	,, ,,	(NEAΠ OΛEITΩN)

Trebonianus Gallus.

4	Æ ·9	AVTTPEBΩNIANOC ΓΑΛΛΟC Bust of Trebonianus Gallus r., laur., wearing paludamentum.	NEAΠO ΛEITΩN Same type.
5	Æ ·8	AVT TPEBΩNIANOC ΓΑΛΛΟC Similar type.	NEAΠO Λ EITΩN Tyche standing l., wearing modius, holding rudder and cornucopiae.

No.	Metal. Size.	Obverse.	Reverse.
		Volusian.	
6	Æ 1·15	AVT K Γ OVIB·OVO ΛOVCIANOC Bust of Volusianus r., laur., wearing cuirass and paludamentum. (Countermark Γ ?)	ΕΠΙ ΚΑΝΔΙΔΟΥ ΓΡ ☩ Δ ΝΕΑΠΟΛΕΙΤΩ Ν Apollo standing l., clad in long chiton and himation, holding in r. plectrum, and with l. supporting lyre, which rests on column.

ORTHOSIA.

No.	Metal. Size.	Obverse.	Reverse.

ORTHOSIA.

BRONZE.

Second Century B.C. ?

1	Æ ·7	Head of Zeus r., laur.	ΟΡΟΩΣΙΕΩΝ Athena standing r., clad in long chiton and chlamys; armed with helmet and shield, and wielding spear. in field r., helmet ? behind, ΑΡΤΕΜΙΔ ΙΑΣ [Pl. XXIII. 3.]

First Century B.C.

2	Æ ·55	ΟΡΟΩΣΙΕΩΝ Head of Dionysos r., wearing ivy-wreath.	ΑΡΙΣΤΕΑΣ ΟΠΛΕΙΤΟΥ Thyrsos filleted. [Pl. XXIII. 4.]
3	Æ ·55		

Imperial Times.

(a) Without heads of Emperors.

4	Æ ·85	Head of Dionysos l., wearing ivy-wreath: border of dots.	Pantheress standing r., with fore-paw raised and head turned back; behind her, a filleted thyrsos placed transversely: border of dots. [Pl. XXIII. 5.]

144   CARIA.

No.	Metal. Size.	Obverse.	Reverse.
5	Æ ·65	OP ΘΩ CIΕΩN Similar type r.: border of dots.	Similar.
6	Æ ·65		[Pl. xxiii. 6.]
7	Æ ·6	(Ο ΡΩΩ CIΕΩN)	(type l.)
8	Æ ·75	OP ΘΩ CI ΕΩN Bust of Senate r., laur., wearing chlamys fastened on shoulder: border of dots.	ΟΡΘΩCI ΕΩN Zeus clad in chiton and himation, standing l., holding thunderbolt, resting on sceptre: border of dots.
9	Æ ·8	CYNKΛΗ ΤΟC Youthful bust of the Senate r., as above, diademed: border of dots.	ΟΡΘΩCI ΕΩN Zeus clad in long chiton, standing l.; r. hand extended, holding thunderbolt; l. resting on sceptre: border of dots.
10	Æ ·7	ΣΥΝΚΛΗ ΤΟΣ Youthful bust of the Senate r., laur.	ΟΡΘΩ ΣΙΕ ΩN Zeus clad in long chiton, standing l.; r. extended, holding thunderbolt; l. resting on sceptre.
		[Pl. xxiii. 7.]	
		(β) With heads or names of Emperors.	
		Vespasian.	
11	Æ ·7	ΟΥΕΣΠΑΣ[ΙΑ] ΝΟΣ ΚΑΙΣΑΡ Head of Vespasian r., laur.	ΟΡΘΩ ΣΙΕ ΩN Zeus standing r., clad in long chiton; r. extended, holding thunderbolt, l. resting on sceptre ?

ORTHOSIA. 145

No.	Metal. Size.	Obverse.	Reverse.
		M. Aurelius.	
12	Æ 1·4	AY KAI M AYAN[T ΩNEINOC] Bust of M. Aurelius r., laur., wearing paludamentum.	OPΘΩ CIEΩN Herakles naked, standing at rest r., leaning on club, over which is lion's skin.

PLARASA.

See APHRODISIAS, p. 25.

U

No.	Metal. Size.	Obverse.	Reverse.
		SEBASTOPOLIS.	
		BRONZE.	
		Time of Vespasian.*	
1	Æ ·65	CEBACTOΠO ΛI TΩN Bust of Zeus r., laur.: border of dots.	ΠAΠIAC AΠOΛΛΩ NIOY Thyrsos filleted, border of dots.
		[Pl. xxiii. 8.]	
		Later Imperial Times.	
2	Æ ·75	Head of young Dionysos r., bound with ivy-wreath: border of dots.	CEBACT OΠOΛEITΩN Cista mystica with half-open lid from which serpent issues r.: border of dots.
		[Pl. xxiii. 9.]	
3	Æ ·75		
4	Æ ·95	IEPACVN KΛHTO[C] Bust of the Senate l.: border of dots.	CEBACTO Π OΛEITΩN Tyche, wearing modius or turreted, standing l., holding rudder and cornucopiae: border of dots.
5	Æ ·85	ΔHMOC Head of youthful Demos r., border of dots.	CEBACTO ΠOΛEITΩN Goddess standing facing, wearing kalathos, veil, and long chiton, with ἀπόπτυγμα; her r. arm bent beneath her breast, her l. hanging at her side: border of dots.
		[Pl. xxiii. 10.]	

* See Introduction.

STRATONICEA.

SILVER.

Rhodian Standard.

Circ. B.C. 166—88.

Hemidrachms.

No.	Wt.	Metal. Size.	Obverse.	Reverse.
1	21·3	AR ·55	Head of Zeus r., laur.	Shallow incuse square, within which, Σ T Eagle l., wings open; above, ΛΕΩΝ; in front, serpent coiled. [Pl. xxiii. 11.]
2	21·9	AR ·5		Σ T Eagle r.; above, ΝΙΚΟΛ ΑΟΣ; in front, star of eight rays.
3	21·3	AR ·45		Σ T Eagle r.; above, ΔΙΟΓΝ ΗΤΟ[Σ]: in front, cornucopiae.
4	19 9	AR ·45		Σ T Eagle r.; above, [Μ]ΕΝΕ ΚΛΗ[Σ]; in front, torch.
5	19·3	AR ·55	(hair in formal curls.) [Pl. xxiii. 12.]	C T Eagle r.; above, ΜΕΝΟΙ ΤΙ ΟC; in front, torch and quiver. [Bank Coll.]

No.	Wt.	Metal. Size.	Obverse.	Reverse.
6	22· pierced	AR ·55	Head of Hekate r., laur., surmounted by crescent; around, ЄKA [T]AIOC CW C ANΔPOY : border of dots.*	Shallow incuse square, within which, CTPATO NIKЄ[W]N Nike advancing r., holding wreath and palm. [Pl. xxiii. 13.]
7	19·8	AR ·6	(inscr. obscure).	C T above, ZWIΛOY P A
8	24·	AR ·55	(no inscr.)	C T above, ΔIONYCIOC; in front, torch.

BRONZE.

9		Æ ·6	Head of Zeus r., laur.	ΣTPATO Eagle, wings open, standing r. on torch. [Pl. xxiii. 14.]
10		Æ ·45	Head of Zeus r., laur.: border of dots.	ΣTPA Eagle, wings open, standing r. on T O ing r. on torch : the whole within shallow incuse square.
11		Æ ·45		
12		Æ ·55		Σ T

* Respecting the magistrate 'Εκαταῖος Σωσάνδρου, see *Introd.* The late form of the omega (ω) on this and the following coin raises the question whether they ought not to be assigned to Imperial Times.

STRATONICEA.   149

No.	Metal. Size.	Obverse.		Reverse.
13	Æ ·5		Ϲ Τ Ρ Α	
14	Æ ·5		C T P A	
		Pl. xxiii. 15.]		
15	Æ ·5	Head of Hekate r., laur., surmounted by crescent: border of dots.	ΣΤΡΑΤΟ ΝΙΚΕΩΝ	Torch: the whole within shallow incuse square.
16	Æ ·45			
17	Æ ·45	[Pl. xxiii. 16.]		
18	Æ ·4	Similar.	ΣΤΡΑ ΙΝΟΤ	Similar.
19	Æ ·35	Torch: border of dots.	ΣΤΡΑΤΟ ΝΙΚΕΩΝ	Torch: border of dots.
20	Æ ·35			
21	Æ ·35			
22	Æ ·35		ΣΤ P[A] TON	

150   CARIA.

No.	Wt.	Metal. Size.	Obverse.	Reverse.
			SILVER.	
			After circ. B.C. 81.	
			Drachm.	
23	52·3	AR ·75	Head of Zeus r., laur.	ΣT PA Hekate standing to front, wearing kalathos and long chiton with peplos; she holds in r. patera, and in l. torch; beside her, altar: border of dots. across field, ΛE ΩN [Pl. xxiii. 17.]
			BRONZE.	
24		Æ ·65	Head of Zeus r., laur.: border of dots.	[ΣTPATO] Pegasos galloping r. NIKEΩN [Pl. xxiii. 18.]
25		Æ ·55	Similar.	ΣTPATO Forepart of Pegasos r. NIKEΩN
26		Æ ·4		
27		Æ ·65	Head of Hekate r., laur., wearing kalathos?: border of dots.	ΣTPATO Pegasos galloping r.: NIKEΩN border of dots. [Pl. xxiii. 19.]
			Head of Hekate r., laur., surmounted by crescent: border of dots.	ΣTPATO Pegasos galloping l. NIKEΩN
28		Æ ·65		in field r., ℞
29		Æ ·65		,, B
30		Æ ·65		,, [,,]

STRATONICEA. 151

No.	Wt.	Metal. Size.	Obverse.	Reverse.
31		Æ ·75	Head of Hekate r., laur., surmounted by crescent: border of dots.	ΣΤΡΑΤΟ Nike advancing r., ΝΙΚΕШΝ holding wreath and palm.
32		Æ ·75		

Imperial Times.

SILVER.

Didrachm.

Augustus to Domitian?

| 33 | 99· | ℞ ·95 | Bust of Augustus? r., laur.: the whole within laurel-wreath. | ΠΥΘΕΑΣ [ΣΑ]ΒΕΙΝΙΑΝ Ο[Υ]* Zeus Panamaros (?) on horseback r.; holding in r. patera (?), and in l. sceptre; in front, lighted altar: in ex. ΣΤΡ ΑΤΟ...... |

[Pl. xxiv. 1.]

BRONZE.

(a) Without heads of Emperors.

Trajan to Sept. Severus?

| 34 | | Æ ·65 | Nike advancing r., holding wreath and palm: border of dots. | CTPA   within a wreath. TONI ΚΕΩΝ |

* Ti. Claudius Sabinianus was a priest of the temple of Zeus Panamaros (*Bull. Corr. Hell.*, xii. 256, no. 37). It is probable that Pytheas was a member of the same priestly family.

No.	Metal. Size.	Obverse.	Reverse.
35	Æ ·75	ЄΠΙC ΑΙΛ ΘЄΟΞЄ ΝΟV Nike advancing l., holding wreath and palm : border of dots.	CTPA TONЄI KЄΩN within laurel-wreath.
36	Æ ·75	[ЄΠΙC]ΑΙΛ ΘЄΟΞЄΝ ΟV Bellerophon naked, standing to front, holding galloping Pegasos l. by the bridle : border of dots.	CTPATONЄIKЄΩN Lighted altar, garlanded, between two tall torches.
37	Æ ·85	CTPATONЄI KЄ Similar type : border of dots.	CTPA TONЄI KЄωN Similar type : border of dots.
38	Æ ·8	BЄΛ Pegasos galloping l. : border of dots. [Pl. xxiv. 2.]	CTPA TONI KЄΩN Similar type, border of dots.
39	Æ ·7	ΙЄPACVN KΛHTOC Bust of the Senate r., laur. : border of dots.	ΙΝΔЄΙ ΘЄA PΩMH Head of Roma r., turreted : border of dots.*
40	Æ ·7	Head of Zeus r., laur. : border of dots.	CTPATO NIKЄΩN Artemis huntress, wearing short chiton, with quiver at shoulder, pulling down stag r. : border of dots. [Pl. xxiv. 3.]
41	Æ ·65		CTPATO NIK ЄΩN

* For the epithet Indica, see *Introduction*.

STRATONICEA.   153

No.	Metal. Size.	Obverse.	Reverse.
42	Æ 1·05	CTPATONI KEΩN Zeus Panamaros (?) as bearded horseman r., radiate, carrying sceptre over l. shoulder, and holding in r. patera ?: border of dots.	ΨΗΦICAMENOY ΦΛΑΥΒΙΟΥ ΔΙΟΜΗΔΟΥC Hekate, with inflated veil, riding l. on lion with radiate head and dog's tail: border of dots.*
			[Pl. xxiv. 4.]
43	Æ ·8	Inscr. illegible.	Inscr. illegible.

Time of Sept. Severus and family.

44	Æ ·85	CTPA TO NIKE.. Similar type; in front, lighted altar: border of dots.	EΠΙ ZΩ CIM O V B Hekate, with inflated veil, riding l. on lion: border of dots.
45	Æ ·85	ΔΗΜΟC Bust of youthful Demos r., laur.: border of dots.	C TP ATON [IKEΩ]N Hekate, with inflated veil, riding l. on lion : border of dots.

(β) With heads of Emperors.

Trajan.

46	Æ ·7	AVNEPBAN TPAIANONCE Head of Trajan r., laur.	INΔEIC TPATONE I Nike advancing l., holding wreath and palm.†

* For the meaning of ΨΗΦICAMENOY, see *Introduction*.
† Respecting INΔEI, see *Introduction*.

x

154 CARIA.

No.	Wt.	Metal. Size.	Obverse.	Reverse.
			Hadrian.	
47		Æ ·7	AVTPAI AΔPIAN [OC] Bust of Hadrian r., laur., wearing cuirass and paludamentum.	CVNKΛHTOC INΔI CTPA Youthful bust of Senate r.
48		Æ ·7		(CVNKΛH [//////////])
			Antoninus Pius.	
49	32·4	Æ ·75	.... AI·T·AIΛ·AΔPI ANOC ANTΩNI NO C Head of Antoninus Pius r., laur. (Countermark, club and lion's skin ?)	ΦΛ APICTOΛAOC Zeus Panamaros (?) CTPATO (in ex.) as bearded horseman r., clad in short chiton; holds in l. long sceptre over shoulder, and in r. patera ?: beneath horse's fore-leg, lighted altar? [Pl. xxiv. 5.]
50		Æ 1·1	AVTKAITAIΛ AΔP IANOC ANTΩN EINOC Head of Antoninus Pius r., laur.	CTPATONEIK EΩ NEΠI C [AIΛ ΘEOΞENOY (in ex.) Hekate standing l., wearing long chiton and peplos, her head surmounted by a crescent and kalathos; she holds in r. patera, and in l. torch: at her feet, dog looking up.

STRATONICEA. 155

No.	Metal. Size.	Obverse.	Reverse.
		Sept. Severus.	
51	Æ 1·4	AV KAΛCE· CEOVH POC Π Bust of Sept. Severus r., laur.; wearing cuirass and paludamentum.	EΠIΠPYΛE ONTO CAΛK [AIOY CT PATONIK E ΩN Zeus seated l. on throne, holding in r. Nike, and resting with l. on sceptre; at his feet, eagle.* [Pl. xxiv. 6.]
		Sept. Severus and Julia Domna.	
52	Æ 1·5	AVKAIC ... PO .... IAΔOMNA Busts face to face of Severus r., laur., wearing cuirass and paludamentum, and of Domna l. (Two countermarks, oblong and circular; in the one, ΘEOV; in the other, a head of Athena r.)	EΠIΦAΛEONTOCAC[?]NAA[P X?]CTPATONIK EΩN Cultus-statue of Artemis Ephesia wearing kalathos, fillets hanging from her hands; at her feet, two stags with heads turned back, looking up to goddess.† [Pl. xxiv. 7.]
53	Æ 1·45	AVKA VHP OC IO VΛ IAΔOMNA (Same type and countermarks.)	Same.
54	Æ 1·5	AVKAICEO .... CIO VΛ IAΔO[MN]A Same type and countermarks.	EΠIΦAΛEONTOC .... AAPX CTPATONIKEΩN Hekate standing to front, head l.; she wears long chiton with peplos; holds in r. patera, and in l. torch; on her head, crescent and kalathos; at her feet, dog looking up.

* At Stratonicea there appear to have been seven Prytaneis in office during each year. (*Bull. Corr. Hell.*, xii. 92.)

† The late M. Waddington told me that he possessed a coin reading EΠI ΠPY ACENA.

156   CARIA.

No.	Metal. Size.	Obverse.	Reverse.
55	Æ 1·5	ΑΥΚΑΙСС ΕΥΗΡΟ C .....ΑΔΟΜΝΑ (Same type and countermarks.)	ΕΠΠΡΥΛΕΟΝΤΟС ΑΛΚΑΙС [ΤΡ [ΑΤ]ΟΝΙΚΕ (in ex.) Ω Ν (in field.) Zeus Panamaros as bearded horseman r., wearing chlamys, and with long sceptre over l. shoulder; in front, flaming altar.
56	Æ 1·4	·ΑΥ·ΚΑΙ ΛΟΥСΕΠС ΕΥΗΡ .... Same type and countermarks.	...... ΛΕΟΝΤΟ С СΤΡΑΤΟ ΝΙΚΕΩΝ Hekate standing to front, head l.; she wears long chiton with peplos, holds in r. patera, and in l. torch; on her head, crescent and kalathos; at her feet, dog looking up.
57	Æ 1·5	ΑΥ .... ΗΡΟ ... C· ΙΟΥ .... ΔΟΜ Same type and countermark (ΘΕΟΥ not legible).	[ΕΠΙΓΡΑΙΑС]ΟΝΟС ΤΟΥ ΚΛΕ ΟΡΟΥ·СΤΡΑΤΟ ΝΙΚ [ΕΩΝ] (in ex.) Hekate as on preceding coin.*
58	Æ 1·45	.,......CΕ ΥΗΡ...... Same type. (Countermark, head of Athena r.)	...... ΙΕΡΟ ΚΛΕ [ΟΥ]С Β С ΤΡΑΤΟΝΙΚ[ΕΩΝ] Nike advancing l., holding wreath and palm.

* In the *Bull. Corr. Hell.*, xii., pp. 257 sq., are several inscriptions dedicated by a Kleobulos, son of Jason, to Zeus Panemerios and Hera. The Grammateus recorded on this coin doubtless belongs to the same family. It is noteworthy that the form Ρ for the letter Β occurs also on coins of Alabanda, of the time of Caracalla, see *supra*, p. 8.

STRATONICEA. 157

No.	Metal. Size.	Obverse.	Reverse.
59	Æ 1·5	...... ЄVHPO C·IOV ΛΙΑΔΟΜΝΑ Same type. (Countermarks, Head of Athena r., and ΘЄΟΥ.)	ЄΠΙ ... ΛΑΝ . ΤЄΟV (?) CΤΡΑΤΟΝΙΚЄ ΩΝ Sacrifice of an ox. Man ($βουθύτης$) wearing short chiton with chlamys and endromides, standing l. on a garlanded platform, holding in l. sceptre, and in r. dagger, which he is about to plunge into the head of a humped bull standing r. beneath a tree. [Pl. XXIV. 8.]

Julia Domna.

60	Æ 1·45	.... O MNANCЄ BA CT[HN] Bust of Julia Domna r. (Countermark, head of Athena r.)	ЄΠΙΑ ΡΧΙЄΡΟΚΛЄ V C B C ΤΡΑΤΟΝΙΚЄ ΩΝ (sic) Male figure naked to waist, wearing helmet, and himation over lower limbs and l. shoulder, seated l. on throne; holds in extended r. statuette of Athena (armed with helmet, spear and shield), and rests with l. on sceptre; behind his throne, shield.
61	Æ 1·15	ΙΟVΛΙΑΔΟ MNANC ЄΒΑ (sic) Bust of Julia Domna r.	ЄΠΙΑΡΧΙЄΡΟΚΛ ... C ΤΡΑΤΟ ΝΙΚЄΩΝ Hekate standing, as on nos. 50, 56, 57 above, but lighted altar before her in place of dog.

Caracalla.

62	Æ ·95	ΑVΤΚΑΙΜΑ ΑΝΤW ΝЄΙΝΟC Bust of Caracalla r., laur.; wearing cuirass and paludamentum.	ЄΠΙCΤΡΑ Φ ΙΛΟCΤΡΑΤ Ǝ Ж IƎ ИO (in field.) WN (in ex.) Cultus-statue of Artemis Ephesia, wearing kalathos, fillets hanging from her hands.
63	Æ ·95		

158 CARIA.

No.	Metal. Size.	Obverse.	Reverse.
		Caracalla and Julia Domna.	
64	Æ 1·4	·AY· ·KM·AAV ANTΩNINOC Bust of Caracalla r., laur., wearing cuirass and paludamentum.	IOV·ΔOM CER·ΘPATONIKEΩN (sic) Bust of Julia Domna r.
		Caracalla and Plautilla.	
65	Æ 1·45	A .... KAIMA VP[A]ИK[A]I ΘE· CE BΛΛEΠΛΑΥΤΙΛΑΝ * Busts face to face of young Caracalla laur., r., and of Plautilla l. (Countermark, bust r.)	ΕΠΙΤΩИ ΠΕΡΤΒΚΛΔΙΟИVCΙΟИCΤΡΑΤΟИΙΚΕΩИ* Hekate standing to front, head l.; she wears long chiton with peplos, holds in r. patera, and in l. torch ; on her head, crescent and kalathos ; at her feet, dog looking up. [Pl. xxiv. 9.]
66	Æ 1·45	Same inscr. Busts in opposite directions. (Countermark, ΘΕΟV)	Same inscr. Zeus Panamaros (?) as bearded horseman, r., wearing chlamys, and with sceptre over l. shoulder ; in front, flaming altar.
67	Æ 1·45		
		Caracalla and Geta.	
68	Æ 1·55	AVKMAPAVP AN TΩNEIN[OC]·ΛCEΠΓΕΤΑC ΚΑΙCΑΡ Busts face to face of young Caracalla l., laur., wearing cuirass and paludamentum, and of Geta r., the latter purposely obliterated. (Countermarks, head of Athena r., and ΘΕΟV.)	ΠPY ZΩCIMO YΠOCITTOVB [CTPATO NIKEΩN Zeus Panamaros, as bearded horseman r., as above, nos. 66, 67, &c. ; in front, flaming altar. [Pl. xxiv. 10.]

* ΘΕ·CΕΒ·ΝΕ· = Θεὰν Σεβαστὴν νέαν : cf. another coin of Plautilla, struck at Alinda, reading ΠΛΑΥΤΙΛΛΑ ΝΕΑ ΘΕΑ ΗΡΑ Mion., iii., p. 313. The reverse legend stands for Επὶ τῶν περὶ Τι.β. Κλ. Διονύσιον.

STRATONICEA. 159

No.	Metal. Size.	Obverse.	Reverse.
69	Æ 1·4	AV KAI MAPAVAИ ...... KAICAP Similar type, but busts in opposite directions, Caracalla r. and Geta (obliterated) l. (Same two countermarks.)	ΕΠΙ[ΓΡΑ?]ΙΑCΟ ΝΟCCΤΡΑ ΤΟИΙΚΕΩΝ Hekate standing to front, head l.; she wears long chiton with peplos, holds in r. patera over flaming altar?, and in l. torch; on her head, crescent and kalathos.
70	Æ 1·4	AV KAIMA AV PAN TΩN ..... KAIΠO(?) CEΠ(?) ..... Similar type, but bust of Caracalla r., *bearded*, that of Geta l., obliterated. (Same two countermarks.)	ΕΠΙ ΠΡΥΙΟΥΛΙΑ ΔΟΜΝΟΙΕΡ ΟΚΛΕΟΥCΤΡΑΤΟИΙΚ ΕΩИ Same type.
71	Æ 1·5	Inscr. illegible. Similar.	ΕΠΙΤΥΓΧΑΝΟΝΤΟ CΓ ΦΙΛΩ [ΝΟC]CΤΡΑΤΟΝΙΚ[ΕΩΝ] Same type.

Severus Alexander.

72	Æ ·8	ΑΛΕΞΑ ΝΔΡΟ C Head of Severus Alexander r., laur.	CΤΡΑΤΟΝ Ι ΚΕΩΝ Zeus seated l. on throne, wearing himation over legs; he holds in extended r. patera, and rests with l. on sceptre. [Pl. XXIV. 11.]

160 CARIA.

No.	Wt.	Metal. Size.	Obverse.	Reverse.
			TABAE. *First Century* B.C. (?) SILVER. Attic Standard. **Drachm.**	
1	58·	AR ·75	Head of young Dionysos r., wearing band across forehead and ivy-wreath.	ΤΑΒΗΝΩΝ Homonoia (?), ΚΞΤ ΤΑ wearing long chiton and kalathos, standing l., holding patera and cornucopiae.* [Pl. xxv. 1.]
			BRONZE.	
2		Æ ·55	Head of Zeus r., laur.	ΤΑΒ ΗΝ Caduceus between caps of the Dioskuri surmounted by stars. [Pl. xxv. 2.]
3		Æ ·6	Head of Zeus r., laur.	Inscr. obscure. Caps of the Dioskuri surmounted by stars. in field above, ΘΕ
4		Æ ·6	Head of Zeus r., laur.: border of dots.	ΤΑΒΗ Similar type: border ΝΩΝ of dots. in field, ΠΑ—ΠΙ—ΑΣ [Pl. xxv. 3.]
5		Æ ·55		in field, ΠΑ—ΠΙ
6		Æ ·55		,, Ζ—Η—Ν ω——Ν

* The first letter Κ of this unexplained reverse inscription is doubtful. Imhoof Blumer (*Mon. Gr.*, p. 316) has read on another specimen, ΚΕ ΤΤΑ Β

TABAE.

No.	Metal. Size.	Obverse.	Reverse.
7	Æ ·7	Head of Zeus r., laur.	TABHNΩN Similar type. in field, Γ O P
8	Æ ·7		,, ,,
9	Æ ·7		TABHNΩN in field, K O
10	Æ ·7		,, ,, ,,
11	Æ ·7		,, ,, ,,
12	Æ ·65		,, ,, M I
13	Æ ·65	Bust of Athena r., wearing crested helmet.	TABHNΩ[N] Humped bull, butting l. above, K
14	Æ ·6	Bust of Athena r., wearing crested helmet; spear over shoulder.	TABHNΩN Humped bull, butting r. in ex. Φ(?)IM [Pl. xxv. 4.]
15	Æ ·35	Veiled female head r., Aphrodite (?).	TA Forepart of humped bull r.
16	Æ ·4		[Pl. xxv. 5.]

Y

No.	Wt.	Metal. Size.	Obverse.	Reverse.
			SILVER.	
			Early Imperial Times to Nero.	
17	31·	𝆄 ·7	Head of bearded Herakles r. : border of dots.* [Pl. xxv. 6.]	ΑΡΤΕΜΩΝ ΠΑΠΙΟΥ Α ΤΑΒΗΝΩΝ Cultus-statue of Aphrodite, facing and wearing polos, a fillet hangs from each extended hand; in field l. and r., crescent and star. †
18	37·5	𝆄 ·75	Same die. [Pl. xxv. 7.] (Broken Coin.)	Α[Ρ]ΤΕΜΩΝ ΠΑ[ΠΙΟΥ] ΑΡ ΤΑΒΗΝΩΝ Artemis clad in short chiton standing r., holding in r. torch, and in l. bow: at her shoulder, quiver.
19	37·5	𝆄 ·75	Bearded head r. (Herakles?) : border of dots.	Similar.
20	39·5	𝆄 ·65	Similar. [Pl. xxv. 8.]	ΤΑΒΗΝΩΝ Zeus naked, advancing r., hurling thunderbolt with r. arm and holding eagle on extended l. ΑΡΤΕΜΩΝ ΠΑΠΙΟΥ ΑΡ

* Cf. the head of Herakles on these coins with a similar head on bronze coins of Nero, struck at Heraclea Salbace (Pl. xx., fig. 5).

† Cf. with this type the coins of Aphrodisias of the age of Augustus, on which the statue of Aphrodite appears precisely as on this coin.

TABAE. 163

No.	Wt.	Metal. Size.	Obverse.	Reverse.
21	26·2	R ·6	Bust of Athena r., wearing crested Corinthian helmet : border of dots.	APTEMWN TABHNWN ΠA Nike advancing r., holding wreath and palm.
22	30·4	R ·55		[APTEMWN ΠA] TABHN- AP WN
23	24·2	R ·55		.... ἱ TABHNΩ[N] AP
24	27·6	R ·6		[A]TTAΛ[OΣ]? TABHNWN AP [Pl. xxv. 9.]
25	26·5	R ·6		[B P]AXYΛΛIΔAΣ T A B H- KAΛ NWN
26	53·7	R ·65	Head of bearded Herakles r. : border of dots.	[T A B H N]WN Homonoia (?) COΛWN standing l., MOY holds patera APICTOΔH and cornu- copiae.
27	44·8	R ·7		
28	51·2	R ·75		TABHNWN CO ΛWN API CTO [Pl. xxv. 10.]

No.	Wt.	Metal, Size.	Obverse.	Reverse.
29	54·3	AR ·75	ΤΑΒΗΝΩΝ Head of young Dionysos r., wearing wreath of ivy: border of dots. [Pl. xxv. 11.]	ΣΕΛΕΥΚΟΣ Poseidon naked, ΒΡΑΧΥΛΛΙ standing r., his ΔΟΥ left foot on prow, and resting with left arm on a trident: behind him a dolphin.
30	48·3	AR ·75		

BRONZE.

(a) Without heads of Emperors.

Time of Nero.

31		Æ ·85	ΤΑΒΗΝΩΝ Head of young Dionysos r., wearing wreath of ivy: border of dots.	ΚΑΛΛΙΚΡΑ ΤΗΣΒ ΡΑΧΥΛ ΙΔ ΟΥ Two filleted thyrsi crossed: the whole in linear circle.
32		Æ ·85		
33		Æ ·8		(ΚΑΛΛΙΚΡ[ΑΤΗΣ] ΒΡΑΧΥΛ ΙΔΟΥ)
34		Æ ·75		[Pl. xxv. 12.]
35		Æ ·65	Similar.	ΚΑΛΛΙΚΡΑΤΗΣ ΒΡΑ Altar, garlanded, on which are the caps of the Dioskuri, and between them a dwarf column; the whole in linear circle.*
36		Æ ·65		
37		Æ ·65		[Pl. xxv. 13.]

* Cf. an identical type on coins of Nero with Magistrate's name ΚΑΛΛΙ (no. 66). This goes to show that the Magistrate, Καλλικράτης Βραχυλλίδου, held office in Nero's reign, and that in all probability the silver coins bearing the name of Σέλευκος Βραχυλλίδου (nos. 29, 30) belong to about the same period.

TABAE. 165

No.	Metal. Size.	Obverse.	Reverse.
38	Æ ·5	Stag r. : border of dots.	TABHN ΩN Caps of the Dioskuri.
39	Æ ·85	TABH NΩN Bust of Bacchante or young Dionysos r., wearing ivy-wreath (?) ; shoulders draped : border of dots.	TABH NΩN Poseidon naked, standing l., his right foot on prow, holding on his extended r., dolphin, and resting with left arm on trident placed upon a dolphin : border of dots.
		[Pl. xxv. 14.]	
40	Æ ·85		

Time of Domitian.

41	Æ ·7	ΔHMOCTABH NωN Bust of youthful Demos r., laur. : border of dots.	ΔIAOP· IE Capricorn r. : border of dots.
42	Æ ·75		
43	Æ ·7		
		[Pl. xxv. 15.]	
44	Æ ·65	TABH NΩN Bust of goddess r., wearing polos : border of dots.	ΔIAO P·IE Altar, on which are the caps of the Dioskuri, surmounted by stars : border of dots.

Time of Sept. Severus and family?

45	Æ ·7	TABH NΩN Bust of Zeus r., laur. : border of dots.	TABH NΩN Nemesis standing l., in usual attitude, holding bridle : border of dots.

166 OLBIA.

No.	Metal. Size.	Obverse.	Reverse.
46	Æ ·75	BOVΛH Bust of Boule r., veiled : border of dots. [Pl. xxv. 16.]	TAB H NΩN Male pantheistic divinity radiate, standing l., naked, holding in r. torch, and in l. lotus-headed sceptre, caduceus, and bow.*
47	Æ ·75	BOVΛH Bust of Boule r., without veil: border of dots.	TABH NΩN Nike advancing r., carrying wreath and palm: border of dots.

Time of Valerian and Gallienus.

No.	Metal. Size.	Obverse.	Reverse.
48	Æ ·9	IЄPOC ΔHMOC Bust of youthful Demos r., laur.; in front, ℞	TABH NΩN Tyche standing l., wearing modius, and holding rudder and cornucopiae : border of dots.
49	Æ ·9		
50	Æ ·8		(TAB HNΩN)
51	Æ ·85		(TAB H NΩN)
52	Æ ·85		(,,)
53	Æ ·85		(,,)
54	Æ ·95		(,,)
55	Æ ·9		(,,)

* Cf. same type on coin of Geta below (no. 88).

TABAE. 167

No.	Metal. Size.	Obverse.	Reverse.
56	Æ ·9	Similar; in front, ℞. [Pl. xxv. 17.]	TAB HNΩN Pan with goat's legs dancing l., snapping the fingers of his right hand, and holding pedum in l.
57	Æ ·9	Similar; in front, ℞.	TABH NΩN Agonistic table, on which, urn; beneath table, amphora: border of dots.
		Time of Gallienus?	
58	Æ ·75	Head of bearded Herakles r., club behind neck: border of dots.	T AB HNΩN Panther l., head raised and turned back as if howling: border of dots.
59	Æ ·75		
60	Æ ·55	Head of bearded Herakles l.: border of dots. [Pl. xxv. 18.]	TABH NΩN Similar type.*
		Imperial Coinage.	
		(β) With heads of Emperors.	
		Germanicus and Drusus.	
61	Æ ·8	...ΑΔΕΛΦΟΙ..... (rest illegible). Heads of Germanicus and Drusus bare, face to face.	TABH NΩNA ΘHNAΓ OPAΣ in four lines within oak-wreath.
62	Æ ·75		

* Cf. similar reverse type on coin of Saloninus, no. 110 (infra, p. 175.)

168   CARIA.

No.	Metal. Size.	Obverse.	Reverse.
		Nero.	
63	Æ ·8	ΣΕΒΑΣΤΟΣ Head of Nero r., laur.	ΤΑΒΗ ΝΩΝ Stag standing l.; in front, ⚔ (Καλλικράτης?)
64	Æ ·75	ΝΕΡΩΝ Head of Nero r., laur.	ΤΑΒΗ ΝΩΝ in two lines, surmounted by two stars; the whole within a wreath of oak and laurel leaves, alternating.
65	Æ ·75		
66	Æ ·7	ΝΕ ΡΩΝ Head of Nero r., laur. [Pl. xxvi. 1.]	ΤΑ ΒΗ ΝΩΝ Altar garlanded, on which are the caps of the Dioskuri, each surmounted by a star, and between them a dwarf column.
67	Æ ·65	[ΝΕΡΩΝ] ΚΑΙΣΑΡ Head of Nero r., laur.	ΤΑΒΗ ΝΩΝ ΚΑΛΛΙ Similar type.
68	Æ ·65		
		Domitian.	
69	Æ 1·05	ΔΟΜΙΤΙΑΝΟΣ ΚΑΙΣΑΡ ΣΕΒΑΣΤΟΣ Head of Domitian r., laur. [Pl. xxvi. 2.]	ΔΙΑΟΡΘΡΙ ΟΥ ΙΕΡΩΝΟΣ ΤΑΒΗ ΝΩΝ Artemis huntress, wearing short chiton, running r., holding in l. bow, and with r. drawing arrow from quiver at her shoulder.
70	Æ 1·		first part of inscr. in opposite direction.

TABAE. 169

No.	Metal. Size.	Obverse.	Reverse.
		Domitia.	
71	Æ ·75	ΔΟΜΙΤΙΑ ϹΕΒΑϹΤΗ Bust of Domitia r. [Pl. xxvi. 3.]	[Δ]ΙΑΟΡΘΡΙ Ο ΥΙΕΡΩΝΟϹ ΤΑ ΒΗ ΝΩΝ Nike standing r., holding wreath and palm.
72	Æ ·75		ΔΙΑ ΟΡΘΡΙ ΟΥΙΕΡΤΑΒΗ type 1.
73	Æ ·75		ΔΙΑ ΟΡΘΡΙ ΟΥΙΕΡΤΑΒΗ type 1.
		Trajan.	
74	Æ ·95	ΑΥΚΑΙΤΡΑΙΑ ΝΟϹ ΑΡΙΓΕΔΑ Head of Trajan r., laur.	ΤΑΒΗ ΝΩΝ Demeter? standing to the front, clad in long chiton with apoptygma; on her head is a kalathos; she holds in r. a bunch of grapes and two ears of corn, and rests with l. on sceptre.
75	Æ ·95	[Pl. xxvi. 4.]	
76	Æ ·95	ΑΥ ΚΑΙ ΤΡΑΙΑΝ ΟϹ ΑΡΙΓΕΡΔΑ Bust of Trajan r., laur.; wearing cuirass and paludamentum.	ΤΑ ΒΗ ΝΩΝ Two identical figures, side by side, of Artemis huntress to the front, wearing short chiton with apoptygma, and holding bow in l., and with r. drawing arrow from quiver at her shoulder.
77	Æ ·9	bust undraped. [Pl. xxvi. 5.]	

z

No.	Metal. Size.	Obverse.	Reverse.
		Plotina.	
78	Æ ·75	ΠΛΩΤΕΙΝ CΕΒΑC ΤΗ Bust of Plotina r., draped.	ΤΑΒΗ ΝΩΝ Nike advancing r., holding wreath and palm.
79	Æ ·8	Similar.	ΤΑΒΗ ΝΩΝ Stag standing r.
		Antoninus Pius.	
80	Æ 1·4	ΑΥΤΚΑΙCΑΡ ΑΝΤΩ ΝΕΙΝΟC Head of Antoninus Pius l., laur.	ΤΑΒΗ ΝΩΝ Artemis and Mên face to face, each wearing Phrygian cap, short chiton with apoptygma, and endromides; Artemis r., holds bow in l., and with r. draws arrow from quiver at her shoulder; Mên l., who wears in addition a long cloak, holds patera, and rests with l. on sceptre.
		M. Aurelius.	
81	Æ 1·5	ΑΥΤ·ΚΑΙ·Μ·ΑΥΡΗΛΙ ΑΝΤΩΝΙΝΟC Head of M. Aurelius r., laur.	ΤΑΒΗ ΝΩΝ Same type as preceding, but altar between divinities.
		Faustina Junior.	
82	Æ 1·	ΦΑΥCΤΕΙΝΑC ΕΒΑC ΤΗ Bust of Faustina Junior r.	ΤΑΒΗ ΝΩΝ Tyche standing l., holding rudder and cornucopiae.

TADAE. 171

No.	Metal. Size.	Obverse.	Reverse.
		Julia Domna.	
83	Æ 1·05	IOVΔO MNACЄB Bust of Julia Domna r. (Countermark, ℞)	TABH NΩN Tyche standing l., holding rudder and cornucopiae.
84	Æ ·95		(TAB HNΩN)
85	Æ ·95	(IOVΛIA CЄBACTH)	
		Caracalla.	
86	Æ 1·45	[AV]TOK·KAI·M· AV ANTΩNЄINOC Bust of young Caracalla r., laur.; wearing cuirass and paludamentum.	APX·APT ЄMI ΔΩPOY (and in ex.) TABHNΩN Artemis and Mên as on no. 80. [Pl. xxvi. 6.]
87	Æ 1·15	AVT·KAI·M·AY· AN TΩNЄINOC Similar.	APXAPTЄMI Δ ΩPOYTABHN Ω N Dionysos wearing long chiton and himation standing l., holding in r. bunch of grapes, and resting with l. on thyrsos bound with fillet; at his feet, panther.
		Geta.	
88	Æ ·8	·Λ·CЄΠ ΓЄTAC·K· Bust of Geta r., bareheaded; wearing cuirass and paludamentum. [Pl. xxvi. 7.]	TAB H NΩN Male pantheistic divinity radiate, standing l., naked, holding in r. torch, and in l. lotus-headed sceptre, caduceus and bow. [Bank Coll.]

172   CARIA.

No.	Metal. Size.	Obverse.	Reverse.
89	Æ ·8	AVT ... ΓΕΤΑC Head of Geta r., bearded and laur.	ΤΑΒ ΗΝΩΝ Nike advancing r., holding wreath and palm.
		Severus Alexander.	
90	Æ 1·45	AV K MAVPCEVAΛE ΞΑΝΔΡΟC Bust of Severus Alexander r., laur.; wearing cuirass and paludamentum. (Countermark, B)	ΑΡΧ·Μ·ΑVΡ· ΙΟV ΛΙΟV in ex. ΤΑΒΗΝΩΝ Hexastyle temple containing statue of Artemis huntress r., in usual attitude.
		Valerian.	
91	Æ 1·4	ΑVΚΑΙΠΟΛΙ ΟVΑΛΕ ΡΙΑΝΟC Bust of Valerian r., radiate; wearing cuirass and paludamentum. (Countermark, B)	ΕΠΙΑΡΧCΤΑΙΑΤΡΟΚ ΑΕΟVC ΤΑΒΗΝΩΝ Artemis and Mên as on no. 80.
92	Æ 1·35	,, ,,	(ΕΠΙΑΡΧCΤΑ ΙΑΤΡΟ ΚΛΕΟ- ΤΑΒΗΝΩΝ) VC
93	Æ 1·45	,, ,,	(ΕΠΙ ΑΡΧΟΝCΤ ΙΑ[ΤΡΟΚ]ΛΕ- ΤΑΒΗΝΩΝ) ΟVC
		Gallienus.	
94	Æ 1·45	ΑVΚΑΙΠΟΛΙ ΓΑΛΛΙ ΗΝΟC Bust of Gallienus r., radiate; wearing cuirass and paludamentum: behind head, Ƃ	ΕΠΙΑΡΧΜΑΡΑVΡ ΔΟ ΜΕCΤ ΧΟVΓ (sic), (in ex.) ΤΑΒΗΝΩΝ Artemis and Mên as on no. 80, but Mên rests on spear instead of sceptre.

TABAE. 173

No.	Metal. Size.	Obverse.	Reverse.
95	Æ ·95	ΑVΚΑΙΠΟΛΙ ΓΑ/ι.ΛΙ HNO[C] Similar.	ΕΠΙΑΡΧ ΙΑCON OCCΙΛ[B]- (in ex.) ΤΑΒΗΝΩΝ ΟΥ Hexastyle temple of Artemis as on no. 90.
96	Æ 1·2	ΑVΚΑΙΠΟΛΙ ΓΑΛΛΙ HNOC Bust of Gallienus r., laur.; wearing cuirass and paludamentum: in front, Ɛ	ΑΡΧ ΙΑCONOC CΙΛΡΟVΤΑ- ɃΗΝΩΝ Tyche, wearing modius and holding rudder and cornucopiae, standing l.
97	Æ 1·15	(ΑVΤΟΚΡ ΚΑΙ ΠΟΠ ΛΓΑΛΛΙΗ ΝΟC)	(ΑΡΧΟ ΙΑCONOC Τ ΑΒΗ ΝΩΝ)
98	Æ 1·2	Similar to 96, but Ɛ behind head.	ΕΠΙ ΑΡΧΙΑCON OCCΙΛΒΟV ΤΑΒΗΝΩΝ Similar type. [Bank Coll.]
99	Æ 1·15	ΑVΤΟΚΡΚΑΙCΑ ΠΟΠ ΛΓΑΛΛΙΗΝΟC Bust of Gallienus r., laur.; wearing cuirass and paludamentum: in front, Β	ΑΡΧΙΑCONOC ΤΑΒΗΝΩΝ Dionysos naked but for himation hanging behind his back, stands to the front, head l., holding in r. kantharos, and resting with l. on thyrsos; at his feet, panther.
100	Æ 1·15	ΑVΤ ΚΑΙ ΠΟΛΙ ΓΑΛ ΛΙΗΝΟC Bust of Gallienus r., laur.; wearing cuirass and paludamentum.	ΕΠΙ ΑΡΧ ΔΟΜΕC ΤΙΧΟΥ ΤΑ ΒΗΝΩΝ Dionysos standing l., wearing long chiton and himation, holding in r. bunch of grapes, and resting with l. on thyrsos; at his feet, panther. [Pl. xxvi. 8.]

No.	Metal. Size.	Obverse.	Reverse.
101	Æ 1·25	AV KAIΠOΛI ΓA[ΛΛI H]NOC Bust of Gallienus r., laur.; wearing cuirass and paludamentum. (Countermark, B)	EΠIAPXIATPOKΛE O VCTA BHNΩN Same type: in field l. C, r. T
102	Æ 1·25	AV KAI ΠOΛI ΓAΛΛI HNOC Bust of Gallienus r., laur.; wearing cuirass and paludamentum: behind, R	EΠI APX ΔO MECTIXOV TABHNΩN Poseidon naked, standing l., with r. foot on dolphin; he rests with l. on trident, and holds on extended r. a seated female figure, resting on sceptre. [Pl. xxvi. 9.]
103	Æ 1·3	AY KAI ΠOΓAΛIH (sic). Bust of Gallienus r., laur.; wearing cuirass and paludamentum: in front, R	APXIA CONOC TABH NΩN Pan with goat's legs dancing l., snapping the fingers of his r. hand, and holding pedum in l. [Pl. xxvi. 10.]

Salonina.

104	Æ ·95	IOYΛ KOPN CAΛΩ NINAC Bust of Salonina r., wearing stephane. (Countermark, B)	TABHNΩN Agonistic urn containing two palms? standing on table: urn inscribed OΛYMΠIA; beneath table, ΠV ΘIA
105	Æ ·95	IOYΛ KOPN CAΛΩ NIN[AC] Similar. (Countermark, B)	TABH NΩN Tyche standing l., wearing modius, and holding rudder and cornucopiae.

TABAE. 175

No.	Metal. Size.	Obverse.	Reverse.
106	Æ ·85	ΙΟΥΛΙ ΚΟΡ ΣΑΛΩΝΙΝΑ Bust of Salonina r., wearing stephane: behind, ℞	ΤΑΒ Η ΝΩΝ Similar.
107	Æ 1·0	Similar, but crescent behind shoulders: behind, ℞	ΤΑΒ Η ΝΩΝ Similar.
108	Æ ·95		
109	Æ ·9	Similar: behind, ℞	ΤΑΒΗ ΝΩΝ Poseidon naked, standing r., his l. foot on prow, and resting with l. arm on trident: behind, dolphin.
110	Æ ·7	ΕΠΙΦΑΚ ΣΑΛΩΝΙΝΟΣ Bust of Saloninus r., laur.	Τ ΑΒ ΗΝΩΝ Panther l., head raised and turned back as if howling. (Cf. same type, nos. 58-60, supra.)

Saloninus.

[Pl. xxvi. 11.]

CARIA.

No.	Wt.	Metal. Size.	Obverse.	Reverse.
			TERMERA. *Circ.* B.C. 500—480. SILVER. Persic Standard? **Tetrobol.**	
1	55·6	AR ·55	Herakles naked (?) kneeling r. on one knee, and holding in l. hand bow, and with r. hand, behind his back, club, the lower end of which projects between his legs: border of dots: style very archaic. [Pl. xxvii. 1.]	Incuse square, containing lion's head r., with open jaws and tongue protruding. [Borrell.]
			TYMNES, TYRANT OF TERMERA. *Circ.* B.C. 480—447. **Drachm.**	
2	72·4	AR ·6	T VMNO Herakles, clad in lion's skin, kneeling r. on one knee, holding in his raised right hand a club above his head, and in his extended left hand a strung bow; at his waist, sword in scabbard; the tail of the lion's skin is twisted up beneath his belt: border of dots. [Pl. xxvii. 2.]	TEPMEPIK ON Incuse square, within which lion's head l., with open jaws. [Newton.]

TRAPEZOPOLIS.

BRONZE.

Imperial Time.

(a) Without heads of Emperors.

No.	Metal. Size.	Obverse.	Reverse.
1	Æ ·9	ΔΗΜΟC Bust of Demos r., laur.; border of dots.	ΤΡΑΠΕΖΟ ΠΟΛΙΤΩΝ Young Dionysos naked, standing l., holding kantharos and resting on thyrsos; at his feet, panther: border of dots. [Pl. XXVII. 3.]
2	Æ ·9	Same die.	ΤΡΑΠΕΖΟΠ ΟΛΙΤΩΝ Mên wearing Phrygian cap, short chiton, cloak, and endromides; holding in r. patera over lighted altar, and resting with l. on sceptre; behind his shoulders, crescent: border of dots. [Pl. XXVII. 4.]
3	Æ ·9	ΒΟΥΛΗΤΡΑ ΠΕΖΟΠ ΟΛΙΤΩΝ Head of Boule r., veiled: border of dots.	ΔΙΑΤΦΛ ΜΑ ΛΥC Ι ΟΥ Kybele, wearing polos and long chiton, standing to front between two lions: border of dots. [Pl. XXVII. 5.]
4	Æ ·75	ΙΕΡΑ ΒΟΥΛΗ Bust of Boule r., veiled: border of dots.	ΤΡΑΠΕΖΟ ΠΟΛΙΤΩ[Ν] Asklepios standing r., looking back, and resting on serpent-staff: border of dots.

No.	Metal. Size.	Obverse.	Reverse.
5	Æ ·75	ΤΡΑΠΕΖΟ ΠΟΛΕΙΤΩΝ Bust of Mên r., wearing laureate Phrygian cap; crescent behind shoulders: border of dots.	Δ ΙΑ ΠΟ ΑΙ ΑΔΡΑΣΤΟΥ Winged Nemesis standing l., r. arm bent at elbow, and plucking chiton at neck; l. hanging down holding bridle: border of dots. [Pl. xxvii. 6.]
6	Æ ·85	ΤΡΑΠΕΖΟΠ ΟΛΕΙΤΩΝ Bust of Demeter r., wearing wreath of corn: border of dots.	ΔΙΑ ΜΚΛΑ [Υ ΔΙΑΝΟΥ](?) Apollo naked, standing r., holding in l. bow, and with right drawing arrow from quiver at his shoulder: border of dots.
7	Æ ·75	ΤΡΑΠΕΖ ΟΠΟΛΕΙΤΩΝ Bust of Mên .r., wearing laureate Phrygian cap; crescent behind shoulders: border of dots.	.... ΔΙΑΝΟΥ Tyche standing l., holding rudder and cornucopiae: border of dots.

(β) With heads of Emperors.

Augustus.

8	Æ ·75	ΣΕΒΑΣΤΟΣ Head of Augustus r., laur.; in front, lituus.	ΤΡΑΠΕΖΟΠΟΛΕΙΤΩΝ ΑΠΟΛΛΟΔΟΤΟΣ ΝΕ shoulder, l. hanging down branch. Apollo naked, standing l., r. hand raised to quiver at holding in field l., ⚹ [Pl. xxvii. 7.]
9	Æ ·75		

TRAPEZOPOLIS. 179

No.	Metal. Size.	Obverse.	Reverse.
10	Æ ·6	ΣΕΒΑΣΤΟΣ Capricorn l., with cornucopiae.	ΑΝΔΡΟΝΙΚ[ΟΣ]* ΓΟΡΓΙΠΠΟΥ Bearded head r., below, ΤΡΑΕ
11	Æ 1·3	Septimius Severus. ΑΥ ΚΑΙ Λ Ο ...... ΟΥ ΗΡΟC ΠΕΡ Bust of Sept. Severus r., laur.; wearing cuirass and paludamentum.	... ΑΡΧ ΤΚΛΑΔΡ ΑCΤΟΥ ΑΡ- ΤΡ ΑΠ ΧΙΠΠΟΥ ΕΖ ΟΠ ΟΛ ΙΤ Ω Ν Kybele standing, facing, wearing polos and long chiton, between two lions, each with forepaw on tympanum. [Pl. xxvii. 8.]
12	Æ ·75	ΑΥ ΚΑΙ Λ CΕΟΥΗΡ ΟC Π ΕΡ Head of Sept. Severus r., laur.	ΤΡΑΠΕΖΟ ΠΟΛΕΙΤΩ· Mên wearing Phrygian cap, short chiton, chlamys, and endromides, and with crescent behind shoulders; holding in r. patera over lighted altar, and resting with l. on sceptre.
13	Æ 1·15	Julia Domna. ΙΟΥΛΙΑΔΟ ΜΝΑ CΕΒΑCΤ Bust of Julia Domna r.	ΕΠΙΑΡΤΑΔΡΑ C ΤΟΥΚΕΖΕ- ΥΞΙ ΝΟϴΟ Ρ Τ Ε ΑΠ Π ΖΟ Ο ΛΙ Τ Ω Ν Kybele enthroned l., wearing polos, at her feet, lion with forepaw raised. [Pl. xxvii. 9.]
14	Æ ·75	ΙΟΥ ΛΙΑ CΕΒΑCΤ Bust of Julia Domna r.	ΤΡΑΠΕΖ ΟΠΟΛΕΙ Kybele standing facing, wearing polos and long chiton; her arms extended over two lions at her sides.

* This magistrate's name occurs on a coin of Augustus reading ΤΡΑ ΠΕΖΟΠΟΛΙΤΩΝ, *Rev.* Thyrsos. (Mion., iii. p. 389, no. 494.)

No.	Wt.	Metal. Size.	Obverse.	Reverse.
			SATRAPS OF CARIA.	
			HECATOMNUS, B.C. 395—377.	
			SILVER.	
			Rhodian Standard.	
			Tetradrachm.	
1	221·	𝓡 1·0	Zeus Stratios or Labraundos standing r., clad in chiton and himation, holding double-axe (labrys) over r. shoulder and long spear in l. [Pl. xxvIII. 1.]	EKATOM Lion standing r.: whole in incuse circle.*

* The coins of Hecatomnus and Mausolus reading EKA and MA and with Milesian types are described in British Museum Cat. Ionia, p. 187 sq.

No.	Wt.	Metal. Size.	Obverse.	Reverse.
			MAUSOLUS, B.C. 377—353.	
			SILVER.	
			Rhodian Standard.	
			Tetradrachms.	
1	233·	Æ ·9	Head of Apollo facing, laur., with flowing hair; chlamys fastened round neck.	MAYΣΣΩΛΛO Zeus Stratios or Labraundos standing r., clad in chiton and himation, holding double-axe (labrys) over r. shoulder and long spear in l., point downwards.
2	230·4	Æ ·9		
3	229·2	Æ 1·0		between Zeus and spear, A [Bank Coll.]
				[Pl. xxviii. 2.]
4	228·	Æ ·95		[Bank Coll.]
5	225·2	Æ ·85		
6	232·7	Æ ·9		in field l., wreath.
				[Pl. xxviii. 3.]
7	332·5	Æ ·95		in field l., Ж
8	229·5	Æ 1·0		„ ME [Bank Coll.]

CARIA.

No.	Wt.	Metal. Size.	Obverse.	Reverse.
				Drachms.
9	56·3	AR ·6	Similar.	Similar.
10	55·9	AR ·55		[Pl. xxviii. 4.]
11	56·6	AR ·55		
12	54·5	AR ·6		
13	46·2 (plated)	AR ·6		
14	56·5	AR ·55		in field l., wreath.
15	49·5	AR ·55		,, ME

SATRAPS OF CARIA.

No.	Wt.	Metal. Size.	Obverse.	Reverse.
			HIDRIEUS, B.C. 351—344. Rhodian Standard. **Tetradrachm.**	
1	232·6	AR 1·0	Head of Apollo facing, laur., with flowing hair; chlamys fastened round neck.	ΙΔΡΙΕΩΣ Zeus Stratios or Labraundos standing r., clad in chiton and himation, holding double-axe (labrys) over r. shoulder and long spear in l., point downwards. between Zeus and spear, E [Pl. xxviii. 5.]
			Didrachms.	
2	104·8	AR ·75	Similar.	Similar. between Zeus and spear, ⋛? [Pl. xxviii. 6.]
3	100·	AR ·8		,, ,, ⋛
4	96·	AR ·7		
			Drachms.	
5	55·7	AR ·55	Similar.	Similar. in field l., Μ [Pl. xxviii. 7.]
6	51·4 (plated)	AR ·6		
			Trihemiobol or Quarter Drachm.	
7	11·6	AR ·4	Similar.	Ι—Δ—Ρ—Ι between the rays of an ornamented star, as on coins of Miletus (cf. Cat. Ion., Pl. xxi. 5—7). [Pl. xxviii. 8.]

No.	Wt.	Metal. Size.	Obverse.	Reverse.
			PIXODARUS, B.C. 340—334.	
			GOLD.	
			Euboic-Attic Standard.	
			Hemistater.	
1	64·1	𝐴𝑉 ·5	Head of Apollo r., laur., hair hanging loose behind. [Pl. xxviii. 9.]	ΠΙΞΩΔΑΡΟ Zeus Stratios or Labraundos standing r., as on silver coins. between Zeus and spear, Ǝ ?*
			Hecte.	
2	21·4	𝐴𝑉 ·35	Similar.	ΠΙΞΩΔ Similar. [Pl. xxviii. 10.]
			Hemihekton.	
3	10·8	𝐴𝑉 ·25	Similar, head l.	ΠΙΞΩΔΑ Similar. [Pl. xxviii. 11.]
			Twenty-fourth.	
4	5·2	𝐴𝑉 ·2	Similar, head l.	Π Ι Double-axe (labrys). [Pl. xxviii. 12.]

* The style and execution of this coin are not altogether beyond suspicion.

No.	Wt.	Metal. Size.	Obverse.	Reverse.
			SILVER.	
			Rhodian Standard.	
			Didrachms.	
5	107·8	ᴙ ·75	Head of Apollo facing, laur., with flowing hair; chlamys fastoned round neck.	ΓΙΞΩΔΑΡΟ[Y] Zeus Stratios or Labraundos standing r., holding labrys and spear.
6	107·1	ᴙ ·8		
				[Pl. xxviii. 13.]
7	106·2	ᴙ ·8		
8	101·7	ᴙ ·65		(Y visible in inscr.)
9	101·3	ᴙ ·8		(„ „)
10	99·	ᴙ ·75		(„ „)
			Drachms.	
11	56·	ᴙ ·6	Similar.	ΓΙΞΩΔΑΡΟΥ Similar.
12	54·8	ᴙ ·65		
13	54·6	ᴙ ·6		
				[Pl. xxviii. 14.]
14	49·6	ᴙ ·55 (plated)		
			Trihemiobol or Quarter Drachm.	
15	11·8	ᴙ ·35	Similar.	ΟϞΑΔΩΞΙϞ between the eight rays of an ornamented star.
				[Pl. xxviii. 15.]

186 CARIA.

No.	Metal. Size.	Obverse.	Reverse.
		# ISLANDS. ## ASTYPALAEA. BRONZE. *Third Century* B.C.	
		Head of Perseus r., wearing winged helmet of Phrygian form.	Harpa.
1	Æ ·45		ΣA [Pl. xxix. 1.]
2	Æ ·45		A Σ
3	Æ ·4		A Σ T Y Π
		Second Century B.C.	
4	Æ ·5	Head of Apollo r., laur.	A beneath which, harpa. [Pl. xxix. 2.]
5	Æ ·6	Head of Perseus r., wearing winged helmet of Phrygian form.	ΑΣΤΥ Head of Medusa facing.
6	Æ ·55		
7	Æ ·55		
8	Æ ·55		[Pl. xxix. 3.]

ASTYPALAEA.   187

No.	Metal. Size.	Obverse.		Reverse.
9	Æ ·5	Head of Medusa facing.	ΑΣΤΥ	Harpa.
10	Æ ·45	[Pl. xxix. 4.]		

First Century B.C.

No.	Metal. Size.	Obverse.		Reverse.
11	Æ ·65	Head of young Dionysos r., wreathed with ivy.	ΑΣΤΥ ΠΑ	Veiled female head r. (Astypalaea ?) : border of dots.
12	Æ ·7	[Pl. xxix. 5.]		
13	Æ ·75	Veiled female head r. (Astypalaea ?)	ΑΣ ΤΥ ΠΑΛ	Male ? head r., in crested helmet.
		[Pl. xxix. 6.]		
14	Æ ·55	Head of Asklepios r.	ΑΣΤΥ ΠΑΛ	Staff of Asklepios with serpent coiled round it.
		[Pl. xxix. 7.]		

Imperial.

Tiberius.

No.	Metal. Size.	Obverse.	Reverse.
15	Æ 1·3	Head of Tiberius r., laur.	ΑΣΤΥ[ΠΑ]ΛΑ //// ΩΝ Nike advancing l., holding wreath.

CARIA.

No.	Wt.	Metal. Size.	Obverse.	Reverse.
			CALYMNA.	
			Early Sixth Century B.C.	
			SILVER.	
			Babylonic Standard.	
			Staters.	
1	156·	R 1·0	Rude archaic head of bearded warrior l., wearing crested helmet, with vizor and cheek-piece.	Lyre (chelys) with seven strings and tortoise-shell bowl, within an incuse adapted to the form of the lyre.
			(pierced.) [Pl. xxix. 8.]	
2	162·2	R ·95		
			Circ. B.C. 300—190.	
			Rhodian Standard.	
			Didrachms.	
3	102·4	R ·8	Head of beardless warrior r., wearing close-fitting crested helmet with vizor over forehead, chin-piece and neck-piece.	KAΛYMNION Lyre (kithara), the whole within dotted square.
4	101·8	R ·8		
5	101·8	R ·8		
6	101·2	R ·75		
			[Pl. xxix. 9.]	

CALYMNA. 189

No.	Wt.	Metal. Size.	Obverse.	Reverse.
7	100·5	AR ·75		
8	99·7	AR ·75		
9	99·6	AR ·75		
				Drachm.
			Similar.	KAΛY MNION Lyre (kithara).
10	49·	AR ·6		
				[Pl. xxix. 10.]
11	37·5 (worn)	AR ·55		
				Hemidrachm.
			Similar.	Similar.
12	22·7	AR ·5		KAΛY [MNION]
				[Pl. xxix. 11.]
				BRONZE.
			Similar.	MYΛ[AK] ΝΩƎN Lyre (kithara).
13		Æ ·8		
14		Æ ·65	Similar.	KAΛY (in field l.). Lyre (kithara).
15		Æ ·55		
16		Æ ·55		
17		Æ ·6		

CARIA.

No.	Metal. Size.	Obverse.	Reverse.
18	Æ ·5	Similar, head l.	KAΛY (beneath). Lyre (kithara).
19	Æ ·5		
20	Æ ·5		[Pl. xxix. 12.]
21	Æ ·45		
22	Æ ·5	(varied).	(KAΛ Y MN ... around)
23	Æ ·5	„	(„ „)
24	Æ ·4	Similar, head r.	KAΛY (in field l.). Lyre (kithara).
25	Æ ·35	Similar.	Lyre (kithara) between two branches.
26	Æ ·3		
27	Æ ·5	Similar, head r.: border of dots.	KAΛY Female head r., veiled.
28	Æ ·55		
29	Æ ·55		[Pl. xxix. 13.]
30	Æ ·45	Similar.	KA within wreath of laurel.

CALYMNA.   191

No.	Metal. Size.	Obverse.	Reverse.
31	Æ ·5	Similar, head r.	KAΛY below wreath of laurel.
32	Æ ·5		
33	Æ ·5		
34	Æ ·5		
35	Æ ·55		
36	Æ ·45		

CARPATHOS.

Posidium.

SILVER.

Phœnician Standard.

Sixth Century B.C.

Staters.

No.	Wt.	Metal. Size.	Obverse.	Reverse.
1	212·	AR ·8	Linear square, containing dotted square, within which two dolphins in opposite directions (the upper one l., the lower r.); beneath them a third smaller dolphin r.: in the two upper corners of the square a flower. Above the back of the upper dolphin traces of ΓO Ϟ? (Cf. Z. f. N., i., pl. iii., 20.) [Pl. XXIX. 14.]	Incuse square, divided by broad band into two oblong compartments, with rough surface. [Carfrae.]
2	208·4	AR ·8	(the larger dolphins in opposite directions (upper one r., lower one l.); no traces of inscr.)	
3	203·	AR ·85	(double linear square enclosing dotted square: no flowers in corners and no inscr.) [Pl. XXIX. 15.]	(The dividing band consists of three parallel lines.)

[For other varieties see Imhoof, *Mon. Grecques*, p. 317.]

C O S.

Seventh Century B.C.

SILVER.

Aeginetic Standard.

Stater.

No.	Wt.	Metal. Size.	Obverse.	Reverse.
1	189·5	AR ·85	Crab.	Rough incuse square irregularly divided into six (?) triangular compartments. Beside it, countermark, small incuse square quartered. [Pl. xxx. 1.] (Cf. also *Num. Chron.*, 1890, pl. ii. 16.)

Diobols.

2	25·	AR ·45	Crab.	Rough incuse square containing irregular markings. [Dorrell.] [Pl. xxx. 2.]
3	24·	AR ·4		
4	21·9	AR ·4		

Obol ?

5	10·7	AR ·3	Crab.	Rough incuse square.

c c

194   CARIA.

No.	Wt.	Metal. Size.	Obverse.	Reverse.
			After B.C. 479. Attic Standard. **Tetradrachms.**	
			ΚΟΣ Naked athlete preparing to hurl the discus; behind him the prize tripod: border of dots.	Incuse square divided diagonally; in centre, crab: border of dots within square.
6	240·4	ℛ ·95	(The tripod stands on a basis.)	
			[*Coins of the Anc.*, pl. xi. 86.]	
7	252·5	ℛ 1·0		(Wreath? border inside square in place of dots.)
			[Pl. xxx. 3.]	
8	258·2	ℛ 1·0	(**ΚΩΣ**) no border visible.	(no border within square.)
			[Pl. xxx. 4.]	
			Late Fifth Century. Attic Standard. **Tetradrachm.**	
			ΚΩΙΟΝ Similar to preceding.	Incuse square, within which border of dots; in centre, crab.
9	253·3	ℛ ·95	(The tripod stands on a basis.)	
			[Pl. xxx. 5.]	
			Circ. B.C. 366—300. Rhodian Standard. **Tetradrachms.**	
			Head of bearded Herakles l., in lion's skin.	**ΚΩΙΟΝ** Incuse square, within which dotted square containing crab and club.
10	235·5	ℛ ·9		above, **ΦΙΛΕΩΝΙΔΑΣ**
			[Pl. xxx. 6.]	

No.	Wt.	Metal. Size.	Obverse.	Reverse.
11	220·7	AR 1·0		KΩION, beneath, ΓPAΞIAN AΞ [Bank Coll.]
12	228·4	AR 1·0		no incuse square; beneath, AΛKI MAXOΣ [Pl. xxx. 7.]
13	230·	AR 1·0		no incuse square; beneath, ΔIΩN
14	229·9	AR ·9	head r.	,, ,, ,, [Pl. xxx. 8.]

Didrachms.

(α) Earlier style.

			Head of young Herakles r., wearing lion's skin.	Incuse square, within which dotted square containing crab; above which, KΩION; and beneath, magistrate's name and club.
15	105·	AR ·75		APIΣTIΩN [Pl. xxx. 9.]
16	99·9	AR ·75		APICTIΩN
17	96·5	AR ·75		APXIΔAMOΣ
			Head of bearded Herakles r., in lion's skin.	KΩION Veiled female head, l. (Demeter?)
18	97·	AR ·8		behind, AΓ or AΓ [Pl. xxx. 10.]
19	95·6	AR ·75		|behind, ΦI

(β) Later style.

| 20 | 104·2 | AR ·75 | | \|behind, ΦIΛ [Pl. xxx. 11.] |

CARIA.

No.	Wt.	Metal. Size.	Obverse.	Reverse.
21	93·2	AR ·75		behind, ΦIΛ
22	102·	AR ·75		,, BITΩN
23	103·7	AR ·75		in front, ,, (head r.) [Bank Coll.]
24	98·5	AR ·75	[Pl. xxx. 12.]	,, ,, (,,)

BRONZE.

25		Æ ·4	Bare head of bearded Herakles r.	KΩI Crab. [Pl. xxx. 13.]
26		Æ ·35	(head beardless.)	[Pl. xxx. 14.]
27		Æ ·55	Female head r., veiled (Demeter ?)	KΩION Crab, beneath which, magistrate's name and usually club. ANAΞANΔ [Pl. xxx. 15.]
28		Æ ·5		ANAΞAN
29		Æ ·5		ΔAMΩN and club below.
30		Æ ·5		[ΔI]AΓO[PAΣ]?
31		Æ ·55		EKATOΔΩP
32		Æ ·45		HPAΓ and club below.
33		Æ ·45		OP[Θ]AΓO? and club below.

No.	Wt.	Metal. Size.	Obverse.	Reverse.
34		Æ ·45		ΓΑΥΣΑΝ? and club above.
35		Æ ·4		ΓΟΛΥΧΑ[ρμος?] and club below.
36		Æ ·5		[ΦΙ]ΛΙΣΚΟΣ
37		Æ ·5		ΦΙΛΙΣΤ[ος]
38		Æ ·55		. . ΑΣΙΜ . . . . (Φρασιμήδης? cf. Paton, 310).
39		Æ ·45		illegible, and club below.
40		Æ ·45		,,
41		Æ ·5		,,

Circ. B.C. 300—166.

(a) *Earlier.* B.C. 300—190.

Tetradrachms.

			Obverse	Reverse
42	222·3	Ɑ 1·1	Head of young Herakles r., wearing lion's skin.	Incuse square, within which dotted square containing crab; above which, ΚΩΙΟΝ; and beneath, bow in case and magistrate's name. (Κ ΩΙΟ Ν) ΤΙΜΟΛΥ ΚΣ [Pl. xxxi. 1.]
43	231·3	Ɑ 1·1	Similar (later style).	ΚΩΙΟΝ no incuse square, similar type. ΜΟΣΧΙΩΝ [Pl. xxxi. 2.]

198   CARIA.

No.	Wt.	Metal. Size.	Obverse.	Reverse.
			Didrachms.	
			Head of young Herakles r., wearing lion's skin.	Incuse square, within which dotted square containing crab; above which, KΩION; and beneath, magistrate's name and club.
44	98·9	Æ ·75		ΔHMHTPIOC [Pl. xxxi. 3.]
45	102·2	Æ ·8		EMΓPEΓΩN
46	102·4	Æ ·75		ΞENOMBPOTOΣ (no inc. sq.) snail between crab's claws. [Pl. xxxi. 4.]
47	98·	Æ ·75		ΠΟΛΥΑΡΧΟ[.]
48	101·2	Æ ·8		CTEΦANOC
49	101·5	Æ ·85		ΙΞΩΙΛΟΣ (no inc. sq.) [Pl. xxxi. 5.]
50	98·2	Æ ·8		KAΛΛIΣTPATOΣ (no inc. sq.)
51	98·8	Æ ·8		KΛEINOΣ (,,) [Pl. xxxi. 6.]
52	105·2	Æ ·85		NIKΩN (no inc. sq.)
53	101·5	Æ ·8	(Same die.)	,, (different die.)
54	102·6	Æ ·8		ΦIΛIΣTOΣ (no inc. sq.)
55	103·	Æ ·8		ΦIΛΩN (,,)

[NOTE.—Nos. 49 55 are later in style than nos. 44–48. Cf. figs. 3, 4 with 5, 6, on the Plate.]

No.	Wt.	Metal. Size.	Obverse.	Reverse.

Drachms.

			Head of bearded Herakles r., in lion's skin.	Incuse square, within which dotted square containing crab; above which, ΚΩΙΟΝ; and beneath, magistrate's name and club.
56	51·9	AR ·55		ΑΡΧΙΔΑΜΟΣ (inc. sq. not visible)
57	46·3	AR ·65		ΕΜΓΡΕΓΩΝ („)
58	50·4	AR ·6		ΙΑΤΡΟΚΛΗΣ [Pl. xxxi. 7.]
59	49·0	AR ·55		ΙΔΟΜΕΝΕΥΣ
60	51·5	AR ·6		ΙΓΓΟΛΟΧΟΣ
61	53·5	AR ·6		ΛΥΚΩΝ
62	54·8	AR ·6		ΜΟΣΧΙ[ΩΝ]
63	47·5	AR ·65		ΓΟΛΥΑΡΧΟΣ (inc. sq. not visible) [Pl. xxxi. 8.]
64	45·2	AR ·65	(Different die.)	ΓΟΛΥΑΡΧΟΣ (diff. die) (inc. sq. not visible)
65	45·2	AR ·65		ΑΜΦΙΔΑΜΑΣ? (obscure) (snail? in place of club under crab).
66	47·5	AR ·65		ΣΩΣΙΣΤΡΑΤΟΣ (incuse square not visible) (snail? in place of club under crab).

No.	Wt.	Metal. Size.	Obverse.	Reverse.
			Hemidrachms.	
67	23·7	ℛ ·5	Head of young Herakles r., in lion's skin.	ΚΩΙΟΝ Crab; beneath, magistrate's name. [Δ]ΗΜΗΤΡΙΟ[C] [Pl. xxxi. 9.]
68	21·3	ℛ ·55	Similar.	ΚΩΙΟΝ Crab; beneath, club and magistrate's name. CTEΦANOC [Pl. xxxi. 10.]
69		ℛ ·5 (plated)		ΕΛΛΑΝΙΚ[ΟΣ]?
70	16·5	ℛ ·45		ΕΓΙΝΙΚΟΣ

(β) *Later.* Circ. B.C. 190—166 ?

[For tetradrachms of Alexander's types, with symbols Crab and club, and with magistrates' names or monograms, see Paton and Hicks, *Inscr. of Cos*, p. 311.]

Didrachms.

No.	Wt.	Metal. Size.	Obverse.	Reverse.
			Head of young Herakles in lion's skin, three-quarter face towards r.	ΚΩΙΟΝ Crab, beneath which club and magistrate's name : the whole within dotted square.
71	104·5	ℛ ·8		ΔΑΜΟΞΕΝΟC [Pl. xxxi. 13.]
72	100·2	ℛ ·8		ΕΥΔΩΡΟΣ
73	98·8	ℛ ·8		ΙΩΙΛΟΣ
74	102·5	ℛ ·8		ΜΙΚΩΝ [Pl. xxxi. 14.]
75	91·2	ℛ ·8		ΜΙΚΩΝ (different dies.)

No.	Wt.	Metal. Size.	Obverse.	Reverse.
			Drachm.	
			Head of bearded Herakles r., in lion's skin.	ΚΩΙΟΝ Crab, beneath which club and magistrate's name: type not enclosed in square.
76	49·8	R ·65		ΑΝΑΞΑΝΔΡΟ[Σ]
77	49·	R ·65		,,
78	47·	R ·6		ΒΑΤΙΩΝ
79	47·	R ·6		ΛΑΕΡΤΑΣ
80	46·5	R ·65		ΞΑΙΓΡΕΤΟΣ [Pl. xxxi. 15.]
81	46·4	R ·65		ΞΑΙΓΡΕΤΟΣ
82	47·4	R ·6		ΓΥΘΙΩΝ
83	44·	R ·55		ΦΙΛΙΝΟ[Σ]
			Hemidrachm.	
			Head of young Herakles r., in lion's skin.	ΚΩΙΩΝ Club and Bow in case; between them magistrate's name.
84	23·	R ·45		ΔΙΟΓΕΝΗΣ; beneath, A [Pl. xxxi. 16.]
			Trihemiobol.	
			Similar.	ΚΩΙΩΝ Similar type.
85	13·	R ·45		ΕΚΑΤΟΔΩ; beneath, coiled serpent.

No.	Metal. Size.	Obverse.	Reverse.
		BRONZE.	
		(a) *Earlier*. B.C. 300—190 ?	
		Head of young Herakles l., in lion's skin.	ΚΩΙΟΝ Crab and club with magistrate's name.
86	Æ ·55		ΑΙΣΧΡΙΩΝ
87	Æ ·55		ΑΝΑΞΑΝ
			[Pl. xxxi. 11.]
88	Æ ·6		ΑΡΑΤοΣ
89	Æ ·55		ΑΡΧΕΠοΛ
90	Æ ·6		[Ε]ΛΛΑΝΙΚοΣ
91	Æ ·6		ΗΡοΔοΤοΣ
92	Æ ·6		,,
93	Æ ·55		ΙΠΠΑΡΧ
94	Æ ·55		ΚΑΦΙΣΙΟ[Σ]?
95	Æ ·6		ΜΙΚΥΘοΣ
96	Æ ·6		[Ξ]ΑΙΓΡΕΤοΣ
97	Æ ·6		ΠΑΥΣΙΜΑΧοΣ
98	Æ ·7		. . . ΣΙ . . . . .

No.	Metal. Size.	Obverse.	Reverse.
99	Æ ·5	Head of young Herakles l., in lion's skin.	K above which, Crab.
100	Æ ·45	type r.	
101	Æ ·45	Head of young Herakles r., in lion's skin.	KΩI Incuse square, within which crab and magistrate's name. ΔΑΜΩΝ [Pl. xxxi. 12.]
102	Æ ·45		ΘΑΥΜΙ (no inc. sq.)

(β) *Later. Circ.* B.C. 190—166?

		Head of young Herakles, three-quarter face towards r., wearing lion's skin.	KΩION Bow in case, and club; beneath, magistrate's name.
103	Æ ·65		ΑΡΧΩΝ [Pl. xxxi. 17.]
104	Æ ·65		ΘΕΥΔΟΤ[ΟΣ]
105	Æ ·7		[Θ]ΕΥΦΙΛΗΤ[ΟΣ]
106	Æ ·65		,,
107	Æ ·7		[Λ]ΑΜΠΙΑΣ
108	Æ ·7		ΠΑΡΜΕΝΙΣΚ[ΟΣ] [Pl. xxxi. 18.]

204 OLBIA.

No.	Metal. Size.	Obverse.	Reverse.
109	Æ ·7		ΦΙΛΙΝΟΣ
110	Æ ·65		,,
111	Æ ·45	Head of Helios, full face.	ΚΩΙΟΝ Club and Bow in case; between them, magistrate's name. ΑΙΣΤΙΩΝ
112	Æ ·45		[Ε]ΠΙΔΑΥΡΙΟΣ
113	Æ ·5		ΜΙΚΥΘΟΣ [Pl. xxxi. 19.]
114	Æ ·5		ΞΑΝΘΙΓΓΟΣ
115	Æ ·55	Head of young Herakles l., in lion's skin.	ΚΩΙΩΝ Bow in case and magistrate's name. (name obscure, ΑΡΧΙΑΣ ?) [Pl. xxxi. 20.]
116	Æ ·45	Head of young Herakles r., in lion's skin.	ΚΩΙ Bow in case and magistrate's name. ΦΙΛΩΝ ?

No.	Wt.	Metal. Size.	Obverse.	Reverse.
			Circ. B.C. 166—88. SILVER. Rhodian Standard. Drachms.	
			Head of young Herakles r., in lion's skin.	KΩIΩN Incuse square, containing crab and club; beneath, magistrate's name.
117	44·3	Æ ·65		APXIAΣ, in field l., Δ [Pl. xxxii. 1.]
118	46·5	Æ ·65		|APXIAΣ, in field r., K
			Drachms of reduced weight, or Tetrobols. (α) With KΩIΩN and one Magistrate's name.	
			Head of Asklepios r., laur.	KΩIΩN Incuse square, containing coiled serpent and magistrate's name.
119	31·7	Æ ·65		ANΘEΣT
120	28·6	Æ ·65		ANΘEΣ beneath serpent, A
121	31·	Æ ·7	(near lower margin A ?)	APIΣTΩ outside inc. sq. HI ?
			(β) With KΩN and one Magistrate's name.	
			Head of Asklepios r., laur.	KΩN Incuse square, containing coiled serpent and magistrate's name.
122	25·7	Æ ·55		ANΔPOΣ Star behind serpent; outside inc. sq. A

CARIA.

No.	Wt.	Metal. Size.	Obverse.	Reverse.
123	34·8	AR ·55	ΑΣ? beneath head.	ΑΝΔΡΟ[Σ] Star behind serpent; outside inc. sq. Δ
124	31·3	AR ·55		ΝΙΚΩΝ Uncertain letter outside inc. sq. [Pl. xxxii. 2.]

(γ) With ΚΩΙ or ΚΩ, one name and title προστάτης.

			Head of Asklepios r., laur.	ΚΩΙ or ΚΩ Incuse square, containing coiled serpent and magistrate's name and title.
125	30·7	AR ·65		ΠΡΟCΤ ΕΥΔΑΜ ΚΩΙ; outside inc. sq. Δ
126	33·5	AR ·7		ΠΡΟΣΤ ΘΕΥΔΟΤ ΚΩΙ; outside, Δ
127	30·7	AR ·6		ΠΡΟΣΤΑ ΘΕΥΔΟΤ ΚΩΙ
128	31·	AR ·55		ΠΡΟΣ ΚΛΕΩ ΚΩ outside inc. sq. Δ
129	29·6	AR ·6		ΠΡΟCΤ ΝΙΚΙΑC ΚΩ outside inc. sq. Δ [Pl. xxxii. 3.]
130	32·	AR ·55		ΠΡΟCΤ ΝΙΚΙΑ ΚΩ outside inc. sq. ΙΑ
131	28·4	AR ·55		ΠΡΟΣΤ ΦΙΛΙΩΝ ΚΩΙ outside inc. sq. Δ?

COS. 207

No.	Wt.	Metal. Size.	Obverse.	Reverse.

(δ) With ΚΩΙ, ΚΩ, or ΚΩΝ and two names.

Head of Asklepios r., laur. | ΚΩΙ, ΚΩ or ΚΩΝ Incuse square containing coiled serpent and two magistrates' names.

No.	Wt.	Metal. Size.	Reverse.
132	31·1	AR ·6	ΑΓΗΣΙΑ } beneath, ΚΩΙ ΘΕΥΦΑΜ } outside square, Δ
133	31·4	AR ·55	ΘΕΥΦΑΜ } beneath, ΚΩ ΑΓΗΣΙΑ } outside square, Δ
134	25·4	AR ·55	ΤΙΣΑΧ } beneath, ΚΩ ΑΛΚΙΔΑ } outside square, Ε
135	30·6	AR ·55	ΑΛΚΙΔΑΜ } beneath, ΚΩΙ ΔΕΙΝΙΑΣ } outside square, Δ
136	31·2	AR ·55	ΔΕΙΝΙΑΣ } beneath, ΚΩ ΝΙΚΟΣΤ } outside square, Ε [Pl. XXXII. 4.]
137	32·	AR ·55	ΝΙΚΟΣΤΡ } beneath, ΚΩ ΔΕΙΝΙΑΣ } outside square, Η ?
138	31·5	AR ·55	ΑΡΙΣΤΟΜ } beneath, ΚΩΙ ΛΟΧΟΣ } outside square, Δ
139	32·8	AR ·6	ΝΙΚΟΜ } beneath, ΚΩΝ ΑΡΙΣΤ } outside square, Δ
140	29·	AR ·6	ΕΥΑΡΑ } beneath, ΚΩΙ ΗΛΙΟΔΩ } outside square, Η
141	30·	AR ·65	ΗΛΙΟΔΩ } beneath, ΚΩ ΕΥΑΡΑΤ } outside square, Η

No.	Wt.	Metal. Size.	Obverse.	Reverse.
142	32·2	AR ·6		Η ΛΙΟΔΩ } beneath, ΚΩΙ ΕΥΑΡΑΤ } outside square, Η
143	32·8	AR ·55		Η ΛΙΟΔ } beneath, ΚΩΙ ΕΥΑΡΑΤ } outside square, Η
144	24·4	AR ·55		Η ΛΙΟΔΩ } beneath, ΚΩΝ ΕΥΑΡΑΤ }
145	31·2	AR ·65		ΝΙΚΑΡΧΟΣ } beneath, ΚΩΝ ΑΣΚΛΗΠΙ }
146	30·7	AR ·55		ΠΑΡΜΕ } beneath, ΚΩ ΓΕΝΟΚΛΗ } outside square, Δ
147	29·3	AR ·55		Π ΑΡΜΕ } beneath, ΚΩ ΓΕΝΟΚ } outside square, Δ
148	28·4	AR ·6		Τ ΙΜΟΓ } beneath, ΚΩΙ ΕΥΔΑ } outside square, Η
149	31·	AR ·6		ΤΙΜΟΞΕΝ } beneath, ΚΩΝ ΕΚΑΤΑΙΟΥ } (star behind serpent.)
150	28·7	AR ·6	beneath head, Δ	ΤΙ ΜΟΞ } beneath, ΚΩΙ ΕΚΑΤΑ } outside square, Δ (star behind serpent.)
			[Pl. xxxii. 5.]	
151	25·1	AR ·55	,, ,, ,,	,, ,, ,,
152	25·3	AR ·55		ΕΚΑΤΑΙ } beneath, ΚΩΙ ΞΕΙΝΟΣ } (star behind serpent.)
153	30·5	AR ·6		Φ ΙΛΟΦΡ } beneath, ΚΩΝ ΜΕΝΩΝ } outside square, Δ

No.	Wt.	Metal. Size.	Obverse.	Reverse.
154	30·4	AR ·55		Φ ΙΛΟΦ } beneath, ΚΩ· ΜΕΝΩΝ } outside square, E ?
155	29·4	AR ·6		ΦΙΛΟΦ } beneath, ΚΩ ΜΕΝΩΝ } outside square, H ?
			BRONZE.	
			Head of young Herakles, three-quarter face towards r., wearing lion's skin.	ΚΩΙΩΝ Bow in case and club, and magistrate's name.
156		Æ ·65		ΑΓΛΑΟΣ
157		Æ ·6		,,
158		Æ ·65		,,
159		Æ ·6		ΔΙΟΜΕ
160		Æ ·65		ΔΙΟΦΑΝ [Pl. xxxii, 6.]
161		Æ ·65		ΕΥΚΡΑ
162		Æ ·6		,,
163		Æ ·65		ΣΩΠΑΤ
164		Æ ·65		illegible.

Nos. 156—164 closely resemble nos. 103—110 of the previous period, but they are distinctly later in style and the inscription is ΚΩΙΩΝ in place of ΚΩΙΟΝ

E E

No.	Wt.	Metal. Size.	Obverse.	Reverse.
			Circ. B.C. 88—50.	
			SILVER.	
			Rhodian (?) Standard.	
			Triobols.	
			Head of Apollo r., laur.	ΚΩΙΩΝ Lyre (kithara) and magistrate's name.
165	20·7	AR ·45		ΑΡΙΣΤΑΙΟΣ
166	19·4	AR ·55		ΑΡΙΣΤΑ[ΙΟΣ]
167	24·1	AR ·45		,,
168	19·1	AR ·5		[ΚΑ]ΛΛΙΠ
			Diobol (?)	
			Head of Apollo r., laur.	ΚΩΙΩΝ Lyre (kithara) and magistrate's name.
169	16·5	AR ·55		ΙΕΡΩΝ [Pl. xxxii. 7.]
			BRONZE.	
			Head of Apollo r., laur.	ΚΩΙΩΝ Lyre (chelys); and magistrate's name: the whole within laurel-wreath.
170		Æ ·95		ΑΛΚΙΔΑΜ
171		Æ ·95		,,

No.	Wt.	Metal. Size.	Obverse.	Reverse.
172		Æ ·9		EMMENI
173		Æ 1·0		EMMEN
174		Æ 1·0		EYKPAT
175		Æ ·95	[Pl. xxxii, 8.]	EYKPAT
176		Æ ·95		EYKPA

SILVER.

Drachm.

177	39·	Æ ·6	Head of Asklepios r., laur.	KΩI Serpent-staff and magistrate's name: the whole within laurel ? wreath. ΑΓΗΣΙΑΣ K [Pl. xxxii. 9.]

BRONZE.

178		Æ ·9	Head of Asklepios r., laur.	KΩIΩN Serpent-staff and magistrate's name: border of dots. ΑΓΗΣΙΑΣ [Pl. xxxii. 10.]
179		Æ ·85		ΑΓΛΑΟΣ
180		Æ ·85		,,
181		Æ ·8		,,

212 CARIA.

No.	Wt.	Metal. Size.	Obverse.	Reverse.
182		Æ ·85		ΑΓΝΩΝ (?)
183		Æ ·9		ΔΙΟΦΑΝ
184		Æ ·85		ΔΙΟΦΑ
185		Æ ·85		ΚΛΕΥΜΑ
186		Æ ·85		ΝΙΚΟΜΗ
187		Æ ·85		ΠΟΛΥΔΑ
188		Æ ·85		ΠΟΛΥΧ(άρης ?)
189		Æ ·85		ΣΑΤΥΡΟΣ
190		Æ ·85		ΦΙΛΙΝΟΣ
191		Æ ·85		ΧΑΡΙΔΑ

SILVER.

Drachm.

			Head of Asklepios r., laur. : border of dots.	ΚΩΙ ΟΝ Coiled serpent r.; beneath, magistrate's name : border of dots.
192	36·2	Æ ·6		ΠΥΘΟΚΛΗΣ
193	32·0	Æ ·6	[Pl. xxxii. 11.]	,, star behind serpent.

COS. 213

No.	Metal. Size.	Obverse.	Reverse.

BRONZE.

Head of Asklepios r., laur. : border of dots. | ΚΩΙΩΝ Coiled serpent r., and magistrate's name : border of dots.

| 194 | Æ ·85 | | ΕΥΑΡΑΤΟΣΔΙ |
| 195 | Æ ·85 | | ΠΥΘΟΚΛΗΣ |

[Pl. xxxii. 12.]

NIKIAS, TYRANT OF COS.

Circ. B.C. 50 *to time of Augustus.*

ΝΙΚΙΑΣ Head of Nikias r., diademed : border of dots. | ΚΩΙΩΝ Head of Asklepios r., laur.; behind, magistrate's name : border of dots.

196	Æ 1·25		ΑΝΤΙΟΧΟΣ
197	Æ 1·2		ΕΥΚΑΡΠΟΣ
198	Æ 1·2		ΚΑΛΛΙΠΠΙΔΗΣ
199	Æ 1·2		ΧΑΡΜΥΛΟΣ

[Pl. xxxii. 13.]

| 200 | Æ 1·2 | | |ΧΑΡΜΥΛΟΣ |

Imperial Times.

(a) Without heads of Emperors.

Bust of Asklepios (?) l., laur. : border of dots. | Inscr. obscure. (ΚΩΙΩΝ ΠΥΘΟ ΚΛΗΣ ?) Coiled serpent r. : border of dots.

| 201 | Æ ·7 | | |

214 CARIA.

No.	Metal. Size.	Obverse.	Reverse.
202	Æ ·95	Bust of Asklepios r., laur.; in front, serpent-staff: border of dots. [Pl. xxxIII. 1.]	ΚΩΙ ΩΝ Lyre (kithara); the whole within laurel-wreath: border of dots.
203	Æ ·8	Head of Asklepios r., laur.: border of dots.	ΚΩΙ ΩΝ Similar.
204	Æ ·8	ΑΣΚΛΑΠΙΟ[Σ] Head of Asklepios r., laur.: in front, serpent-staff: border of dots. [Pl. xxxIII. 2.]	ΚΩΙ ΩΝ Veiled female figure, seated l., resting her chin upon her r. hand: border of dots.
205	Æ ·65	ΚΩΙΩΝ Bust of Asklepios r., laur.; in front, serpent-staff: border of dots.	Palladium l., wielding spear and armed with shield: in front, altar and olive-tree: border of dots. behind, ΚΑΛΥΜΝΙΟΣ
206	Æ ·85	Head of Poseidon r.; in front, dolphin: border of dots.	ΚƱ ΙƱΝ in laurel-wreath: border of dots.
207	Æ ·7		ΚƱ ΙƱΝ [Bank Coll.]
208	Æ 1·05	Bust of Herakles r., bearded; club over l. shoulder: border of dots. [Pl. xxxIII. 3.]	ΚΩΙ ΝΩ Lebes on tripod stand: perched on the rim are two doves, drinking: border of dots.

No.	Metal. Size.	Obverse.	Reverse.
209	Æ ·95	ΟΔΑ ΜΟC Bust of Demos r., bearded; border of dots.	ΚΩΙ ΩΝ Herakles bearded, naked, standing to front, head r., holding on l. arm infant and lion's skin; at his feet, crab: border of dots. [Pl. xxxiii. 4.]
210	Æ ·85	ΑΒΟ ΥΛΑ Bust of Boule r., veiled: border of dots.	ΚΩΙ ΩΝ Herakles bearded, naked, seated to front on rock, head r., turned towards infant, whom he holds upon his l. knee; r. arm of Herakles raised above his head; in field r., above infant's head, star, on l. foot, crab ?: border of dots. [Pl. xxxiii. 5.]
211	Æ ·85		
212	Æ ·85	ΞΕΝΟ ΦΩΝ Head of Xenophon the Physician r., bare: border of dots.	ΚΩΙ ΩΝ Hygieia standing r., feeding serpent from patera: border of dots.
213	Æ ·8		
214	Æ ·75		[Pl. xxxiii. 6.]
215	Æ ·55	ΞΕΝΟΦѠΝ [Ι]ΕΡΕΥ [C] Head of Xenophon the Physician r., bare: border of dots.	ΚΩ Ι ΩΝ Serpent-staff: border of dots.

CARIA.

No.	Metal. Size.	Obverse.	Reverse.
216	Æ ·55	ΙΠ Head of Hippokrates the Physician r., bearded : in front, serpent-staff : border of dots. [Pl. xxxIII. 7.]	ΚΩ ΙΩΝ Serpent-staff: border of dots. Same die as preceding.
217 218	Æ ·5 Æ ·55	Bust of City Tyche r., turreted : border of dots. [Pl. xxxIII. 8.]	ΚΩΙΩΝ Kalathos containing poppy-head and two ears of corn ; on either side, a torch : border of dots.

Imperial.

(β) With heads and names of Emperors.

Augustus.

		ΣΕΒΑΣΤΟΣ Head of Augustus r., laur.	ΚΩΙΩΝ Head of Asklepios r., laur., and magistrate's name.
219	Æ ·8		ΝΙΚ[ΑΓΟΡΑΣ] ΔΑ
220	Æ ·85	[Pl. xxxIII. 9.]	ΝΙΚΑΓΟ[ΡΑΣ ΔΑ]
221	Æ ·75		ΝΙΚ[ΑΓΟΡΑΣ ΔΑ]
222	Æ ·75		[ΝΙΚΑΓΟ]ΡΑΣ ΔΑ
223	Æ ·85		ΧΑΡΜΥΛΟΣ Β
224 225	Æ ·75 Æ ·85	ΣΕΒΑΣΤΟΣ Head of ΚΩΙΩΝ Augustus r., laur.	ΕΙΡΑΝΑ Head of Eirene r., laur., hair rolled : around, magistrate's name. ΣΟΦΟΚΛΗΣ ΤΙΜΟΞΕΝΟΥ

No.	Metal. Size.	Obverse.	Reverse.
226	Æ ·65	ΣΕΒΑΣΤΟΣ Head of Augustus r., laur.	ΚΩΙΩΝ Club, serpent-staff, and name. ΣΟΦΟΚΛΗΣ
227	Æ ·65		,,
228	Æ ·6		,,
229	Æ ·75	ΣΕΒΑΣΤΟΣ Head of Augustus r., laur.	ΚΩΙΩΝ Serpent-staff and magistrate's name. ΠΥΘΟΝΙΚΟΣΤΙΜΟΞΕΝΟΥ
230	Æ ·6	ΣΕΒΑΣΤΟΣ Head of Augustus r., laur.	ΚΩΙΩΝ Head of Herakles r., in lion's skin, and magistrate's name. ΠΥΘΟΝΙΚΟΣ
231	Æ ·55		,,
232	Æ ·6		,,
233	Æ ·6		,,
234	Æ ·55		,,
		Caius (Caligula).	
235	Æ 1·	ΓΑΙΟΣ ΚΑΙΣΑΡΣΕΒΑΣΤΟΣ ΓΕΡΜΑΝΙΚΟΣ Head of Caligula r., laur.	ΚΩ ΙΩΝ Serpent coiled r., around, [ο] ΟΠΤΙΜΟΣ ΕΥΔΑΜΟΣ B̄

[Pl. xxxiii. 10.]

218   CARIA.

No.	Metal. Size.	Obverse.	Reverse.
		Domitian.	
236	Æ ·6	.... ЄΒΑΣΤ .. Head of Domitian r., laur.	ΚΩ [Ι]ΩΝ Serpent-staff.
		Domitia.	
237	Æ ·5	ΔΟΜΙΤΙΑ ΣΕΒΑΣΤΗ (obscure) Bust of Domitia r.	ΚΩΙΩΝ Two long torches apparently bound with wreaths.
238	Æ ·5		
		Trajan (?)	
239	Æ ·9	Inscr. obscure. Head of Trajan r., laur.	ΚΩΙ ΩΝ Herakles, naked, standing to front, head l., holding in outstretched r. patera ?, and on l. arm club and lion's skin.
240	Æ ·7	Inscr. obscure. Head of Trajan r., laur.	ΚΩΙ ΩΝ Club.
		Hadrian.	
241	Æ 1·1	.... ΚΑΙCΑΡΑΔ ΡΙΑΝΟC ΟΛΟΝ (?) ///////// Bust of Hadrian r., laur., wearing paludamentum.	ΚΩΙ ΩΝ Asklepios facing, head l., resting with r. on serpent-staff.

No.	Metal. Size.	Obverse.	Reverse.
242	Æ ·85	AVTOK AΔPIANOC CЄB Similar.	KΩI ΩN Statue on basis of Herakles naked, to front, head r., resting on club covered with lion's skin.
243	Æ ·5	Inscr. obscure. Head of Hadrian r., laur.	KΩIΩN Helmeted bust of Athena? l.

Antoninus Pius.

244	Æ 1·2	AY KAIΣAΔPI AN TΩNINOΣ Head of Antoninus Pius r., laur.	KΩI ΩN Veiled female figure standing l., resting on sceptre and holding patera over portable lighted altar. [Pl. xxxiii. 11.]
245	Æ 1·15	Similar, but C in place of Σ	Similar.

L. Verus.

246	Æ 1·4	AV·K·ΛOV·AVP·OVH POC. CЄBAC·AP MENIAKOC Bust of L. Verus r., laur., wearing cuirass and paludamentum.	KΩIΩN in ex. Distyle temple, containing statues of Asklepios l. and Hygieia r., with usual attributes.

Julia Domna.

247	Æ ·8	IOVΛIA CЄBACTH Bust of Domna r.	KΩI ΩN Veiled female figure standing l., resting on sceptre and holding patera over portable lighted altar.

220   CARIA.

No.	Metal. Size.	Obverse.	Reverse.
		Caracalla.	
248	Æ 1·25	AV·K·MAP·AY AN TΩNEINOC Bust of Caracalla r., laur., wearing cuirass and paludamentum.	KΩI ΩN Statue on basis of naked Herakles l., holding in outstretched r. patera, and on l. arm club and lion's skin. [Pl. xxxiii. 12.]
249	Æ 1·	MAP AVP ANTΩNI NOC Similar.	KΩI Ω[N] Nike standing l., holding wreath and palm; around, AP XHC ME NE [KPATOVC]
		Geta.	
250	Æ ·1	AV KAI ΠOΠ CEΠTI ΓETAC Bust of Geta r., laur., wearing cuirass and paludamentum.	KΩI ΩN Nike standing l., holding wreath and palm; around, [AP XHC] ME N E KPA TOVC
		Philippus Senior.	
251	Æ 1·15	AVT·K·M·IOV· ΦIΛIΠ ΠOC Bust of Philip r., laur., wearing cuirass and paludamentum.	KΩI ΩN Female figure turreted, facing, resting on sceptre with r., and holding cornucopiae on l. arm; she wears long chiton, peplos and veil (City Tyche ?) [Pl. xxxiii. 13.]

(For Alliance Coin with Halicarnassus, see supra p. 112.)

No.	Wt.	Metal. Size.	Obverse.	Reverse.
			MEGISTE. *Circ.* B.C. 333—304. Rhodian Standard. **SILVER.** **Drachms.**	
1	43·	R ·6	Head of Helios l., with short hair, on radiate disk.	M E Rose with bud on either side: whole in incuse circle. [Pl. xxxiv. 1.]
2	46·	R ·55		[Pl. xxxiv. 2.]
3	48·5	R ·55		[Pl. xxxiv. 3.]
			BRONZE.	
4		Æ ·4	Similar head r.	M E Rose.

NISYROS.

Circ. B.C. 350—300.

BRONZE.

No.	Metal. Size.	Obverse.	Reverse.
1	Æ ·5	Bearded head r. (Poseidon).	NI Dolphin r., and trident crossed.
2	Æ ·4	Similar. [Pl. xxxiv. 4.]	Dolphin r.: beneath, trident r.
3	Æ ·4	Head of Zeus Ammon, r., laur.	NI Dolphin r. and trident ?
4	Æ ·55	Female head r., in stephane, hair rolled. [Pl. xxxiv. 5.]	Dolphin r.; beneath, trident l.
5	Æ ·5		ΝΙΣΥ
6	Æ ·45		,,
7	Æ ·5		,,

RHODES.

CAMIRUS.

Circ. B.C. 600—500.

ELECTRUM.

Aeginetic Standard.

Twenty-fourth.

No.	Wt.	Metal. Size.	Obverse.	Reverse.
1	8·1	El. ·3	Fig-leaf. [Pl. xxxiv. 6.]	Incuse square, within which a deeper small incuse depression. (Lawson, Smyrna.)

SILVER.

Aeginetic Standard.

Staters.

No.	Wt.	Metal. Size.	Obverse.	Reverse.
2	189·6	Æ ·75	Fig-leaf with sprouts in the form ψ in the intervals of the lobes. [Pl. xxxiv. 7.]	Incuse divided into two oblong compartments, with rough surfaces.
3	187·	Æ ·85	(two young figs sprouting from stalk of leaf.) [Pl. xxxiv. 8.]	
4	181·	Æ ·8	(two young figs sprouting from stalk of leaf.)	
5	185·	Æ ·8		(surfaces scored with irregular lines.)

CARIA.

No.	Wt.	Metal. Size.	Obverse.	Reverse.
6	181·	AR ·85	(leaf more realistic, no sprouts between lobes, A-Ж beside stalk.) [Pl. xxxiv. 9.]	(surfaces scored with irregular lines.)
7	184·7	AR ·8	(leaf more realistic, no sprouts between lobes; without inscr.)	(surfaces scored with irregular lines.)

Drachma.

8	93·1	AR ·6	Fig-leaf with sprouts between lobes, as on no. 2. [Pl. xxxiv. 10.]	Incuse square divided into two oblong compartments.
9	92·8	AR ·65	(Stalk of leaf ends in volutes.) [Pl. xxxiv. 11.]	(Rough incuse square.)

Tritemorion.

10	9·1	AR ·3	Fig-leaf.	Incuse square.

Hemiobol.

11	7·6	AR ·25	Fig-leaf.	Incuse square.

Circ. B.C. 500—408.

Persic ? Standard.

Stater.

12	175·2	AR ·75	Fig-leaf with sprouts in the form of Y in the intervals of the lobes. [Pl. xxxiv. 12.]	KAMI PEΩN within an incuse square divided into two oblong halves.

No.	Wt.	Metal. Size.	Obverse.	Reverse.
			Trihemiobol.	
13	18·3	AR ·4	Fig-leaf.	K A within incuse square divided into two oblong halves. [Pl. xxxiv. 13.]
			Obol.	
14	11·2	AR ·4	Rose.	KA Griffin's head l.: the whole in incuse square.* [Pl. xxxiv. 14.]
				BRONZE.
15		Æ ·35	Fig leaf.	K A in two quarters of a wheel of four spokes: the whole within circular incuse. [Pl. xxxiv. 15.]

* This coin is conjecturally attributed by Imhoof-Blumer (*Mon. Gr.*, p. 321) to the small island of Casos, about 70 stadia W. of Carpathos (Strab., x. 18). As the types differ from those of the contemporary coins of Camirus, and as Casos seems to have been a prosperous port, as it was assessed at 1000 drachms in the Athenian tribute lists, there is something to be said in favour of M. Imhoof-Blumer's hypothesis. On the other hand it seems very improbable that the Rose, the characteristic symbol of the island of Rhodes, should make its first appearance as a coin-type at Casos.

No.	Wt.	Metal. Size.	Obverse.	Reverse.
			IALYSUS.	
			Circ. B.C. 500—408.	
			SILVER.	
			Phoenician Standard.	
			Staters.	
1	222·8	AR ·8	Forepart of winged boar l.	IEΛVΣIΟΝ Eagle's head r. within dotted square; in r. upper corner a floral volute : whole in incuse square. [Pl. xxxv. 1.]
2	229·4	AR ·9	(type r.)	I(IΛΛVΣIΟΝ type l.) [Pl. xxxv. 2.]
3	233·4	AR 1·05	IAΛV Σ I ON Forepart of winged boar l.; beneath, helmet with cheek pieces: border of dots: flat fabric.	IAΛVΣIΟΝ Eagle's head l. within dotted square; volute as above in l. corner: whole in incuse square. [Pl. xxxv. 3.]
			Diobols.	
4	16·1	AR ·35	Forepart of winged boar l.	No inscr. Eagle's head l. in dotted square: whole in incuse square.
5	14·8	AR ·35		
			Obol.	
6	7·8	AR ·25	Similar.	Similar.

IALYSUS.   227

No.	Wt.	Metal. Size.	Obverse.	Reverse.
			Persic Standard.	
			Drachm.	
7	75·9	Æ ·6	Forepart of winged boar l. [Pl. xxxv. 4.]	No inscr. Eagle's head l. in dotted square; volute in l. upper corner as above: whole in incuse square.
			Triobol?	
8	31·6	Æ ·45	Similar. [Pl. xxxv. 5.]	Similar.
			Hemiobol.	
9	6·5	Æ ·3	Forepart of winged horse r. A [Pl. xxxv. 6.]	Rose within dotted square: whole in incuse square.

CARIA.

No.	Wt.	Metal. Size.	Obverse.	Reverse.

LINDUS.

Circ. B.C. 600—500.

SILVER.

Phoenician Standard.

Staters.

1	210·3	𝔄 ·85	Lion's head r., with open jaws, within dotted square. [Pl. xxxv. 7.]	Incuse divided into two oblong compartments, the surfaces of which are scored with irregular lines. [Bank Collection.]
2	213·	𝔄 ·8	(tuft of hair on lion's forehead, dotted square not seen.) [Pl. xxxv. 8.]	(ΛΙΝΔΙ on bar dividing incuses; surfaces maculated.)

Diobols.

3	16·1	𝔄 ·35	Lion's head r., with open jaws. [Pl. xxxv. 9.]	Incuse square divided into two oblong halves; surfaces irregular.
4	15·2	𝔄 ·35		
5	13·7	𝔄 ·35		[Newton.]

No.	Wt.	Metal. Size.	Obverse.	Reverse.
			Circ. B.C. 500—408.	
			Phoenician Standard.	
			Tetrobols.	
			Forepart of horse r.*	Lion's head l., with open jaws, within dotted square: whole in incuse square.
6	33·2	Æ ·45		
7	33·	Æ ·45		(type r.)
8	32·7	Æ ·45		(,,)
9	32·3	Æ ·45		(,,)
				[Pl. xxxv. 10.]
10	32·	Æ ·45		(type r.)
11	31·6	Æ ·4		(,,)
			Obol.	
			Forepart of horse r.	Lion's head l., with open jaws, within dotted square: whole in incuse square.
12	7·9	Æ ·25		

* Most of these coins have a faint inscription in front of the horse, apparently [Λ]ΙΝΔΙ. Nos. 6—12, with the exception of no. 8, were procured from M. Biliotti during the time that he was consul at Rhodes. M. J. P. Six's attribution of them to Mylasa (*Num. Chron.* 1890) is untenable.

CARIA.

No.	Wt.	Metal. Size.	Obverse.	Reverse.
			RHODUS.	
			Circ. B.C. 408—400.	
			SILVER.	
			Attic Standard.*	
			Tetradrachm.	
1	258·8	Æ ·95	Head of Helios three-quarter face towards r., hair flying loose; rough work. [Pl. xxxvi. 1.]	POΔION Rose; on either side, vine tendril and bunch of grapes symmetrically arranged: the whole in incuse square.
			Hemidrachms.	
2	27·2	Æ ·45	Similar type. [Pl. xxxvi. 2.]	[P]ΘΔIΘɪ (*sic*) Similar.
3	29·5	Æ ·5	Head of Helios three-quarter face towards r., and inclined on one side as if looking over shoulder; hair flying loose.	P O Rose: incuse square.
4	28·7	Æ ·45		
5	28·4	Æ ·45	[Pl. xxxvi. 3.] [Pl. xxxvi. 4.]	
6	28·3	Æ ·5		
7	28·3	Æ ·45		
8	28·6	Æ ·45		(Astragalos in place of letter O)†

* The coins of Samos of this period are also of Attic weight.
† Cf. Imhoof-Blumer, *Zeit. f. Num.* 1880, p. 28, no. 9.

RHODUS.   231

No.	Wt.	Metal. Size.	Obverse.	Reverse.
9	27·6	Æ ·45	Similar.	P O Head of Rhodos r., hair in sphendone: whole in incuse square.*

Circ. B.C. 400—333.

GOLD.

Euboic Standard.

Stater.

10	132·6	N ·7	Head of Helios three-quarter face towards r., hair falling in locks suggesting rays.	POΔION Rose with vine-branch, grapes, and E on l., and rose bud on r.: traces of incuse square.

[Pl. xxxɪv. 5.]

SILVER.

Rhodian Standard.

Tetradrachms.

11	234·2	Æ ·95	Head of Helios three-quarter face towards r., hair loose.	POΔION Rose with bud; in field, varying letter and symbol: whole in incuse square. l., sphinx seated l.; r., pendent† bud.
12	233·3	Æ ·9		l., bud and A; r., eye in profile, with eyebrow, r.

* Imhoof-Blumer, *l.c.*, no. 10, describes a specimen with the letter Λ (Δ?) behind the head of Rhodos in the left upper corner of the square, and with stars upon the sphendone of the goddess.

† The bud on all the other specimens (nos. 11—25) is in an upright position.

No.	Wt.	Metal. Size.	Obverse.	Reverse.
13	229·	R ·95		l., bud and A; r., ⊢⊕
14	233·	R ·95		l., ear of corn; r., bell-shaped flower in place of bud, and A
15	228·4	R ·9		l., bud and Δ; r., dolphin downwards.
16	232·5	R ·95		l., bud and ⊥; r., lyre (kithara). [Pl. xxxvi. 6.]
17	233·2	R ·9		l., bud and ⊥; r., caduceus.
18	229·7	R ·9		l., bud and ⋜; r., owl r.
19	233·6	R ·95		l., bud and T; r., aplustre(?) of unusual form. [Pl. xxxvi. 7.]
20	235·	R ·95		(POΔ ION); l., Φ and obscure symbol; r., bud.
21	229·7	R ·95		l., bud and Φ; r., Y and shell (pecten).
22	236·6	R 1·		l., bud and Φ; r., grain of corn.
23	233·6	R ·95		(POΔ ION); l., grain of corn and Φ r., bud.
24	229·8	R ·95		l., bud and Φ; r., kylix.
25	235·8	R ·95		l., bud and Φ; r., Boeotian shield.

No.	Wt.	Metal. Size.	Obverse.	Reverse.
			Didrachms.	
			Head of Helios three-quarter face towards r., hair loose.	POΔION Rose with bud; in field, varying symbol and letter: whole in incuse square.
26	104·6	Æ ·75		l., thunderbolt and Δ; r., bud. (incuse square not apparent.)
27	105·5	Æ ·8		l., bunch of grapes and E; r., bud. [Pl. xxxvi. 8.]
28	106·2	Æ ·7		Similar.
29	103·5	Æ ·7		,,
30	100·5	Æ ·75		,, (incuse circular.)
31	104·4	Æ ·75		l., grapes hanging from stalk attached to rose, and E; r., bud; (incuse not apparent).
32	102·7	Æ ·7		Similar (?) (,,).
33	103·9	Æ ·7		Similar, but E in field r.
34	104·8	Æ ·7		E Y l., grapes; r., bud; (incuse not apparent). [Pl. xxxvi. 9.]
35	99·8	Æ ·8		l., grapes and EY; r., bud (incuse not apparent). [Pl. xxxvi. 10.]
36	103·3	Æ ·75		E Y l., grapes hanging from stalk attached to rose; r., bud; (incuse not apparent).
37	100·9	Æ ·75		l., bee and NI; r., bud; (incuse not apparent).

No.	Wt.	Metal. Size.	Obverse.	Reverse.
			Drachms.	
			Head of Helios three-quarter face towards r., hair loose.	ΡΟΔΙΟΝ Rose; details varied: whole in incuse square.
38	52·1	𝐴𝑅 ·6		l., grapes and Δ; r., bud.
39	56·	𝐴𝑅 ·6		bud pendent from stalk on either side; in field r., I
			[Pl. xxxvi. 11.]	
40	53·8	𝐴𝑅 ·55		Similar.
			Didrachm.	
			Head of Helios in profile r., hair bound with radiate taenia.	ΡΟΔΙΟΝ Rose.
41	101·3	𝐴𝑅 ·75		l., cornucopiae and ΕΥ; r., bud.
			[Pl. xxxvi. 12.]	
			Diobol.	
			Similar.	P [O] Two rosebuds springing from opening leaves: whole in incuse.
42	17·3	𝐴𝑅 ·4		between buds, E
			[Pl. xxxvi. 13.]	

Circ. B.C. 333—304.

Didrachms.

			Head of Helios three-quarter face towards r., hair loose.	P O Rose with bud on r. side, varying symbol on l., and magistrate's name above.
43	101·4	𝐴𝑅 ·75		ΑΝΤΙ..... ear of corn.

No.	Wt.	Metal. Size.	Obverse.	Reverse.
44	97·8	R ·75		ΑΡΙΣΤΟΒΙΟΣ ivy-wreath suspended from rose: (whole in well marked incuse circle).
45	102·5	R ·8		ΑΡΙΣΤΟΝΟΜΟΣ prow. [Pl. xxxvii. 1.]
46	97·1	R ·75		ΑΡΙΣΤΟΛΟ[ΧΟ]Σ harpa.
47	99·	R ·7		ΕΡΑΣΙΚΛΗΣ helmet. [Pl. xxxvii, 2.]
48	101·5	R ·75		ΦΙΛΩΝΙΔΑΣ?* lamp suspended from rose.

Didrachms.

			Head of Helios radiate, three-quarter face towards r.	ΡΟΔΙΟΝ Rose with bud on r. side, varying symbol on l., (usually) initials of magistrate's names: border of dots.
49	99·6	R ·75		pileus surmounted by star.
50	102·6	R ·75		star and ΔΙ
51	99·7	R ·8		„ „
52	101·8	R ·8		harpa and Υ [Pl. xxxvii. 3.]
53	101·8	R ·75		harpa and ΕΥ
54	101·	R ·8		„ „
55	100·2	R ·8		„ „

* ΦΙΛΩΝΙΔΑΣ is scarcely legible on this specimen, but it can be read on the drachm (no. 60) bearing the same symbol.

CARIA.

No.	Wt.	Metal. Size.	Obverse.	Reverse.
			Drachms.[*]	
			Head of Helios unradiate, three-quarter face towards r., hair loose.	[PO]ΔIO[N] Rose with bud on r. side, and on l. symbol and letter.
56	51·5	ᴭ ·55		star and Δ
57	51·	ᴭ ·55	[Pl. xxxvii. 4.]	,, ,,
			Head of Helios three-quarter face towards r., hair loose.	P O Rose with bud on r. side, varying symbol on l., and magistrate's name above.
58	40·9	ᴭ ·5		name illegible. Trident.
59	49·7	ᴭ ·55	[Pl. xxxvii. 5.]	ΕΡΑΞΙΚ[ΛΗ] helmet.
60	47·3	ᴭ ·6		ΦΙΛΩΝΙΔΑΞ Lamp suspended from rose.
			Triobols or Hemidrachms.	
			Head of Helios three-quarter face towards r., hair loose.	P O Rose with bud on r. side.
61	23·2	ᴭ ·5		l., grapes.
62	25·9	ᴭ ·5	[Pl. xxxvii. 6.]	l., Δ (inscr. PO in field l.)

[*] These drachms are distinctly earlier in style than nos. 153 sqq. *infra*, which bear the same types.

RHODUS.

No.	Wt.	Metal. Size.	Obverse.	Reverse.
			Trihemiobols or Quarter-drachms.	
			Head of Helios in profile, r., radiate.	P O Two rosebuds springing from opening leaves ; between them, varying symbol : border of dots.
63	14·6	Æ ·4		symbol uncertain. [Pl. xxxvii. 7.]
64	13·2	Æ ·4		Artemis with torch, running r.
65	13·6	Æ ·4		lyre.
66	13·3	Æ ·4		,, [Pl. xxxvii. 8.]
67	13·8	Æ ·4		shell (pecten).
68	13·7	Æ ·4		lamp.*
69	15·5	Æ ·4		ivy-wreath.†
			BRONZE.	
			P O Rose.	Rose with bud.
70		Æ ·35		traces of letters or symbol in field l.
71		Æ ·4		,, ,, ,,
72		Æ ·45	([P] O) ,,	,, ,,
73		Æ ·4	in field l., Σ	[Pl. xxxvii. 9.]

* Cf. drachm no. 60 and didrachm no. 48.
† Cf. didrachm no. 44.

238   CARIA.

No.	Metal. Size.	Obverse.	Reverse.
		Head of Rhodos r., wearing stephane, earring and necklace.	P O Rose with bud on r., and varying symbol on l., or letter.
74	Æ ·45		grapes. [Pl. xxxvii. 10.]
75	Æ ·45		grapes.
76	Æ ·45		,,
77	Æ ·45		,,
78	Æ ·45		,, (on r., bud on l.)
79	Æ ·45		ear of corn.
80	Æ ·45		,,
81	Æ ·45		,,
82	Æ ·45		thunderbolt. [Pl. xxxvii. 11.]
83	Æ ·45		thunderbolt.
84	Æ ·45		,,
85	Æ ·45		ivy-leaf. [Pl. xxxvii. 12.]
86	Æ ·45		dolphin.
87	Æ ·45		,,
88	Æ ·45		trident.
89	Æ ·45		,,

No.	Metal. Size.	Obverse.	Reverse.
90	Æ ·5		cornucopiae.
91	Æ ·45		race-torch.
92	Æ ·45		,,
93	Æ ·45		shell (pecten). [Pl. xxxvii. 13.]
94	Æ ·45		shell (pecten).
95	Æ ·45		,, (on r., bud on l.)
96	Æ ·45		,, (,, ,,)
97	Æ ·45		star.
98	Æ ·45		,,
99	Æ ·45		horse's head r.
100	Æ ·45		spear-head ?
101	Æ ·5		,,
102	Æ ·45		shell ?, funnel-shaped (on r., bud on l.)
103	Æ ·45		,, ,, (,, ,,)
104	Æ ·45		strung bow ?
105	Æ ·45		bee ?

240   CARIA.

No.	Wt.	Metal. Size.	Obverse.	Reverse.
106		Æ ·35		no symbol visible.
107		Æ ·4		,, ,,
108		Æ ·45		A/
109		Æ ·45		E
110		Æ ·45		I
111		Æ ·45		,,
112		Æ ·45		M [Pl. xxxvii. 14.]
113		Æ ·45		M
114		Æ ·45		Γ
115		Æ ·45		,,
116		Æ ·45		X
117		Æ ·45		,,

[The average weight of these bronze coins is about 23 grains.]

Circ. B.C. 304—166.

Tetradrachms.

			Head of Helios radiate, three-quarter face towards r.	P O (in field) Rose with bud on r., varying symbol on l., and magistrate's name above: border of dots.
118	202·3	AR ·95		AETIΩN; symbol, vase (skyphos).

No.	Wt.	Metal. Size.	Obverse.	Reverse.
119	207·5	R 1·05	Similar.	POΔION (above); magistrate's name in field. AKEΣIΣ; symbol, dolphin.
120	208·	R ·9		AMEIN IAΣ; symbol, prow, r. [Pl. xxxviii. 1.]
121	206·4	R ·95		AMEINI AΣ; symbol, prow, r.
122	206·7	R 1·1		APIΣTOK PITOΣ; symbol, aplustre.
123	198·1	R ·95	Similar.	P O (in field), magistrate's name above. APIΣTOKPITOΣ; symbol, aplustre.
124	205·7	R 1·	Similar.	POΔION (above); magistrate's name in field. EYKPA THΣ; symbol, thunderbolt.
125	204·8	R 1·05	Similar. (Countermark, bull's head facing.)*	POΔI ON (in field); magistrate's name above. EYKPATHΣ; symbol, thunderbolt. [Pl. xxxviii. 2.]

* This Bull's head countermark may have been placed on the coin at Cnidus. Cf. Bull's head as a coin-type on Cnidian bronze coins of this period. (Pl. xv. 19.)

No.	Wt.	Metal. Size.	Obverse.	Reverse.
			Similar.	P O (in field); magistrate's name above.
126	206·4	AR 1·05		ΘΑΡΣΥΤΑΣ; symbol, eagle with raised wing r. on thunderbolt.
127	199·5	AR 1·05		,, ,, ,,
128	204·	AR 1·		ΤΕΙΣΥΛΟΣ; symb., female figure standing to front, clad in long chiton and peplos, her l. hand raised to her breast, holding dove(?); on her head polos. (Aphrodite?)* [Pl. xxxviii. 3.]

Didrachms.

			Head of Helios radiate, three-quarter face towards r.	P O (in field) Rose with bud on r., varying symbol on l., and magistrate's name above: border of dots.
129	95·7	AR ·8		ΑΓΕΜΑΧΟΥ; symb., wreath.
130	103·6	AR ·8		ΑΓΗΣΙΔΑΜΟΣ; symb., Artemis running l., holding torch. [Pl. xxxviii. 4.]
131	103·4	AR ·8		ΑΓΗΣΙΔΑΜΟΣ; symb., Artemis running l., holding torch.
132	101·7	AR ·75		,, ,, ,,
133	94·2	AR ·75		ΑΕΤΙΩΝ; symb., thyrsos bound with fillet. [Pl. xxxviii. 5.]

* Cf. terra cotta statuettes of Aphrodite from Camirus, in the Brit. Mus.

RHODUS. 243

No.	Wt.	Metal. Size.	Obverse.	Reverse.
134	105·	R ·8	Similar.	ΡΟΔΙΟΝ (above); magistrate's name in field. AMEIN IAΣ; symb., aplustre.
135	100·4	R ·8	Similar.	P O (in field); magistrate's name above. ΑΝΑΞΑΝΔΡΟΣ; symbol, oval shield.
136	101·4	R ·8		ΑΡΙΣΤΑΚΟΣ; symb.cultus-statue of Aphrodite? to front. (cf. no. 128.) [Pl. xxxviii. 6.]
137	101·2	R ·8		ΑΡΙΣΤΟΒΟΥΛΟΣ; symb., ear of corn.
138	101·4	R ·8		ΑΡΙΣΤΟΚΡΙΤΟΣ; symb.,aplustre.
139	103·4	R ·8		ΕΡΑΣΙΚΛΗΣ; symbol, helmet. (cf. no. 47, didrachm with same name and symbol, but with un-radiate head.) [Pl. xxxviii. 7.]
140	98·5	R ·75		ΕΡΑΣΙΚΛΗΣ; symb., helmet.
141	104·4	R ·75	Similar.	ΡΟΔΙΟΝ (above); magistrate's name in field. ΕΥΚΡΑ ΤΗΣ; symb., anchor.
142	97·5	R ·75	Similar.	P O (in field); magistrate's name above. ΘΑΡΣΥΤΑΣ; symb., eagle with raised wing r. on wreath.

No.	Wt.	Metal. Size.	Obverse.	Reverse.
143	104·8	AR ·75		ΜΝΑΣΙΜΑΧΟΣ Athena standing l., helmeted, holds in r. aplustre, in l. mast or trophy-stand.
144	103·5	AR ·75		,, ,, ,,
145	102·4	AR ·75		ΜΝΑΣΙΜΑΧΟΥ Nike in place of Athena; r. hand raised, holding aplustre ?
146	101·9	AR ·75		,, ,, ,,
147	88·6	AR ·75		ΞΕΝΟΚΡΑΤΗΣ serpent ?
148	98·5	AR ·75		ΟΝΑΣΑΝΔΡΟΣ eagle on thunderbolt.
149	104·2	AR ·8		ΣΤΑΣΙΩΝ bow in case and club, crossed.
150	103·9	AR ·8		ΤΙΜΟΘΕΟΣ terminal figure facing. (Silenos drinking from askos ?)
151	103·6	AR ·85		,, ,,
152	100·1	AR ·75	[Pl. xxxviii. 8.]	,, ,,
			Drachms.	
			Head of Helios unradiate, three-quarter face towards r., hair loose.	P O Rose with bud on r., varying symbol on l., and magistrate's name above.
153	40·6	AR ·55		ΑΙΝΗΤΩΡ butterfly.
154	39·	AR ·65		,, ,,

RHODUS. 245

No.	Wt.	Metal. Size.	Obverse.	Reverse.	
155	40·4	Ṛ ·65	(head towards l.) [Pl. xxxix. 1.]	ΑΙΝΗΤΩΡ	caduceus.
156	39·2	Ṛ ·65	(head towards l. Counter-mark uncertain object.)	ΑΙΝΗΤΩΡ	,,
157	37·5	Ṛ ·55	(head towards l.)	,,	,,
158	35·6	Ṛ ·6	(,,)	,,	,,
159	35·5	Ṛ ·6	(head towards l. Countermark K-Y, and lyre.)*	,,	,,
160	27·9	Ṛ ·6	(head towards l.)	,,	,,
161	38·5	Ṛ ·6	(,,)	,, caduceus and Ⱶ	
162	39·4	Ṛ ·55		ΑΜΕΙΝΙΑΣ	trident.
163	40·2	Ṛ ·55		ΑΡΙΣΤΑΚΟΣ	caduceus.
164	38·	Ṛ ·65		ΓΟΡΓΟΣ	bow in case.
165	40·2	Ṛ ·6		,,	,,
166	43·6	Ṛ ·6		,, [Pl. xxxix. 2.]	,,
167	40·3	Ṛ ·55		ΓΟΡΓΟΣ	bow in case.
168	42·2	Ṛ ·6		,,	,,
169	36·2	Ṛ ·55		ΓΟΡΓΟΥ	,,

* This countermark was evidently placed upon the coin at Cyaneae in Lycia after B.C. 168,

No.	Wt.	Metal. Size.	Obverse.	Reverse.
170	27·	Ɑ̃ ·6	(head towards l.)	ΓΟΡΓΟΣ butterfly.
171	39·	Ɑ̃ ·6		,, caduceus.
172	39·2	Ɑ̃ ·6		,, (caduceus on r., and tendril? on l.)
173	37·8	Ɑ̃ ·6		ΔΑΜΟΚΡΙΤΟΣ ⚹ on l.
174	36·	Ɑ̃ ·55		ΔΙΟΚΛΗΣ no symbol; tendril on both sides.
175	40·7	Ɑ̃ ·55		ΕΥΚΡΑΤΗΣ tripod.
176	40·6	Ɑ̃ ·6		,, ,,
177	42·0	Ɑ̃ ·65	(head towards l.)	ΚΑΛΛΙΣΘΕΝΗΣ club. [Pl. xxxix. 3.]
178	40·3	Ɑ̃ ·6	(head towards l.)	[ΛΥ]ΣΩΝ? bee? or shell?
179	33·5	Ɑ̃ ·6		ΜΟΥΣΑΙΟΣ caduceus on r., tendril on l.
180	37·7	Ɑ̃ ·65		,, caduceus on r., B and tendril on l.
181	42·3	Ɑ̃ ·6		ΠΕΙΣΙΚΡΑΤΗΣ Athena r., armed with shield, and wielding spear. [Pl. xxxix. 4.]
182	42·7	Ɑ̃ ·6		ΣΤΑΣΙΩΝ club and bow crossed.
183	41·	Ɑ̃ ·65		,, ,,

RHODUS. 247

No.	Wt.	Metal. Size.	Obverse.	Reverse.
184	37·7	Æ ·55	(head towards l.)	ΣΩΠΟΛ[ΙΣ] thunderbolt.
185	39·0	Æ ·55		ΣΩΣΙΚΡΑΤΗΣ caduceus and uncertain object.
186	36·9	Æ ·6		ΤΕΙΣΥΛΟΣ serpent.
187	37·4	Æ ·55		name illegible; palm.

Hemidrachms.

			Head of Helios unradiate, three-quarter face towards r.	P O Rose with bud on r., varying symbol on l., and magistrate's name above.
188	18·1	Æ ·45		ΑΚΕΣΙΣ dolphin. [Pl. xxxix. 5.]
189	18·	Æ ·5		ΑΜΕΙΝΙΑΣ bearded ithyphallic term r. [Pl. xxxix. 6.]
190	20·6	Æ ·4		ΑΜΕΙΝΙΑΣ bearded ithyphallic term r.
191	17·8	Æ ·5		,, ,,
192	20·5	Æ ·45		ΑΝΑΞΑΝΔΡΟ[Σ] trident.
193	18·5	Æ ·45		ΓΟΡΓΟΣ fish-hook.
194	17·9	Æ ·45		ΕΥΚΡΑΤΗΣ anchor.
195	20·2	Æ ·45		,, ,,
196	17·4	Æ ·4		,, (?) tripod. [Pl. xxxix. 7.]
197	18·3	Æ ·5		ΠΕΙΣΙΚΡΑΤΗΣ spear-head.

248 CARIA.

No.	Wt.	Metal. Size.	Obverse.	Reverse.
			Drachms without name of Rhodes.	
198	38·6	ℛ ·65	Head of Helios unradiate, three-quarter face towards l.	※ ⋔ Rose with bud on r. in field r. ⟝ above, ΒΑΒΩΝ [Pl. xxxix. 8.] [Struck at Miletus. Cf. Hunter Cat., p. 203, no. 1, and Imhoof, *Mon. Gr.*, p. 323.]
199	39·3	ℛ ·55	Similar.	Rose with bud on r. above, ΔΗΜΟΚΛΗΣ on l., dolphin.
200	30·8	ℛ ·55	(head facing.)	,, ,,
201	38·8	ℛ ·65		Rose with bud on l. above, ΔΙΟΚΛΗΣ on r. ⋈ beneath, winged thunderbolt. [Pl. xxxix. 9.] [Cf. the specimen published by Imhoof-Blumer in *Num. Zeit.* iii., pl. x. 27, on which he reads Λ—⋈, and which he attributes to the Carian town of Lepsimandus. There is no trace of the letter Λ on the B.M. specimen.]
202	36·2	ℛ ·6	(head towards r.)	above, [Ε]ΥΒΙΟΣ on r., dolphin and Α
203	31·3	ℛ ·6	(head towards r.) Countermark lion r., with head turned back in incuse square.	above, ΙΑΣΩΝ on r., caduceus. [Pl. xxxix. 10.]
204	38·7	ℛ ·6	(head towards l.)	bud on either side of rose. above, ΚΑΛΛΙΠΠΟΣ on l., prow.

RHODUS.

No.	Wt.	Metal. Size.	Obverse.	Reverse.
205	31·9	AR ·65	(head towards l.) Countermark, head of Helios r., radiate.	similar, but ΚΑΛΛΙΠΟΣ
206	40·5	AR ·65	(head towards l.)	above, ΚΗΦΙΣΟΔΩ[ΡΟΣ] on l., bucranium.
207	42·1	AR ·6	(head towards r.)	on r., two buds. above, ΣΤΑΣΙΩ[Ν] on l., bunch of grapes. [Pl. xxxix. 11.]
208	41·	AR ·6	(head towards r.)	above, ΣΤΡΑΤΩΝ on l., uncertain symbol. on r., bud.
209	33·5	AR ·7	(,,)	above, ΣΤΡΑΤΩΝ dolphin on either side. border of dots.

Drachms without name of Rhodes and with various letters in the field.

			Head of Helios unradiate, facing, and with right cheek covered by an eagle r.	Rose.
210	33·4	AR ·6		no letters, branch and bud on r. [Pl. xxxix. 12.]
211	29·	AR ·6		Δ Υ (?) Δ Δ
212	25·9	AR ·55		Θ Α / Ξ Α branch and bud on both sides.
213	38·	AR ·65		Π Α / Ξ Α ,, ,,
214	28·5	AR ·5		Π Α / Σ R ,, ,,

K K

No.	Wt.	Metal. Size.	Obverse.	Reverse.
215	34·5	AR ·55		Π A R Є branch and bud on r.
216	30·2	AR ·6		Π E torch on r. Ƕ Λ
			[Pl. xxxix. 13.]	
217	39·1	AR ·5		ME wreath ? I
218	27·2	AR		Y—Π branch on each side. M I
			[Pl. xxxix. 14.]	

BRONZE.

			Head of Zeus r., laur.: border of dots.	P O Rose with bud on r.
219		Æ ·75		in field l., Φ|
			[Pl. xxxix. 15.]	
220		Æ ·75		in field l., Φ|
221		Æ ·7		,, ,,
222		Æ ·65		in field l., 🛕

			Head of Zeus r., laur.	P O Rose surmounted by radiate solar disk.
223		Æ ·65		in field l., branch; r., dolphin.
			[Pl. xxxix. 16.]	
224		Æ ·55		in field r., aplustre ?
225		Æ ·5		no symbol.

No.	Wt.	Metal. Size.	Obverse.	Reverse.
			Veiled female head r., wearing stephane and earring.	P O Rose with bud on r.
226		Æ ·5		in field l., TE [Pl. xxxix. 17.]
227		Æ ·65		in field l., TE
			Veiled female head r., wearing stephane and earring.	PO Prow r.; above it, rosebud.
228		Æ ·6		[Pl. xxxix. 18.]

Circ. B.C. 189—166.

GOLD.

Staters.

			Head of Helios radiate, three-quarter face towards r.	Shallow incuse square, containing P O Rose with bud on l. and varying symbol on r.; above, magistrate's name.
229	131·2	N ·8		ΑΝΤΑΙΟΣ symbol, bee. [Pl. xxxix. 19.]
230	131·	N ·75		ΑΝΤΑΙΟΣ symbol, aplustre.

Quarter Staters.

			Head of Rhodos r., radiate, wearing stephane, earring and necklace.	P O Rose with bud on l. and varying symbol on r.; above, magistrate's name: border of dots.
231	28·8	N ·45		ΑΝΤΑΙΟΣ symbol, star.

No.	Wt.	Metal. Size.	Obverse.	Reverse.
232	31·4	N ·5		ΔΙΟΓΕΝ symbol, dolphin? [Pl. xxxix. 20.]
233	81·5	N ·5		ΜΕΛΑΝΤ symbol on l., ear of corn.
234	33·4	N ·45		ΤΙΜΟΚΡΑ symbol, aplustre.*

[To this period also belongs the gold Philip (Müller, 308), with P. O and adjunct symbol Rose, and magistrate's name ΜΝΑΞΙ-ΜΑΧΟΞ; also gold staters bearing the name and types of Lysimachus, symbols rose and trident, and magistrate's name ΑΡΙΣΤΟ-ΒΟΥΛΟΣ (Müller, Lysim., nos. 450, 451), and the Alexandrine tetradrachms (Müller, nos. 1154—1167) of two series, (α) with monograms, and (β) with magistrate's names in the field. The known names are ΑΙΝΗΤΩΡ, ΑΡΙΣΤΟΒΟΥΛΟΣ, ΔΑΜΑ-ΤΡΙΟΣ, ΔΑΜΟΚΡΙΝΗΣ, ΔΙΟΦΑΝΗΣ, ΗΦΑΙΣ-ΤΙΩΝ, ΣΤΑΣΙΩΝ, ΤΕΙΣΥΛΟΣ and ΤΙΜΑΙΟΣ.]

Circ. B.C. 166—88.

Drachms.

			Head of Helios r., radiate.	Shallow incuse square, containing P—O Rose with bud on r. and varying symbol on l.; above, magistrate's name.
235	44·2	Æ ·6		ΑΓΑΘΑΡΧΟΣ symbol, trident.
236	39·6	Æ ·6		,, ,, ,,
237	43·5	Æ ·55		ΑΓΕΜΑΧΟΣ symbol, aplustre.
238	48·1	Æ ·55		ΑΓΗΣΙΔΑΜΟΣ ,, helmet.
239	41·7	Æ ·55		,, ,, ,,

* Mr. Lawson has also a specimen with the name ΔΑΜΑΣ. Wt. 26 grs.

No.	Wt.	Metal. Size.	Obverse.	Reverse.
240	40·8	AR ·6		ΑΕΤΙΩΝ symbol, grapes.
241	45·3	AR ·6		ΑΘΑΝΟΔΩΡΟΣ ,, wing.
242	48·5	AR ·65		,, ,, ,,
243	48·3	AR ·65		,, ,, spear-head.
244	38·4	AR ·6		ΑΙΝΗΤΩΡ ,, race-torch.
245	46·6	AR ·55		ΑΝΑΞΑΝΔΡΟΣ ,, butterfly.
246	47·	AR ·55		ΑΝΑΞΙΔΙΚΟ[Σ] ,, fish-hook.
247	46·	AR ·6		ΑΝΑΞΙΔΟΤΟΣ ,, serpent twined round omphalos. [Pl. XL. 1.]
248	46·	AR ·6		ΑΝΑΞΙΔΟΤΟΣ symbol, serpent twined round omphalos. [Pl. XL. 2.]
249	46·	AR ·55		ΑΝΤΙΓΕΝΗΣ symbol, prow.
250	46·3	AR ·6		ΑΡΙΣΤΟΒΟΥΛΟΣ ,, club.
251	42·7	AR ·65		ΑΡΤΕΜΩΝ ,, shield.
252	40·5	AR ·7		,, symbol, ivy-wreath.
253	44·2	AR ·55		,, ,, head-dress of Isis. [Pl. XL. 3.]
254	43·4	AR ·6		ΑΡΤΕΜΩΝ ⳁ symbol, head-dress of Isis.

No.	Wt.	Metal. Size.	Obverse.	Reverse.
255	41·6	Ꭺ ·6		ΔΑΜΑΤΡΙΟΣ symbol, dolphin.
256	40·3	Ꭺ ·6		ΔΕΞΙΚΡΑΤΗΣ ,, thyrsos bound with fillet.
257	47·3	Ꭺ ·6		,, ,, winged caduceus.
258	41·	Ꭺ ·65		,, ,, ,,
259	48·	Ꭺ ·65		,, ,, open right hand.
				[Pl. xl. 4.]
260	44·3	Ꭺ ·55		ΔΙΟΓΝΗΤΟΣ symbol, lighted altar.
				[Pl. xl. 5.]
261	47·9	Ꭺ ·65		ΕΥΦΑΝΗΣ symbol (on r.), head-dress of Isis.
262	41·6	Ꭺ ·55		,, ,, ,,
263	35·7	Ꭺ ·6		ΙΗΝΩΝ ,, ,,
264	36·4	Ꭺ ·55		ΗΡΑΓΟΡΑΣ ,, serpent twined round omphalos, surmounted by star.
265	41·4	Ꭺ ·7		ΘΡΑΣΥΜΕΝΗΣ Τ symbol, rising sun.
				[Pl. xl. 6.]
266	50·4	Ꭺ ·65		ΘΡΑΣΥΜΗΔ[ΗΣ] symbol (on r.), head-dress of Isis.
				[Pl. xl. 7.]
267	30·2	Ꭺ ·6		ΚΑΛΛΙΞΕ[ΝΗΣ] symbol, caduceus.

No.	Wt.	Metal. Size.	Obverse.	Reverse.
268	39·7	AR ·55		MAHΣ symbol (on r.), head-dress of Isis.
269	37·5	AR ·6		,, ,, ,,
270	31·2	AR ·6		,, ,, ,,
271	29·	AR ·65		MHNOΔΩPO[Σ] symbol (on r.), star.
272	39·3	AR ·6		MNHMΩN symbol, cornucopiae.
273	40·8	AR ·65		NEΩN symbol (on r.), cornucopiae.
274	36·5	AR ·6		NIKAΓOPAΣ no symbol.
275	34·5	AR ·6		,, ,,
276	32·3	AR ·55		NIKHΦOPOΣ symbol, hand holding ear of corn.
277	32·4	AR ·6		,, ,, ,,
278	33·7	AR ·55		,, ,, ,, [Pl. XL. 8.]
279	37·1	AR ·65		NIKHΦOPOΣ symbol, hand holding ear of corn.
280	39·8	AR ·6		ΞENOKPATHΣ symbol, lyre (chelys).
281	46·	AR ·6		ΞEN . . . . symbol, ram's head r., and caduceus.

256   CARIA.

No.	Wt.	Metal. Size.	Obverse.	Reverse.
282	44·4	Ɑʀ ·55		ΠΕΙΣΙΣΤΡΑΤοΣ symbol, thyrsos. [Bank Coll.]
283	34·2	Ɑʀ ·65		ΠΕΡΙΤΑΣ symbol (on r.), coiled serpent.
284	44·0	Ɑʀ ·6		ΣΤΑΣΙΩΝ ,, serpent twined round omphalos, surmounted by star ?
285	44·6	Ɑʀ ·6		ΣΤΑΣΙΩΝ symbol, star. [Pl. xl. 9.]
286	44·6	Ɑʀ ·6		ΣΩΣΑΝΔΡ[ΟΣ] ,, butterfly.
287	37·2	Ɑʀ ·65		ΤΙΜοΣΤΡΑΤ[ΟΣ] symbol, uncertain. [Pl. xl. 10.]
288	45·8	Ɑʀ ·6		ΦΙΛΟΚΡΑΤΗΣ symbol, bucranium. [Pl. xl. 11.]
289	26·5	Ɑʀ ·6		ΦΙΛΩΝ symbol (on r.), ear of corn.
290	45·	Ɑʀ ·6		Illegible; ,, human head r.
			Hemidrachms (Triobols).	
			Head of Helios radiate, three-quarter face towards r.	Shallow incuse square, containing P O Rose with budding branch on r. and varying symbol on l.; above, magistrate's name.
291	22·5	Ɑʀ ·5		ΑΝΑΞΙΔοΤΟΣ symbol, omphalos surmounted by star. [Pl. xl. 12.]
292	17·	Ɑʀ ·5		ΑΝΤΑΙΟΣ symbol (on r.), half radiate disk.

RHODUS. 257

No.	Wt.	Metal. Size.	Obverse.	Reverse.
293	20·3	AR ·5		ΑΡΤΕΜΩΝ symbol, aplustre.
294	21·3	AR ·45		,, ,, club.
295	18·5	AR ·5		,, ,, ,,
296	21·8	AR ·5		ΓΟΡΓΙΑ symbol (on r.) uncertain. [Pl. XL. 13.]
297	19·	AR ·5		ΔΑΜΑΣ symbol (on r.) grapes.
298	21·3	AR ·5		ΔΑΜΑΤΡΙΟΣ symbol (on r.) acrostolium.
299	17·2	AR ·5		ΔΕΞΑΓΟΡΑΣ symbol, grapes.
300	21·7	AR ·5		ΔΕΞΙΚΡΑΤΗΣ symbol, ear of corn.
301	22·1	AR ·45		ΔΕΞΙΚΡΑΤΗΣ symbol, caduceus.
302	18·1	AR ·5		ΔΙΟΓΝΗΤΟΣ symbol (on r.) Arion? on dolphin r.
303	20·6	AR ·5		ΔΙΟΝΥΣΙΟΣ symb., cornucopiae.
304	19·6	AR ·55		ΘΡΑΣΥΜΕΝΗ[Σ] symb., rising sun. [Pl. XL. 14.]
305	19·4	AR ·5		ΘΡΑΣΥΜΕΝΗ[Σ] symbol, racetorch on both sides.

L L

No.	Wt.	Metal. Size.	Obverse.	Reverse.
306	19·	AR ·5		ΘΡΑΣΥΜΕΝ[ΗΣ] symbol, thunderbolt.
307	21·	AR ·55		ΜΗΝΟΔΩΡΟ[Σ] symbol (on r.) star. [Pl. XL. 15.]
308	20·2	AR ·5		ΜΗΝΟΔΩΡΟ[Σ] symbol (on r.) star.

Quarter Drachms (Trihemiobols).

			Head of Helios r., radiate.	P O Rose with budding branch on l. and varying symbol on r.: border of dots.
309	12·7	AR ·45		symbol, star.
310	11·1	AR ·4		,, ,,
311	12·7	AR ·45		,, ear of corn. [Pl. XL. 16.]

BRONZE.

			Head of Helios r., radiate.	P O Rose with budding branch or branches, varying symbol on each side : border of dots.
312		Æ 1·1		on l., fish-hook; on r., dolphin and trident. [Pl. XL. 17.]
313		Æ 1·1		on l., fish-hook; on r., dolphin and trident.
314		Æ 1·		on l., fish-hook; on r., sword in sheath.
315		Æ 1·05		,, ,, ,, ,,

RHODUS. 259

No.	Metal. Size.	Obverse.	Reverse.
316	Æ 1·05		on l., fish-hook; on r., sword in sheath.
317	Æ 1·05		on l., acrostolium; on r., palm ?
318	Æ 1·2		on l., thunderbolt; on r., cista.
319	Æ 1·1		on l., helmet; on r., thunderbolt.
320	Æ 1·1		,, ,, ,, ,,
321	Æ 1·15		on l., head-dress of Isis; on r., thunderbolt.
322	Æ 1·05		on l., head-dress of Isis; on r., winged caduceus.
323	Æ 1·05		on l., owl; on r., winged caduceus.
324	Æ ·5	Head of Helios r., radiate.	P O Rose with budding branch or branches.
325	Æ ·4		
326	Æ ·45		
		[Pl. xl. 18.]	
327	Æ ·5	Head of Rhodos r., radiate, wearing stephane, earring and necklace.	Incuse square, containing P O Rose with branch on each side.
328	Æ ·5		

260   CARIA.

No.	Wt.	Metal. Size.	Obverse.	Reverse.
329		Æ ·45		
330		Æ ·5		
331		Æ ·5		
332		Æ ·5		
333		Æ ·5	[Pl. XL. 19.] [Pl. XL. 20.]	(magistrate's name above rose, illegible.)

SILVER.

Circ. B.C. 88—43.

Cistophoric Standard (?) 1½ Drachm.

334	68·4	AR ·8	Head of Helios, radiate, three-quarter face towards l. [Pl. XLI. 1.]	P O Full-blown rose to front; above and below, palm: border of large dots.*

Attic Drachms (?)

335	63·9	AR ·85	Head of Helios, radiate, three-quarter face towards r., of more youthful type than that on the previous coin. [Pl. XLI. 2.]	P O Full-blown rose to front; magistrate's name and varying symbol. ΑΡΙΣΤΟΜΑΧΟΣ symb., aplustre.

* To this time I would also ascribe two remarkable coins in the Hunter and Paris Collections. From casts of these coins in the British Museum, I am able to correct the description in the Hunter Cat., p. 247, no. 11, as follows :—

Head of Helios or Medusa (?), three-quarter face towards r., with winged diadem tied beneath chin.   P O Rose with budding branch on r.; above, ΓΟΡΓΟΣ; in field l., star: border of dots.

AR (Hunter Coll.) 68·25 grs. Size Æ ·8.   (Plate XLV. 3. Paris Coll.)

No.	Wt.	Metal. Size.	Obverse.	Reverse.
336	53·8 (broken)	Ꭱ ·8		ΙΑΣΩΝ symb., wreath and cornucopiae.
337	62·	Ꭱ ·75		ΚΡΙΤΟΚΛΗΣ symb., ear of corn.
338	63·	Ꭱ ·75		,, ,, ,,
339	64·2	Ꭱ ·8		ΛΕΩΝΙΔΑΣ symbol, three stars (without P O)
340	61·7	Ꭱ ·8		ΝΙΚΟΦΩΝ symbol, owl.
341	66·7	Ꭱ ·8		ΤΙΜΟΞΕΝΟΣ symbol, oenochoe and tripod. (ΡΟΔΙ in place of P O)

BRONZE.

342		Æ 1·4	Head of Helios, radiate, facing.	P O Full-blown rose to front, within an oak-wreath; above or below, magistrate's name. ΖΗΝΩΝ (above). [Pl. XLI. 3.]
343		Æ 1·4		ΞΗΝΩΝ (beneath).
344		Æ 1·25		ΣΩΣ[ΘΕ]ΝΗ[Σ] (beneath).
345		Æ 1·4		ΣΦΑΙ ΡοΣ (beneath). Star between syllables. [Pl. XLI. 4.]

262　CARIA.

No.	Metal. Size.	Obverse.	Reverse.
		Head of Helios r., radiate.	P O　Full-blown rose to front; around, magistrate's name: border of dots.
346	Æ ·7		ΕΠΙΤΥΧΗΣ symbol, caduceus.
347	Æ ·7		,,　　,,　　,,
		[Pl. xli. 5.]	
348	Æ ·7		ΕΠΙΤΥΧΗΣ symbol, caduceus.
349	Æ ·7		,,　　,,　　,,
350	Æ ·85		ΣΑΤΥΡΟΣ symbol, caduceus?
351	Æ ·75		ΣΦΑΙΡΟΣ symb., winged caduceus.
352	Æ ·7		,,　　,,　　,,
353	Æ ·75		,,　　,,　　,,
354	Æ ·75		,,　　,,　　,,
355	Æ ·7		ΣΩΣΘΕΝΗΣ without P O? or symbol.
356	Æ ·75		,,　　,,　　,,　　,,
		Head of Helios r., radiate: border of dots.	ΡΟΔΙΩΝ Full-blown rose to front; beneath, symbol: border of dots.
357	Æ ·75		symbol, club.
358	Æ ·7		,,　dolphin and branch.
		[Pl. xli. 6.]	

RHODUS. 263

No.	Metal. Size.	Obverse.	Reverse.
359	Æ ·7		symbol, term.
360	Æ ·7		,, ,,
361	Æ ·7		,, palm and dolphin.
362	Æ ·5	ΡΟΔ ΙѠΝ Bust of Helios? r., radiate(?) border of dots.	ΡΟΔΙѠΝ Full-blown rose to front: border of dots.
363	Æ ·55	[Pl. XLI. 7.]	,, ,, ,,

Early Imperial Times.

Circ. B.C. 43—A.D. 96.

LARGE BRONZE COINS.

		Head of Dionysos, wearing ivy wreath, often radiate: border of dots.	Nike, holding wreath (or sometimes aplustre) and palm, standing on prow, rose, globe, or basis; in field, ΡΟ ΔΙΩΝ and magistrate's name: border of dots.
364	Æ 1·45	(head l., radiate.)	(Nike on rose) ΕΠΙ ΝΟΥ ΑΝΤΙ ΡΟΔ ΓΟ ΙΩΝ
365	Æ 1·4	(head r., radiate.)	(Nike on prow) ΕΠΙ ΑΝΤΙΠΑ[ΤΡΟΥ]?
366	Æ 1·4	(head l., unradiate.)	ΡΟ ΑΝ ΔΙ ΤΙΠΑ ΩΝ ΤΡΟΥ ΕΠΙ

No.	Metal. Size.	Obverse.	Reverse.
367	Æ 1·3	(head l., unradiate.)	(Nike on basis.) ΡΟ ΑΝΤΙ ΔΙ ΤΑ ΩΝ ΤΡΟΥ ΕΠΙ
368	Æ 1·45	(head l., unradiate.)	(Nike on [?].) inscr. as on last.
369	Æ 1·3	(head r., unradiate.)	(Nike l. on rose ?) ΡΟΔΙ ΩΝ ΕΠΙ ΑΠΟΛΛ ΩΝΙΟΥ
370	Æ 1·4	(head r., radiate.)	(Nike on prow ?) ΡΟΔΙΩΝ ΔΑΜΑ ΕΠΙ ΡΑ ΤΑ
371	Æ 1·35	(head l., radiate.)	(Nike on prow, holds aplustre.) ΡΟΔΙΩΝ ΕΠΙ ΔΑ ΜΑΡΑ ΤΟΥ
372	Æ 1·4	(head l., radiate.)	(Nike on prow, holds aplustre.) ΡΟΔΙ ΩΝΕΠΙ ΔΑ ΜΑΡΑ ΤΟΥ
373	Æ 1·35	(head l., radiate.)	(Nike on prow, holds aplustre.) ΡΟΔΙΩ ΕΠΙ Ν ΔΑ ΛΑΡ[Α] [Pl. XLII. 1.] Τ[ΟΥ]
374	Æ 1·5	(head l., unradiate.)	(Nike on globe, ΕΠΙΕΥΔΩΡΟΥ with rose in front.) ΡΟΔΙΩΝ [Pl. XLII. 2.]
375	Æ 1·45	(head r., radiate.)	(Nike on rose.) ΡΟΔΙ ΩΝ ΕΠΙ ΤΑΜΙΑ [ΟΑΡΑ] ΤΟΥ

RHODUS.

No.	Metal. Size.	Obverse.	Reverse.
376	Æ 1·4	(head r., radiate.)	(Nike without support, holds aplustre.) Po ΔΙ ΩΝ TAMIA TEIMOΣTPATOY [Pl. XLII. 3.]
377	Æ 1·4	(head r., unradiate.)	no Nike, rose; above, POΔIΩN TA MIA TEI MO ΣTP ATOY [Pl. XLII. 4.]
378	Æ 1·35	(head r., radiate.)	(Nike l. on prow, holds aplustre ?) POΔI ΩN ΦAIN[I] EΠI ΛA
379	Æ 1·35	(head l., unradiate.)	(Nike l. on prow ?) POΔI ΩN EΠI ΦAINI [ΛA] [Pl. XLII. 5.]
380	Æ 1·4	(head l., unradiate.)	(Nike l. on ?, double-struck.) PoΔI ΩN EΠI ΦAINI ΛA
381	Æ 1·4	(head r., unradiate.)	(Nike l. on prow, with rose in front.) POΔI EΠI ΩN XAPEI NOY

SMALLER BRONZE COINS.

382	Æ ·7	Head of Dionysos l., wearing ivy-wreath and radiate. [Pl. XLII. 6.]	POΔIΩN Rose.
383	Æ ·55	Bust of Dionysos l., wearing ivy-wreath; at shoulder, thyrsos: border of dots.	POΔIΩN Rose: border of dots.
384	Æ ·55	bust r. [Pl. XLII. 7.]	

266   CARIA.

No.	Metal. Size.	Obverse.	Reverse.
385	Æ ·5	Head of Dionysos r., wearing ivy-wreath: border of dots. [Pl. XLII. 8.]	PO Δ IΩN Rose: beneath, palm: border of dots.
386	Æ ·7	Head of Dionysos r., wearing ivy-wreath.	PO Nike holding wreath and palm, standing on prow r.: in field r., amphora: border of dots.
387	Æ ·85	Head of Helios r., radiate: border of dots. [Pl. XLII. 9.]	POΔIωN Nike standing l., holding wreath and palm: border of dots.
388	Æ ·85		
389	Æ ·7	Bust of Helios r., radiate, neck draped: border of dots. [Pl. XLII. 10.]	POΔI ωN Nike standing r., holding wreath and palm; in front, acrostolium: border of dots.
390	Æ ·6	Head of Helios r., radiate.	P O Nike standing l., holding wreath and palm: border of dots.
391	Æ 65	Head of Alektrona r., wearing stephane, radiate. [Pl. XLII. 11.]	P O Nike standing l., holding wreath and palm: border of dots. symbol in field l., rising sun.
392	Æ ·55	[Pl. XLII. 12.]	
393	Æ ·55		

RHODUS.

No.	Metal. Size.	Obverse.	Reverse.
		Bronze Didrachms.	
394	Æ 1·4	PoΔIoIYΠEPTΩNCE BA CTΩN Head of Helios r., radiate; chlamys round neck: border of dots. [Pl. xliii. 1.]	Nike, with wreath and palm, advancing l., to crown a trophy which stands upon a pile of shields: between figures, ΔI ΔPAXM : border of dots. ON
395	Æ 1·35	(PoΔIoI YΠEP TΩN CE BAC TΩN)	(Δ IΔPAX MoN)
396	Æ 1·35	(,,)	
397	Æ 1·35	(,,)	(ΔIΔPA XMoN)
398	Æ 1·4	(PoΔIoI YΠEP TΩN CEB ACTΩN)	(Δ IΔPAXM O N)
		(The average wt. of these 5 specimens is 317 grs.)	
399	Æ 1·3	Head of Helios r., radiate: border of dots. [Pl. xliii. 2.]	PoΔIΩN Nemesis? standing ΔIΔPAXMoN to front between two thymiateria, and beneath a canopy supported on either side by flying Nike: border of dots. Wt. 273 grs.
400	Æ ·65	Bust of Helios r., radiate: border of dots. [Pl. xliii. 3.]	PoΔI ΩN Similar type.
401	Æ ·6	[Pl. xliii. 4.]	(canopy and supporters not visible.)

CARIA.

No.	Metal. Size.	Obverse.	Reverse.
402	Æ ·7	Head of Helios r., radiate: border of dots.	POΔ IΩN Nemesis? standing to front: border of dots.
403	Æ ·6	Similar.	POΔI ΩN Similar type.
404	Æ ·65	POΔI ΩN Bust of Helios r., radiate: border of dots.	POΔ Bust of Sarapis r., radiate and wearing modius: border of dots.
405	Æ ·6	Similar.	POΔI ΩN Similar.
406	Æ ·65	Similar.	POΔI ΩN Similar.
407	Æ ·6		
408	Æ ·65	Head of Helios r., radiate; in front, star.	POΔI ΩN Head of Sarapis r., wearing modius.
409	Æ ·65		
410	Æ ·65		[Pl. XLIII. 5.]

RHODUS.

No.	Metal. Size.	Obverse.	Reverse.
411	Æ ·7	Head of Helios r., radiate; in front, crescent: border of dots.	ΡΟΔΙ ΩΝ Asklepios standing to front, resting on serpent-staff. [Pl. XLIII. 6.]
412	Æ ·6		
413	Æ ·6		
414	Æ ·45	Head of young Dionysos or Bacchante r., with thyrsos at shoulder: border of dots.	Ρ ΟΔ ΙΩ Ν Bunch of grapes: border of dots.
415	Æ ·5	Head of Tyche (?) r., turreted: border of dots.	ΡΟΔ ΙΩΝ Thyrsos, bound with taenia: border of dots.

Imperial Coinage.

Nerva.

416	Æ 1·35	ΑΥΤΟΚΡΑΤΩΡ ΚΑΙ CAP ΝЄΡΟΥΑΝ CЄ ΒΑCΤΟC (? sic) Head of Nerva r., laur.	ΡΟΔΙΩΝ Helios, radiate, ΔΙΔ ΡΑΧΜΟΝ standing l., giving his r. hand to female figure (Rhodos?) who stands facing him, and holding spear in l.
417	Æ 1·4		ΔΙΔΡ ΑΧΜΟΝ ΡΟΔΙΩΝ [Pl. XLIII. 7.]

No.	Metal. Size.	Obverse.	Reverse.
		Trajan.	
418	Æ 1·8	ΑΥΤΟΚΡΑΤΟΡΑ ΚΑΙ CAPA[NEP OYAN TPAIAN] Head r., laur., of Trajan.	POΔIΩN Dionysos, wearing himation, standing l., caressing with r. a pantheress, and resting with l. on thyrsos. [Pl. XLIII. 8.]
		(The average weight of these three last didrachms is 263 grs.)	
		Antoninus Pius.	
419	Æ ·75	ΑΝΤΩΝΙΝΟC ΚΑΙ CAP Head of Antoninus Pius r., laur.	POΔI ΩN Head of Helios r., radiate.
		M. Aurelius.	
420	Æ ·65	BHP OC Head of young M. Aurelius r., bare.	POΔ IΩN Head of young Dionysos r., wearing ivy-wreath.
421	Æ ·6		
		Commodus.	
422	Æ ·55	POΔ IΩN Bust of Commodus r., bearded, radiate, in cuirass and paludamentum.	POΔ IΩN Bust of Helios r., radiate, chlamys over shoulders.
		[Pl. XLIII. 9.]	

APPENDIX.

No.	Wt.	Metal Size.	Obverse.	Reverse.
			ALABANDA.	
			Tetradrachms.	
			Before B.C. 197 ?	
1	246·	AR 1·25	Head of Apollo l., laur.: border of dots.	ΑΛΑΒΑΝΔΕΩΝ Pegasos r., beneath quiver with strap and magistrate's name, ΔΗΜΗΤΡ ΙΟΣ (Montagu Sale. Pl. viii. 594.)
			Under name of Antiochia, B.C. 197—189 ?	
1A	252·	AR 1·1	Head of Apollo l., laur.: border of dots.	ΑΝΤΙΟΧΕ[ΩΝ] Pegasos l., beneath Σ (Montagu Sale. Lot 595.)
			PLARASA AND APHRODISIAS.	
			First Century B.C. (*temp. Augusti*) ?	
			Drachms.	
6A	53·	AR ·6	Bust of Aphrodite veiled r., as on p. 26, no. 6.	[ΠΛΑΡΑ]ΣΕΩΝ ΚΑΙ Α[ΦΡΟ ΔΕΙΣΙΕΩΝ] Eagle l., on thunderbolt, as on p. 26, no. 6. [Α] ΠΟ ΜΕ ΛΛΟ ΝΑΝ ΔΟ ΔΡ ΤΟ ΟΥ Σ
8A	51·	AR ·7		ΧΡΥ ΧΡΥ ΣΙΠ ΣΙΠ ΠΟΣ ΠΟΥ (outer inscr. almost off the flan.)
10A	54·6	AR ·7		ΑΡ ΤΕ ΜΩΝ ✕ ΣΗ ΑΡΤΕ ΝΩΝ ΜΙΔΩ ΡΟΣ

No.	Wt.	Metal. Size.	Obverse.	Reverse.
			CNIDUS. Tetradrachms. Circ. B.C. 390—300.	
28A	225·5	R ·95	Head of Aphrodite Euploia l., wearing earring and necklace; hair gathered up and tied at back of head, ends loose: behind, prow, l.	KNI Forepart of Lion r. above, [K]ΑΛΛΙΦΡΩΝ (Montagu Sale. Pl. viii. 599.)
			Circ. B.C. 300—190.	
39A	227·5	R 1·	Head of Aphrodite r., wearing stephane, earring and necklace; behind, helmet : border of dots. [Pl. XLV. 7.]*	KNI Forepart of lion r. above, [ΘΕ]ΥΜΕΛΩΝ (Montagu Sale. Pl. viii. 600.)
			Cos. Tetradrachm. Circ. B.C. 300.	
41A	219·5	R 1·05	Head of young Herakles r., wearing lion's skin.	Incuse square, within which dotted square containing crab; above which K ΩΙΟ N and beneath, bow in case and magistrate's name ΓΝΩΣΙΔΙΚοΣ (Montagu Sale. Lot 611.)
			RHODES. Circ. B.C. 189—166. GOLD. Half-Stater.	
A 230	65·6	N ·65	Head of Helios, radiate, three-quarter face towards r.	Shallow incuse square containing P O Rose; above magistrate's name ΑΝΤΑΙΟΣ, symbol in field r., winged caduceus. (Montagu Sale. Pl. viii. 620.)

* This specimen, though included on Pl. xlv. no. 7, among the coins not in the British Museum, has since been purchased at the Montagu Sale.

INDEXES.

I. Geographical.
II. Types.
III. Symbols and Countermarks.
IV. A. Kings and Rulers.
IV. B. Magistrates' Names on Autonomous Coins.
IV. C. Magistrates' Names on Imperial Coins.
V. Roman Magistrates' Names.
VI. Engravers' Names.
VII. Remarkable Inscriptions.

INDEX I.

GEOGRAPHICAL.

The numbers in this and the following Indexes refer to the *pages* in the Catalogue.

A.

Alabanda (Antiochia), 1, 271.
Alabanda, 2, 271.
Alinda, 10.
Amyzon, 13.
Antiochia (Alabanda), 1, 271.
Antiochia ad Maeandrum, 14.
Aphrodisias and Plarasa, 25, 271.
Aphrodisias, 28.
Aphrodisias and Ephesus, 53.
Aphrodisias and Antiochia, 53.
Apollonia Salbace, 54.
Astypalaea, 186.
Astyra, 59.
Attuda, 62.

B.

Bargasa, 70.
Bargylia, 71.

C.

Calymna, 188.
Camirus, 223.
Carpathos, 192.
Caunus, 74.
Ceramus, 77.
Chalcetor ? 79.
Chersonesus Cnidia, 80.
Cidramus, 81.
Cnidus, 84, 272.
Cos, 193, 272.

E.

Euippe, 98.
Euromus, 99.

G.

Gordiuteichos, 101.

H.

Halicarnassus, 102.
Halicarnassus and Samos, 112.
Halicarnassus and Cos, 112.
Harpasa, 113.
Heraclea Salbace, 116.

Hydisus, 122.
Hyllarima, 123.

I.

Ialysus, 226.
Iasus, 124.
Idyma, 127.

L.

Lindus, 228.

M.

Megiste, 221.
Mylasa, 128.
Myndus, 134.

N.

Neapolis Myndiorum ? 140.
Neapolis ad Harpasum, 141.
Nisyros, 222.

O.

Orthosia, 143.

P.

Plarasa and Aphrodisias, 25, 271.
Posidium Carpathi, 192.

R.

Rhodus, 223, 230, 272.

S.

Sebastopolis, 146.
Stratonicea, 147.

T.

Tabae, 160.
Termera, 176.
Trapezopolis, 177.

INDEX II.

TYPES.

A.

Adonis, Birth of.—Aphrodisias, 34.
Adonis charging at wild boar.—Aphrodisias, 50.
Agonistic Table.—Aphrodisias, 37, 38, 47, 50, 51 ; Tabae, 167.
Agonistic Urn.—Tabae, 174.
Alektrona, Head of.—Rhodus, 266.
Alexander the Great, Head of.—Caunus, 75.
Altar.—Antiochia, 18.
Altar, on which, Eagle.—Antiochia, 24.
Altar, lighted, between bunches of grapes.—Cnidus, 97.
Altar, lighted, garlanded.—Stratonicea, 152.
Altar of the Dioskuri.—Tabae, 164, 165, 168.
Amazon (or Sabazios?) on horseback.—Apollonia Salbace, 54.
Amphora.—Astyra, 59, 60, 61.
Amphora and grapes.—Astyra, 60.
Antiochia, City of, seated, turreted.—Antiochia, 18.
Aphrodisias and Antiochia, Demoi of.—Aphrodisias and Antiochia in alliance, 53.
Aphrodisias and Ephesós seated face to face.—Aphrodisias and Ephesus in alliance, 53.
Aphrodite, Head of.—Aphrodisias, 40 ; Plarasa and Aphrodisias, 26, 27, 28, 271 ; Astyra, 61 ; Cnidus, 84 — 87, 89 — 91, 272.
Aphrodite ? Head of, veiled.—Tabae, 161.
Aphrodite of Praxiteles, Head of.—Cnidus, 96, 97.
Aphrodite of Praxiteles and Asklepios.—Cnidus, 97.
Aphrodite, seated, Erotes playing around her.—Aphrodisias, 46.
Aphrodite standing, carrying infant Eros and sceptre.—Aphrodisias, 30, 42.
Aphrodite standing, holding mirror ? around her, Erotes.—Aphrodisias, 82.
Aphrodite standing, r. arm extended, holds mirror in l. hand.—Heraclea Salbace, 121.

Aphrodite standing, embracing Ares.
—Aphrodisias, 43.
Aphrodite, Eros extracting thorn from foot of.—Aphrodisias, 31.
Aphrodite, Cultus-statue of.—Aphrodisias, 28, 31, 39—41; Cidramus, 81, 82; Gordiuteichos, 101; Tabae, 162.
Aphrodite, Cultus-statue of, saluted by M. Aurelius and L. Verus.—Aphrodisias, 41.
Aphrodite, Cultus-statue of, between seated Priestess and altar.—Aphrodisias, 42—44, 51.
Aphrodite, Cultus-statue of, with Priestess and altar, between two Erotes on cippi, pointing torches towards head of goddess.—Aphrodisias, 46.
Aphrodite, Cultus-statue of, between two geese.—Aphrodisias, 44.
Aphrodite Eleutheria, standing, holding apple and sceptre.—Aphrodisias, 30, 31; holding patera and sceptre.—Aphrodisias, 30, 31.
Aphrodite Euploia, Head of.—Cnidus, 87, 88, 272.
Apollo, Head of.—Alabanda-Antiochia, 1, 2, 271; Alabanda, 2—4, 271; Antiochia, 14, 15; Apollonia-Salbace, 54; Caunus, 76; Cnidus, 93, 95, 107; Halicarnassus, 104, 107—109; Iasus, 124, 125; Myndus, 136—138; Neapolis Myndiorum, 140; Astypalaea, 186; Cos, 210, 211.
Apollo, Head of, facing.—Halicarnassus, 102; Mausolus, 181, 182; Hidrieus, 183; Pixodarus, 184, 185.

Apollo, Bust of, with lyre.—Alabanda, 5.
Apollo standing.—Neapolis ad Harpasum, 142.
Apollo, naked, standing holding branch and bow.—Attuda, 63.
Apollo, standing, holding arrow.—Iasus, 126.
Apollo standing, holding bow, and drawing arrow from quiver.—Trapezopolis, 178.
Apollo standing, quiver at shoulder, and holding branch.—Trapezopolis, 178.
Apollo standing, holding raven and laurel-branch.—Alabanda, 7.
Apollo, draped, standing to front, holding raven and laurel-branch.—Apollonia Salbace, 56; holding uncertain object and resting on lyre.—Apollonia Salbace, 57.
Apollo standing, resting on column and holding uncertain object.—Attuda, 62.
Apollo naked, standing, holding branch and resting on column.—Attuda, 64.
Apollo Kitharoedos.—Alinda, 12; Apollonia Salbace, 58; Harpasa, 113.
Apollo Kitharoedos and Asklepios.—Halicarnassus and Cos in alliance, 112.
Apollo and Artemis? standing face to face.—Apollonia Salbace, 55.
Apollo and Artemis with tripod and serpent between them, and fire-altar beside Artemis.—Myndus, 139.
Apollonia, City, Bust of.—Apollonia Salbace, 55.

Ares naked, standing, embraced by Aphrodite.—Aphrodisias, 43.
Artemis, Bust or head of.—Amyzon, 13; Cnidus, 91, 94; Euippe, 98; Heraclea Salbace, 116; Iasus, 125; Myndus, 138.
Artemis standing, drawing arrow from quiver and holding bow.—Iasus, 126.
Artemis standing, holding torch and bow.—Tabae, 162.
Artemis Ephesia, Cultus-statue of.—Stratonicea, 155, 157.
Artemis Ephesia, Cultus-statue of, between stags.—Antiochia, 20.
Artemis Huntress.—Tabae, 168.
Artemis Huntress and Stag.—Stratonicea, 152.
Artemis Huntress, Two identical figures of.—Tabae, 169.
Artemis Kindyas, Head of.—Bargylia, 71, 72; Statue of.—Bargylia, 72.
Artemis and Mên face to face.—Tabae, 170–172.
Asiatic goddess (Artemis?), Cultus-statue of.—Attuda, 64; Harpasa, 113.
Asklepios, Bust or head of.—Attuda, 62; Astypalaea, 187; Cos, 205—209, 211—214, 216, 219.
Asklepios or Zeus, Head of.—Heraclea Salbace, 118.
Asklepios seated.—Heraclea Salbace, 116; holding patera over serpent, and crooked staff.—Heraclea Salbace, 120.
Asklepios standing.—Alabanda, 4; Aphrodisias, 33; Bargylia, 73; Trapezopolis, 177; Cos, 218; Rhodus, 269.
Asklepios and Hygieia.—Apollonia Salbaco, 55, 56; Attuda, 65; Bargasa, 70.
Asklepios and Telesphoros.—Attuda, 67.
Asklepios with Aphrodite.—Cnidus, 97.
Asklepios, Serpent-staff of.—Astypalaea, 187.
Astypalaea?, Head of, veiled.—Astypalaea, 187.
Atesh-gah (Persian fire-altar).—Myndus, 137.
Athena (or Roma?), Bust of.—Antiochia, 16.
Athena, Bust or head of.—Aphrodisias, 29, 37; Apollonia Salbace, 55; Attuda, 62; Caunus, 75; Cnidus, 96, 107; Halicarnassus, 103, 106, 107—110; Harpasa, 113; Hydisos, 122; Tabae, 161, 163; Cos, 219.
Athena, advancing.—Harpasa, 113, 114.
Athena, standing.—Antiochia, 18, 21; Attuda, 69; Harpasa, 115; Neapolis ad Harpasum, 141; Orthosia, 143.
Athena standing, holding Nike and spear.—Alabanda, 8.
Athena standing, turreted, with spear, shield, and owl.—Heraclea, 119.
Athena standing, holding olive-branch, shield, and spear.—Hyllarima, 123.
Athena standing, holding patera and spear.—Alabanda, 6.
Athena standing, holding patera, shield, and spear.—Antiochia, 17.
Athena sacrificing.—Antiochia, 20.
Athena, Terminal figure of, armed

with shield and spear.—Halicarnassus, 110.
Athletes, three, drawing lots.—Aphrodisias, 47.
Attuda, City, Head of, turreted.—Attuda, 62—64.

B.

Bacchante or Dionysos, Bust of.—Aphrodisias, 33.
Bacchante, Head or bust of.—Myndus, 138; Tabae, 165.
Bellerophon on Pegasos.—Bargylia, 72.
Bellerophon standing, holding Pegasos.—Stratonicea, 152.
Boar, winged, Forepart of.—Ialysus, 226, 227.
Boule, Bust of.—Antiochia, 15, 17; Aphrodisias, 31, 32, 34—36; Apollonia Salbace, 56; Attuda, 66; Bargasa, 70; Heraclea Salbace, 116, 117; Tabae, 166; Trapezopolis, 177; Cos, 215.
Bow in case.—Cos, 204.
Bow in case within oak-wreath.—Alinda, 11.
Bow in case, and Club.—Halicarnassus, 106, 107; Cos, 203, 209.
Bow in case, and Crab.—Cos, 272.
Branch.—Myndus, 138.
Bull, Head of.—Chersonesus Cnidia, 80; facing.—Cnidus, 90, 94.
Bull, Head and neck of.—Chersonesus Cnidia, 80, 90, 95.
Bull, Forepart of.—Caunus, 74.
Bull, humped, butting.—Alabanda-Antiochia, 2.

Bull, humped, Forepart of.—Alabanda, 4; Tabae, 161.
Bull, humped, recumbent on Maeander pattern.—Antiochia, 14.
Bull, humped, standing.—Antiochia, 15; Aphrodisias, 38; within circle of Maeander pattern ending in pilei of the Dioskuri.—Antiochia, 14.
Bull, butting.—Caunus, 74.
Bull, humped, butting.—Tabae, 161.
Bull, humped, sacrifice of.—Stratonicea, 157.

C.

Caduceus.—Ceramus, 78.
Caduceus, winged.—Apollonia Salbace, 56; Halicarnassus, 109.
Caduceus, between caps of the Dioskuri.—Tabae, 160.
Capricorn.—Tabae, 165.
Centaur holding bow?—Aphrodisias, 47.
Ceramus, City, Head of, turreted.—Ceramus, 78.
Charites, three, naked.—Aphrodisias, 44.
Cista mystica and serpent.—Sebastopolis, 146.
Club.—Cos, *passim*.
Club and Crab.—Cos. *See* Crab.
Club and Bow in case.—Cos, 201, 203, 204.
Club in oak-wreath.—Alinda, 10.
Club and Bow in case, within oak-wreath.—Alinda, 11.
Club and Serpent-staff.—Cos, 217.
Cnidus, City, Head of, turreted.—Cnidus, 92.

Corn, Three ears of.—Attuda, 63.
Cornucopiae.—Caunus, 75 ; Heraclea Salbace, 116.
Cornucopiae, with grapes and corn.—Heraclea Salbace, 116.
Crab.—Cos, 193—195, 200, 203, 205.
Crab and bow in case.—Cos, 197, 201, 204, 272.
Crab and club.—Cos, 194—203, 205.
Cuirass on trophy-stand.—Plarasa and Aphrodisias, 25.

D.

Demeter, Bust of.—Trapezopolis, 178.
Demeter ? Head of, veiled.—Cos, 195—197.
Demeter standing, holding ears of corn and torch.—Antiochia, 15.
Demeter standing, holding poppy and corn, resting on long torch.—Antiochia, 19.
Demeter ? standing, wearing kalathos and holding grapes, corn, and sceptre.—Tabae, 169.
Democracy (ΔΑΜΟΚΡΑΤΙΑ), Head of.—Cnidus, 92.
Demoi of Aphrodisias and Antiochia, 53.
Demos, youthful, Head or bust of.—Alabanda, 4 ; Antiochia, 16 ; Aphrodisias, 29—31, 33, 35, 38 ; Apollonia Salbace, 56 ; Attuda, 63—65; Harpasa, 113, 114 ; Heraclea Salbace, 117 ; Sebastopolis, 146; Stratonicea, 153 ; Tabae, 165—167 ; Trapezopolis, 177.
Demos, bearded, Head or bust of.—Aphrodisias, 29, 30 ; Attuda, 63 ; Cos, 215.
Demos, bearded and diademed, Head of.—Antiochia, 16.
Dionysos or Bacchante, Bust of.—Aphrodisias, 33.
Dionysos, youthful, Bust or head of.—Alabanda, 6 ; Cnidus, 96; Euromus, 99 ; Myndus, 135 ; Orthosia, 143, 144 ; Sebastopolis, 146 ; Tabae, 160, 164 ; Astypalaea, 187.
Dionysos, youthful, Bust of, with thyrsos.—Aphrodisias, 38.
Dionysos, Head of, often radiate.—Rhodus, 263—265, 269, 270.
Dionysos standing, holding grapes and thyrsos.—Antiochia, 19 ; Apollonia Salbace, 56.
Dionysos standing, holding grapes and thyrsos ; at feet, panther.—Cidramus, 82 ; Tabae, 171, 173, 174.
Dionysos standing beside column, holding grapes and thyrsos; in front, panther.—Aphrodisias, 33.
Dionysos standing, holding kantharos and thyrsos.—Apollonia Salbace, 57 ; Attuda, 64 ; Cnidus, 96.
Dionysos standing beside column, holding grapes and kantharos ; at feet, panther.—Harpasa, 114.
Dionysos, standing, resting on thyrsos and caressing pantheress.—Rhodus, 270.
Dionysos standing, holding kantharos and thyrsos ; at feet, panther.—

Antiochia, 22; Aphrodisias, 33; Attuda, 63; Tabae, 173; Trapezopolis, 177.
Dioskuri standing.—Alinda, 11.
Dioskuri, Altar of the.—Tabae, 164, 165, 168.
Dioskuri, Caps of the.—Tabae, 160, 161, 165.
Discobolus.—Cos, 194.
Dolphin and Trident.—Nisyros, 222.
Dolphins, Two.—Myndus, 138.
Dolphins, Two, and smaller dolphin. —Posidium Carpathi, 192.

E.

Eagle.—Aphrodisias, 38; Ceramus, 77; Euromus, 100; Halicarnassus, 104; Myndus, 137; Stratonicea, 147; Plarasa and Aphrodisias, 271.
Eagle in incuse square.—Halicarnassus, 102.
Eagle on laurel-branch.—Apollonia Salbace, 54.
Eagle on Maeander pattern.—Antiochia, 15.
Eagle holding serpent.—Aphrodisias, 38.
Eagle on thunderbolt.—Myndus, 136; Plarasa and Aphrodisias, 26—28.
Eagle on torch.—Stratonicea, 148.
Eagle, Head of, in incuse square.— Ialysus, 226, 227.
Eirene, Head of.—Cos, 216.
Eleutheria.—See Aphrodite.
Eleutheros Demos.—Aphrodisias, 38.
Emperors and Imperial personages; heads, busts, etc.:—

Augustus.—Alabanda, 5; Alinda, 11; Antiochia, 18; Aphrodisias, 39, 40; Apollonia Salbace, 56; Euromus, 100; Heraclea Salbace, 118; Mylasa, 130, 131; Stratonicea, 151; Trapezopolis, 178, 179; Cos, 216, 217.
Augustus and Livia.—Alabanda, 5; Aphrodisias, 40; Euromus, 100.
Livia.—Alabanda, 5; Aphrodisias, 40; Apollonia Salbace, 57.
Agrippa, Caius, and Lucius—Alabanda, 5.
Caius Caesar.—Aphrodisias, 40.
Germanicus and Drusus.—Tabae, 167.
Tiberius.—Astypalaea, 187.
Caligula.—Cos, 217.
Agrippina Junior.—Alabanda, 6.
Nero.—Alabanda, 6; Apollonia Salbace, 57; Cidramus, 81; Halicarnassus, 110; Heraclea Salbace, 119; Myndus, 138; Tabae, 168.
Vespasian.—Alabanda, 6; Heraclea Salbace, 119; Orthosia, 144.
Titus.—Bargylia, 72.
Domitian. Antiochia, 18; Heraclea Salbace, 120; Tabae, 168; Cos, 218.
Domitia.—Tabae, 169; Cos, 218.
Nerva.—Rhodus, 269.
Trajan.—Alinda, 11; Antiochia, 19; Attuda, 66; Halicarnassus, 110; Stratonicea, 153; Tabae, 169; Cos, 218; Rhodus, 270.
Plotina.—Tabae, 170.
Hadrian.—Aphrodisias, 41; Halicarnassus, 110; Harpasa, 114; Mylasa, 131; Stratonicea, 154; Cos, 218, 219.

Sabina.—Harpasa, 114.
Aelius Caesar.—Alinda, 11.
Antoninus Pius.—Antiochia, 19; Ceramus, 78; Cidramus, 82; Halicarnassus, 110; Heraclea Salbace, 120; Mylasa, 131; Stratonicea, 154; Tabae, 170; Cos, 219; Rhodus, 270.
Faustina Senior.—Myndus, 139.
M. Aurelius. — Antiochia, 19; Aphrodisias, 41; Apol'onia Salbace, 57; Harpasa, 114; Heraclea Salbace, 120; Mylasa, 131; Orthosia, 145; Tabae, 170; Rhodus, 270.
Faustina Junior.—Antiochia, 20; Aphrodisias, 42; Halicarnassus, 111; Mylasa, 131; Tabae, 170.
L. Verus.—Antiochia, 20; Aphrodisias, 42; Cos, 219.
Lucilla.—Euippe, 98.
Commodus.—Antiochia, 20; Attuda, 66; Bargasa, 70; Ceramus, 78; Halicarnassus, 111; Rhodus, 270.
Sept. Severus. — Alabanda, 6; Alinda, 12; Aphrodisias, 43; Aphrodisias and Ephesus, 53; Attuda, 67; Halicarnassus, 111; Heraclea Salbace, 121; Mylasa, 132; Stratonicea, 155; Trapezopolis, 179.
Sept. Severus on horseback, galloping over prostrate foe.—Aphrodisias, 43.
Sept. Severus and Domna.—Bargylia, 73; Halicarnassus and Samos, 112; Myndus, 139; Stratonicea, 155—157.
Sept. Severus, Bust of, between busts of Caracalla and Geta.—Attuda, 67.

Julia Domna. — Alabanda, 7; Aphrodisias, 43—45; Attuda, 67; Bargylia, 73; Heraclea Salbace, 121; Stratonicea, 157; Tabae, 171; Trapezopolis, 179; Cos, 219.
Caracalla.—Alabanda, 7—9; Antiochia, 21; Aphrodisias, 45; Apollonia Salbace, 58; Cnidus, 97; Harpasa, 115; Iasus, 126; Mylasa, 132, 133; Stratonicea, 157; Tabae, 171; Cos, 220.
Caracalla on galloping horse; beneath, two lions.—Apollonia Salbace, 58.
Caracalla galloping over two prostrate foes.—Attuda, 67.
Caracalla and J. Domna.—Stratonicea, 158.
Caracalla and Geta.—Halicarnassus and Cos, 112; Mylasa, 133; Stratonicea, 158, 159.
Caracalla and Plautilla.—Alinda, 12; Cnidus, 97; Stratonicea, 158.
Plautilla.—Alinda, 12.
Geta.—Mylasa, 133; Tabae, 171, 172; Cos, 220.
Macrinus.—Heraclea Salbace, 121.
Elagabalus. — Aphrodisias, 45; Cidramus, 82.
Elagabalus on horseback, galloping over prostrate foe.—Aphrodisias, 45.
Elagabalus, standing, holding cultus-statue of Aphrodite, and crowned by Demos.—Aphrodisias, 45.
Julia Maesa.—Cidramus, 82, 83.
Severus Alexander. — Antiochia, 21; Aphrodisias and Antiochia, 53; Stratonicea, 159; Tabae, 173,

Julia Mamaea.—Aphrodisias, 46; Harpasa, 115.
Maximinus.—Aphrodisias, 46.
Gordianus III.— Antiochia, 21; Aphrodisias, 46, 47; Halicarnassus, 111; Harpasa, 115; Neapolis ad Harpasum, 141.
Tranquillina.—Mylasa, 133.
Philippus Senior.—Cos, 220.
Philippus Junior.—Antiochia, 27; Aphrodisias, 47.
Trajanus Decius.—Antiochia, 22; Aphrodisias, 48.
Trajanus Decius in quadriga.—Aphrodisias, 48.
Etruscilla.—Antiochia, 23.
Trebonianus Gallus.—Neapolis ad Harpasum, 141.
Volusianus.—Neapolis ad Harpasum, 142.
Valerianus.—Antiochia, 23; Tabae, 172.
Gallienus.—Antiochia,23; Aphrodisias, 48—51; Apollonia Salbace, 58; Attuda, 68; Bargasa, 70; Tabae, 172—174.
Gallienus on horseback.—Aphrodisias, 49, 50; Bargasa, 70.
Gallienus in quadriga.—Aphrodisias, 48.
Salonina.—Antiochia, 24; Aphrodisias, 51, 52; Apollonia Salbace, 58; Attuda, 68; Tabae, 174, 175.
Saloninus.—Tabae, 175.
Valerianus Junior.—Attuda, 69.
Eros, Bust of.—Plarasa and Aphrodisias, 25.
Eros, winged, standing with bow and arrow.—Aphrodisias, 32.
Eros, winged, standing, holding torch.—Aphrodisias, 31, 32.
Eros winged, standing, holding torch and bow.—Aphrodisias, 32, 37.
Eros winged, in attitude of Thanatos, with inverted torch.—Aphrodisias, 32.
Erotes, Two, seated, playing with astragali.—Aphrodisias, 32.

F.

Female head or bust.—Alabanda, 5; *veiled.*—Alabanda, 5; Apollonia Salbace, 55; Calymna, 190, 191; Rhodus, 251; *hair rolled.*—Chalcetor ? 79; Hyllarima, 123; *wearing stephane.*—Cnidus, 93; Nisyros, 222.
Female figure *seated*, veiled, resting chin on hand.—Cos, 214.
Female figure *standing, veiled.*—Cos, 219; holding patera? and cornucopiae?—Halicarnassus, 109; sacrificing.—Cos, 219.
Female figure *standing*, holding patera and sceptre.—Antiochia, 17; Cos, 219.
Fig-leaf.—Idyma, 127; Camirus, 223—225.
Fire-altar.—Myndus, 137; on large square altar.—Myndus, 139.
Founder of Antiochia (κτίστης,) standing.—Antiochia, 23.

G.

Gerousia, Bust of.—Antiochia, 17, 18.
Goat's head and foreleg in incuse square.—Halicarnassus, 102.

TYPES. 285

Goat, Forepart of, in incuse circle.—Halicarnassus, 102.
Goddess, Bust of, wearing polos.—Tabae, 165; Cultus-statue of.—Alabanda, 3; veiled, standing, wearing kalathos.—Cidramus, 82; Sebastopolis, 146.
Grapes.—Cnidus, 95; Myndus, 135; Rhodus, 269.
Griffin, Head of, in incuse square.—Camirus, 225.

H.

Harpa.—Astypalaea, 186, 187.
Harpasos, River-god, recumbent.—Harpasa, 114, 115.
Hekate, Head of. — Stratonicea, 148 151.
Hekate, standing.—Stratonicea, 150, 154—159.
Hekate riding on lion.—Stratonicea, 153.
Hekate triformis, with attributes.—Antiochia, 22.
Helios or Apollo? Head of.—Astyra, 60.
Helios, Head of, facing, *unradiate*. —Cnidus, 94; Halicarnassus, 106, 107; Cos, 204; Rhodus, 230—236, 244—249, 252.
Helios, Head of, facing, *unradiate*, eagle covering r. cheek.—Rhodus? 249, 250.
Helios, Head of, in profile, *radiate*.—Aphrodisias, 38; Halicarnassus, 108; Rhodus, 234, 237, 251—256, 258—260, 262, 263, 266—270.
Helios, Head of, facing, *radiate*.—Rhodus, 235, 240—244, 251, 252, 256—258, 260, 261, 272.
Helios, Head of, on radiate disk.—Megiste, 221.
Helios and Rhodos? standing face to face.—Rhodus, 269.
Hemikotylion.—Astyra, 59.
Hera, standing, holding sceptre.—Antiochia, 20.
Herakles, young, Head of.—Alinda, 10, 11; Halicarnassus, 106; Cos, 195—198; 200—205, 209, 217, 272.
Herakles, young, Three-quarter or full-face head of.—Cos, 203, 204.
Herakles, bearded, Head of.—Alinda, 10; Heraclea Salbace, 119; Tabae, 162, 163, 167; Cos, 194—196, 199, 201, 214.
Herakles, kneeling.—Termera, 176.
Herakles, standing. — Attuda, 68; Heraclea Salbace, 118; Orthosia, 145.
Herakles standing, with club and lion's skin.—Heraclea Salbace, 116, 119, 120.
Herakles standing, holding club and bow.—Heraclea Salbace, 120.
Herakles standing, holding patera, club, and lion's skin.—Cos, 218.
Herakles standing, pouring libation on lighted altar.—Heraclea Salbace, 121.
Herakles standing, crowned by Nike, who stands on his shoulder.—Alinda, 12.
Herakles, Infant, strangling serpents.—Cnidus, 88.
Herakles and Keryneian stag.—Alinda, 12.

Herakles standing, holding infant; at his feet, crab.—Cos, 215.
Herakles seated, holding infant with star over head; at his foot a crab.—Cos, 215.
Herakles, Statue of, to front.—Cos, 219.
Herakles, Statue of, on basis, holding patera, club and lion's skin.—Cos, 220.
Hermes? Head of.—Halicarnassus, 109.
Hermes standing, holding caduceus.—Alabanda, 5 ; holding purse and caduceus.—Antiochia, 16 ; Aphrodisias, 36 ; Cidramus, 81 ; Heraclea Salbace, 118.
Hermes dragging ram.—Aphrodisias, 52.
Hermes Agoraios, standing.—Aphrodisias, 36, 52.
Hermias swimming with dolphin.—Iasus, 124—126.
Herodotus, Bust of.—Halicarnassus, 110.
Hippokrates (Physician), Head of.—Cos, 216.
Homonoia? standing.—Tabae, 160, 163.
Homonoia? sacrificing.—Cnidus, 97.
Horse, Forepart of.—Mylasa, 129 ; Lindus, 229.
Horse, free.—Mylasa, 128, 129.
Horse, winged, Forepart of.—Halicarnassus, 102, 105 ; Ialysus, 227.
Hygieia, standing. — Attuda, 62 ; Heraclea Salbace, 117 ; Cos, 215.
Hygieia feeding serpent.—Euippe, 98.

I.

Iasos (founder), Head of.—Iasus, 126.
Incuse circle, containing wheel.—Camirus, 225.
Incuse square, rough.—Cos, 193 ; Camirus, 224.
Incuse square quartered diagonally.—Astyra, 59.
Incuse square in two oblong halves. — Posidonia Carpathi, 192 ; Camirus, 223, 224 ; Lindus, 228.
Incuse square, containing crab and bow in case.—Cos, 272.
Incuse square, containing smaller incuse square.—Camirus, 223.
Incuse square, containing griffin's head.—Camirus, 225.
Incuse squares, Two.—Cnidus, 84.
Incuse squares, Three, in lacunar.—Astyra, 60.
Isis, standing.—Heraclea Salbace, 117.
Isis, Head-dress of.—Halicarnassus, 109 ; Myndus, 134.
Isis.—*See* Sarapis.—Alinda, 11.

J.

Jupiter Capitolinus seated before agonistic table.—Antiochia, 23.
Jupiter Capitolinus seated, holding Nike and sceptre.—Antiochia, 19.
Jupiter Capitolinus seated before Tyche of Antiochia crowned by Nike.—Antiochia, 21.
Jupiter Capitolinus, Tetrastyle temple of.—Antiochia, 20.

K.

Kalathos containing poppy-head and ears of corn.—Cos, 216.
Kybele seated, at her feet lion.—Trapezopolis, 170.
Kybele seated between two lions.—Attuda, 66.
Kybele standing between two lions.—Attuda, 66—68; Trapezopolis, 177, 179.
Kybele riding on lion.—Attuda, 68.
Kyberses, River-god.—Mylasa, 132.

L.

Labrys.—Alinda, 11; Aphrodisias and Plarasa, 25; Euromus, 99; Mylasa, 129; Pixodarus, 184.
Labrys filleted.—Aphrodisias, 38, 39; Heraclea Salbace, 116.
Labrys and filleted palms.—Aphrodisias, 28.
Labrys and trident combined.—Mylasa, 128.
Laurel-branch, filleted.—Alabanda, 5, 7.
Lebes on tripod, with doves sipping.—Cos, 214.
Leto carrying her two children.—Attuda, 64.
Liknophoros with basket on head.—Antiochia, 18.
Lioness or panther. Aphrodisias, 38.
Lion, Head of.—Termera, 176; Lindus, 228, 229.
Lion, Forepart of. — Chersonesus Cnidia, 80; Cnidus, 84—92, 94, 272.

Lion standing.—Hecatomnus, 180.
Lion's skin over club.—Alinda, 10.
Lyre (chelys).—Halicarnassus, 108; Calymna, 188; Cos, 210, 211.
Lyre (kithara).—Alabanda, 3, 8; Apollonia Salbace, 54; Halicarnassus, 107; Iasus, 125; Neapolis Myndiorum ? 140; Calymna, 188—191; Cos, 210, 214.
Lyre between laurel-branches. — Halicarnassus, 103—105.

M.

Maeander, River-god, recumbent, with reed and cornucopiae.—Antiochia, 16, 19, 22, 23.
Male head, young, laur. and diademed.—Amyzon, 13.
Male (?) head, helmeted.—Astypalaea, 187.
Male head, bearded.—Cnidus, 97.
Male figure draped, r. arm raised.—Alinda, 12.
Male figure seated, helmeted, holding statuette of Athena, and resting on sceptre. — Stratonicea, 157.
Male figure running, holding uncertain object and spear. — Apollonia Salbace, 57.
Medusa, Head of.—Astypalaea, 186, 187.
Μήν, Bust of.—Antiochia, 15; Trapezopolis, 178.
Μήν standing.—Cidramus, 83.
Μήν standing, foot on bucranium, holding patera and sceptre.—Aphrodisias, 34.

Μήν standing, holding patera over altar, and resting on sceptre.—Trapezopolis, 177, 179.
Μήν, Altar of.—Attuda, 65, 68.
Μήν and Artemis, face to face.—Tabae, 170—172.
Μήν 'Ασκαινός (?).—Aphrodisias, 34.
Μήν Κάρου, Bust of.—Attuda, 65.
Morsynos, River-god, standing, holding patera(?) and reed.—Antiochia, 16.

N.

Negress, Bust of.—Amyzon, 13.
Nemesis standing.—Attuda, 63, 66; Tabae, 165.
Nemesis, winged, standing.—Antiochia, 20; Aphrodisias, 34; Trapezopolis, 178.
Nemesis (?).—Rhodus, 267, 268.
Nike standing.—Antiochia, 15, 18, 19; Aphrodisias, 37; Mylasa, 133; Stratonicea, 148, 151—153; Cos, 220.
Nike advancing.—Cnidus, 96; Stratonicea, 156; Tabae, 163, 166, 169, 170, 172; Astypalaea, 187.
Nike crowning trophy. — Rhodus, 267.
Nike on prow, rose, globe, &c. —Rhodus, 263-266.
Nikias, Head of.—Cos, 213.

O.

Oenochoë.—Astyra, 59.
Oenochoë and Lyre (chelys).—Astyra, 59.

Owl.—Halicarnassus, 107, 109.
Owl on filleted olive-branch. —Myndus, 186.

P.

Palladium.—Cos, 214.
Pan, Head of.—Idyma, 127.
Pan, dancing, snapping his fingers and holding pedum.—Tabae, 167, 174.
Pantheistic divinity radiate, holding torch, sceptre, caduceus and bow.—Tabae, 166, 171.
Panther.—Tabae, 167, 175.
Pantheress.—Orthosia, 143.
Pegasos, Forepart of.—Bargylia, 72; Stratonicea, 150.
Pegasos.—Alabanda (Antiochia), 1, 2; Alabanda, 2, 271; Alinda, 11; Bargylia, 71, 72; Stratonicea, 150, 152.
Perseus, Head of.—Astypalaea, 186.
Poseidon, Head of.—Halicarnassus, 103, 104, 109; Cos, 214; Nisyros, 222.
Poseidon standing, with foot on prow.—Tabae, 164, 165, 175.
Poseidon standing, one foot on dolphin, holds in r. seated female statuette and in l. trident.—Tabae, 174.
Prow.—Cnidus, 92, 93; Rhodus, 251.
Pyramidal fire-altar.—Myndus, 137.

Q.

Quiver with strap.—Euippe, 98.
Quiver and bow.—Bargylia, 71.

R.

Raven (?).—Alabanda, 3-5.
Rhodos, Head of, in incuse square.—Rhodus, 231.
Rhodos, Head of.—Rhodus, 238-240, 251, 252.
Rhodos, Head of, radiate.—Rhodus, 251.
Roma seated.—Alabanda, 4.
Rose.—Aphrodisias and Plarasa, 25; Astyra, 60; Megiste, 221; Camirus, 225; Rhodus, 234-260, 265, 266, 272.
Rose in incuse circle.—Rhodus, 235.
Rose in incuse square.—Ialysus, 227; Rhodus, 230-234.
Rose, full-blown, to front.—Rhodus, 260-263.
Rose surmounted by radiate solar disk.—Rhodus, 250.
Rose-buds, two.—Rhodus, 234, 237.

S.

Sabazios on horseback, labrys over shoulder.—Attuda, 63, 64.
Sabazios or Amazon on horseback.—Apollonia Salbace, 54.
Sabazios or Sozon standing, holding patera and labrys.—Heraclea Salbace, 119.
Sacrifice of bull.—Stratonicea, 157.
Sarapis, Head or bust of.—Aphrodisias, 36; Harpasa, 114; Heraclea Salbace, 117.
Sarapis, Head of, radiate.—Rhodus, 268.
Sarapis and Isis standing face to face.—Alinda, 11.

Senate, Young male bust of.—Aphrodisias, 30, 31, 33-35, 87; Apollonia Salbace, 56; Attuda, 65; Cidramus, 81; Heraclea Salbace, 117; Orthosia, 144; Sebastopolis, 146; Stratonicea, 152, 154.
Senate, Female bust of.—Antiochia, 17.
Senate seated, with lituus and sceptre.—Alabanda, 4.
Serpent coiled.—Cos, 205-209, 212, 213, 217.
Serpent-staff.—Cos, 211, 212, 215-218.
Shields, Macedonian, three.—Mylasa, 128.
Sozon standing, holding branch.—Antiochia, 16.
Spear-head.—Chalcetor(?), 79.
Sphinx seated.—Caunus, 74.
Stag, Fore-part of.—Bargylia, 72.
Stag standing.—Bargylia, 72; Euromus, 99, 100; Mylasa, 131; Tabae, 165, 168, 170.
Star.—Hidrieus, 183; Pixodarus, 185.
Sword in sheath.—Caunus, 75, 76; Mylasa, 128.

T.

Telesphoros standing.—Bargasa, 70.
Temple, distyle, of Aphrodite or Artemis Ephesia.—Heraclea Salbace, 118.
Temple, distyle, containing cultus-statue of Aphrodite between seated Priestess and altar.—Aphrodisias, 29, 40.

Temple, distyle, of Asklepios and Hygieia.—Cos, 219.
Temple, distyle, of Athena.—Halicarnassus, 111.
Temple, distyle, of Homonoia.—Halicarnassus, 111.
Temple, tetrastyle, of Aphrodite.—Aphrodisias, 37, 41, 48; Heraclea Salbace, 121.
Temple, tetrastyle, containing cultus-statue of Aphrodite between seated Priestess and Altar.—Aphrodisias, 45, 46.
Temple, tetrastyle, of Athena.—Antiochia, 17.
Temple, tetrastyle, of Homonoia.—Halicarnassus, 111.
Temple, tetrastyle, of Jupiter Capitolinus.—Antiochia, 20, 21.
Temple, tetrastyle, of Kybele.—Attuda, 67.
Temple, tetrastyle, of Tyche.—Antiochia, 17, 18, 21.
Temple, tetrastyle, of Tyche and Nemeses.—Apollonia Salbace, 57.
Temple, tetrastyle, of Zeus Labraundos.—Mylasa, 132, 133.
Temple, tetrastyle, of Zeus Osogos.—Mylasa, 132.
Temple, hexastyle, of Artemis Huntress.—Tabae, 172, 173.
Temple, octastyle, containing cultus-statue of Aphrodite.—Aphrodisias, 42.
Term, ithyphallic, bearded.—Myndus, 138.
Thunderbolt, winged.—Apollonia Salbace, 54; Myndus, 135, 136.
Thunderbolt, winged, in laurel-wreath.—Alinda, 10.

Thyrsi, two, crossed.—Tabae, 164.
Thyrsos.—Rhodus, 269.
Thyrsos, filleted.—Orthosia, 143; Sebastopolis, 146.
Timeles (River-god), recumbent.—Aphrodisias, 29.
Torch.—Amyzon, 18; Stratonicea, 149.
Torches, two.—Cos, 218.
Tree before lighted altar.—Attuda, 66.
Tree, leafless, felled by two Phrygians.—Aphrodisias, 34, 85.
Trees, leafless, three, in enclosure of trellis.—Aphrodisias, 35.
Trees, leafless, three, between altars.—Aphrodisias, 35.
Trident.—Halicarnassus, 104, 105, 108; Mylasa, 129, 131.
Trident and Labrys combined.—Mylasa, 128.
Trident and Labrys combined, standing on crab.—Mylasa, 132.
Tripod.—Alabanda, 3; Cnidus, 91, 94; Myndus, 138.
Tripod with ὅλμος.—Halicarnassus, 103.
Tyche of city, Head or bust of.—Alabanda, 4, 6; Heraclea Salbace, 118; Cos, 216; Rhodus, 269.
Tyche, sacrificing.—Alabanda, 8.
Tyche, standing.—Alabanda, 7; Antiochia, 17, 22, 24; Aphrodisias, 42, 45, 47, 50, 52; Apollonia Salbace, 56, 58; Attuda, 62, 68; Cnidus, 97; Heraclea Salbace, 117; Neapolis ad Harpasum, 141; Sebastopolis, 146; Tabae, 166, 170, 171, 173-175; Trapezopolis, 178.

TYPES. 291

Tyche standing, veiled and turreted, resting on sceptre and holding cornucopiae.—Cos, 220.

V.

Vase with one handle.—Astyra, 59, 60.
Vine-branch with grapes.—Cnidus, 96.

W.

Warrior, Archaic head of, bearded and helmeted.—Calymna, 188.
Warrior, Head of, beardless, helmeted.—Calymna, 188-191.
Wheel in circular incuse.—Camirus, 225.

X.

Xenophon (Physician), Head of.—Cos, 215.

Z.

Zeus, Head of.—Antiochia, 14; Aphrodisias, 28; Apollonia Salbace, 54, 56; Ceramus, 77; Euromus, 99; Gordiuteichos, 101; Halicarnassus, 109; Harpasa, 113; Myndus, 134, 136; Orthosia, 143; Sebastopolis, 146; Stratonicea, 147, 148, 150, 152; Tabae, 160, 161, 165; Rhodus, 250.

Zeus seated. — Antiochia, 16; Aphrodisias, 29, 41.
Zeus Nikephoros seated.—Aphrodisias, 36, 46, 48; Apollonia Salbace, 55, 58; Harpasa, 115: at feet, Eagle. — Stratonicea, 155.
Zeus seated, holding patera and sceptre.—Cidramus, 81; Stratonicea, 159.
Zeus seated, holding sceptre and thunderbolt.—Alabanda, 6.
Zeus standing, holding patera and sceptre, at feet, Stag.—Mylasa, 132: at feet, Eagle, and holding patera and sceptre surmounted by Eagle.—Ceramus, 78.
Zeus standing, holding eagle and sceptre.—Alabanda, 6.
Zeus standing, holding thunderbolt and sceptre.—Orthosia, 144.
Zeus hurling thunderbolt and holding eagle.—Attuda, 65; Tabae, 162.
Zeus (?) standing, armed with helmet, cuirass, spear and shield.—Hydisus, 122.
Zeus Ammon, Head of.—Nisyros, 232.
Zeus Askraios (?) standing to front.—Halicarnassus, 110, 111.
Zeus Askraios (?) and Hera, standing.—Halicarnassus, 112.
Zeus Boulaios, Head of.—Antiochia, 16.
Zeus Labraundos, Head of.—Mylasa, 130.
Zeus Labraundos, or Stratios, standing.—Hecatomnus, 180; Maüsolus, 181, 182; Hidrieus, 183; Pixodarus, 184, 185.
Zeus Labraundos, or Stratios, stand-

ing, armed with Spear and Labrys, goat ? behind him.—Ceramus, 78.
Zeus Labraundos, Cultus-statue of.—Euromus, 99, 100.
Zeus Labraundos, Temple of.—Mylasa, 133.
Zeus Kapetolios (*see* Jupiter Capitolinus).
Zeus Lydios, Bust of.—Cidramus, 81.
Zeus Osogos standing, holding eagle ?—Mylasa, 133.
Zeus Osogos and Zeus Labraundos, Statues of.—Mylasa, 133.
Zeus Osogos, Temple of.—Mylasa, 132.
Zeus Panamaros ? on horseback.—Stratonicea, 151, 153, 154, 156, 158.
Zeus Sarapis seated, with Kerberos at his feet.—Iasus, 126.

INDEX III.

SYMBOLS AND COUNTERMARKS.

A.

Acrostolium.—Rhodus, 259, 266.
Altar, lighted.—Rhodus, 254.
Altar.—Cnidus, 94.
Amphora.—Rhodus, 266.
Anchor.—Rhodus, 243, 247.
Aphrodite? standing.—Rhodus, 242, 243.
Aplustre?—Rhodus, 232.
Aplustre.—Rhodus, 241, 243, 250-252, 257, 260.
Arion? on dolphin.—Rhodus, 257.
Artemis running with torch.—Rhodus, 237, 242.
Astragalus.—Rhodus, 230.
Athena holding aplustre and mast.—Rhodus, 244.
Athena Promachos.—Rhodus, 246.

B.

Bee.—Rhodus, 233, 251.
Bee?—Rhodus, 239, 246.
Bow in case.—Rhodus, 245.
Bow in case and Club crossed.—Rhodus, 244.
Bow strung.—Rhodus, 239.
Bucranium.—Rhodus, 249, 256.
Butterfly.—Rhodus, 244, 246, 253, 253.

C.

Caduceus.—Alabanda (Antiochia), 2; Plarasa and Aphrodisias, 26; Caunus, 75; Cnidus, 89, 93; Halicarnassus, 104; Rhodus, 232, 245-248, 254, 257, 259, 262, 272.
Capricorn.—Alabanda, 5.
Cista. Rhodus, 259.
Club.—Rhodus, 246, 253, 257, 262.
Club and bow crossed.—Rhodus, 246.
Corn, Ear of.—Rhodus, 232, 234, 238, 243, 252, 256-258.
Corn, grain of.—Rhodus, 232.
Cornucopiae.—Plarasa and Aphrodisias, 27; Stratonicea, 147; Rhodus, 234, 239, 255, 257, 261.

Countermarks:—
Aphrodite?, Head of.—Cnidus, 96.
Athena, Head of.—Stratonicea, 155 sqq.
Bull's head facing.—Rhodus, 241.
Club and Lion's skin?—Stratonicea, 154.
Female head.—Plarasa and Aphrodisias, 28.
Grapes.—Plarasa and Aphrodisias, 28.
Head, bearded.—Antiochia, 19.
Head, radiate.—Antiochia, 15.
Helios, Head of.—Rhodus, 249.
Emperor, Head of.—Attuda, 64, 65.
Geta, Head of, usually with letters Γ or ΓЄ.—Alabanda, 4, 6, 7, 8; Alinda, 12.
Letters: Λ in wreath—Heraclea Salbace, 121; ΛΚΜ and eagle—Aphrodisias, 29; Β—Attuda, 66; Γ—Attuda, 64; Γ?—Neapolis, 142; ΔΡ—Attuda, 64; Ϛ—Alabanda, 6; Ζ or Ν?)—Aphrodisias, 45; Β—Aphrodisias, 31, 33, 38; Tabae, 171, 172, 174; ΘЄΟV—Stratonicea, 155 sqq.; ΚΥ and Lyre—Rhodus, 245; ж—Heraclea, 119.
Lion.—Rhodus, 248.
Star.—Euippe, 98; Halicarnassus, 108.
Crescent.—Rhodus, 269.
Crux ansata.—Caunus, 75.

D.

Dioskuri, Caps of the.—Euromus, 99.
Dolphin.—Rhodus, 232, 238, 241, 247, 248, 250, 252, 254.
Dolphin and Branch.—Rhodus, 262.
Dolphin and Trident.—Rhodus, 258.
Dolphins, two.—Rhodus, 249.

E.

Eagle on cheek of Helios.—Rhodus, 249.
Eagle on thunderbolt.—Rhodus, 242, 244.
Eagle on wreath.—Rhodus, 243.
Eye.—Rhodus, 231.

F.

Fishhook.—Rhodus, 247, 253, 258, 259.
Floral device.—Cnidus, 85.
Floral volute.—Ialysus, 226, 227.
Flower, Bell-shaped.—Rhodus, 232.

G.

Grapes.—Astyra, 61; Caunus, 75; Cnidus, 92; Myndus, 134; Rhodus, 231, 233, 234, 236, 238, 249, 253, 257.

H.

Hand holding ear of corn.—Rhodus, 255.
Hand open.—Rhodus, 254.
Harpa.—Myndus, 134; Rhodus, 235.
Helmet.—Alabanda, 3; Cnidus, 90, 272; Orthosia, 143; Ialysus, 226; Rhodus, 235, 236, 243, 252, 259.
Horse's head.—Rhodus, 239.

I.

Isis, Head-dress of.—Rhodus, 253-255, 259.
Ivy-leaf.—Rhodus, 238.
Ivy-wreath.—Rhodus, 235, 237, 253.

K.

Kylix.—Rhodus, 232.

L.

Labrys.—Euromus, 99; Mylasa, 128.
Lamp.—Rhodus, 235—237.
Lituus.—Alabanda, 6.
Lyre.—Halicarnassus, 104; Rhodus, 232, 237, 255.

N.

Nike holding aplustre.—Rhodus, 244.

O.

Oenochoë.—Astyra, 60, 61.
Oenochoë and Tripod.—Rhodus, 261.
Olive-spray.—Halicarnassus, 102.
Omphalos and Serpent.—Rhodus, 253, 254.
Omphalos and Star.—Rhodus, 256.
Owl.—Rhodus, 232, 259, 261.

P.

Palm.—Rhodus, 247, 259, 266.
Palm and Dolphin.—Rhodus, 263.
Pentagram.—Rhodus, 246.
Pileus surmounted by Star.—Rhodus, 235.
Prow.—Cnidus, 87, 88, 272; Rhodus, 235, 241, 248, 253.

Q.

Quiver with Strap.—Alabanda, 271.

R.

Race-torch.—Rhodus, 239, 253, 257.
Radiate disk, half of (rising sun).—Rhodus, 256, 257, 266.
Ram's head and Caduceus.—Rhodus, 255.
Rose.—Cnidus, 94; Rhodus, 252.

S.

Serpent.—Rhodus, 244, 247.
Serpent coiled.—Stratonicea, 147; Rhodus, 256.
Serpent twined round omphalos.—Rhodus, 253, 254, 256.
Shell, funnel-shaped.—Rhodus, 239.
Shell (pecten).—Rhodus, 232, 237, 239.
Shield.—Rhodus, 253.
Shield, Boeotian.—Rhodus, 232.

Shield, oval.—Rhodus, 243.
Silenos drinking from askos ?—Rhodus, 244.
Spear-head.—Rhodus, 239, 247, 253.
Sphinx.—Rhodus, 231.
Star.—Halicarnassus, 104; Iasus, 126; Myndus, 134; Stratonicea, 147; Cos, 205, 206, 208, 212; Rhodus, 235, 236, 239, 251, 255, 256, 258, 261, 268.
Star (Milesian).—Rhodus, 248.
Stars, three.—Rhodus, 261.
Sword in sheath.—Rhodus, 258, 259.

T.

Term.—Rhodus, 263.
Term, ithyphallic, bearded.—Rhodus, 247.
Thunderbolt.—Myndus, 134, 135; Rhodus, 233, 238, 241, 247, 248, 258, 259.

Thyrsos.—Rhodus, 242, 254, 256.
Torch.—Stratonicea, 147, 148; Rhodus, 250.
Torch and Quiver.—Stratonicea, 147.
Trident.—Rhodus, 236, 238, 245, 247, 252.
Tripod.—Rhodus, 246, 247.
Tripod and Oenochoë.—Rhodus, 261.

V.

Vase (skyphos).—Rhodus, 240.

W.

Wing.—Rhodus, 253.
Wreath.—Plarasa and Aphrodisias, 26; Caunus, 74; Mausolus, 181, 182; Rhodus, 235, 237, 242, 250, 261.

INDEX IV. A.

KINGS AND RULERS, &c.

E

ΕΚΑΤΟΜ.—Hecatomnus, 180.
ΕΥΠΟΛΕΜΟΥ.—Eupolemus, —Mylasa, 128.

I

ΙΔΡΙΕΩΣ.—Hidrieus, 183.

M

ΜΑΥΣΣΩΛΛΟ.—Mausolus, 181.

N

ΝΙΚΙΑΣ.—Nikias, Coś, 213.

Π

ΠΙΞΩΔΑΡΟ and ΠΙΞΩΔΑΡΟΥ.—Pixodarus, 184, 185.

T

ΤΥΜΝΟ.—Tymnes, Termera, 176.

INDEX IV. B.

MAGISTRATES' NAMES ON AUTONOMOUS COINS.

A.

ΑΓΑΘΑΡΧΟΣ.—Rhodus, 252.
ΑΓΑΘΟΦ[ΑΝΗΣ].—Cnidus, 91.
ΑΓΕΜΑΧΟΣ.—Rhodus, 252.
ΑΓΕΜΑΧΟΥ.—Rhodus, 242.
ΑΓΕΦΩΝ.—Cnidus, *Introd.* li.
ΑΓΗΣΙΑ.—Cos, 207.
ΑΓΗΣΙΑΣ.—Cos, 211.
ΑΓΗΣΙΔΑΜΟΣ.—Rhodus, 242.
ΑΓΗΣΙΔΑΜΟΣ.—Rhodus, 252.
ΑΓΗΤΩΡ.—Cnidus, *Introd.* l.
ΑΓΛΑΟΣ.—Cos, 209, 211.
ΑΓΝΩΝ?—Cos, 212.
ΑΕΤΙΩΝ.—Rhodus, 240, 242, 253.
ΑΘΑΝΟΔΩΡΟΣ.—Rhodus, 253.
ΑΙΘΩΝ.—Halicarnassus, 107.
ΑΙΝΕΑΣ.—Antiochia, 14; *Introd.* xxxi.
ΑΙΝΗΤΩΡ.—Rhodus, 245, 253; *Introd.* cix.
ΑΙΣΧΡΙΩΝ.—Cos, 202.
ΑΚΕΣΙΣ.—Rhodus, 241, 247.
ΑΚΡΟ....—Cnidus, *Introd.* l.
ΑΛΚΙΔΑΜ.—Cos, 207, 210.
ΑΛΚΙΜΑΧΟΣ.—Cos, 195.
ΑΜΕΙΝΙΑΣ.—Rhodus, 241, 243, 245, 247.
ΑΜΦΙΔΑΜΑΣ?—Cos, 199.
ΑΝΑΞΑΝΔΡΟΣ.—Cos, 196, 201, 202; Rhodus, 243, 247, 253.
ΑΝΑΞΙΔΙΚΟ[Σ].—Rhodus, 253.
ΑΝΑΞΙΔΟΤΟΣ.—Rhodus, 253, 256.
ΑΝΑΞΙΠΠΟΣ.—Iasus, 125.
ΑΝΔΡΟΜΕ? — Halicarnassus, 108.
ΑΝΔΡΟΣ.—Cos, 205.
ΑΝΔΡΩΝ ΦΑΝΙΟΥ.—Aphrodisias and Plarasa.—*Introd.* xxxiv.
ΑΝΘΕΣΤ...—Cos, 205.
ΑΝΝΙΚΑ....—Cnidus, *Introd.* l.
ΑΝΤΑΙΟΣ.—Rhodus, 251, 256, 272.
ΑΝΤΙ....—Cnidus, 92; Rhodus, 254.
ΑΝΤΙΓ?—Halicarnassus, 108.

MAGISTRATES' NAMES ON AUTONOMOUS COINS.   299

ΑΝΤΙΓΕΝΗΣ.—Rhodus, 253.
[Α]ΝΤΙΟΧΙΔΑ[Σ].—Cnidus, *Introd*. l.
ΑΝΤΙΟΧΟΣ.—Cos, 213.
ΑΝΤΙΠΑΤΡοΣ. — Cnidus, *Introd*. l.
ΑΝΤΙΠΑΤΡοΣ with ΜΥΩΝ and ΔΙ[ο]ΓΕΝΗΣ.—Aphrodisias and Plarasa, 27.
ΑΓ or ΑΓ.—Cos, 195.
ΑΠΟΛ....—Ceramus, 77 ; Halicarnassus, 104.
ΑΠΟΛΛΟ....,—Halicarnassus, 109.
[Α]ΠοΛΛοΔοΤοΣ ΜΕΝΑΝ ΔΡοΥ.—Aphrodisias and Plarasa, 271.
ΑΠοΛΛΩΝΙοΣ ΑΓΕΛΑοΥ.— Aphrodisias and Plarasa, 26.
ΑΡΑΤοΣ.—Cos, 202.
Ρ—Ε.—Rhodus(?), 250.
ΑΡΙΣΤΑΓΟΡΑΣ.-Cnidus,92,94.
ΑΡΙΣΤΑΙοΣ.—Cos, 210.
ΑΡΙΣΤΑΚοΣ.—Rhodus,243,245.
ΑΡΙΣΤΕΑΣ and ΑΡΙCΤΕΑC. Stratonicea, *Introd*. lxix., lxx.
ΑΡΙΣΤΕΑΣ ΟΠΛΕΙΤοΥ. — Orthosia, 143.
ΑΡΙΣΤΕΥΣ. — Alabanda (Antiochia), *Introd*. xxvii., xxviii.
ΑΡΙΣΤΙΩΝ, ΑΡΙCΤΙΩΝ, and ΑΙΣΤΙΩΝ.—Cos, 195, 204.
ΑΡΙCΤΟ.—Halicarnassus, 109.
ΑΡΙΣΤΟΒΙοΣ.—Rhodus, 235.
ΑΡΙΣΤοΒοΥΛοΣ.—Rhodus,243, 253 ; *Introd*. cix.

ΑΡΙΣΤΟΚΛΗΣ. — Cnidus, *Introd*. l.
ΑΡΙΣΤοΚΡΙΤοΣ.—Rhodus, 241, 243.
ΑΡΙΣΤΟΛΟ[ΧΟ]Σ. — Rhodus, 235.
ΑΡΙΣΤοΜ.—Cos, 207.
ΑΡΙΣΤοΜΑΧοΣ.—Rhodus, 260.
ΑΡΙΣΤοΝοΜοΣ.—Rhodus, 235.
ΑΡΙΣΤΟΠΟΛΙΣ.—Cnidus, 95.
ΑΡΙΣΤΩ.—Cos, 205.
ΑΡΙΦ[ΡΩ]Ν.—Cnidus, 90.
ΑΡΤΕ...? — Halicarnassus, 107, 108.
ΑΡΤΕΜΙΔ ΙΑΣ.—Orthosia, 143.
ΑΡΤΕΜΙΔΩ. — Stratonicea, *Introd*. lxx.
ΑΡΤΕΜΙΔΩΡοΣ. — Aphrodisias and Plarasa, 271.
ΑΡΤΕΜΙΔΩΡοΣ ΑΠοΛΛΩ ΝοΣ.—Aphrodisias and Plarasa, 26.
ΑΡΤΕΜΙΔΩΡοΣ ΑΡΤΕΜΙΔ ΩΡοΥ ΤοΥ ΑΝΔΡΩΝοΣ. —Aphrodisias and Plarasa, 26.
ΑΡΤ. ΣΩ. ΣΗ.—Aphrodisias and Plarasa, *Introd*. xxxiv.
ΑΡΤΕΜΩΝ.—Aphrodisias and Plarasa, 271 ; Rhodus, 253, 257.
ΑΡΧΕΚΡ[ΑΤΗΣ].—Cnidus, 89.
ΑΡΧΕΠοΛ.—Cos, 202.
ΑΡΧΙΑΣ.—Cnidus, *Introd*. lii. ; Cos, 204, 205.
ΑΡΧΙΔΑΜοΣ.—Cos, 195, 199.
ΑΡΧΩΝ.—Cos, 203.
ΑΣ....—Cnidus, 92.

ΑΣΚΛΑΠΙΟ[Σ].—Cos, 214.
ΑΣΚΛΗΠΙ.—Cos, 208.
ΑCΠΑ.—Halicarnassus, 109.
ΑΤΤΑΛΟC ΑΡ.—Stratonicea, Introd. lxix.
ΑΥΤοΚΡΑΤΗΣ.—Cnidus, 90.

B.

ΒΑΒΩΝ.—Rhodus, 248.
ΒΑΙΩΝ.—Cnidus, 90.
ΒΑΤΙΩΝ.—Cos, 201.
ΒΙΤΩΝ.—Cos, 196.

Γ.

ΓΑΙΟC.—Stratonicea, Introd. lxix.
ΓΕΝοΚΛΗ.—Cos, 208.
ΓΝΩΣΙΔΙΚοΣ.—Cos, 272.
ΓοΡ.—Tabae, 161.
ΓοΡΓΙΑ.—Rhodus, 257.
ΓοΡΓοΣ.—Rhodus, 245, 246, 247, 260.
ΓοΡΓοΥ.—Rhodus, 245.

Δ.

ΔΑΜΑΣ.—Rhodus, 257.
ΔΑΜΑΤΡΙοΣ.—Rhodus, 254, 257; Introd. cix.

ΔΑΜοΚΡΙΝ[ΗΣ].—Rhodus, Introd. cix.
[Δ]ΑΜοΝΙΚοΣ.—Plarasa, Introd. xxxiii.
ΔΑΜοΞΕΝοC.—Cos, 200.
ΔΑΜΩΝ.—Cos, 196, 203.
Δ—Δ.—Rhodus? 249.
ΔΕΙΝΙΑΣ.—Cos, 207.
ΔΕΞΑΓοΡΑΣ.—Rhodus, 257.
ΔΕΞΙΚΡΑΤΗΣ.—Rhodus, 254, 257.
ΔΗΜΗΤΡΙοΣ.—Alabanda, 271; Introd. xxvii.
ΔΗΜΗΤΡΙοC.—Amyzon, Introd. xxxi.; Cos, 198, 200; Introd. xciv.
ΔΗΜΟCΘΕΝΗC.—Stratonicea, Introd. lxix.
ΔΗΜοΚΛΗΣ.—Rhodus(?), 248.
ΔΙ.—Rhodus, 235.
[ΔΙ]ΑΓο[ΡΑΣ]?—Cos, 196.
ΟΙΔ.—Halicarnassus, 107.
ΔΙοΓΕΝΗΣ.—Alabanda, Introd. xxvii.; Cos, 201; Rhodus, 252.
ΔΙοΓΕΝΗΣ with ΜΥΩΝ and ΑΝΤΙΠΑΤΡοΣ.—Aphrodisias and Plarasa, 27.
ΔΙοΓΝΗΤοΣ.—Stratonicea, 147; Rhodus, 254, 257.
ΔΙοΚΛΗΣ.—Cnidus, 94, 96; Rhodus, 246, 248.
ΔΙοΚΛΗC ΚΙ.—Stratonicea, Introd. lxix.
ΔΙοΜΕ.—Cos, 209.
ΔΙοΝΥ.—Alinda, 10; Halicarnassus, 108.

MAGISTRATES' NAMES ON AUTONOMOUS COINS. 301

ΔΙΟΝΥΣΙΟΣ.—Alabanda (Antiochia), 1, *Introd.* xxviii.; Antiochia ad Maeandrum, *Introd.* xxxii.; Rhodus, 257.
ΔΙΟΝΥCΙΟC.—Stratonicea, 148.
ΔΙΟCΚ.—Halicarnassus, 108.
ΔΙΟΤΡΕΦΗΣ. — Antiochia ad Maeandrum, *Introd.* xxxii.
ΔΙΟΦΑΝ.—Cos, 209, 212.
ΔΙΩΝ.—Cos, 195.
ΔΡΑΚΩΝ.—Halicarnassus, 106.
Δ—Υ.—Rhodus(?), 249.

E.

ΕΚΑΣ.—Euromus, *Introd.* liii.
ΕΚΑΤΑΙΟΣ· — Cnidus, *Introd.* lii.
ΕΚΑ[Τ]ΑΙΟC CΩCΑΝΔΡΟΥ.—Stratonicea, 148, *Introd.* lxx.
ΕΚΑΤΑΙΟΥ.—Cos, 208.
ΕΚΑΤΟΔΩΡ.—Cos, 196, 201.
ΕΛΛΑΝΙΚΟΣ.—Cos, 200, 202.
ΕΜΜΕΝΙ.—Cos, 211.
ΕΜΓΡΕΓΩΝ.—Cos, 198, 199, *Introd.* xciv.
ΕΞΗΚΕC.—Myndus, 135.
ΕΟΒΩΛΟ[Σ].—Cnidus, 87.
ΕΠΑΓΑΘΟΣ.—Cnidus, 96.
ΗΠ᎒ (= 'Επήρατος ?). — Cnidus, *Introd.* xlix.
ΕΠΙ(?)ΣΟ.—Halicarnassus, 103.
ΕΠΙΓΟΝΟΣ.—Myndus, 134.
[Ε]ΠΙΔΑΥΡΙΟΣ.—Cos, 204.

ΕΠΙΚΡΑΤΗΣ Ξ[Ε]ΝΟΚΡΑΤΟΥ[Σ] (Ιερεύς δήμου).—Aphrodisias and Plarasa, 26.
ΕΓΙΝΙΚΟΣ.—Cos, 200.
ΕΠΙΤΥΧΗΣ.—Rhodus, 262.
ΕΡΑΞΙΚΛΗΣ.—Rhodus,235, 236, 243.
[Ε]ΡΜΑΓΟΡ[ΑΣ] ? — Alabanda (Antiochia), *Introd.* xxviii.
ΕΡΜΙΑΣ.—Myndus, 136.
ΕΡΜΟΓΕ.—Antiochia, *Intr.* xxxii.
ΕΡΜΟΛΥΚ[ΟΣ].—Myndus, 184.
ΕΡΜΟΦΑΝΤΟC.—Ceramus, 77.
ΕΡΜΩΝ.—Halicarnassus, 106.
ΕCΤΙ.—Halicarnassus, 104.
ΕΥ.—Rhodus, 233, 234, 235.
ΕΥΑΡΑΤΟΣ.—Cos, 207, 208, 213.
[Ε]ΥΒΙΟΣ.—Rhodus ? 248.
ΕΥΒΟΥΛ[ΟC].—Cnidus, 96.
ΕΥΔΑΜ· (προστάτης).—Cos, 206, 208.
ΕΥΔΗ(?)—Antiochia, 15.
ΕΥΔΩΡΟΣ (?[Θ]ΕΥΔΩΡΟΣ).—Cnidus, *Introd.* 1.; Cos, 200.
ΕΥΚ.—Cnidus, *Introd.* lii.
ΕΥΚΑΡΠΟΣ.—Cos, 213.
ΕΥΚΡΑΤ.—Cos, 209, 211.
ΕΥΚΡΑΤΗΣ.—Rhodus, 241, 243, 246, 247.
ΕΥΝ.—Cnidus, *Introd.* lii.
ΕΥΓΟΛΕΜΟΥ.—Mylasa, 128.
ΕΥΦΑΝΗΣ.—Rhodus, 254.
ΕΥΦΡΑ[ΝΩ]Ρ.—Cnidus,*Introd.*lii.
ΡΦΥ᎒ (? Εὔφρων).—Cnidus, *Introd.* xlix.
ΜΩ᎐ΦΥ᎑.—Cnidus, 91.
ΕΥΦΡΩΝ.—Cnidus, 89.

Ι.

ΖΗΝΩΝ.—Tabae, 160.
ΣΗΝΩΝ.—Aphrodisias and Plarasa, 271.
ΖΗΝΩΝ.—Rhodus, 261.
ΣΗΝΩΝ.—Rhodus, 254.
ΣΗΝΩΝ.—Rhodus, 261.
ΣΩΙΛΟΣ.—Cos, 198, 200.
ΖΩΙΛΟΥ.—Stratonicea, 148.

H.

ΗΛΙΟΔΩ.—Cos, 207, 208.
ΗΡΑΓ.—Cos, 196.
ΗΡΑΓΟΡΑΣ.—Rhodus, 254.
ΗΡΟΔΟΤΟΣ.—Cos, 202.
ΗΡΟΔΩΡΟΣ.—Myndus, 134.
ΗΡΩΔΗΣ.—Cnidus, *Introd.* lii.
ΗΦΑΙΣΤΙΩΝ ΧΑΡΙΞΕΝΟΥ.
—Aphrodisias and Plarasa, *Introd.* xxxiv.

Θ.

Θ—Α.—Rhodus? 249.
ΘΑΡΣΥΤΑΣ.—Rhodus, 242, 243.
ΘΑΥΜΙ.—Cos, 203.
ΘΕ.—Tabae, 160.
ΘΕΟΓΝΩΤΟΣ (or ΘΕΥΓΝΩ
ΤΟΣ?).—Cnidus, *Introd.* lii.

ΘΕΟΔΟΤΟΣ.—Myndus, 134,135.
ΘΕΟΔΩΡΟΣ.—Myndus, 134.
ΘΕΟΚΛΗΣ.—Myndus, 137. •
ΘΕΟΞΕ.—Antiochia, *Introd.* xxxii.
ΘΕΟΦΑΝΗΣ.—Cnidus, *Introd.* l.
ΘΕΥΔΟΤ[ΟΣ].—Cos, 203.
ΘΕΥΔΟΤ[ΟΣ] (προστάτης).—Cos, 206.
ΘΕΥΜΕΛΩΝ.—Cnidus, 90, 272.
ΘΕΥΦΑΜ[ΙΔΑΣ].—Cos, 207.
[Θ]ΕΥΦΙΛΗΤ[ΟΣ].—Cos, 203.
ΘΡΑΣΥΜΕΝΗ[Σ]. — Rhodus, 257, 258.
ΘΡΑΣΥΜΕΝΗΣ Τ.—Rhodus, 254.
ΘΡΑΣΥΜΗΔ[ΗΣ]. — Rhodus, 254.

Ι.

ΙΑ (numeral ?).—Alabanda, 2.
ΙΑΣΩΝ.—Halicarnassus, 104.
ΙΑΣΩΝ.—Rhodus? 248, 281.
ΙΑΣΩΝ ΣΚΥΜΝΟΥ.—Aphrodisias and Plarasa, *Intro.* xxxiv.
ΙΑΤΡΟΚΛΗΣ.—Cos, 199.
ΙΔΟΜΕΝΕΥΣ.—Cos, 199.
ΕΙ (numeral ?).—Alabanda, 3.
ΙΕΡΟ.—Halicarnassus, 109.
ΙΕΡΟΚΛ[Η].—Halicarnassus,104.
ΙΕΡΟΚΛΗΣ.—Myndus, 135.
ΙΕΡΩΝ.—Cos, 210.
ΙΜΕΡΑΙΟΣ. — Nisyros, *Introd.* xcix.

MAGISTRATES' NAMES ON AUTONOMOUS COINS. 303

ΙΠ.—Cos, 216.
ΙΠΠΑΡΧ.—Cos, 202.
ΙΠΠΟΔΑ.—Cnidus, *Introd.* li.
ΙΓΓΟΛΟΧΟΣ.—Cos, 199.
ΙΣΙΔΩΡΟΣ.—Myndus, 136.
ΙΣΟΚΡΑΤΗΣ.—Alabanda (Antiochia), 1 ; *Introd.* xxvii., xxviii.

K.

ΚΑΛΛΙΞΕ[ΝΗΣ].—Rhodus,254.
[ΚΑ]ΛΛΙΠ.—Cos, 210.
ΚΑΛΛΙΠΠΙΔΗΣ.—Cos, 213.
ΚΑΛΛΙΠΟΣ.—Rhodus ? 249.
ΚΑΛΛΙΠΠΟΣ. — Cnidus, 91 ; Rhodus ? 248.
ΚΑΛΛΙΠΠΟΣ ΛΕΟΝΤΕΩΣ ... ΠΕΙΤΟΥ. — Aphrodisias and Plarasa, 27.
ΚΑΛΛΙΣΘΕΝΗΣ.—Rhodus,246.
ΚΑΛΛΙCΤΟΣ.—Myndus, 135.
ΚΑΛΛΙΣΤΡΑΤΟΣ.—Cos, 198.
ΚΑΛΛΙΦΡΩΝ.—Cnidus, 89, 272.
ΚΑΛΥΜΝΙΟΣ.—Cos, 214.
ΚΑΡΝΕΙΣΚΟΣ.—Cnidus, 91, 93.
ΚΑΦΙΣΙΟ[Σ]?—Cos, 202.
ΚΑΦΙCΟ.—Cnidus, 95.
ΚΗΦΙΞΟΔΩ[ΡΟΞ]. — Rhodus ? 249.
ΚΛΕΙ.—Halicarnassus, 104, 106.
ΚΛΕΙΝΙΓΓΟΣ.—Cnidus, 89.
ΚΛΕΙΝΟΣ.—Cos, 198.
ΚΛΕΙΤΟΦΩ[Ν].—Cnidus, 92.

ΚΛΕΟΣΘΕΝΗΣ. — Cnidus, *Introd.* 1.
ΚΛΕΥΜΑ.—Cos, 212.
ΚΛΕΩ· (προστάτης).—Cos, 206.
ΚΟ.—Tabae, 161.
ΚΟΛΒΑ.—Neapolis Myndiorum ? 140.
ΚΡΙΤΟΚΛΗΣ.—Rhodus, 261.
[Κ]ΤΗΣΙΑΣ.—Iasus, 125.
ΚΤΗΤΟΣ.—Caunus, 75.
ΚΥΔΟΚΛΗ[Σ].—Cnidus, 91.

Λ.

ΛΑΕΡΤΑΣ.—Cos, 201.
ΛΑΜΠΙ.—Halicarnassus, 105.
[Λ]ΑΜΠΙΑΣ.—Cos, 203.
ΛΑΜΠΙΤΟΣ.—Iasus, 124.
ΛΑΜΓΩΝ.—Cnidus, 87.
[ΛΑ]ΧΑΡΤΟΣ.—Cnidus, 93.
ΛΕΩΝ.—Stratonicea, 147, 150.
ΛΕ[Ω]Ν with [ΣΩ]Σ[ΙΠ]ΟΛΙΣ and ΧΑΡΜΙΔΗΣ.—Attuda, 62.
ΛΕΩΝΙΔΑΣ.—Rhodus, 261.
ΛΟΧΟΣ.—Cos, 207.
ΛΥΚΩΝ.—Cos, 199 ; Antiochia, *Introd.* xxxii.
[ΛΥ]ΣΩΝ ?—Rhodus, 246.

M.

Μ.—Alabanda (Antiochia), 2.
ΜΑΗΣ.—Rhodus, 255.

M—E.—Rhodus ? 250.
ΜΕΛΑ.—Myndus, 136.
ΜΕΛΑΝ.—Halicarnassus, 105.
ΜΕΛΑΝΘΙΟΣ.—Stratonicea, Introd. lxx.
ΜΕΛΑΝΤ.—Rhodus, 252.
ΜΕΛΕ.—Antiochia, 14.
ΜΕΝΑΝ.—Antiochia, 15.
ΜΕΝΑΝΔΡΟC.—Apollonia Salbace, 54.
ΜΕΝΕΚ.—Halicarnassus, 109.
ΜΕΝΕΚΛΗΣ.—Alabanda (Antiochia), 2, Introd. xxvii., xxviii.; Stratonicea, 147.
ΜΕΝΕΣΘΕΥΣ.—Alabanda (Antiochia), 2, Introd. xxvii., xxviii.; Iasus, 124.
ΜΕΝΕΦΡΩΝ.—Antiochia, 14.
ΜΕΝΙCΚΟΥ.—Antiochia, Introd. xxxii.
ΜΕΝΟΙΤΙΟC.—Stratonicea, 147.
ΜΕΝΩΝ.—Cos, 208, 209.
ΜΗΝΟΔΟΤΟΣ.—Alabanda, Introd. xxvii.; Myndus, 135, 136.
ΜΗΝΟΔΟΤΟΣ ΑΓΕΛΑΟΥ. —Aphrodisias and Plarasa, Introd. xxxiv.
ΜΗΝΟΔΩΡΟΣ.—Rhodus, 255, 258.
ΜΙ.—Tabae, 161.
M - I.—Rhodus ? 250.
ΜΙΚΥΘΟΣ.—Cos, 202, 204.
ΜΙΚΩΝ.—Cos, 200.
ΜΝΑΣΙΜΑΧΟΣ.—Rhodus, 244; Introd. cix.

ΜΝΑΣΙΜΑΧΟΥ.—Rhodus, 244.
ΜΝΗΜΩΝ—Rhodus, 255.
ΜοΙΡΙΧ[οΣ].—Cnidus, 93.
ΜΟΡΦΙΩΝ.—Cnidus, Introd. li.
ΜΟCΧΙ.—Halicarnassus, 109.
ΜΟΣΧΙΩΝ.—Cos, 197, 199; Introd. xciv.
ΜΟΣΧΟ[Σ].—Cnidus, 95; Halicarnassus, 106.
ΜΟΥΣΑΙΟΣ.—Rhodus, 246.
ΜΥΩΝ with ΔΙΟΓΕΝΗΣ and ΑΝΤΙΠΑΤΡΟΣ.—Aphrodisias and Plarasa, 27.
ΜΥΩΝ ΚΑΛΛΙΠΠΟΥ.—Aphrodisias and Plarasa, 27.

N.

ΝΕΟΚΛΗ.—Halicarnassus, 107.
ΝΕΩΝ.—Rhodus, 255.
ΝΙ.—Rhodus, 233.
ΝΙΚΑΓΟΡΑΣ.—Rhodus, 255.
ΝΙΚΑΡΧοΣ.—Cos, 208.
ΝΙΚΗΦοΡΟΣ.—Rhodus, 255.
ΝΙΚΙΑΕ (προστάτης).—Cos, 206.
ΝΙΚΟΛΑοΣ.—Stratonicea, 147.
ΝΙΚΟΜ.—Cos, 207.
ΝΙΚΟΜΗ.—Cos, 212.
ΝΙΚΟΣΤΡ.—Cos, 207.
ΝΙΚΟΣΤΡΑΤοΣ.—Cos, Introd. xcv.
ΝΙΚΟΦΩΝ.—Rhodus, 261.
ΝΙΚΩΝ.—Cos, 198, 206.

Ξ.

Ξ--Α.—Rhodus ? 249.
ΞΑΙΓΡΕΤΟΣ.—Cos, 201, 202.
ΞΑΝΘΙΠΠΟΣ.—Cos, 204.
ΞΕΙΝΟΣ.—Cos, 208.
ΞΕΝΟΚΡΑΤΗΣ. — Aphrodisias, Introd. xxxiv.; Rhodus, 244,255.
ΞΕΝΟΚΡΑΤΗΣ ΞΕΝΟΚΡΑΤΟΥ.—Aphrodisias and Plarasa, Introd. xxxiv.
ΞΕΝΟΜΒΡΟΤΟΣ.—Cos, 198.
ΞΕΝΟΦΩΝ and ΞΕΝΟΦΩΝ. —Cos, 215.

Ο.

ΟΛΥΜ...?—Halicarnassus, 106.
ΟΝΑΣΑΝΔΡΟΣ.—Rhodus, 244.
ΟΡ[Θ]ΑΓΟ?—Cos, 196.

Π.

Π—Α.—Rhodus ? 249, 250.
ΠΑΙ? —Apollonia Salbace, 54.
ΠΑΜΦΙΛΟΣ.—Alabanda, Introd. xxviii.
ΠΑΝΘΑΛΗΣ.—Cnidus, 90.
ΠΑΝΤΑ[Ι]ΝΟΣ.—Iasus, 124.
ΠΑΝΤΑΛΕΩΝ.—Cnidus, 95.
ΠΑΠΙΑΣ.—Tabae, 160.
ΠΑΠΙΑC ΚΑΛΛΙΠΠΟΥ. — Apollonia Salbace, Introd. xxxvii.
ΠΑΡΜΕ.—Cos, 208.

ΠΑΡΜΕΝΙΣΚ[ΟΣ].—Cos, 203.
ΓΑΥΞΑΝ?—Cos, 197.
ΠΑΥΣΑΝΙΑΣ.—Iasus, 125.
ΠΑΥΣΙΜΑΧΟΣ.—Cos, 202.
Π—Ε.—Rhodes ? 250. .
ΠΕΙΣΙΚΡΑΤΗΣ.—Rhodus, 246, 247.
ΠΕΙΣΙΣΤΡΑΤΟΣ.—Rhodus,256.
ΠΕΡΙΤΑΣ. Rhodus, 256.
ΠΟ...—Iasus, 125.
ΠΟΛΕ.—Euromus, 99.
ΠΟΛΙΤΗC.—Ceramus, 77.
ΠΟΛΥΑΡΧΟΣ.—Cos, 198, 199; Introd. xciv.
ΠΟΛΥΔΑ.—Cos, 212.
ΠΟΛΥΧ[ΑΡΗΣ?].—Cos, 212.
ΠΟΛΥΧΑ[ΡΜΟΣ?].—Cos, 197.
ΠΟCΙΤΤΟΥ, see ΖΩCΙΜΟΥ.
ΠΡΑΞΙΑΝΑΞ.—Cos, 195.
?ΩϘΠ.—Myndus, 136.
ΠΥΘΕΑΣ. — Stratonicca, Introd. lxx.
ΠΥΘΙΩΝ.—Cos, 201.
ΠΥΘΙΩΝ ΠΟΛΥΚΡΑΤΟΥ.— Aphrodisias and Plarasa, Introd. xxxiv.
ΠΥΘΟΚΛΗΣ.—Cos, 212, 213.
ΠΥΘΩΝ.—Cnidus, 92.

Σ.

ΣΑΤΥΡΟΣ.—Cos, 212 ; Rhodus, 262
ΣΟ (ἐπὶ) —Halicarnassus, 103.
ΣΟΛ[ων ?]—Antiochia, Intro. xxxi.

R R

ΣΤΑΣΙΩΝ.—Rhodus, 244, 246, 249, 256, Introd. cix.
ϹΤΕΦΑΝΟϹ.—Cos, 198, 200, Introd. xciv.
ΣΤΗΣΙΟΧΟΣ.—Iasus, 125.
ΣΤΡΑΤΩΝ.—Rhodus ? 249.
ΣΥΜΜΑΧοΣ.—Alabanda (Antiochia), Introd. xxviii.; Myndus, 136.
ϹΥΜΜΑΧΟϹ.—Myndus, 135.
ΣΦΑΙΡοΣ.—Rhodus, 261, 262.
ϹΩΔ?—Halicarnassus, 109.
ΣΩΠΑΤ.—Cos, 209.
ΣΩΠοΛ[ΙΣ].—Rhodus, 247.
ΣΩΣΑΝΔΡΟ[Σ].—Rhodus, 256.
ΣΩΣΘΕΝΗΣ.—Rhodus,261,262.
ΣΩΣΙΓΕΝΗΣ.—Cnidus, Introd. 1.
ϚΩϚΙΚΡΑΤΗϚ.—Rhodus, 247.
ϚΩϚΙΜΑΧ[ΟϚ]. — Cnidus, Introd. 1.
[ΣΩ]Σ[ΙΠ]ΟΛΙΣ with ΧΑΡΜΙΔΗΣ and ΛΕ[Ω]Ν.—Attuda, 62.
ϚΩϚΙϚΤΡΑΤοϚ.—Cos, 199.
ϹΩϹΤ.—Myndus, 136.

T.

ΤΕ.—Rhodus, 250.
ΤΕΙΣΥΛοΣ.—Rhodus, 242, 247, Introd. cix.
ΤΕΛΕΑΣ.—Cnidus, 91.
ΤΕΛΕΑΣ and Ε.—Cnidus, Introd. 1.
ΤΕΛΕΣΙΠΠΟΣ.—Cnidus, 96.

ΤΕΛΕΣΙΦΡΩΝ. — Cnidus, Introd. 1.
[Τ]ΕΛΕϹΙΦ[ΡΩΝ].—Cnidus, 89.
ΤΕΛΕϹΙΦΡΩΝ and Ε.—Cnidus, Introd. 1.
ΤΙΜοΓ.—Cos, 208.
ΤΙΜοΘΕοΣ.—Rhodus, 244.
ΤΙΜοΚΛΗΣ. — Alabanda (Antiochia), 1; Introd. xxvii. xxviii.
ΤΙΜοΚΡΑ.—Rhodus, 252.
ΤΙΜοΛΥΚοΣ.—Cos, 197.
ΤΙΜοΞΕΝοΣ.—Cos, 208; Rhodus, 261.
ΤΙΜοΣΤΡΑΤ[οΣ]. — Rhodus, 256.
ΤΙΣΑΧ.—Cos, 207.
ΤΡΑ.—Cnidus, 93.
ΤΥΜΝΟ.—Termera, 176; Introd. lxxviii.

Y.

Υ—Π.—Rhodes ? 250.
ΥΨΙΚΛΗΣ ✖ ΑΔΡΑΣΤΟΥ, — Aphrodisias and Plarasa, Introd. xxxiv.

Φ.

ΦΑΝΙΑϹ ΚΙΘΑ.—Stratonicea, Introd. lxx.
ΦΑΡοΣ.—Caunus, 75.
ΦΙ.—Rhodus, 250.

MAGISTRATES' NAMES ON AUTONOMOUS COINS. 307

ΦΙΛ.—Cos, 195, 196.
ΦΙΛΕΩΝΙΔΑΣ.—Cos, 194.
ΦΙΛΙΝΟΣ.—Cos, 201, 204, 212.
[ΦΙ]ΛΙΣΚΟΣ.—Cos, 197.
ΦΙΛΙΣΤ[ΟΣ].—Cos, 197, 198.
ΦΙΛΙΩΝ (προστάτης).—Cos, 206.
ΦΙΛΟΚΡΑΤΗΣ.—Rhodus, 256.
ΦΙΛΟΚΡΑΤΙΔΑC.—Cnidus; 94.
ΦΙΛΟΦΡ.....—Cos, 208, 209.
ΦΙΛΤΟΓΕΝΗΣ.—Alabanda (Antiochia), Introd. xxviii.
ΦΙΛΩΝ.—Cos, 198; Rhodus, 256.
ΦΙΛWΝ?—Cos, 204.
ΦΙΛΩΝΙΔΑΣ.—Rhodus, 235,236.
[Φ?]ΙΜ.—Tabae, 161.

X.

ΧΑΡΙΔΑ.—Cos, 212.
ΧΑΡΜ.—Halicarnassus, 105.
ΧΑΡΜΗΝ?—Halicarnassus, 107.
ΧΑΡΜΙΔΗΣ with [ΣΩ]Σ[ΙΠ]ο
ΛΙΣ and ΛΕ[Ω]Ν.—Attuda, 62.
ΧΑΡΜΥΛΟΣ.—Cos, 213.
ΧΡΥΣΙΠΠΟΣ ΧΡΥΣΙΠΠΟΥ.—
Aphrodisias and Plarasa, 271.
ΧΡΥΣΟΓΟΝΟΣ. — Alabanda
(Antiochia), Introd. xxviii.
ΧΡΥCΟΥ.—Stratonicea,Introd.lxx.

..]ΑΣΙΜ[... (Φρασιμήδης?)—Cos, 197.
..]ΔΕCCΤ[.. (Μόδεστος?).—Cos, 98.
..]ΚΡΑΤΛΑC (sic).—Cnidus, 93.
.....]ΛΑΚΩΝ. — Cnidus, Introd. li.
..]ΜΑΓΟΡ[... ('Ερμαγόρας?). —
Alabanda (Antiochia), 2.
...]ΟΚΡΑΤ[.. (Φιλοκρατίδας). —
Cnidus, 93.
..]ΡΙΛΟΧ[..?—Antiochia, 15.

INDEX IV. c.

MAGISTRATES' NAMES ON IMPERIAL COINS.

A.

ΑΓΑΘΕΙΝΟΥ (στρα.).—*Mamaea*, Apollonia Salbace, *Introd.* xxxviii.
ΑΓΛΑΟΥ.—*Augustus*, Antiochia, 18 ; *Introd.* xxxii.
ΑΓΛΑΟΥ, ΚΛ. ΦΡΟΥΓΙ (ἐπιμελη[θέντος]).—*Domitian*, Antiochia, 18 ; *Introd.* xxxii.
ΑΔΡΑΣΤΟΥ, ΠΟ. ΑΙ. (διὰ).—Trapezopolis, 178.
ΑΔΡΑΣΤΟΥ, Τ. ΚΛ. ΑΡΧΙΠΠΟΥ (ἀρχ.).—*Sept. Severus*, Trapezopolis, 179.
ΑΔΡΑΣΤΟΥ, Τ. ΚΕ ΖΕΥΞΙΘΕΟΥ (ἐπὶ ἄρ.).—*J. Domna*, Trapezopolis, 179.
ΑΘΗΝΑΓΟΡΑΣ.—*Germanicus* and *Drusus*, Tabae, 167.
ΑΘΗΝΑΓΟΡΟΥ.—*Imperial Times*, Harpasa, 113.
ΑΝΔΡΟΝΙΚ[ΟΣ] ΓΟΡΓΙΠΠΟΥ.—*Time of Augustus*, Trapezopolis, 179.
.... Α ΑΝΔΡΩΝΟΣ (ἐπὶ ἀρχ.(?).—Alabanda, 4 ; *Introd.* xxx.
ΑΝΤΙΓΟΝΟΥ (ἐπὶ).—*Imperial Times*, Rhodus, 263.
ΑΝΤΙΠΑΤΡΟΥ (ἐπὶ).—*Imperial Times*, Rhodus, 263.
ΑΝΤΩΝΙ. See ΡΟΥΦΟΥ.
ΑΠΕΛΛΑ (ἐπὶ ἀρ[χοντος]).—*Gallienus*, Aphrodisias, 49.
ΑΠΟΛΛΟΔΟΤΟΣ.—*Augustus*, Trapezopolis, 178.
ΑΠΟΛΛΩΝΙΑΝΟΥ ΠΟ. ΑΙΛ. (ἐπὶ ἀρχ[οντος]).—*Philip Junior*, Aphrodisias, 47 ; *Introd.* xxxv.

ΑΠΟΛΛΩΝΙΟC (υἱὸς Ἀφροδισιέων).—*Augustus* and *Livia*, Aphrodisias, 29, 39, 40 ; *Introd.* xxxv.
ΑΠΟΛΛΩΝΙΟΣ ΑΠΟΛΛΩΝΙΟΥ.—*Augustus*, Heraclea Salbace, 118 ; *Introd.* lvii.
ΑΠΟΛΛΩΝΙΟΣ ΚΩΚΟΥ.—*Caligula*, Apollonia Salbace, *Introd.* xxxvii.
ΑΠΟΛΛΩΝΙΟΥ (ἐπὶ).—*Imperial Times*, Rhodus, 264.
ΑΠΟΛΛΩΝΙΟΥ CT. (ἀρχ.).—*Caracalla* and *Geta*, Tabae, *Introd.* lxxvii.
ΑΡΙCΤΕΑC ΚΛΑΥ.—*Antoninus Pius*, Stratonicea, *Introd.* lxxii., lxxiv.
ΑΡΙCΤΕΟΥ ΚΛΑΥΔΙΟΥ (ἐπὶ).—*Imperial Times*, Stratonicea, *Introd.* lxxiv.
ΑΡΙCΤΕΑ ΤΙ. (ἐπιμελη[θέντος]).—*Imperial Times*, Stratonicea, *Intr.* lxxiv.
ΑΡΙCΤΕΑC ΧΙΔ?—*Augustus*, Stratonicea, *Introd.* lxxi.
ΑΡΙΣΤΟ[ΓΕ]ΝΗΣ (ἱππάρχης).—*Augustus*, Alabanda, *Introd.* xxx.
ΑΡΙCΤΟΛΑΟC ΦΛ.—*Antoninus Pius*, Stratonicea, 154 ; *Introd.* lxxi.
ΑΡΠΑΛ.—*Trajan*, Halicarnassus, 110.
ΑΡΡΙ. See ΦΛΑΒΙΑC.
ΑΡΤΕΜΙΔΩΡΟΥ (ἀρχ.).—*Caracalla*, Tabae, 171.
ΑΡΤΕΜΩΝ ΠΑΠΙΟΥ (ἀρ.).—*Imperial Times*, Tabae, 162.
ΑΡΧΙΠΠΟΥ. See ΑΔΡΑCΤΟΥ.
ΑCΕΝΑ(?) (ἐπὶ πρυ.).—*Imperial Times*, Stratonicea, *Introd.* lxxiv.
ΑΤΤΑΛΟC, CT. (ἀρχίατρος Νέοις [ἀνέθηκε]).—*Antoninus Pius* and *M. Aurelius*, Heraclea Salbace, 120 ; *Introd.* lvii.
[Α]ΤΤΑ[ΛΟΣ]? (ἀρ[χων]).—*Early Imperial Times*, Tabae, 163.

B.

[ΒΡ]ΑΧΥΛΛΙΔΑΣ ΚΑΛ[λικράτους].—*Early Imperial Times*, Tabae, 163.

Γ.

ΓΛΥΚΩΝ (ἱερεύς).—*Nero*, Heraclea Salbace, 119 ; *Introd.* lvii.

Δ.

ΔΑΜΑΡΑΤΑ (ἐπὶ).—*Imperial Times*, Rhodus, 264.
ΔΑΜΑΡΑΤΟΥ (ἐπὶ).—*Imperial Times*, Rhodus, 264.
ΔΗΜΗΤΡΙοΥ ΙΟΥΛ. Τ. ΦΛ. (ἀρχ.).—*Caracalla* and *Geta*, Halicarnassus and Cos, 112.
ΔΙΟΔΟ (ἐπὶ ἀρξ[αντος]).—*Commodus*, Ceramus, 78.
ΔΙοΜΗΔοΥC, ΦΛΑΥΒΙοΥ (ψηφισαμένου).—*Time of Trajan or Hadrian*, Stratonicea, 153; *Introd*. lxxiii.
ΔΙΟΝΥCΙΟΝ, ΤΒ. ΚΛ. (ἐπὶ τῶν περὶ).—*Caracalla* and *Plautilla*, Stratonicea, 158.
ΔΙΟΝΥCΙΟΥ ΑΥΡ. (ἐπὶ).—Stratonicea, *Introd*. lxxiv.
ΔΙΩΝΟC ΤΟΝ ΔΙΟΦΑΝΤΟΝ (ἀρχ.).—*Sept. Severus* and *J. Domna*, Myndus, 139.
ΔΟΜЄCΤΙΧΟΝ, ΜΑΡ· ΑΥΡ. (ἐπὶ ἀρχ. γ').—*Gallienus*, Tabae, 172--174.
ΔΟΜΝΟ, ΙΟΥΛΙΑ· ΙЄΡΟΚΛЄΟΥ (ἐπὶ πρυ.).—*Caracalla* and *Geta*, Stratonicea, 159.

E.

ЄΠΙΤΥΓΧΑΝΟΝΤΟC Γ ΦΙΛΩ[ΝΟC].—*Caracalla* and *Geta*, Stratonicea, 159.
ЄΡΜΟΓЄΝΟΥC ΑΠЄΛΛΑ.—*Gallienus*, Aphrodisias, 49; *Introd*. xxxv.
ЄΡΜШΝΟC ΑΥ. (ἐπὶ).—*Gallienus*, Bargasa, 70.
ЄΥΑΝΔΡΟC Β., Μ.ΑΥ. (ἀρχίατρος).—*Caracalla*, Harpasa, *Introd*. lvi.
ΕΥΔΑΜΟΣ Β̄, ꟼ ΟΠΤΙΜΟΣ.—*Caligula*, Cos, 217.
ЄΥΔШΡΟΥ (ἐπὶ).—*Imperial Times*, Rhodus, 264.
ΕΥΠΟΛΕΙΤΑ, Τ·Κ·Τ· (ἐπὶ).—*Imperial Times*, Cnidus, 97.
ΕΥΛ̂†ΚΑΜΫ CΤΡΑ†ΚΛЄΟΥC? ([ἀρ]χ.) —*Septimius Severus*, Halicarnassus, 111.

Z.

ΖΕΥΞΙΘΕΟΥ. See **ΑΔΡΑCΤΟΥ.**
ΖΗΛΟC, Τ.Κ. (ἀνέθ[ηκε]).—*Time of M. Aurelius*, Aphrodisias, 30, 35.
ΖΗΛΟC, Τ.Κ. (ἱερεὺς ἐπινίκιον ἀνέ[θηκε]).—*M. Aurelius* and *L. Verus*, Aphrodisias, 41, 42.
ΖΗΛΟC, Τ.ΚΛ. (ἱερεὺς).—*Time of M. Aurelius*, Aphrodisias, *Intr.* xxxv.
ΖΗΝΩΝ, ΤΙ.Κ.—*Time of Sept. Severus*, Aphrodisias, 33.
ΖΗΝΩΝ, ΤΙ. ΚΛ. (ἀνέ[θηκε]).—*Time of Sept. Severus*, Aphrodisias, 34.
ΖΗΝΩΝ, ΤΙ.ΚΛ. (ἀρχιε[ρεὺς] ἀρχινεοκ[όρος] ἀνέθ[ηκε]).—*Julia Domna*, Aphrodisias, 44; *Introd.* xxxv.
ΖΗΝΩ. ΚΛ. (ἀρχ[ιερέως]).—*Time of Sept. Severus*, Aphrodisias, 35.
ΖΗΝΩΝ with **ΜΕΝΙΠΠΟC.** (See **ΜΕΝΙΠΠΟC.**)
ΣΩΠΥΡΟΣ.—*Imperial Times*, Stratonicea, *Introd.* lxxi.
ΖΩCΙΜΟΥ ΠΟCΙΤΤΟΥ (πρυ. τὸ β'.).—*Caracalla* and *Geta*, Stratonicea, 158; *Introd.* lxxiv.
ΖΩCΙΜΟV (ἐπὶ β'.).—Stratonicea, 153.

Θ.

ΘΕΜΙCΤΟΚΛΗC, ΑΙΛΙ. (πρῶτον ἄρξ[ας]).—*Antoninus Pius*, Ceramus, 78.
ΘΕΟΞΕΝΟΥ, C.ΑΙΛ. (ἐπὶ).—*Antoninus Pius*, Stratonicea, 152, 154.
ΘΛΑΣΤΟΣ (ἀνέθηκεν).—*Augustus*, Mylasa, 130.

Ι.

ΙΑCΟΝΟC ΤΟΥ ΚΛΕΟΒΟV[λου] (ἐπὶ γρα.).—*Sept. Severus* and *Domna*, Stratonicea, 156.
ΙΑCΟΝΟC (ἐπὶ γρα. ?).—*Caracalla* and *Geta*, Stratonicea, 159.
ΙΑCΟΝΟC (ἀρχ.).—*Gallienus*, Tabae, 173, 174.
ΙΑCΟΝΟC CΙΛΒΟV (ἐπὶ ἀρχ.).—*Gallienus*, Tabae, 173.

ΙΑΤΡΟΚΛΕΟΥC, CTA[τιλίου] (ἐπὶ ἄρχον[τος]).—*Valerian* and *Gallienus*, Tabae, 172, 174.

ΙΕΡΟΚΛΕΟΥ. See ΙΟΥΛΙΑ ΔΟΜΝΟ.

ΙΕΡΟΚΛΕΟΥC B (ἐπὶ ἄρχ.).—*Sept. Severus* and *Domna*, Stratonicea, 156, 157.

ΙΟΥΛΙΑ ΔΟΜΝΟ. ΙΕΡΟΚΛΕΟΥ (ἐπὶ πρυ.).—*Caracalla* and *Geta*, Stratonicea, 159.

ΙΟΥΛΙΟΥ, Μ.ΑΥΡ. (ἄρχ.).—*Severus Alexander*, Tabae, 172.

ICOBOVNON. See ΜΕΝΕCΘΕΑ.

K.

ΚΑΛΙCΠΟΥ? ΚΕΚΙΝΕΟΥ, Δ.—*M. Aurelius*, Apollonia Salbace, 57.

ΚΑΛΛΙ. ,—*Nero*, Tabae, 168.

ΚΑΛΛΙΚΡΑΤΗΣ ΒΡΑΧΥΛΙΔΟΥ.—*Time of Nero*, Tabae, 164.

ΚΑΛΛΙΚΡΑΤΗΣ ΒΡΑΧΥΛΛΙΔΟΥ.—*Nero*, Tabae, *Introd.* lxxvi.

ΚΑΛΛΙΚΡΑΤΗΣ.—*Faustina Jun.*, Cnidus, *Introd.* lii. ; *Caracalla?*, Cnidus, *Introd.* lii.

ΚΑΛΛΙΠΠοΣ ΑΡΤΕΜΙΔΩΡΟΥ.—*Augustus*, *Livia*, Apollonia Salbace, 56, 57 ; *Introd.* xxxvii.

ΚΑΛΛΙΠΠΟΥ (διὰ . . . .).—*Temp. Trajan—Antonines*, Apollonia Salbace, 55.

ΚΑΛΛΙΠΠΟΥ (στρα.).—*Faustina*, Apollonia Salbace, *Introd.* xxxviii.

ΚΑΛΛΙΠΠΟΥ (στρα. γ'.).—*Trajan*, Apollonia Salbace, *Introd.* xxxvii.

ΚΑΛΛΙΠΠΟΥ (στρα. δ'.). — *Temp. Trajan—Antonines*, Apollonia Salbace, 55.

ΚΑΝΔΙΔΟΥ (ἐπὶ γρ.).—*Gordian*, *Volusian*, Neapolis ad Harpasum, *Introd.* lxvi.

ΚΑΝΔΙΔΟΥ (ἐπὶ γρ. τὸ δ'.).—*Volusian*, Neapolis ad Harpasum, 142.

ΚΑΝΔΙΔΟΥ ΚΕΛCΟΥ (ἐπὶ).—*M. Aurelius*, Harpasa, 113, 114.

Κ[ΑΡΜΙΝΙ]ΟΥ ΚΛΑΥΔΙΑΝΟΥ (διὰ ἀσιάρχου).—*M. Aurelius* and *L. Verus*, Attuda, *Introd.* xlii.

ΚΕΛCΟΥ. See ΚΑΝΔΙΔΟΥ.

ΚΛΑΥΔΙΑΝΟΥ, Μ. (διά).—Trapezopolis, 178.

MAGISTRATES' NAMES ON IMPERIAL COINS. 313

Λ.

ΛΑΧΙΝΟΥC (ἐπὶ).—Stratonicea, *Introd.* lxxiv.
ΛΕΟΝΙΔΟΥ (ἐπὶ).—Stratonicea, *Introd.* lxxiv.
ΛΕΟΝΤΟC ΑΛΚΑΙΟΥ (ἐπὶ πρυ.).—*Sept. Severus*, Stratonicea, 155, 156; *Introd.* lxxiii.
ΛΕΟΝΤΟC ΦΛ. AC[.]NA (ἐπὶ ἀρχ. ?) —*Sept. Severus* and *Domna*, Stratonicea, 155.

M.

ΜΑΛΥCΙΟΝ Τ. ΦΛ. (διὰ).—Trapezopolis, 177.
ΜΕΝΑΝΔΡΟΥ ΠΗΛΙ ... (στρα.).—*Gallienus*, Apollonia Salbace, 58.
ΜΕΝΕΚΡΑΤΟΥC (ἀρχῆς).—*Caracalla, Geta*, Cos, 220.
ΜΕΝΕCΘΕΑ ΙCΟΒΟΥΝΟΝ (ἐπὶ ἀρχ[όντων] τῶν περὶ).—*Sept. Severus* and *Domna*, Aphrodisias, 43—45; *Introd.* xxxv.
ΜΕΝΙΠΠΟC (ἀνέθη[κε]).—*Julia Domna*, Aphrodisias, 43; *Introd.* xxxv.
ΜΕΝΙΠΠΟC ΚΑΙ ΣΗΝΩΝ (ἀνέθεσ[αν]).—*Julia Domna*, Aphrodisias, 44.
ΜΕΝΙΠΠΟC ΚΑΙ ΣΗΝΩΝ (τῇ πατρίδι).—*Sept. Severus*, Aphrodisias, 43.
ΜΕΝΙΠΠΟΥ (ἐπὶ ἄρχον[τος]).—*Sept. Severus*, Alinda, 12; *Introd.* xxxi.
ΜΕΝΙΠΟΥ ΑΠΟΛΩΝΟΥ (sic) (διὰ).—*Time of Trajan*, Attuda, 63.
ΜΕΝΙΠΠΟΥ (διὰ).—*Time of Trajan*, Attuda, 62, 63.
[ΜΕΝΙΠΠΟΥ], Μ. ΑΙΛΙ. (διὰ).—*Time of Trajan*, Attuda, 63.
ΜΕΝΙΠΠΟΥ (διὰ υἱοῦ πόλεος).—*Trajan*, Attuda, 66.
ΜΟΥΣΑΙΟΣ ΚΑΛΛΙΚΡΑΤΟΥΣ (πρ[ύτανις]).—*Augustus*, Cidramus, *Introd.* xlvii.
ΜΥΩΝΟΣ ΦΛΑ. (ἀρ[χιερέως] [ἐπ]ιμεληθέντος).—Aphrodisias, 34.

N.

ΝΙΚΑΓΟΡΑΣ ΔΑ.—*Augustus*, Cos, 216.
ΝΙΚΟCΤΡΑΤΟΥ (στρα.).—*Caracalla*, Apollonia Salbace, *Introd.* xxxviii.
ΝΙΚΟCΤΡΑΤΟΥ (ἐπὶ).—*Geta*, Apollonia Salbace, *Introd.* xxxviii.

Ξ.

ΞΕΝΟΦΩΝ (ἱερεύς).—*Imperial Times*, Cos, 215.
ΞΕΡΞΗC ΕΥΓΕΝΕΤωΡ ΑΠοΛΛοΔοΤοϽ.—*Tiberius*, Antiochia, *Introd.* xxxii.

O.

ΟΡΘΡΙΟΥ ΙΕΡωΝΟC (διά).—*Domitian*, Tabae, 168, 169.
ΟΡ. ΙΕ. (διά).—*Time of Domitian*, Tabae, 165.
ΟΥΛΙΑΔΟΥ Μ. ΟΥΛ. (ἀρχ.).—*Caracalla* and *Plautilla*, Alinda, 12; *Introd.* xxxi.
ΟΥΛ/... ///ΤΟC, Μ. (ἀρχ.).—*Caracalla* and *Plautilla*, Alinda, 12.

Π.

ΠΑΙΩΝΙΟΥ.—*Augustus*, Antiochia, 18; *Introd.* xxxii.
ΠΑΜΦΙΛΟC CΕΛΕΥΚΟΥ.—*Vespasian*, Cidramus, *Introd.* xlvii.
ΠΑΝΦΙΛοΥ ΚΑΙ Π[οΛΕΜΩΝοC?] (διά).—*Hadrian*, Cidramus, *Introd.* lxvii.; *Ant. Pius*, Cidramus, 82.
ΠΑΠΙΑC ΑΠοΛΛΩΝΙοΥ.—*Vespasian*, Sebastopolis, 146; *Intr.* lxvii.
ΠΑΠΙΑC ΚΑΛΛΙΠΠΟΥ.—*Temp. Hadrian—Antonines*, Apollonia Salbace, 55.
ΠΑΠΙΟΥ ΚΑΛΛΙΠΠΟΥ.—*Temp. Hadrian—Antonines*, Apollonia Salbace, 55; *Temp. Trajan—Gallienus*, Apollonia Salbace, *Int.* xxxvii.
ΠΕΡ[ΙΤΟΥ?] ΦΛ. (ἀρχ[οντος]).—*Sept. Severus*, Aphrodisias and Ephesus, 53.
ΠΟΛΕΜΩΝ CΕΛΕΥΚΟΥ.—*Nero*, Cidramus, 81; *Introd.* xlvii.
ΠΟΛΕΜΩΝΟC (διά [Πανφίλου καὶ]).—*Antoninus Pius*, Cidramus, 82.
ΠΟΛΥΔ. See ΡοΥΦοΥ.
ΠΥΘΕΑΣ [CΑ]ΒΕΙΝΙΑΝο[Υ].—*Augustus—Domitian ?* Stratonicea, 151.
ΠΥΘοΝΙΚοΣ.—*Augustus*, Cos, 217.
ΠΥΘοΝΙΚοΣ ΤΙΜοΞΕΝοΥ.—*Augustus*, Cos, 217.

P.

ΡΟΥ[φου] ΚΛΑΥΔΙ· (στρα.).—*M. Aurelius*, Apollonia Salbace, *Introd.* xxxvii.
ΡΟΥΦΟΥ, ΠΟΛΥΔ. ΑΝΤΩΝΙ. (ἐπιμε[ληθέντος]).—*Sept. Severus*, Attuda, 67.

Σ.

CAPATOY (ἐπὶ ταμία).—*Imperial Times*, Rhodus, 264.
ΣΕΛΕΥΚΟΣ ΒΡΑΧΥΛΛΙΔΟΥ. *Early Imperial Times*, Tabae, 164.
CΕΛΕΥΚο[Υ] ΠΟΛΕΜΩ[ΝοC] (διὸ).—*M. Aurelius*, Cidramus, *Introd.* xlvii.
ΟΙΛΒΟΥ. See IACONOC.
COΛΩΝ APICTOΔHMOY.—*Imperial Times*, Tabae, 163.
ΣΟΦΟΚΛΗΣ.—*Augustus*, Cos, 217.
ΣΟΦΟΚΛΗΣ ΤΙΜοΞΕΝοΥ.—*Augustus*, Cos, 216.
CTPATONIKOV (ἐπὶ ἄρχ.).—*Trajan Decius*, Aphrodisias, 48 ; *Introd.* xxxv.
CΥΝΑΡΧΙΑ ΑΝ[ΤΙΟΧΕΩΝ] ΑΓΛΑΟV.—*Augustus*, Antiochia, 18.
CΥΝΑΡΧΙΑ Α[ΝΤΙ]ΟΧΕΩΝ ΠΑΙΩΝΙΟΥ. *Augustus*, Antiochia, 18.

Τ.

ΤΕΙΜΟΘΕΟΥ (ἐπὶ ἄρχοντος).—*Imperial Times*, Hyllarima, 123 ; *Introd.* lviii.
ΤΕΙΜΟΘΕΟΥ, Λ. (ἐπὶ στρ.).—*Hadrian*, Apollonia Salbace, *Intr.* xxxvii.
ΤΕΙΜοCΤΡΑΤΟΥ (ταμία).—*Imperial Times*, Rhodus, 265.
Τ.Κ.Τ. ΕΠΙ ΕΥΠΟΛΕΙΤΑ.—*Imperial Times*, Cnidus, 97.
ΤΩΝ ΠΕΡ[ὶ] ΤΒ. ΚΛ. ΔΙΟΝΥCΙΟΝ (ἐπὶ).—*Caracalla* and *Plautilla*, Stratonicea, 158.

Y.

YBPEOY (γραμματεύοντος).—*Augustus,* Mylasa, 130.

Φ.

ΦΑΙΝΙΛΑ (ἐπὶ).—*Imperial Times,* Rhodus, 265.
ΦΙΛΟ. (Φιλοστράτου ?) (ἐπὶ στρα.).—*Caracalla,* Stratonicea, 157.
ΦΙΛΩ[ΝΟC]. See **ΕΠΙΤΥΓΧΑΝΟΝΤΟC.**
ΦΛΑΒΙΑC (διὰ ἱερίας).—*Time of Sept. Severus,* Attuda, 64.
ΦΛΑΒΙΑC ΑΡΡΙ. ΚΛ. (διὰ ἱερείας).—*Sept. Severus,* Attuda, 67.

Χ.

ΧΑΡΕΙΝΟΥ (ἐπὶ).—*Imperial Times,* Rhodus, 265.
ΧΑΡΜΙΔΗC ΝΕΙΚΟCΤΡΑΤ. (στρατηγῶν).—*Hadrian to the Antonines,* Apollonia Salbace, 56.
ΧΑΡΜΥΛΟΣ Β.—*Augustus,* Cos, 216.

..... **ΛΑΝ. ΤΕΟV**(?) (ἐπὶ).—*Sept. Severus* and *J. Domna,* Stratonicea, 157.
..... **ΝΙΟC. Γ. ΦΙΛΩΝΟC** (ἐπὶ πρυ.).—*Imperial Times,* Stratonicea, Introd. lxxiv.

INDEXES V. AND VI.

ROMAN MAGISTRATES' NAMES
AND
ENGRAVERS' NAMES.

No names of Roman Magistrates or of Engravers occur on the coins described in this volume.

INDEX VII.

REMARKABLE INSCRIPTIONS.

A.

Α ΒΟΥΛΑ.—Cos, 215.
ΑΔΕΛΦΟΙ . . . . .—Tabae, 167.
ΑΚΜ (countermark).—Aphrodisias, 29.
ΑΝΕΘΗΚΑ.—Neapolis Aureliu, Ioniae, *Introd.* lxvi.
ΑΝΕΘΗΚΕ ΑΦΡΟΔΕΙCΙΕΩΝ Τ. Κ. ΖΗΛΟC.—Aphrodisias, 30, 35, 42.
ΑΝΕ(θηκε) ΑΦΡΟΔΕΙCΙΕΩΝ Τ. Κ. ΖΗΛΟC ΙΕΡΕΥC ΕΠΙΝΙΚΙΟΝ.—Aphrodisias, 41, 42.
ΑΝΕΘΗ(κε) ΑΦΡΟΔΙCΙΕΩΝ Μ[ΕΝΙΠΠΟC]. — Aphrodisias, 43.
ΑΝΕΘΗΚΕΝ ΘΛΑΣΤΟΣ.— Mylasa, 130.
ΑΝΕΘΕC(αν) ΑΦΡΟΔΙCΙΕΩΝ ΜΕΝΙΠΠΟC ΚΑΙ ΣΗΝΩΝ.—Aphrodisias, 44.
ΑΝΕΘ(ηκε) ΑΦΡΟΔΙCΙΕΩΝ ΤΙ. ΚΛ. ΣΗΝΩΝ ΑΡΧΙΕ. ΑΡΧΙΝΕΟΚ.—Aphrodisias, 44.
ΑΝΤΙΟΧΕΙΑ. — Antiochia ad Maeandrum, 18.
ΑΡΧ. Γ. ΦΛ. ΔΗΜΗΤΡΙΟΥ, ΙΟΥΛ. — Halicarnassus and Cos, 112.
ΑΡΧ. ΔΙΩΝΟC ΤΟΥ ΔΙΟΦΑΝΤΟΥ.—Mylasa, 139.
ΑΡΧΗC ΜΕΝΕΚΡΑΤΟΥC.—Cos, 220.
ΑΡΧΙΑΤΡΟC. — Heraclea Salbace, 120.
ΑΣΚΛΑΠΙΟ[Σ].—Cos, 214.
ΑΤΕΛΕΙΑC.—Alabanda, 4.
ΑΤΕΛΕΙΟC.—Alabanda, 4.
ΑΤΤΑΛΗΑ. — Aphrodisias, 37, 38, 47.
ΑΦΡΟΔΕΙCΙ(έων) ΑΝΤΙΟΧΕΩΝ ΔΗΜΟΙ ΟΜΟΝΟΙΑ.
—Aphrodisias and Antiochia, 53.

REMARKABLE INSCRIPTIONS. 319

ΑΦΡΟΔΕΙCΙΑC ΕΦΕCΟC ΟΜΟΝΟΙΑ. — Aphrodisias, 53.

B.

ΒΕΛ.—Stratonicea, 152.
ΒΟΥΛΗ.—Antiochia, 15; Aphrodisias, 34; Tabae, 166; Trapezopolis, 177.

Γ.

ΓΟΡΔΙΑΝΗΑ.—Aphrodisias, 37, 38, 47, 50.
ΓΡΑΜΜΑΤΕVΟΝΤΟC VBP ΕΟV.—Mylasa, 130.

Δ.

ΔΗΜΟC.—Antiochia, 16; Aphrodisias, 29, 30, 33, 38; Apollonia Salbace, 56; Attuda, 63—65; Παρπασα, 113, 114; Heraclea Salbace, 117; Sebastopolis, 146; Stratonicea, 153; Tabae, 165; Trapezopolis, 177.
ΔΙΑ ΜΕΝΙΠΠΟΥ ΥΙΟΥ ΠΟΛΕΟC.—Attuda, 66.
ΔΙΑ ΦΛΑΒΙΑC ΙΕΡΙΑC.— Attuda, 64.

ΔΙΑ ΚΛ. ΦΛΑΒΙΑC ΑΡΡΙ. ΙΕΡΕΙΑC.—Attuda, 67.
ΔΙΑ [CΕΛΕΥΚΟΥ] ΠΟΛΕΜΩΝΟC.—Cidramus, 82.
ΔΙΑ ΟΡΘΡΙΟΥ ΙΕΡWΝΟC. —Tabae, 165, 168, 169.
ΔΙΑ Τ. ΦΛ. ΜΑΛVCΙΟV.— Trapezopolis, 177.
ΔΙΑ Μ. ΚΛΑΥΔΙΑΝΟΥ.— Trapezopolis, 178.
ΔΙΑ ΠΟ. ΑΙ. ΑΔΡΑCΤΟΥ.— Trapezopolis, 178.
ΔΙΔΡΑΧΜΟΝ.—Rhodus, 267, 269, 270; Introd. cxvii.
ΔΡ (countermark). Attuda, 64.
ΔΥ(?)—ΔΔ.—Rhodus(?), 249.

Ε.

ΕΙΕΡΑ ΒΟΥΛΗ.—Aphrodisias, 31, 32, 36.
ΕΙΡΑΝΑ.—Cos, 216.
ΕΛΕΥΘ[ΕΡΟC] ΔΗΜΟC.— Aphrodisias, 38.
ΕΠΙ ΔΙΟΔΟ. ΑΡΞ.—Ceramus, 78.
ΕΠΙ ΤΕΙΜΟΘΕΟΥ ΑΡΧΟΝΤΟC.—Hyllarima, 123.
ΕΠΙ ΚΑΝΔΙΔΟΥ ΓΡ. ✝ Δ. Neapolis ad Harpasum, 142.
ΕΠΙ ΤΑΜΙΑ, &c.—Rhodus, 264.
ΕΠΙΜΕ(ληθέντος?) ΡΟΥΦΟΥ ΠΟΛΥΔ. ΑΝΤΩΝΙ.— Attuda, 67.
ΕΥΠΟΛΕΜΟΥ.—Mylasa, 128.

Z.

Z[ЄVC] BoVΛAIoC. — Antiochia, 16.
ZЄVC KAΠЄTΩΛIOC.—Antiochia, 19—21.
ZЄVC ΛVΔIOC.—Cidramus, 81.

H.

H[P]A.—Antiochia, 20.
HPAKΛIA.—Heraclea Salbace, 118.

Θ.

CA—ΞA. —Rhodus? 249.
ΘЄA [PΩ]MH.—Alabanda, 4.
ΘЄοΣ ΣΕΒΑΣΤοΣ.— Aphrodisias, 40.
ΘЄOV (countermark). — Stratonicea, 155 *sqq.*

I.

IACOC KTICTHC.—Iasus, 126.
IЄPA BOVΛH.—Antiochia, 15, 17; Aphrodisias, 31, 32, 35, 36; Apollonia Salbace, 56; Attuda, 66; Bargasa, 70; Heraclea Salbace, 116; Trapezopolis, 177.

IЄPA ΓЄPOVCIA.—Antiochia, 17, 18.
IЄPA CVNKΛHTOC. — Antiochia, 17; Aphrodisias, 30, 33—35, 37; Apollonia Salbace, 56; Attuda, 65; Cidramus, 81; Heraclea Salbace, 117; Sebastopolis, 146; Stratonicea, 152.
IЄPΕYΣ ΔHMοY.—Plarasa and Aphrodisias, 26.
IЄPΕYΣ ЄΠINIKION ANE-(θηκε).—Aphrodisias, 41, 42.
IЄPοC ΔHMοC.—Aphrodisias, 31; Tabae, 166.
INΔЄI ΘЄA PΩMH.—Stratonicea ad Caicum, *Introd.* lxxii.
INΔ. ΘЄOC CVNKΛHTοC. Stratonicea ad Caicum, *Introd.* lxxiii.
INΔЄI CTPATONЄI.—Stratonicea ad Caicum, *Introd.* lxxii.

K.

KAΠЄTΩΛIA.—Aphrodisias, 47.
KAΠЄTΩΛI(a) ΠVΘIA.—Aphrodisias, 51, 51.
KЄ TTA B.—Tabae, 160 (*note*).
KΞT TA.—Tabae, 160.
KOΛBA.—Neapolis Myndiorum, 140.
KTICTHC.—Antiochia, 23.

REMARKABLE INSCRIPTIONS. 321

M.

ΜΑΙΑΝΔΡΟC.—Antiochia, 16, 19.
ΜΕΑΝΔΡΟC.—Antiochia, 22.
ΜΕ—Ι.—Rhodus(?), 250.
ΜΗΝ ΚΑΡΟV.—Attuda, 65.
ΜοΡCVΝοC.—Antiochia, 16.

Ν.

ΝΕΑ ΘΕΑ ΗΡΑ.—Alabanda, 12.
ΝΕΑΠολΙ ΜΥΝ? — Neapolis Myndiorum (?), 140.
ΝΕΟΙC.—Heraclea Salbace, 120.
ΝΙΚΙΑΣ.—Cos, 213.

ΟΜΟΝΟΙΑ. — Aphrodisias and Ephesus, 53 ; Aphrodisias and Antiochia, 53 ; Halicarnassus and Cos, 112.

Π.

ΠΑ—ΑΕ.—Rhodus? 250.
ΠΑ—ΣR.—Rhodus? 249.
ΠΑ—ΞΑ.—Rhodus? 249.
ΠΕ—ΝΛ.—Rhodus? 250.
ΠΟΛΙC.—Attuda, 63.
ΠΡΟΣΤΑ(της).—Cos, 206.
ΠΡΩΤΟΝ ΑΡΞ(ας?).—Ceramus, 78.
ΠΥΘΙΑ.—Aphrodisias, 50, 51.

P.

Ξ.
ΞΕΝΟΦΩΝ.—Cos, 215.
ΞΕΝΟΦΩΝ [Ι]ΕΡΕΥ[C]. — Cos, 215.

ΡοΔΙοΙ ΥΠΕΡ ΤΩΝ CΕΒΑC ΤΩΝ.—Rhodus, 267 ; Introd. cxvii.

Σ.

Ο.
Ο ΔΑΜΟC.—Cos, 215.
ΟΙΚΟΥΜΕΝΙΚΟC. — Aphrodisias, 50, 51.

CΤ. ΑΤΤΑΛΟC ΑΡΧΙΑ ΤΡΟC.— Heraclea Salbace, 120.
[ΣΥ]Ν(μαχικόν).—Cnidus, 88.
CΥΝΑΡΧΙΑ.—Antiochia, 18.

T T

CΥΝΚΛΗΤΟC. — Aphrodisias, 31, 35; Orthosia, 144.
ΣΥΝΚΛΗΤοΣ.—Orthosia, 144.
CΥΝΚΛΗΤΟC ΙΝΔΙ. CΤΡΑ. Stratonicea ad Caicum, 154; *Introd.* lxxii.
CΩΖΩΝ.—Antiochia, 16; Aphrodisias, 39.

Τ.

ΤΑΜΙΑ, &c.—Rhodus, 264, 265.
ΤΕΡΜΕΡΙΚΟΝ.—Termera, 176.
ΤΗ ΠΑΤΡΙΔΙ.—Aphrodisias, 43.
ΤΙΜΕΛΗC.—Aphrodisias, 29.
Τ.Κ.Τ. ΕΠΙ ΕΥΠΟΛΕΙΤΑ.— Cnidus, 97.
ΤΥΜΝΟ.—Termera, 176.
ΤΩΝ ΠΕΡΙ ΜΕΝΕCΘΕΑ ΙCΟΒΟΥΝΟΝ (ἐπὶ ἀρχόντων).—Aphrodisias, 43—45.

ΤΩΜ ΠΕΡ[Ι] ΤΒ. ΚΛ. ΔΙΟ ΜΥCΙΟΜ (ἐπί).—Stratonicea, 158.
[ΤΩΝ ΠΡΟΣ] ΜΑΙΑΝΔΡΩ. —Antiochia, 15.

Υ.

ΥΙΟC ΑΦΡΟΔΙCΙΕΩΝ.—Aphrodisias, 39, 40.
ΥΙΟΥ ΠΟΛΕΟC.—Attuda, 66.
ΥΠ—ΜΙ.—Rhodus? 250.

Ψ.

ΨΗΦΙCΑΜΕΝΟΥ ΦΛΑΥΒΙΟΥ ΔΙΟΜΗΔΟΥC.—Stratonicea, 153.

TABLE
FOR
CONVERTING ENGLISH INCHES INTO MILLIMETRES
AND THE
MEASURES OF MIONNET'S SCALE.

TABLE
OF
THE RELATIVE WEIGHTS OF ENGLISH GRAINS AND FRENCH GRAMMES.

Grains.	Grammes.	Grains.	Grammes.	Grains.	Grammes.	Grains.	Grammes.
1	·064	41	2·656	81	5·248	121	7·840
2	·129	42	2·720	82	5·312	122	7·905
3	·194	43	2·785	83	5·378	123	7·970
4	·259	44	2·850	84	5·442	124	8·035
5	·324	45	2·915	85	5·508	125	8·100
6	·388	46	2·980	86	5·572	126	8·164
7	·453	47	3·045	87	5·637	127	8·229
8	·518	48	3·110	88	5·702	128	8·294
9	·583	49	3·175	89	5·767	129	8·359
10	·648	50	3·240	90	5·832	130	8·424
11	·712	51	3·304	91	5·896	131	8·488
12	·777	52	3·368	92	5·961	132	8·553
13	·842	53	3·434	93	6·026	133	8·618
14	·907	54	3·498	94	6·091	134	8·682
15	·972	55	3·564	95	6·156	135	8·747
16	1·036	56	3·628	96	6·220	136	8·812
17	1·101	57	3·693	97	6·285	137	8·877
18	1·166	58	3·758	98	6·350	138	8·942
19	1·231	59	3·823	99	6·415	139	9·007
20	1·296	60	3·888	100	6·480	140	9·072
21	1·360	61	3·952	101	6·544	141	9·136
22	1·425	62	4·017	102	6·609	142	9·200
23	1·490	63	4·082	103	6·674	143	9·265
24	1·555	64	4·146	104	6·739	144	9·330
25	1·620	65	4·211	105	6·804	145	9·395
26	1·684	66	4·276	106	6·868	146	9·460
27	1·749	67	4·341	107	6·933	147	9·525
28	1·814	68	4·406	108	6·998	148	9·590
29	1·879	69	4·471	109	7·063	149	9·655
30	1·944	70	4·536	110	7·128	150	9·720
31	2·008	71	4·600	111	7·192	151	9·784
32	2·073	72	4·665	112	7·257	152	9·848
33	2·138	73	4·729	113	7·322	153	9·914
34	2·202	74	4·794	114	7·387	154	9·978
35	2·267	75	4·859	115	7·452	155	10·044
36	2·332	76	4·924	116	7·516	156	10·108
37	2·397	77	4·989	117	7·581	157	10·173
38	2·462	78	5·054	118	7·646	158	10·238
39	2·527	79	5·119	119	7·711	159	10·303
40	2·592	80	5·184	120	7·776	160	10·368

TABLE

OF

THE RELATIVE WEIGHTS OF ENGLISH GRAINS AND FRENCH GRAMMES.

Grains.	Grammes.	Grains.	Grammes	Grains.	Grammes.	Grains.	Grammes.
161	10·432	201	13·024	241	15·616	290	18·79
162	10·497	202	13·089	242	15·680	300	19·44
163	10·562	203	13·154	243	15·745	310	20·08
164	10·626	204	13·219	244	15 810	320	20·73
165	10·691	205	13·284	245	15·875	330	21·38
166	10·756	206	13·348	246	15·940	340	22·02
167	10·821	207	13·413	247	16·005	350	22·67
168	10·886	208	13·478	248	16·070	360	23·32
169	10·951	209	13·543	249	16·135	370	23·97
170	11·016	210	13·608	250	16·200	380	24·62
171	11·080	211	13·672	251	16·264	390	25·27
172	11·145	212	13·737	252	16·328	400	25 92
173	11·209	213	13·802	253	16·394	410	26·56
174	11·274	214	13·867	254	16·458	420	27·20
175	11·339	215	13·932	255	16·524	430	27·85
176	11·404	216	13 996	256	16·588	440	28·50
177	11·469	217	14·061	257	16 653	450	29·15
178	11·534	218	14·126	258	16·718	460	29·80
179	11·599	219	14·191	259	16·783	470	30 45
180	11·664	220	14·256	260	16·848	480	31·10
181	11·728	221	14·320	261	16·912	490	31·75
182	11·792	222	14 385	262	16·977	500	32·40
183	11·858	223	14·450	263	17·042	510	33·04
184	11·922	224	14·515	264	17·106	520	33·68
185	11·988	225	14·580	265	17·171	530	34·34
186	12·052	226	14·644	266	17·236	540	34·98
187	12·117	227	14 709	267	17·301	550	35·64
188	12·182	228	14·774	268	17·366	560	36·28
189	12·247	229	14·839	269	17·431	570	36·93
190	12·312	230	14·904	270	17·496	580	37·58
191	12·376	231	14·968	271	17·560	590	38·23
192	12·441	232	15·033	272	17·625	600	38·88
193	12·506	233	15·098	273	17·689	700	45·36
194	12·571	234	15·162	274	17·754	800	51·84
195	12·636	235	15·227	275	17·819	900	58·32
196	12·700	236	15·292	276	17·884	1000	64·80
197	12·765	237	15·357	277	17·949	2000	129 60
198	12·830	238	15·422	278	18·014	3000	194·40
199	12·895	239	15·487	279	18·079	4000	259·20
200	12·960	240	15·552	280	18·144	5000	324·00

LONDON:
PRINTED BY GILBERT AND RIVINGTON, LIMITED,
ST. JOHN'S HOUSE, CLERKENWELL.

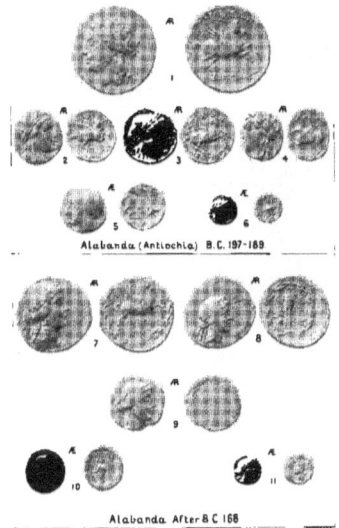

Alabanda (Antiochia) B.C. 197-189

Alabanda After B.C. 168

ALABANDA

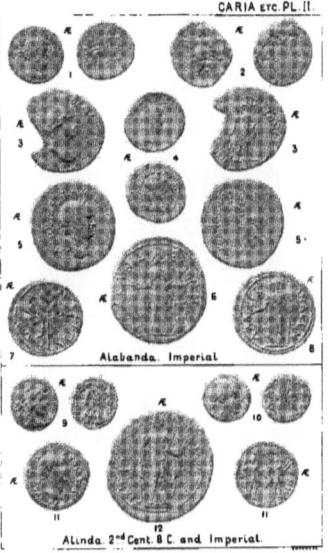

ALABANDA ALINDA.

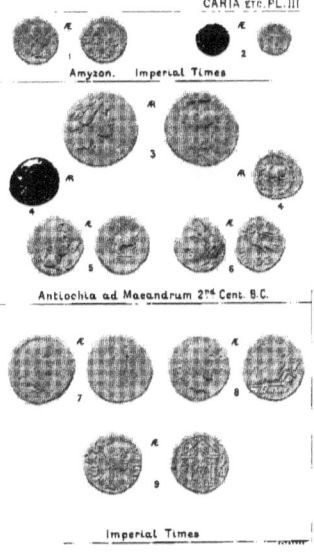

AMYZON. ANTIOCHIA

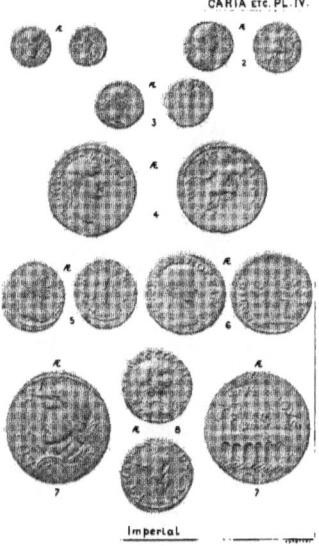

ANTIOCHIA.

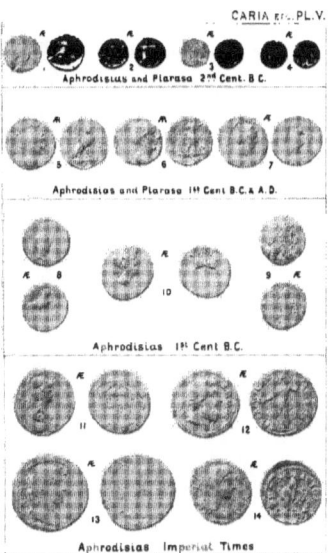

APHRODISIAS and PLARASA.

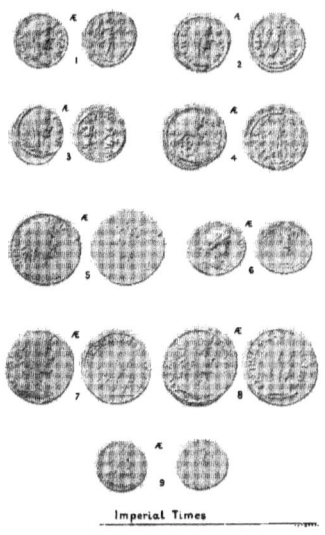

Imperial Times

APHRODISIAS.

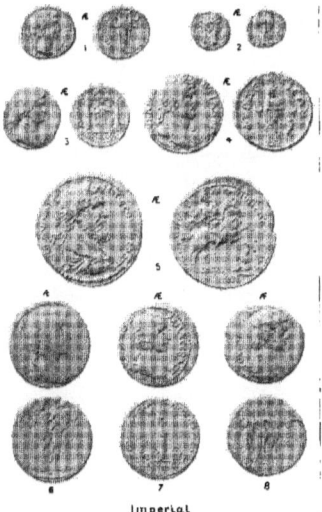

APHRODISIAS.

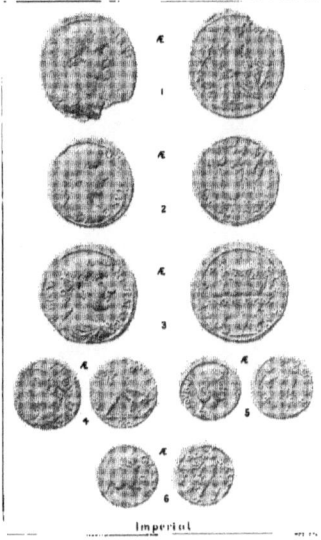

APHRODISIAS.

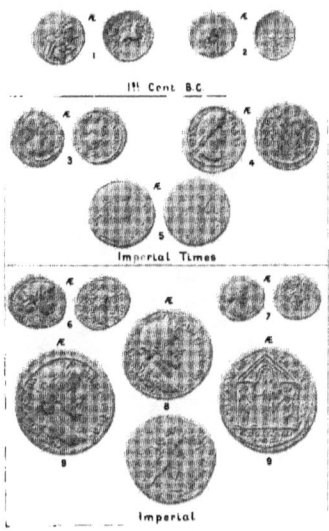

APOLLONIA-SALBACE.

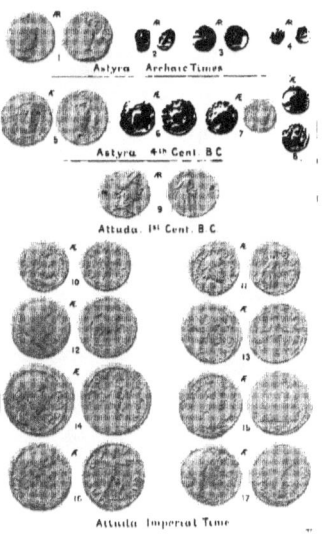

ASTYRA. ATTUDA.

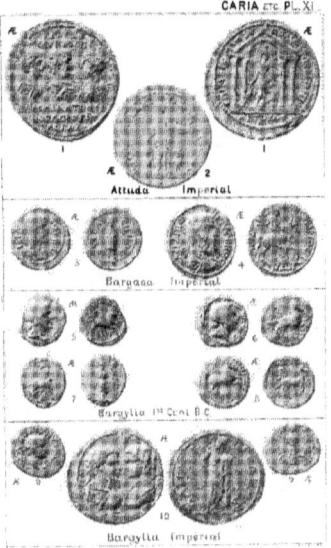

ATTUDA. BARGASA. BARGYLIA.

CARIA etc PL. XII

Caunus. Before B.C. 309

Caunus. B.C. 309-189

Caunus. After B.C. 166

Ceramus. 2nd or 1st Cent. B.C.

Imperial

CAUNUS, CERAMUS.

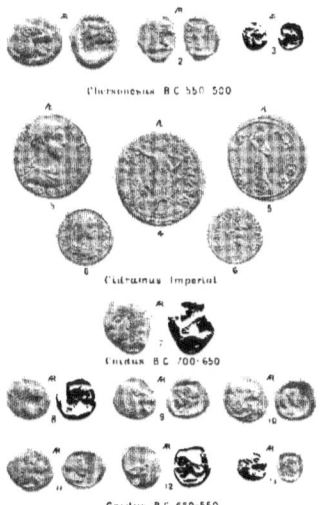

CHERSONESUS, CIDRAMUS, CNIDUS

CARIA Pl. XIV.

B.C. 550-500

B.C. 500-480

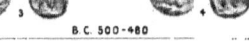

B.C. 412-400

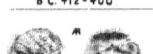

B.C. 400-390

CNIDUS.

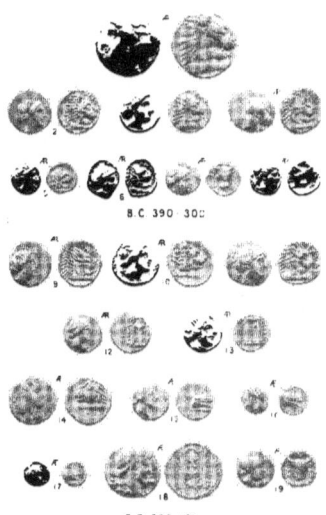

B.C. 390-300

B.C. 300-190

CNIDUS

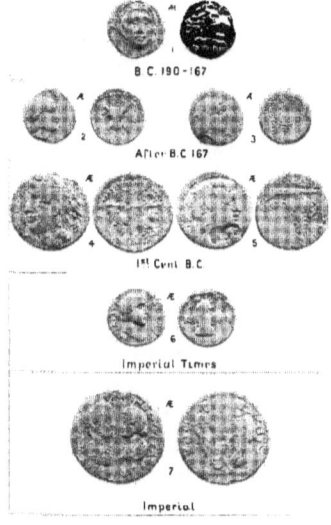

CNIDUS

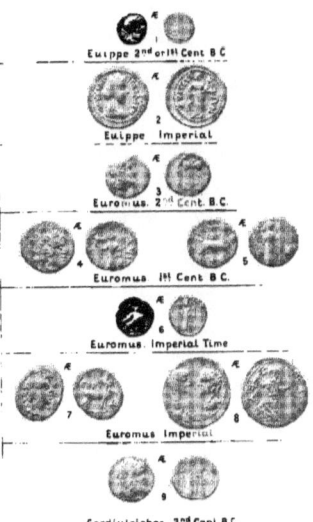

EUIPPE, EUROMUS, GORDIUTEICHOS.

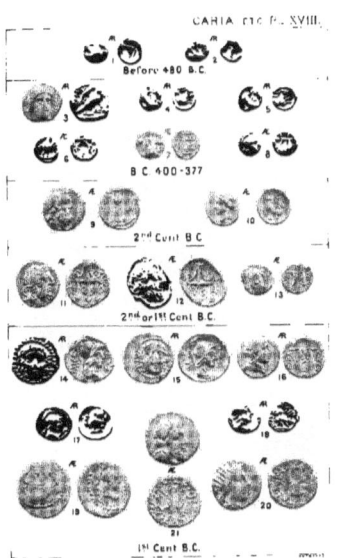

HALICARNASSUS.

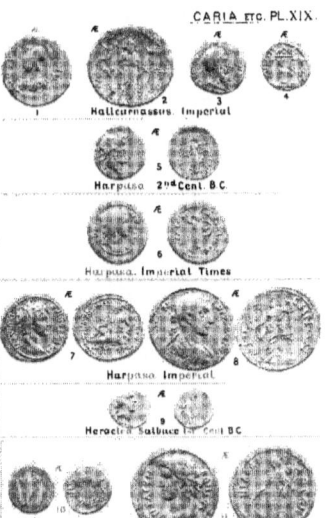

CARIA ETC. PL. XIX.

Halicarnassus. Imperial

Harpasa. 2nd Cent. B.C.

Harpasa. Imperial Times

Harpasa. Imperial

Heraclea Salbace 1st Cent. B.C.

Heraclea Salbace. Imp. Times

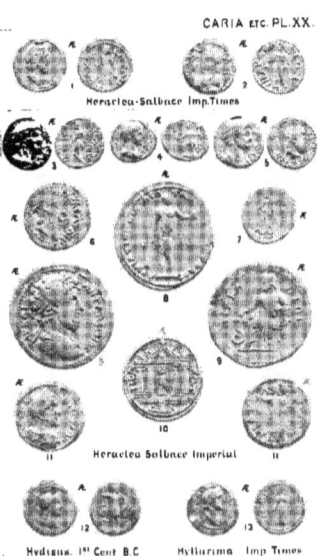

HERACLEA-SALBACE, HYDISUS, HYLLARIMA.

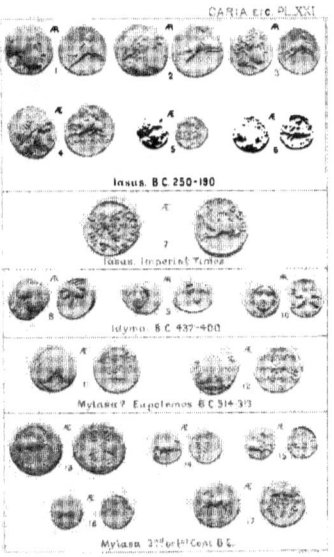

IASUS, IDYMA, MYLASA

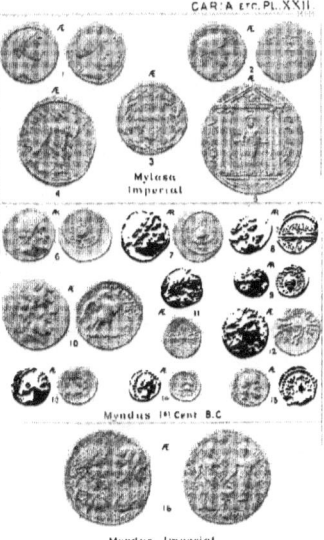

MYLASA   MYNDUS.

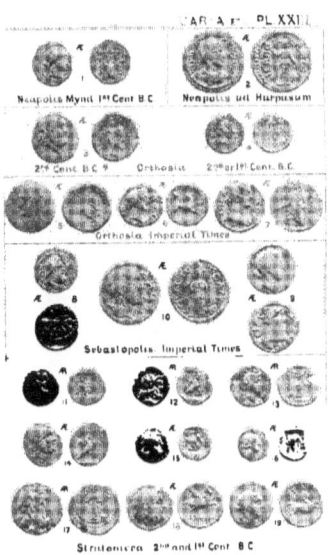

NEAPOLIS, ORTHOSIA, SEBASTOPOLIS
STRATONICEA

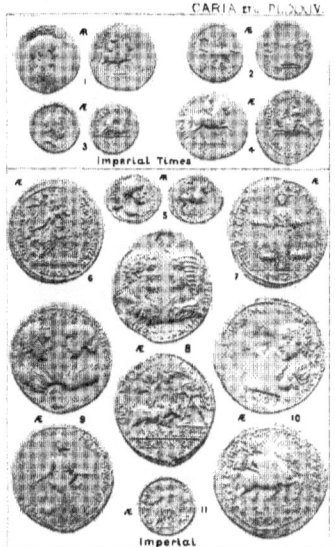

STRATONICEA

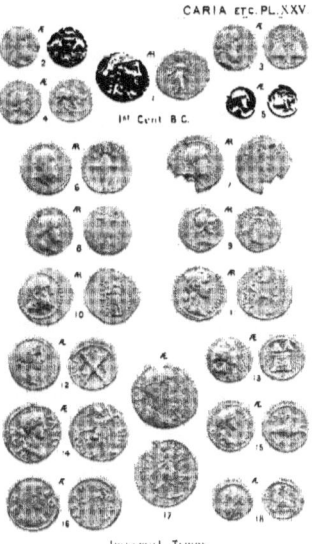

TABAE.

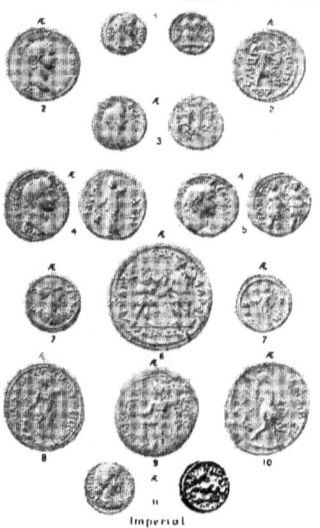

TABAE.

CARIA etc PL.XXVII

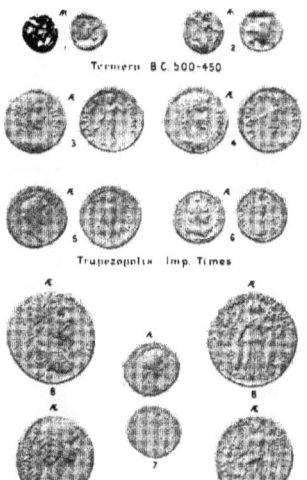

Termera B.C. 500-450

Trapezopolis Imp. Times

CARIA etc. PL. XXVIII.

Hekatomnus B.C 395-377

Maussolus B.C 377-353

Hidrieus B.C 353-344

Pixodarus B.C 340-334

SATRAPS OF CARIA.

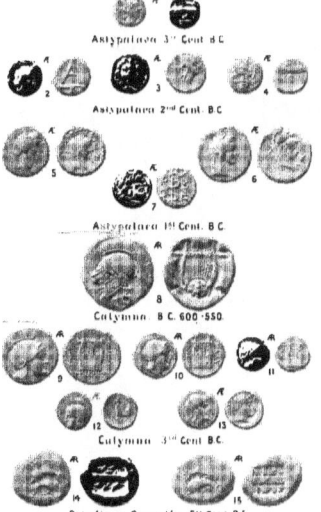

ASTYPALAEA, CALYMNA, CARPATHOS

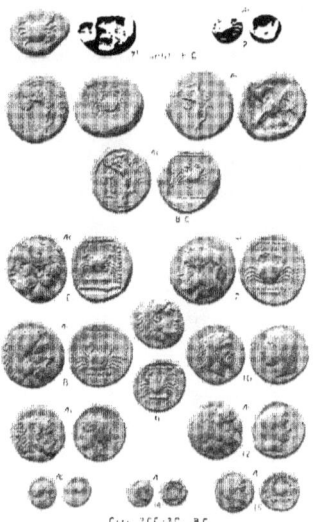

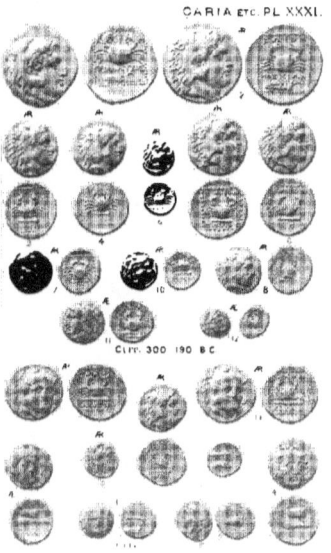
COS

CARIA etc. PL. XXXII.

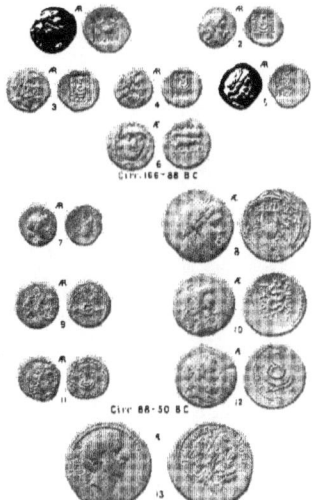

Circ. 166-88 B.C.

Circ. 88-50 B.C.

Nikias B.C. 50 - Augustus

COS

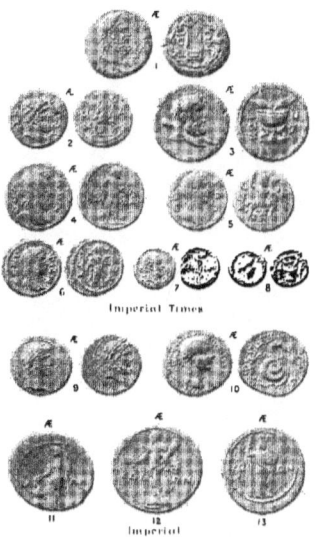

Imperial Times

Imperial

COS

ARIA ETC PL XXXIV.

Medeste Circ 333-304 B.C.

Nisyrus Circ 350-300 B.C.

Cumitian 600-500 B.C.

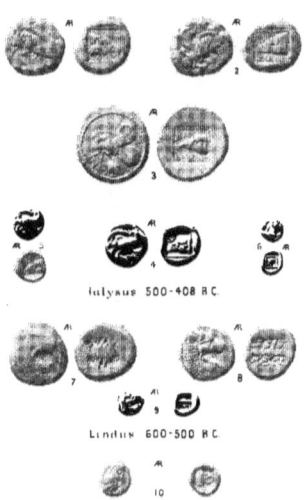

Ialysus 500-408 B.C.

Lindus 600-500 B.C.

Lindus 500-408 B.C.

IALYSUS, LINDUS

CARIA ETC. PL. XXXVI

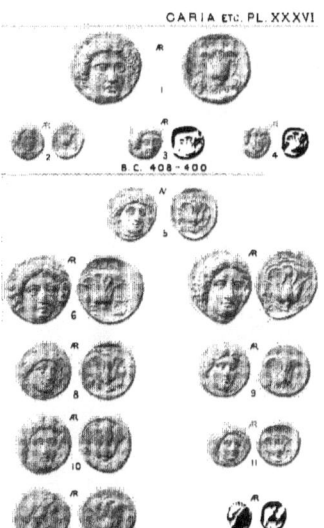

B.C. 408-400

B.C. 400-333

RHODUS.

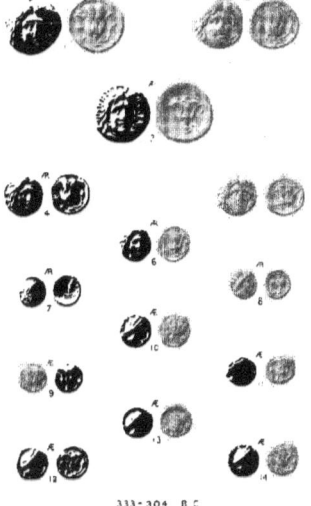

333-304 B.C.

RHODUS

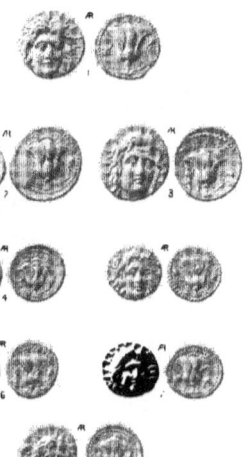

304-166 B.C.

RHODUS

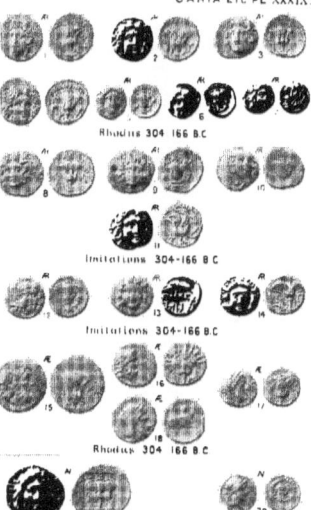

CARIA ETC. PL. XL

166-88 B.C

RHODUS.

CARIA ETC PL XLI.

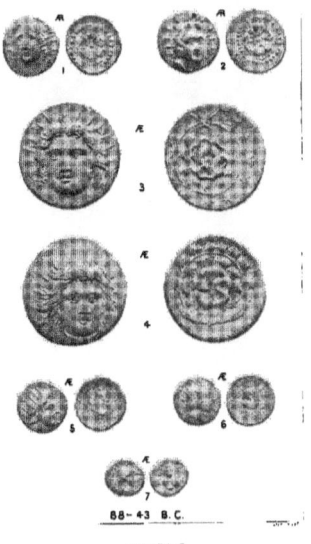

88-43 B.C.

RHODUS

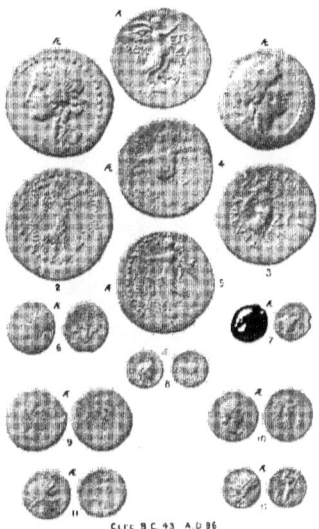

Circ B.C. 43 A.D. 96

RHODUS

CARIA ETC PL.XLIII

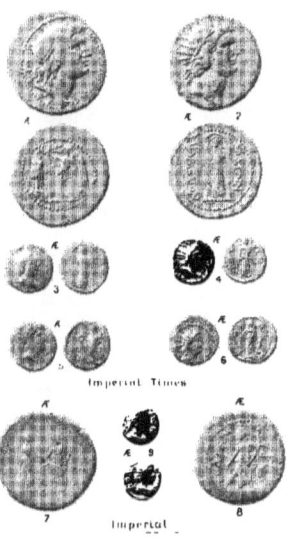

RHODUS

CARIA I.TC. PL. XLIV

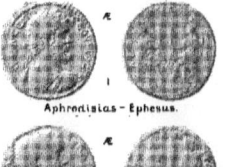

Aphrodisias – Ephesus.

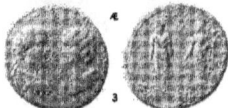

Aphrodisias – Antiochia.

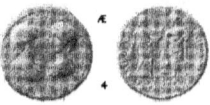

Halicarnassus – Samos

Halicarnassus – Cos

CARIA.—ALLIANCE COINS

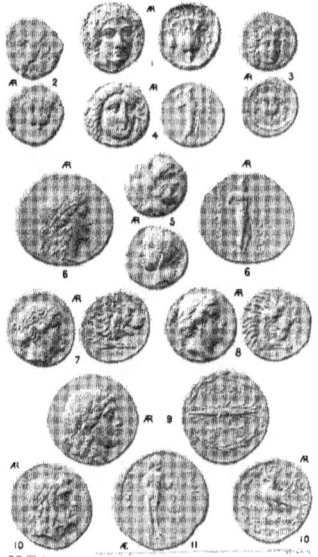

COINS NOT IN THE BRIT. MUS.

www.ingramcontent.com/pod-product-compliance
Lightning Source LLC
Chambersburg PA
CBHW030300010526
44108CB00038B/680